The Interrogation Rooms of the Korean War

THE UNTOLD HISTORY

MONICA KIM

PRINCETON UNIVERSITY PRESS

PRINCETON & OXFORD

Library of Congress Control Number: 2018938277
First paperback printing, 2020
Paperback ISBN 978-0-691-21042-1
Cloth ISBN 978-0-691-16622-3

British Library Cataloging-in-Publication Data is available

Editorial: Amanda Peery, Eric Crahan, and Pamela Weidman
Production Editorial: Mark Bellis
Cover Design: Faceout Studio, Lindy Martin
Cover Credit: Shutterstock
Production: Erin Suydam
Publicity: James Schneider
Copyeditor: Dawn Hall

This book has been composed in Arno

For my mother, 장재순
and my father, 김정한

CONTENTS

NOTE ON LANGUAGE

FOR ALL REFERENCES TO and mention of places and people in Korean that come from the files of the United States military or government at the time, I have kept the spelling of Korean and Chinese names according to the Romanized versions appearing in the archived documents for ease of possible later reference in the archives. US military Romanization of Korean did not consistently follow any format at this particular time, so spelling can be highly idiosyncratic and vary greatly.

The names of Korean, Japanese, and Chinese persons appear via the usual practice of placing the family name first, then the personal name. I have used the McCune-Reichauer system for the transliteration of the other references in Korean, with the noted exceptions of well-known figures like Syngman Rhee, who are often associated and referenced with particular renderings of their names.

"Orientals" or "Asiatics" were terms commonly used in the United States to refer to East Asians, whether in Korea, Japan, or the United States. Whenever archival material or an oral history employs such terms, I have kept the term intact. However, I do use "Japanese Americans" in my discussion of the POW interrogators and their history. Using "Japanese Americans" for this time period is indeed anachronistic, as "Asian American" would later be created by student movements in the 1960s as a term for expressing the political solidarity of students from different Asian backgrounds. Although "Japanese American" is awkward to use in a sense, the use of only "Oriental" within this chapter would replicate much of the conflation between the Asian citizen of the United States and the Asian subject of US projects in East Asia. As a result, I have decided to use "Japanese American" to help initially parse a divergent, but ultimately converging, history.

ABBREVIATIONS

ACYL Anti-Communist Youth League

ATIS Allied Translator and Interpreter Section

CFI Custodian Force of India

CI Civilian Internee

CIC Counterintelligence Corps

CID Criminal Investigation Detachment

CIE Civilian Information and Education

CM Compound Monitor

CPV Chinese People's Volunteers

DPRK Democratic People's Republic of Korea

DZ Demilitarized Zone

FBI Federal Bureau of Investigation

GHQ General Headquarters

ICRC International Committee of the Red Cross

JAG Judge Advocate General

JCS Joint Chiefs of Staff

KATUSA Korean Augmentation to United States Army

KPA Korean People's Army

MIS Military Intelligence Section

NC Northern Command

NNRC Neutral Nations Repatriation Commission

NSC   National Security Council

NWYMA   North West Young Men's Alliance

POW   Prisoner of War

PRK   People's Republic of Korea

PSB   Psychological Strategy Board

PSYWAR Psychological Warfare

PW   Prisoner of War

ROK   Republic of Korea

ROKA   Republic of Korea Army

SD   Special War Problems Division

SKLP   South Korean Labor Party

SOP   Standard Operating Procedures

UN   United Nations

UNC   United Nations Command

UNCREG United Nations Command Repatriation Group

UNTCOK United Nations Temporary Commission on Korea

US   United States

USAFIK United States Armed Forces in Korea

USAMGIK United States Army Military Government in Korea

THE INTERROGATION ROOMS
OF THE KOREAN WAR

Introduction

War and Humanity

IT WAS OCTOBER 1, 1950, and twenty-year-old Oh Se-hŭi was making his way back to his home in Kyŏngsang Province, after multiple stints with the northern Korean People's Army (KPA). After General Mac-Arthur's successful landing at the port of Inchon two weeks earlier on September 15, the KPA had been in steady retreat, and Oh had seized on a chance to return home. Oh stepped out of the wooded hills onto a road that wound around a cabbage field and began to walk north.

A voice barked out from behind him—"Hands in the air!" Oh raised his hands slowly in the air. He had already deemed it inevitable that he would eventually run into a soldier of the Republic of Korea Army (ROKA), the United Nations Command (UNC), or even the KPA again—and in preparation for such encounters he had stashed away four different pieces of paper in strategic places on his body. The first, a handwritten "patriot certificate" attesting to his true dedication to the KPA, he had folded carefully and placed into the lining of his beret-like hat, one worn often by guerilla fighters. The second, a leaflet dropped by UN reconnaissance planes, guaranteed his safe surrender, and he had placed it, like "precious cargo," in the inside pocket of his coat. The third, tucked away in the right back pocket of his pants, was his student papers stating that he was enrolled at Seoul University, the prominent, national university of South Korea. In the left back pocket of his pants the fourth piece of paper—a slim notebook—contained the registered names of his students when he had been a middle school teacher in the countryside. He had rehearsed over and over in his mind what he would do when he met a member from the KPA, or a US soldier, a guerilla fighter, or an ROKA soldier. The certificate would hold him in good stead with the KPA and the communist guerilla fighters; the UN surrender leaflet appeared to have the most wide-ranging application since the military forces of sixteen different nations, including the Republic of Korea (ROK), were operating on the Korean peninsula under the auspices of the UNC, led by the US military; the student and teacher papers attested to his civilian status and ROK citizenship, possible necessary evidence for someone of the ROKA.

Car brakes screeched to a halt. An ROKA soldier stepped out of the jeep, pointing his rifle at Oh. "What are you?" barked the soldier. Taking out the "precious cargo" of the UN leaflet from his jacket, Oh gave the leaflet to the ROKA soldier, who promptly scoffed at him, declaring, "This doesn't mean anything here," ripping up the paper. Oh then gave him his student paper, and the soldier yelled out, while ripping up the paper, "What the hell is a college student doing here?" Not knowing if he would live or die, he then offered the teacher papers to the soldier. "What's a teacher doing here?" the soldier asked, and he tossed aside the papers. Impatient, the soldier pointed his rifle at Oh's chest and commanded, "Take off your hat!" Nervously, Oh removed his hat, praying that the Communist certificate would not fall out. It did not. The ROKA soldier examined Oh's hair, which had grown quite long and unruly during the past few weeks, unlike the short, cropped hair of the guerilla fighters. Satisfied that Oh was not an enemy, the soldier finally called out to the others in the jeep: "Someone come take care of this!" "This" was Oh Se-hŭi—he had now become a prisoner of war.[1]

The Script of War

War, we assume, is a part of the universal human condition. And when war converges with another age-old human impulse—storytelling—war emerges from the story more akin to a force of nature than a mere manmade event. The horror, the violence, and the rapture of war distill into allegories and meditations on the nature of humankind. To tell a story about war is to tell a story about humanity.

But if we unclasp war from humanity, our assumption that the sheer human drama of war echoes timeless truths about humanity falls to the side, and we can see more clearly that stories of war hold allegorical power because at their most fundamental, they are stories about intimate encounter. It is the small, rather than the epic, that moves the story of war forward. These stories pivot around critical moments where life and death hang in the balance depending on one person's intimate recognition of another person's humanity. In front of the barrel of a gun, a person begging for food, the indiscriminate bombing of villages—every action hinges on imagining the partial or full humanity of the other. And as Oh Se-hŭi's four pieces of paper make evident, the material with which one vies for recognition is utterly specific and inescapably historical.

In the mid-twentieth century, it was precisely this decisive pause before a person committed an act of violence or mercy in war that became the focus of intense international debate. This moment of recognition was the very social encounter that international organizations, nation-states, and revolutionary groups wanted to institutionalize, to render into a formal process. The aftermath of the devastation from the world wars pushed the question of how to define and regulate warfare, while the surge in anticolonial movements across the globe pushed the question of how to define the limits of humanity. To rewrite the script of legitimate warfare was to re-create the template for the legitimate human subject for a post-1945 global order. Who was worthy of life?

The stories of war and humanity intersected at this historical moment not by virtue of their universal nature, but because of a specific institution that was the central concern of the postwar international world: the nation-state. In the conferences at Geneva or Washington, DC, the stories about war and humanity revealed themselves to be scripts for state action. To regulate war, one had to control state behavior—and to protect the individual human, one had to control state behavior. With the founding of the United Nations in October 1945, the writing of the Universal Declaration of Human Rights in 1948, and the drafting of the Geneva Conventions in 1949, the "family of nations" was the central underpinning system facilitating these definitions of war and humanity. In turn, it was the basic element of sovereign recognition that bound and held this system together.

However, people in the colonies demanding liberation and autonomous statehood all around the globe issued a fundamental challenge to this system of sovereign recognition. Whether India, Indochina, or Algeria, the demands for sovereign recognition shook the very foundation of Western colonial power and thus its global reach: its prerogative to deny recognition, whether in terms of humanity or the waging of violence. War, we must remember, was a privilege accorded only to recognized states. Only sovereign entities could engage in what Carl von Clausewitz had conceptualized as a "duel," a legitimate extension of policy making involving two recognizable sides. Violence within the colonies received other monikers—insurgency, riot, rebellion, among others.

The official outbreak of the Korean War on June 25, 1950, revealed an undeniably curious situation between the naming of violence and the taming of violence on the world stage. As Western powers refined and redefined the "laws of war," it began to appear that states were no longer waging "war" anymore. When asked by the press whether or not the United States was at war on the Korean peninsula, President Harry Truman replied succinctly, "We are not at war." He agreed with a later characterization of the military mobilization offered by a member of the press: a "police action under the United Nations."[2] The vocabulary to frame military action quickly multiplied: *police action, intervention, occupation.*

The script of war was changing. Two imperatives that shaped the post-1945 world were in explicit tension. The first imperative was colonial power. Western powers faced an unanticipated quandary: to wage "war" with another entity implied political recognition of its sovereign legitimacy, an act that they desired to defer as long as possible in face of anticolonial movements. The second imperative was moral authority. The criminalization of "aggressive" war shifted the legitimate grounds on which a state could declare and mobilize war. It was no longer sufficient to declare war in the patent interests of the state. Now, war would have to be conducted in the name of "humanity," framed in the terms of a universal conflict rather than a state-specific necessity. War could now only be conducted as a disavowal of war itself.

This book tells a story of the changing script of warfare in the mid-twentieth century through the war that was not a war—the Korean War. At stake in this conflict was not simply the usual question of territorial sovereignty and the nation-state. The heart of the struggles revolved around the question of political recognition, the key relational dynamic that formed the foundation for the post-1945 nation-state system. This book argues that if we want to understand how the act of recognition became the essential terrain of war, we must step away from the traditional landscape of warfare—the battlefield—and into the interrogation room.

The mandate for war exceeded sovereign territorial borders and delved into the most intimate corner of humanity—the individual human subject. The geography of war was no longer limited to a traditional sense of sovereignty in the state-territorial sense. Rather, the locus of war in the "new" postwar era was the interior worlds of individual people. Whether American psychologists in the US military or Communist revolutionaries on the Korean peninsula, people in the postwar world focused their attention on the interior human world, as both empires and revolutions claimed the central project of decolonization. To quote Frantz Fanon, "Decolonization is truly the creation of new men."[3] The ambitions of empire, revolution, and international solidarity converged on an intimate meeting of military warfare: the interrogator and the interrogated prisoner of war. Who would fashion the new human subject for the world after 1945? It was a vast, impossible question, but one that had immediate, urgent consequences on the ground as the forms of violence multiplied as quickly as the language for war fragmented. In the middle between the tides of violence and the unreliability of language were people—whether Korean, American, "Oriental," Chinese, Communist, or anti-Communist. What unfolds in the pages that follow is a history of a war over humanity on the ground, following two generations of people from both sides of the Pacific as they created and negotiated interrogation rooms from World War II through the Korean War and into the McCarthy era.

The Korean War on the Stage of History

It is no small irony of history that the most identifiable marker of the Korean peninsula to people outside of Korea is an abstract line that cuts across the peninsula on most maps of Korea. The 38th parallel, first drawn by two US officials late at night on August 14, 1945, as the proposed line of division between the US and Soviet military occupations on the Korean peninsula, had no correlation to any geographical or cultural boundary on the ground.[4] On the ground, in the years after 1945, Koreans, Soviets, and Americans were all uncertain about exactly where the 38th parallel was, and smugglers and refugees followed multiple trails northward and southward. After June 25, 1950, the 38th parallel had gone from being a temporary, even arbitrary, border to being a sacred sovereign border in this story of the war. On June 26, 1950, when President Harry Truman delivered a statement explaining his decision to mobilize US troops on the Korean peninsula, he focused on the 38th parallel, lambasting the southward crossing of the northern Korean People's Army on June 25, 1950, as "an act of aggression" and a "[threat] to the peace of the world."[5] Responding to Truman's statement with their own press release, Soviet officials accused the "South Korean puppet government" of provoking the June 25 attack over the 38th parallel, which in turn was clear evidence of the US "imperialist warmongers."[6] According to these accusations, the 38th parallel functioned as a line of sovereignty drawn on the Korean peninsula and as a symbol of the borders of the emerging global order.

From the vantage point of the White House, the Korean War was a front line in the larger "Cold War" conflict between the United States and the Soviet Union, where the 38th parallel enabled Truman to tell the story of the conflict on the Korean peninsula according to a familiar script of war, one where the violation of a sovereign border provided the impetus and reason for entrance into a war. The standard story of the Korean War closely hews to the 38th parallel as its major pivot. The northern Korea People's Army (KPA) moved swiftly down the peninsula after June 1950, and the KPA troops and personnel also quickly instituted planned programs of land reform, as well as claiming Democratic People's Republic of Korea (DPRK) sovereignty over the southern half of the peninsula. From his command post in US-occupied Japan, General Douglas MacArthur orchestrated the landing at the port city of Inchon on the western coast of the Korean peninsula in mid-September, which turned the military tides for the United States and the United Nations from surprising defeat to possible success. In late September 1950, General MacArthur requested and received permission from President Harry Truman for the US-led United Nations Command (UNC) forces to cross over the 38th parallel and continue northward. Truman gave him the green light, and the UNC forces proceeded across the 38th parallel. The war of Cold War containment had become a war of rollback.

This "police action" soon changed again. In November 1950, the People's Volunteer Army of the People's Republic of China entered the war, crossing the Yalu River from China into North Korea. Once again, the military tides turned, and the United States and UN forces found themselves pushed back against the 38th parallel. By July 1951, the 38th parallel became the agreed-on site for cease-fire negotiations between the United Nations Command, the People's Republic of China, and the Democratic People's Republic of Korea. In the early 1950s, politicians and diplomats could barely sustain the usual trope of a violated border as a meaningful reason for the violence sanctioned and continuing on the Korean peninsula. That is, the traditional script of warfare requiring the transgression of a sovereign, territorial border was no longer sufficient for what was actually at stake in the conflict. Thus, while the Korean War began in June 1950 as a war waged over the violation of a border—the 38th parallel, by early 1952, it was becoming a war waged over the violation of a human subject—the prisoner of war.

Through the history of the Korean War, we can acutely see the story of how, in the middle of the twentieth century, official warfare moved from being waged over geopolitical territory to being waged over human interiority. This shift had happened in plain sight on the 38th parallel, where the armistice negotiations were taking place in a small village called Panmunjom. On January 2, 1952, the US delegate representing the United Nations Command placed a new proposal on the negotiating table—voluntary POW repatriation. Immediately, the Chinese and North Korean delegates pointed out that the 1949 Geneva Conventions on the Treatment of Prisoners of War stipulated *mandatory* repatriation at the end of the war, and they refused the proposal.

According to the US-proposed plan, at the end of the conflict, a soldier would be able to "exercise his individual option as to whether he will return to his own side or join the other side." In his argument, Admiral Ruthven Libby, the US delegate, used phrases such as "principle of freedom of choice" and "the right of individual self-determination."[7] Or in other words Libby put forth—the voluntary repatriation proposal was essentially "a bill of rights" for the prisoner of war. "As regards repatriation, it permits freedom of choice on the part of the individual, thus insuring that there will be no forced repatriation against the will of an individual." In Libby's choice of words, we can see how the prisoner of war, previously a bureaucratic category of wartime personhood, had become a political subject. The once-vulnerable subject of war, who required the protection and regulation of states, now was a political subject, one invested with desires and the capacity for choice-making. American-style liberalism had come to the interrogation room, and in such a space, the prisoner of war could supposedly express his or her desire, and therefore exercise a freedom to choose.

Historians of the Korean War have often dismissed the POW repatriation controversy as a propaganda ploy used by all sides to gain the upper hand in the armistice negotiations, relegating the story to the footnotes. However, the controversy over POW repatriation became so heated that the signing of the cease-fire was effectively delayed for eighteen months, while the fighting continued across the Korean peninsula. The duration and scope of the debate were unexpected. The United States created a stark binary between "voluntary" repatriation versus "forced" repatriation at the negotiation tables. On closer examination, we can see that the United States was, in fact, making a stunning assertion. The United States was claiming that the most opaque and most coercive space of warfare—the interrogation room—could be transformed by the United States into a liberal, bureaucratic space.

The US delegate at Panmunjom and the Truman administration insisted on the seemingly self-evident transparent nature of their screening process; the US military interrogation room would be a space where Korean and Chinese prisoners of war would be free to express individual choice regarding whether or not they would return to their "homeland." A simple "yes" or "no" was to be recorded by the interrogator. The interrogation room, rather than being a peripheral, invisible space, suddenly became the public, explicit site of the workings of US liberal power. The conduct of warfare—and not the elimination of war—was evidence on the global stage of history, a demonstration of one's capacity for governance.

But the choice offered to the Korean prisoner of war was not a simple matter of a "yes" or "no." The Korean prisoners of war understood that the deceptively straightforward question of repatriation was, in fact, another form of the "What are you?" question asked by the ROKA soldier to Oh Se-hŭi on the path by the cabbage field in October 1950. Were they anti-Communists or Communists? Were they pro-American or anti-American? The presence of two states on the Korean peninsula, one created under Soviet military occupation, the other under US military occupation after liberation from Japanese colonial rule in 1945, literally created a competition between which type of putative "decolonization" was valid, effective, and democratic. After the 1948 elections in the south, the United States and the United Nations declared the southern Republic of Korea the only sovereign state on the peninsula. For the United States, to have prisoners of war choose to *not* repatriate to the northern Democratic People's Republic of Korea would be to validate the US project of liberation through military occupation in the south. For the Korean prisoner of war, it would be another moment of negotiating political recognition for survival.

The supposed moral compass of politics in the war had moved its needle from the 38th parallel to the prisoner of war. And the debate over the nature of the conflict found expression in the controversy around the interrogation room. The issue of POW repatriation captured the attention of the international press and immediately became the flash point of a global debate involving the United Nations, the International Committee of the Red Cross, and the state governments of India, Mexico, and Brazil. This seemingly one-dimensional issue of POW repatriation was, in fact, a dense node of global politics. When Indian General Kodandera Subayya Thimayya met with Prime Minister Jawaharlal Nehru for last-minute instructions on his mission to create a system for POW repatriation along the 38th parallel in 1953, Nehru offered him the following words: "Your job is to find some solution to the problem that is plaguing the world in Korea. A solution to that problem may mean that similar problems in other parts of Asia can be solved as well. Thus, your job can well mean peace in Asia and perhaps in the world."[8] The high political stakes of decolonization had reconfigured the site of the interrogation room, bringing it out of the shadows of exception and into the limelight of diplomatic politics as the US-Soviet Cold War dynamics began to assert its primacy on the international stage.

The nature of the intimate meeting that took place within the interrogation room became a measure of the respective state's legitimacy in its claims or challenges to ideals of liberal governance in the decolonizing post-1945 world. In the interrogation rooms of the Korean War, the templates for this encounter essentially served as allegorical scripts for idealized processes of decolonization of the individual subject by the state. Which state could reinvent the most intimate relations of the colonizer and the colonized, to transform the relationship between the state and subject into one of liberation, democracy, or freedom?

This book foregrounds the landscape of interrogation during the US occupation of Korea and the Korean War, tracing a matrix of interrogation rooms created by the United States, the southern Republic of Korea, the northern Democratic People's Republic of Korea alongside the People's Republic of China, and also India. When we look at the Korean War from the inside of these interrogation rooms, we see a set of stakes not wholly bound to the imperatives of the early Cold War. The figure of the prisoner of war was essentially a distillation of the relationship between the state and its subject. A soldier was ideally the manifestation of two core elements legitimating the state's mobilization of warfare. The soldier was both a citizen and a weapon of the state. The soldier's participation was, on one hand, proof of the national public's consent for the war. At the same time, the soldier's performance in the war was supposed to be evidence of the state's superior technologies of warfare. In the Korean War, states challenged the legitimacy of other states via the POW issue. To have the POW renounce his or her state would shake the legitimacy of that state's governance, and to criticize the state's exploitation of its own soldiers would undermine the superiority of the enemy state's conduct of warfare.

The POW controversy of the Korean War touched off a constellation of political anxieties and ambitions because it resonated with a very basic question confronting the decolonizing world. In the post-1945 crucible of mass militarization of US total warfare, the retreat of Japanese imperialism, and broad anticolonial movements across Asia, the question arose about how to configure a relationship between a state and its subject that could serve as the viable basis for a kind of national or international governance in the post-1945 world. In other words, how did one configure a person for state-building, revolution, or imperial warfare? And who would then be the agent in history that would usher in a new era of a decolonized future?

Enter the interrogation room of the Korean War at this crossroads of empire and revolution. Different states and militaries were claiming that they were able to mitigate the human impulse of fear, violence, and power in the interrogation room. The idealized interrogation room exposed the assumptions held by those who had configured the encounter regarding what legitimate governance looked like. Whether it was American ideas of liberal governance and its demand for a transparent subject desiring free market choice, or Korean Communist philosophies about individual revolutionary subjectivity for collective self-determination, or Indian notions of nonalignment to position the postcolonial Asian as already holding the potential to be the ideal national citizen—all of these questions about the individual's place on the global historical stage of postcolonial nation-building were in play within the interrogation rooms throughout the Korean peninsula. The interrogation room, in this story of the Korean War, was not only supposed to produce information, but also subjects.

The Interrogation Room in the Landscape of War

We often think of the interrogation room as hidden, invisible, and separate from the lives of ordinary people. In fact, a rather specific image might come to mind for many of us: a cloistered darkened room somewhere that serves as a site for extraordinary human drama, whether in terms of physical violence or intellectual wits. The interrogation room is a symbol of the cloaked underbelly of the social order, the exceptional periphery that enables the maintenance of everyday norms. In the following pages, the interrogation rooms that appear are more ordinary and idiosyncratic. Interrogation can look like the meeting between Oh Se-hŭi and the ROKA soldier; it can be a hastily arranged group interrogation for surrendered POWs after a battle; it can be questioning at a checkpoint for refugees; and it can be even a highly formal and ritualized interrogation in the explanation rooms organized by the Indian-led Neutral Nations Repatriation Commission (NNRC) at the 38th parallel. With such variation and improvisation, "interrogation"— as practiced and negotiated by those on the ground—was a landscape rather than a contained space. And once we are able to see more adequately how interrogation was embedded—sometimes even in plain sight—into the everyday, we are also able to comprehend how the encounter mediated between the interrogator and the prisoner of war was only one node of a complex ecosystem of violence, intimacy, and bureaucracy.

This book explores how the individual person became the terrain for warfare and also its *jus ad bellum* in the mid-twentieth century during the postcolonial war that was officially not a war. And I argue that it was the interrogator who became critical to fashioning the POW for these dual purposes. In the calculus of modern warfare, the very existence of a prisoner of war was supposed to be proof of the humanity— the benevolence, the compassion, and the rational morality—of the capturing soldier, the military, and the state. Which side treated the prisoners of war more humanely? Under whose custody was the POW population larger? The POW was a constant demonstration of the state's mercy and ability to transcend the evils of war. From the standpoint of the interrogation room, the discussion around the POW during the Korean War belied the deeper stakes at hand in the controversy. This controversy was not a discussion about the humanity of the prisoner of war. Instead, this controversy revolved around who had the capacity to recognize another's humanity. For the United States, interrogators needed to provide the POW as justification for war.

Parallel to how the Korean War was the war that was not a war, the United States was the aspiring empire that had no imperial ambitions. In the wake of World War II, the United States insisted that it would be the harbinger of an era different from the colonialism of the British or the French. In October 27, 1945, Truman declared in a speech, "We seek no territorial expansion of selfish advantage.... We believe in the eventual return of sovereign and self-government to all peoples who have been deprived of them by force."[9] On March 12, 1947, Truman addressed Congress in a bid for the United States to give aid to Turkey and Greece, and his speech encapsulated certain tenets of what is now considered to be the Truman Doctrine on US foreign policy. Notably, Truman gave two statements that characterized the projected role of the United States on the post-1945 global stage. The first statement was on the freedom of choice: "At the present moment in world history nearly every nation must choose between alternative ways of life." The Cold War storyline of the Soviet Union as representing slavery and the United States representing freedom was the clearest, simplest delineation of US self-presentation as a benevolent power. The second statement highlighted the threat to freedom: "If we falter in our leadership, we may endanger the peace of the world—and we shall surely endanger the welfare of our own nation."[10] The United States was now, according to Truman's narrative, the self-declared guardian of the world. In her work on US war-making, Mimi Nyugen notes how "freedom is precisely the idiom through which liberal empire acts as an arbiter for *all* humanity."[11] For the Korean War, it was the figure of the POW that facilitated this ideological reconfiguring of liberal warfare. And this sociocultural shift went hand in hand with a massive structural shift in American empire-making.

US historians point to the Korean War as a pivotal event for the United States in global Cold War history. The Korean War operated as the catalyst for the mobilization and rise of what we now call the US national security state. In April 1950, the Policy Planning Staff, headed by Paul Nitze, presented to Truman what historians have called the "blueprint" or the "bible of American national security," the National Security Council Paper 68 (NSC-68).[12] The fifty-eight-page report was an assessment of the state of national security, and at the heart of this report's narrative was "the conviction that a new era of total war had dawned on the United States," to use the words of historian Michael Hogan.[13] NSC-68 proposed a militarized state for a permanent state of war, one that followed the Truman Doctrine of how an attack anywhere in the world could be seen as an attack on the United States. Casting the Soviet Union as an implacable enemy, the writers of NSC-68 effectively called for "a substantial increase" in both military expenditures and military assistance programs as well as the development of "overt" and "covert psychological warfare" programs to "encourage mass defections" or the "fomenting and supporting [of] unrest and revolt."[14] But for Truman and Congress, the NSC-68 called for an exponential budgetary increase that seemed prohibitive. Then the Korean War broke out. As Dean Acheson and Paul Nitze reflected in 1953 on those early months of 1950, they both agreed: "Korea came along and saved us."[15]

Or as Acheson stated in more detail: "Korea moved a great many things from the realm of theory and brought them right into the realm of actuality and the realm of urgency."[16] The cost of bringing the NSC-68 proposal into "the realm of actuality" required an estimated $40 billion, which was three times more than the $13 billion slotted for 1950 military spending. With the Korean War, the military budget exponentially increased to $48 billion by May 31, 1951.[17] Korea soon became a focal point for the expansionist strategies of the United States over the globe. In 1953, there were 813 military bases under US command, and President Dwight Eisenhower's first term would oversee the creation of sixty-eight more bases.[18] "The war in Korea brought about a radical revision of postwar strategic planning," note Seungsook Moon and Maria Höhn, and according to their work, "the bulk of the US overseas military empire" was concentrated in South Korea, Japan, Okinawa, and West Germany.[19] This infrastructure and network laid the grounds to facilitate interventionist US operations on a global scale.

But what historian Bruce Cumings has called the "archipelago of empire" was a refashioning of US ambition against the backdrop of decolonization.[20] As in the late nineteenth century with the Spanish-American Wars when the United States annexed the Philippines, Puerto Rico, Guam, and also Hawai'i and American Samoa, in the post-1945 era the United States turned to the 130 Pacific Islands as valuable sites for military testing and bases, using tactics such as "leasing instead of annexing territory" from Western colonial powers, which the Department of Defense stated enhanced "our reputation for integrity of international agreement and traditional lack of imperialistic ambition."[21] With the military bases, the United States could argue that it had no designs on supposed colonial settlement. This extensive base network undergirded another strategy to extend US military reach over the globe: military assistance agreements and mutual defense treaties.

The interrogation room was a compressed site for the configuring and inventing of the labor, infrastructure, and policy required for this new liberal empire. Under Truman, the United States had installed Military Assistance Aid Groups (MAAGs) in the Philippines, Korea, and Taiwan, and in 1952 fifteen countries signed defense agreements with the United States. Counterinsurgency and military training were also essential tactics of the United States in the post-1945 era, with entities like the Central Intelligence Agency (CIA) established in 1947 and charged with conducting "covert operations ... which are so planned and executed ... that if uncovered the US Government can plausibly disclaim any responsibility for them."[22] The military bases, the covert operations, and the POW controversy in the Korean War—all of these framed an empire that disavowed its imperial nature and its colonial past and present.

Mapping out the experiences in the interrogation room lays bare the projects of militarized surveillance in the post-1945 era, and the intricate interdependencies of the labor involved. Just as people were forced to move through interrogation networks, people also moved and created these flexible networks across territories and the Pacific. Both the interrogator and the prisoner of war became the terrain on which the reinscription of meaning took place at this contested node between empire, revolution, and state-building. The simple, high-stakes question posed to Oh Se-hŭi by the ROKA soldier—"What are you?"—was, in essence, the question every state or organization was demanding of the interrogator and the prisoner.

The US military interrogation room that one meets in this study was neither monolithic nor absolute in its hegemonic project. Nor was it the sole form of interrogation that the Korean or US prisoner of war encountered in the years before, during, and after the three years of the Korean War. The invention of multiple, different types of interrogation serves as the central framing for this study, and I examine how these historically configured interrogation rooms revealed, in turn, multiple visions and interpretations of the project of formal decolonization and its relation to another project—modern warfare. The different visions of either Secretary of State Dean Acheson, Indian President Jawaharlal Nehru, or President Syngman Rhee regarding Korea's significance to the post-1945 global order were contingent on thousands of acts of interrogation, translation, and disciplining of possible subjects. It was interrogation that provided the proper narrative needed, that assured policy makers of the availability of a willing, desirous subject. What follows is not meant to be a comprehensive story of the Korean War as an event, nor is it a comprehensive account of the prisoner of war experience on all sides of the war.[23] Rather, it is a history of how people remade warfare in front of formal decolonization through historically specific sites, technologies, and experiences.

From within the interrogation room, the cast of unexpected historical actors within this story multiplies—Japanese American young men, who had spent their adolescence in the internment camps of World War II, were often the translators for or first-level interrogators of the Korean prisoners of war, the Korean prisoners of war themselves were from both sides of the 38th parallel or even from the farther reaches of the Korean diaspora, like Uzbekistan or the northern regions of the Soviet Union. Members of the Custodian Force of India had fought under the British colonial military forces during World War II, and some of them had gone on to consolidating the national Indian Forces through the violent Partition of India and Pakistan. The US prisoners of war formed a generational cohort who had grown up through the Great Depression and came to the Korean peninsula with experiences under Jim Crow segregation and the US "warfare state" forged during the mass mobilization of both the home and foreign fronts of World War II.[24]

Both the interrogator and the prisoner of war understood that war-making was fundamentally also empire- or state-building. Between the mass demobilization of the Japanese imperial army, which had used Korean conscripts and volunteers in its expansionist projects through-out Asia, and the Cold War configuring of the US total warfare state of World War II, states and organizations were eager to mark and claim the labor of these moving populations.[25] As for the Chinese and North Korean interrogators, whether through the Chinese revolution of 1949 that brought the Chinese Communist Party into power or the Korean anticolonial guerilla militias in Manchuria during the 1930s, they had participated in the creation of military forces as a claim to legitimate nation-state status.

The vantage point of the interrogation room affords us a different time frame for the beginning and ending of this story of the Korean War. This story of the war positions the significance of the Korean War beyond the usual Cold War binary power struggle, and not solely within the postcolonial civil war binary of the anti-Communist south versus the Communist north. Rather, through the prism of the interrogation room, we can understand the Korean War as part of a longer history of Japanese colonial legacies and US imperial ambitions within a trans-Pacific frame, as both projects converged on the Korean peninsula in the middle of the twentieth century. From the Philippine-American War of the turn of the century, through the Russo-Japanese War, the

Sino-Japanese War, and the Asia-Pacific theater of World War II, both the United States and Japan were reformulating their claims to being the legitimate future horizon of a new kind of global order. A history of the interrogation room critically becomes a study of projects of subject-making, racial formations, and claims to sovereignty in the wake of 1945, as the former colony of Korea, the former empire of Japan, and the self-disavowing empire of the United States navigated how to present themselves as nation-states. It is an international story of how the Korean War heralded an era of what jurist Carl Schmitt had termed "wars over humanity" in 1950, where nation-states no longer made wars, but rather wars made nation-states.[26]

Violence in the Archive

Paper was also a weapon of war. In September 1950, a month before his capture by the ROKA soldier, Oh Se-hŭi was traveling with his comrades when he heard a plane even before he could see it. Immediately, he rushed for cover. One never knew what to expect from a US airplane. Among the possibilities: napalm or paper. It was either potential death in the form of a jellied gasoline that burned into the skin, or potential safety in the form of a "safe conduct pass"—a leaflet printed in both English and Korean guaranteeing safe surrender to anyone in possession of it. For civilians and soldiers on the ground, the Korean War was one of constant, terrifying bombing, on a scale often lost on the American public. From 1950 to 1953, the United States forces dropped 386,037 bombs and 32,357 tons of napalm. Historian Marilyn Young makes this calculation: "If one counts all types of airborne ordinance, including rockets and machine-gun ammunition, the total tonnage comes to 698,000."[27] Within the three years of continuous active fighting on the Korean peninsula, the US military had dropped more tonnage of bombs than it had in the entire Asia-Pacific theater during World War II. This turn to air war operated hand in hand with the deepening investment in psychological warfare. Both the psyche and the bombing target were useful abstractions for policy makers on which to demonstrate the power of America to the world. The US military dropped over one billion leaflets over the breadth of the Korean peninsula during the war.[28] Psychological warfare was a definite weapon of war, and soldiers like Oh Se-hŭi were its terrain.

The bomb that exploded over Oh Se-hŭi that day in September 1950 was a paper bomb. Oh secretly picked up a "safe conduct pass" leaflet that fell to the ground and stowed it in his inside jacket pocket for possible later use.[29] Paper—and what was written on it—was a vital resource and tool. Between the over one billion leaflets bombed over the Korean peninsula by the US military and the UNC safe surrender leaflet ripped up by the ROKA soldier, paper was not a neutral object in warfare.

To tell the story of the prisoner of war during Korean War, we must also pay close attention to the circulation and meaning of paper on this landscape of napalm and ammunition. Paper was not in ready supply because it was, in fact, quite scarce, but the importance of paper was undeniable. When International Committee of the Red Cross (ICRC) delegate Frederick Bieri visited the camp on Koje-do, he noted in his report that the POWs requested more copies of the 1949 Geneva Conventions to read and post in their compounds. The POWs also asked for more writing utensils, more Japanese-English dictionaries, and more paper. When thirty Korean Communist prisoners of war managed to capture the US camp commander of UNC Camp #1 on Koje Island in early March 1952, one of their first requests was for one thousand sheets of paper. The prisoners of war wrote essays, petitions, and letters, sending these to President Eisenhower, the United Nations, and the ICRC. Others kept their own writing projects. A twenty-four-year-old POW named Lee Pyong Man, who had been attending college at the outbreak of the war, complained that his "notebook that contained the communist history was confiscated" during a search of his compound.[30] Two hundred leaflets had been allegedly picked up by the ROKA soldiers around the POW compounds before a singing demonstration instigated by women Korean Communist POWs at the Koje-do camp.[31]

Much of the prisoners' mobilization of paper in wartime was in response to and engagement with a power structure of warfare and governance that was not located simply in war rooms or military armaments. Oh Se-hŭi's experiences introduce us to a central political concern for our own project of telling the story of the Korean War through the interrogation room: the archive. Beyond the paper used by the prisoner of war was the vast and immense scaffolding of institutional paperwork built around the POW during the Korean War. Indeed, to tell the story of the POW is also to tell the story of this sizable paper archive with its global reach and dense bureaucracy. The idea that bureaucracy was so integral to warfare was not new—but the urgency and necessity in documenting details around the POW does call for our consideration. And tracking the different paper trails following the discussion on prisoners of war leads us through the bureaucracies of multiple states and institutions: the US Army, the Department of State, the United Nations, the International Committee of the Red Cross, and the meetings at Panmunjom, while also following the petitions, letters, and demands of the prisoners of war, all sent to the White House, the United Nations, the ICRC, or different countries. Narratives of the US military in the Korean War have primarily focused on the literal military tactics on the battlefield or the political diplomacy occurring at the highest levels; however, this story of the war is much more interested in the military man as bureaucrat, the interrogator as bureaucrat, and interrogation as a template of bureaucracy.

To create a certain kind of paper archive was to claim a certain kind of legitimacy in international politics. The imperative to produce the documentation needed to support the regulatory effect the ICRC hoped that the Geneva Conventions would have on state warfare merged with another phenomenon. As scholar Karma Nabulsi has noted, the debates over defining war crimes during and after World War II "directly" affected the Geneva negotiations in 1949. Nabulsi singles out the 1942 London Declaration of War Crimes as "one of the most important legal precedents" that undergirded the framing of the Nuremberg Trials of 1946 and the Universal Declaration of Human Rights of 1948.[32] The liberal internationalist order was highly invested in notions of evidence and documentation, and the institutional archive of the POW was created around the express purpose of documenting the treatment of the prisoner of war. On the post-1945 stage of war crimes trials, the question of evidence—and who could judge—had become an encompassing issue. In the Korean War, the POW was the evidence, the measure of a state's conduct in wartime, and states put each other on trial in the court of public opinion. But in front of the sheer volume of records, this book neither takes bureaucratic practices for granted, nor approaches paper as a benign medium. In the following pages, the story of paper and laws of war begins with the letter three Korean emissaries bring from King Kojong to the delegates of the 1907 Hague Convention to protest the Japanese protectorate treaty forced upon Korea and ends with President Dwight Eisenhower signing the Code of Conduct for American troops as Executive Order 10631 in 1955, bringing the colonial era into the same story of the Cold War.

This book tackles the immense paper bureaucracy of the very national security state catalyzed by the Korean War. The policy memoranda, the meeting minutes, military intelligence reports, and correspondence: the US diplomatic and military paper archives housed in the National Archives at College Park, Maryland have provided the foundational grounds on which historical analysis has gained traction in order to analyze US foreign policy. Interrogation generated more paper within this system, as military intelligence provided the "information" for military operations or policy decisions. For a period like the US occupation of southern Korea in the post-1945 era, the reports written and produced by the Counterintelligence Corps and the G2 intelligence sections of the US military have served as the basis for many histories on postliberation southern Korea, and these documents are housed in the National Archives in College Park, Maryland, and not on the Korean peninsula.

The paper archival base for this book extends to files that have never received systematic analytical treatment by scholars. Included in this previously unexamined archive of documents are two important collections: the first is a collection of over three hundred investigation cases containing interrogation transcripts and summaries of incidents in the UNC POW camp located on Koje Island. The second is a collection that was recently declassified through a long-standing Freedom of Information Act request—it is a collection of US Counterintelligence Corps (CIC) interrogations of over one thousand US prisoners of war returning from Chinese and North Korean POW camps after the cease-fire signing, and the CIC specifically focused on the POWs' experiences of interrogation. Alongside military manuals and lecture transcripts on interrogation training techniques, these archives provide us the opportunity to discern not only the idealized templates for the conduct and product of interrogation but also the improvisation and uncertainty that ran through these report narratives. If "interrogation is an art with as many branches as music, or painting," as the 1952 guide for new CIC agents counseled, then for the interrogator, "it is his object to produce a coherent, factual, and readable narrative."[33] What were the standardized narrative templates for "exposing" or "revealing" elements in interrogation, and how can we read them also for how these templates obscured or erased other elements simultaneously?

And sometimes the archive interrupts its own logic. In a high-security, climate-controlled vault at the National Archives in College Park, two large archival boxes sit on a shelf in the company of Lee Harvey Oswald's rifle, Eva Braun's diary, and Mason and Dixon's surveying journal. Rather than housing an iconic object from "American" history, the boxes contain a blood document from a war largely forgotten by mainstream America—a petition covering over a hundred pages written and signed in blood by 487 anti-Communist Korean prisoners of war, members of the Anti-Communist Youth League in the Yŏngch'ŏn POW camp. Meticulously written in Korean and translated into English by the POWs themselves, three sets of petitions, all dated May 10, 1953, were addressed respectively to President Dwight Eisenhower, General Mark Clark, and Lieutenant General William Harrison. This document's residence in the vault, according to one senior archivist, is due to the difficulty in cataloging and preserving the material: how does one categorize and store a blood document? The blood document poses a challenge to the classification system because it forces us to confront language and corporeality at the same time, rupturing basic assumed divisions between the mind (language/text) and the body (blood). This blood petition raises the simple question of, what does blood do to text, and what does text, in turn, do to blood? The writing medium of blood pushes us to approach the document again as an *act* of writing instead of moving immediately to the textual content itself. What kind of political act was this blood petition?

The focus on writing as an act forces us to consider what is not contained or recorded in the paper archive, especially in the interrogation reports.[34] The bureaucratic template for these records erases the conflict and struggle within the interrogation room. Much more complicated questions over translation, physical gestures, the threat of violence— these were moved beyond the frame of the interrogation report. The only archival evidence of the presence and labor of the Japanese American interrogators in the National Archives is in the name noted for the interrogator in the reports. The work of Korean translators or the experiences of Korean prisoners of war in these interrogation rooms is either absent or requires a close, creative reading of the interrogation and investigation reports' narratives. Oral history interviews I conducted with Japanese American former interrogators, Korean former prisoners of war, and also Korean civilians who had lived in the surroundings of the POW camps during the war are central to the framework of the story that follows. These oral history narratives became the basis for focusing on the questions of subject-making vis-à-vis the institutionalization of warfare in this book.

Paper, in the end, was not the most important material in the interrogation room. In practice, the body was the most important text. The very first piece of paper Oh offered to the ROKA soldier was the UN safe surrender leaflet, which the ROKA soldier ripped up rather contemptuously. In the end, none of the paper offered by Oh sufficed. When the soldier saw Oh's long hair, it was in that moment Oh became a person deserving of another moment of life. Both Oh Se-hŭi and the ROKA soldier had their own fluency based on their experiences under Japanese colonial rule and US occupation in how to read the other, how to anticipate the other, and how to negotiate the other's possible readings. The stakes were high regarding how the POWs navigated and negotiated their role—and violence was not held in abeyance, but rather was a constant presence. Their physical bodies were always a part of the equation, and encounter was not something mediated only by paper.

American prisoners of war found themselves facing the same quandary and challenge. After the signing of the cease-fire agreement in July 1953, the American public and government became fascinated and preoccupied with a group of twenty-one American prisoners of war who chose to stay in China at the end of the war. But their choice of China seemed incomprehensible to mainstream America. Why would this motley group of young American men choose to stay in China? In reply, the American public held on to the notion of "brainwashing." In other words, these American POWs had essentially *not* made a choice, and were instead victims of an "Oriental" Communist regime through "brainwashing" techniques used in the interrogation rooms. And the stigma along with the suspicion of having been a prisoner of war interrogated in the North Korean and Chinese POW camps followed the American soldiers long after they ceased being officially prisoners of war.

The cultural phenomenon of "brainwashing" introduces an important theme of thinking about the body alongside the paper archive. The hysteria around the US prisoners of war was energized by an anxiety over how to know what had happened to the POW when there was no definitive external physical marker of change or impact from the experience of captivity. The body, in essence, was also considered an archive. The body was an archive of experience, and people were concerned about how to read the body effectively and efficiently. Physical gestures, speech acts, the body itself—all of these became a kind of text to be read, assessed, and evaluated. The US military experimented with lie detector tests on Koreans, with the basic question of whether or not the "Oriental" body registered and recognized the difference between telling a "lie" or the "truth." Indeed, the kind of body that was key for the US military in developing interrogation techniques was the racialized body. The ability to discern and tell the truth was a question of embodied, biological selfhood. In an era of formal decolonization, this sup-posedly "objective" measuring of a racialized subject's capacity for verac-ity was embedded in the larger political project of assessing of whether or not postcolonial societies had the capacity for self-government. In other words, the struggle over the global geopolitical order that occurred on an intimate scale within the interrogation room was more patently a conflict over the racial order.[35]

American POWs themselves understood that ideas about racial or-ders were fundamentally at stake in the interrogation rooms. In the North Korean and Chinese-run POW camps along the Yalu River, American POWs recreated the Ku Klux Klan. The anxiety that people, states, and societies held around wartime interrogation revolved less around the question of exactly what happened during the interroga-tion, but more around the question of how the experience of interro-gation could have changed the prisoner. The US liberal empire was claiming a space of interrogation where the prisoner could express his or her desire freely. North Korean and Chinese military interrogation rooms were offering the process of self-criticism as a way to refashion one's own will and political consciousness. The Custodian Force of India and the India-led Neutral Nations Repatriation Committee set up "explanation rooms," where state representatives could attempt to persuade prisoners to repatriate. If these interrogation rooms could transform, facilitate, or reveal people's interiors, then another system of interrogation was created to evaluate and control those who passed through these rooms. South Korean paramilitary youth groups within the POW camps began incorporating tattooing practices in their inter-rogations, and American POWs created KKK-similar groups like the "Circle," "which got its name from an incident in which its members surrounded and beat a prisoner who, they discovered, had written pro-Communist articles."[36] Often, those beaten were American POWs from working-class backgrounds, or were black, Filipino, Puerto Rican. The struggles over people's interiors—desires, hopes, politics—were em-bedded in practices and ideologies about race, whether about racial na-tionalism, imperialism, or militarism.

The Map of the Book

"The Elements of War"—part I of this book—charts the project of forging the new paradigm of liberal warfare by delving into the trans-Pacific histories of the interrogation room, the prisoner of war, and the interrogator of the Korean War. The first chapter, "Interrogation," moves from Korea's early twentieth-century struggles for sovereignty through the US occupation of Korea after liberation from Japanese colonial rule in 1945. The story traces how the landscape of surveillance created under American military occupation on the Korean peninsula then transformed into the matrix of interrogation rooms for a war of intervention. The chapter on "The Prisoner of War" moves between the policy makers in Washington, DC, and the prisoners of war in the UNC camp on Koje Island. It focuses on the stakes for both the policy makers and the prisoners of war in rendering the prisoner of war from a bureaucratic category of warfare into a political subject on the Cold War decolonizing stage. The final chapter in this section, "The Interrogator," begins the story in the Japanese American internment camps of World War II, and follows how the Japanese American subject moved from being an "enemy alien" under surveillance to laboring as an interrogator of Koreans during the Korean War. This chapter reconstructs the types of interrogation rooms these Japanese American interrogators invented, what they resisted, and what they reinterpreted.

"Humanity Interrogated"—the second half of this book—lays out the story of the Korean War through four different sites of interrogation. In "Koje Island: A Mutiny or Revolution," we return to the site of the largest US- and UN-run POW camp during the war to go behind the barbed wire fence to follow the event that squarely placed the POW controversy onto the global media map: the kidnapping of the US camp commander by a group of mostly Korean Communist POWs. Questions about sovereignty, diplomacy, and international humanitarian law come to the fore as the chapter places the UNC camp on Koje Island in the same frame as the negotiating table at Panmunjom. The next chapter, "Below the 38th Parallel: Between Barbed Wire and Blood," begins during the US occupation period as the mobilization of Korean

youth groups become key to the rightist regime and US counterintelligence network coming into formation on the peninsula. It then takes
us through a network of US- and UN-run POW camps on the peninsula in order to examine the interrogation practices developed by the
anti-Communist South Korean paramilitary youth groups inside the
camps. The third chapter, "On the 38th parallel: The Third Choice," takes
us to the POW camp on the 38th parallel created by the Custodian
Force of India that housed the neutral "explanation" rooms that the
Indian delegation had proposed as a resolution to the negotiation impasse at Panmunjom over the topic of POW repatriation. Inside these
explanation rooms, prisoners of war would have three choices in terms
of repatriation: repatriation, nonrepatriation, or a "neutral" nation. It
was an interrogation room for "neutrality," an early manifestation of
nonalignment's vision. Moving from inside the explanation rooms the
chapter then traces the journeys of seventy-six Korean prisoners of war
who had chosen a "neutral country," as POWs eventually found their
way to Argentina, Mexico, Brazil, and India. The final chapter, "Above
the 38th Parallel: The US Citizen–POW," takes us into the POW camps
and interrogation rooms created by the Chinese and North Korean
militaries. From inside the interrogation room, the story of decolonization on the Korean peninsula in the mid-twentieth century did not
stop at the question of liberation for the Korean people. This chapter
asks what decolonization meant for American prisoners of war also.
How the US POWs navigated a trans-Pacific surveillance system of
interrogation—North Korean, Chinese, fellow POWs, and the US CIC—
forms the central thread through this chapter.

Many of the historical experiences in this book are not to be found
in either American or Korean history books. The contours of the Korean War's absence from the pages of American history cast a long
shadow over the genealogy of American interventions abroad. Telling
the story of the Korean War requires not simply the offering of a narrative but an examination of the mechanics of our own attachments,
repulsion, and investments in the narratives themselves. Inclusion in
the pantheon of American wars of the twentieth century requires a national mythos, and the Korean War had inspired neither the national,

collective morale of World War II nor the national, collective trauma of the Vietnam War. The Korean War presents us with the singular opportunity to begin not with the question of why we remember or forget a war, but rather how we tell the story of war itself. It is, at its heart, a story about a crisis of political imagination.

FIGURE I.1 Safe Conduct Pass issued
by the United Nations Command—
An example of the safe surrender pass that
Oh Se-hŭi carried (National Archives
and Records Administration)

FIGURE I.2 Safe Conduct Pass issued
by the Korean People's Army and the
Chinese People's Volunteer Forces
(National Archives and Records Administration)

PART I

The Elements of War

1

Interrogation

IN APRIL 1946, a group of three men from the US military arrived at the home of Chang Sung Sum, a Korean peasant farmer. It would have been relatively easy to identify Chang's house in the village of San Su Nai Bi.[1] A large sign hung on the outside of the house for all passersby to see. "Beyond this house is South Korea," declared the sign in three languages: Korean, English, and Russian. Chang's small plot of land was on the 38th parallel.

From the vantage point of Chang's trilingual sign, the 38th parallel was less a stable border than an awkward marker of decolonization deferred. Shooting skirmishes between soldiers from the Soviet-occupied north and the US-occupied south regularly punctuated the air all along the width of the Korean peninsula. The militaries of the two Koreas, the Soviet Union, and the United States could not figure out where the 38th parallel was located, so Chang had taken matters into his own hands.

Chang's three visitors that April 1946 were from an organization with the US military government that would quickly rise to power and influence—the US Counterintelligence Corps. The American CIC agent, the South Korean soldier, and the Korean interpreter were concerned about farmer Chang. The CIC had heard that a Soviet soldier along with four North Korean soldiers had come by his home. What had they wanted to talk about with Chang? According to Chang, he had been working in the fields when they came to his house. They stopped in front of the house and called out to him. "Hearing their call, [Chang] went to the house and the Russians asked him, Why are you taking this

American rice ration? Don't you know they are going to take over Korean property in turn for the rice they give you?"[2] The CIC had sent out three people to interview one peasant farmer, whose home rested on where the 38th parallel might possibly have been at that time. Peasant farmers like Chang Sung Sum were a part of what scholar Bruce Cumings has called "the most numerous of the Korean classes and the class that gave the liberation period its dual characteristics of extensive participation and widespread resistance."[3] For the CIC, the political desires of Korean peasants formed an uncharted landscape, one that was far more ambiguous than the 38th parallel.

Before the prisoner of war became the object of focus, anxiety, and policy planning for the United States during the Korean War, it was the peasant like Chang Sung Sum that concerned the US military government. In histories of the Korean War, the history of struggles over the meanings of decolonization on the peninsula has been subsumed by the Cold War frame manifested by the 38th parallel. Much of the literature on the Korean War either takes the 38th parallel for granted or charts the character of the war primarily as movement over the physical terrain, with the 38th parallel highlighted in the center of the Korean peninsula. By charting out the landscape of "states of emergency," which focused the question of legitimacy on the individual Korean subject, this story challenges the historical primacy scholars have granted to the 38th parallel in narratives of the Korean War. The development of the military government state apparatus around the Korean peasant during the US occupation laid the grounds for the interrogation rooms mobilized for the Korean War. The amount of daily improvisation the CIC undertook in charting out the Korean peasant masses was both staggering and mundane.

From the vantage point of Chang's trilingual sign on the 38th parallel, the traditional temporal and geopolitical bounds of the Korean War fell away. The story of the Korean peasant under US occupation, the development of a US intelligence network, and the proposal for POW voluntary repatriation was part of a longer twentieth-century story of American imperial expansionist ambitions in Asia. From the vantage point of Chang's sign, we can see how the paradigm of warfare was changing over the landscape of deferred decolonization on the Korean peninsula. This chapter begins its story with three Korean emissaries at the Second Hague Convention in 1907 with a letter from King Kojong protesting the illegality of the Japanese protectorate treaty over Korea. The doors at the conference remained closed. The "civilizing mission" as held sacrosanct by the Western colonial powers subsumed Korea's sovereign nation-state status—the Korean was not racially advanced sufficiently for self-government.

In a bid to distinguish its ambitions from those of the European colonial powers, the United States insisted that it respected and indeed recognized the territorial sovereignty of other nations and postcolonies. As a result of this insistence, the United States needed to demonstrate its own benevolence, and thus it needed evidence of its liberatory project. In post-1945 southern Korea, the United States enacted and institutionalized the beginnings of two kinds of military action that would define US militarization in the latter half of the twentieth century and beyond. The first was liberation through military occupation, or to be more specific to the case of Korea, decolonization through military occupation. This project then led to another kind of military action, which was a war of intervention, or in the case of Korea, an international "police action." The individual postcolonial Korean was supposed to be evidence of the rupture the United States had enacted on the Korean peninsula, breaking the historical legacies of Japanese colonialism and ushering in the possibilities an aspirational US liberalism offered.

The CIC, along with the other intelligence sections of the US military, helped translate the "state of emergency" declared by the United States Army Military Government in Korea (USAMGIK) officials into a mundane, everyday plane of experience. Like the peasant farmer Chang Sung Sum with his trilingual signs on the 38th parallel in 1946 and the captured Korean fighter Oh Se-hŭi with his four pieces of paper on his body in 1950, the ordinary Korean living under US occupation was learning how to navigate different potential readings of his or her personhood by different groups. And how each reading would come with its own particular violent consequences, whether physically or socially. Interrogation, in this crucible, was not merely a state-sanctioned technique. Koreans understood how to anticipate and navigate how US military intelligence and different Korean groups could read them politically. It became a relational practice of everyday politics on the ground, and a source of great anxiety for the US military government.

This chapter charts the infrastructure of intelligence created by the US military on the ground in southern Korea and positions this project within a larger story of Korea's position relative to the global shifts of sovereignty, recognition, and warfare through the twentieth century. Language is an especially pivotal realm for power in the following pages, as close readings of diplomatic memoranda and military government ordinances enable us to follow how US agents and officials attempted to fashion and control a Korean subject suitable for their project of military occupation. But the Korean populace were neither passive readers nor silent listeners, and Korean political organizations distributed their own pamphlets and lined walls with posters. In front of the Koreans' undeniable demands and harvest uprisings, the USAMGIK depended on the CIC to provide certainty and knowledge about the Korean individual subject. The professionalization of the CIC, which was reaped through the CIC's criminalization of the Korean political left, was ad hoc, improvised, and dependent on a crucial figure: the Korean informant. By the time Truman sent troops to the peninsula in 1950, the Korean populace already intimately understood how a US-militarized state of emergency operated institutionally on the ground.

The Lacuna of Korea in the Twentieth Century

After an arduous three-month journey from Korea through Vladivostok, Saint Petersburg, and Berlin, three emissaries from Korea arrived finally at The Hague in the Netherlands on June 25, 1907. Yi Sangsŏl, Yi Jun, and Yi Ŭijong had a message for the world from King Kojong. The Second Hague Convention on the international laws of war was underway, with forty-four states participating. Delegates from Korea had attended the first Hague Convention in 1899, but the delegations of the Second Convention refused this time to open the doors of the conference to these three emissaries. Korea had become "illegal" on the world stage, to use the words of historian Alexis Dudden.[4]

In 1905, with military threat and force, Japan had pressured Korean officials to sign a protectorate treaty, essentially giving Japan the right to represent Korea in all foreign diplomatic relations. King Kojong had refused to sign the treaty, and in 1906 Kojong began planning a secret mission for Korean representatives to expose and protest the illegal nature of the protectorate treaty at The Hague in 1907. But Japan, along with the other forty-three delegations, ignored the demands of the three Korean representatives. Korea was no longer a sovereign state on the international stage.

Undeterred, Yi Sangsŏl, Yi Jun, and Yi Ŭijong swiftly moved to send translations in French, the language of Western diplomacy at that time, of their message to all of the delegations in attendance. Quickly, their letter appeared in the Sunday, June 30 issue of the *Courrier de la Conférence de la Paix*, a daily journal produced by William T. Stead, a British "social evangelist and journalist" known on both sides of the Atlantic.[5] Under the heading "Why Exclude Korea?," the letter the three Korean representatives had sent to the different delegates was reproduced in full. The Korean emissaries emphasized that Japan's actions with the protectorate treaty was "in violation of all international law" and had been done "by force." In addition to attaching a detailed summary of all the acts committed by the Japanese in Korea leading up to the forced treaty signing, they laid out three clear points in the letter:

1. The Japanese acted without the consent of the His Majesty, the emperor.
2. In order to achieve their goal, the Japanese employed armed force against the imperial government.
3. The Japanese acted in violation of all the laws and customs of the country.[6]

By Monday, the *Courrier* printed that in response to the Korean emissaries' letter, the Japanese delegation stated that the treaty between Japan and Korea gave Japan the "exclusive right" to represent Korea in foreign affairs. And no other delegation challenged this assertion.[7]

For the colonial powers at the Second Hague Convention, criticizing or condemning Japan's actions would have undermined their own claims over vast colonized territories globally. In addition, toward "the latter part of the nineteenth century, protectorates were a common technique by which European states exercised extensive control over non-European states while not officially assuming sovereignty over those states."[8] These protectorates, according to legal scholar Anthony Anghie, were "essentially a treaty by which uncivilized states placed themselves under the 'protection' of European states."[9] Japan had also won decisive victories against Russia in the Russo-Japanese War (1904–5). Warfare as aggression was not condemned, and instead the prevailing notions of social Darwinism and the civilizing mission framed the debate around Korea. As the jurist Thomas Joseph Lawrence wrote in 1904 after the Russo-Japanese War: "I have no doubt that in the long run Korea will be annexed by one or the other of her powerful neighbours. It is the fate of small, weak, and corrupt states to fade out of the political map," he claimed. But such a colonial possession, he argued, would be beneficial for the Japanese: "if the Japanese receive her as the prize of victory, they will develop an aptitude for governing subordinate peoples which history shows to have been wanting to them in the past."[10] With the defeat of Russia at the hands of Japan, it appeared that Japan would become the nonwhite colonial power at the table. And in order to demonstrate its full capacity as a colonizing power, Japan needed a colony. To have Korea under its "protection," Japan was only fulfilling the principles of the colonial civilizing mission espoused by others at the conference.

Four days after the Japanese statement on the validity of Japan's claims over Korea's external sovereignty, a photographic portrait of Yi Sangsŏl, Yi Jun, and Yi Ŭijong appeared at the top of the front page of the *Courrier de la Conférence de la Paix*, accompanied by a full-page article titled "Interview with the Korean Prince Yi." William T. Stead was a journalist famous for his sensationalist "new journalism," where he used his pen and the press as a way to mobilize public sentiment around moral crises.[11] Stead had supported and reported on the First Hague Peace Conference, and published a weekly *War Against War* and even toured Europe to drum up support for what he called an "International Peace Crusade." After the utter silence from behind the conven-

FIGURE 1.1 Portrait of Yi Sangsŏl, Yi Jun, and Yi Ŭijong on front page of *Courrier de la Conférence de la Paix*. July 5, 1907 (Swarthmore College Peace Collection)

tion doors to the demands of the Korean emissaries, Stead had clearly taken up their cause.

The portrait of Yi Sangsŏl, Yi Jun, and Yi Ŭijong presented them in immaculate Western dress, fully exemplifying what historian Henry Em has called "the (Christian) liberal-bourgeois subjectivity that emerged in Korea at the turn of the century."[12] King Kojong had selected these three men precisely for their extensive experience abroad and fluency in multiple languages. Yi Ŭijong had grown up following his father who worked as a diplomat to Washington, DC, Paris, and Saint Petersburg, and was fluent in English, French, and Russian in addition to Korean. Significantly, Stead decided to plead the case for Korean sovereignty by making Yi a "prince" in the front-page article. "He is a cultivated prince," the article commented, "speaking several languages, an energetic man, full of intense vitality." In Stead's estimation, the outrage of the Western public could be more reliably tapped if the principle of Korean sovereignty was literally embodied by a young Korean man as a prince, rather than a representative. Yi Ŭijong needed to *be* Korea in order for the Western reader to imagine Korea. And Stead's theatrical article, where an unnamed journalist stood in for the reader, was not anticolonial treatise. Stead's barbs were aimed against the use of force and the hypocrisy of Christian society. "Prince Yi" was an embodiment of Christian pacifism: "Korea has been a country without arms. Korea has never held aggressive ambitions. Korea only asks for permission to live in peace and solitude. We practice what you, the pacifists, preach. Where are you now?" It is important to leave space here for the possibility that the three emissaries had deliberately gone to Stead, knowing that he was a famous pacifist journalist.[13] It was a mission to make Korea visible and undeniable on the world stage.

Korean negotiations with the West and Japan had a much longer history than The Hague. The United States had been making military overtures to Korea as early as 1871. In an event scholar Gordon Chang calls "The 1871 American war against Korea," Chang notes that it was "one of the largest, if not the largest, and bloodiest uses of military force overseas by the United States in the fifty years between the Mexican-American War of 1846–1848 and the Spanish-American War of 1898."[14] The US secretary of state, Hamilton Fish, had instructed Frederick F. Low, the US minister of China, and the American fleet's commander, Admiral John Rodgers, to execute an "opening" of Korea in the same manner that Matthew Perry had in terms of Japan. The result of the expedition was the violent death of at minimum 250 Koreans—and absolutely no Perry-like success in forcing the "opening" of Korea. It would not be until 1882 that Admiral Robert Shufeldt successfully brokered a treaty of "amity and commerce" between the United States and Korea. However, the display of military power by the United States was most probably not the deciding factor in the change of Korea's strategy vis-à-vis the insistent West.

In a different reenactment of Perry's opening of Japan, Japanese gunboats arrived at Kanghwa Island in 1875. Exchange of artillery took place, and eventually four hundred Japanese troops landed on the shore after Chinese mediation failed. And although some advisors advised Kojong to mobilize the military, King Kojong decided on a different move—on February 27, 1876, Kojong signed a treaty with Japan. As Bruce Cumings notes, "Article 1 recognized Korea as an "autonomous" (*chaju*) state with sovereign rights the same as Japan's.... The article really meant that Japan no longer found any Chinese position in Korea worthy of its respect."[15] Korea had been a tributary state of China, a relationship that both granted a considerable amount of autonomy and recognized Korea as part of a cosmology centered on China. Henry Em notes that as early as 1883, the officials under King Kojong "were not oblivious to how power determined international relations and the application of international law," and they "understood that international law functioned as the only language with which Choson [Korea] could both engage and deter Japan and the Western powers."[16] With Japan's reinterpretation of Korea's autonomy, King Kojong of Korea then turned to the Western system of sovereignty—the putative fiction of equal nation-states—as a way to contain Japan.

In a move to preserve Korean autonomy, King Kojong performed a critical ritual—the Oath of 1895—which broke Korea's position of "autonomy within a China-centered tributary system" and announced Korea as a sovereign entity in a global nation-state system.[17] With the defeat of China in 1895, Japan facilitated the sovereign status of Korea as a "nation-state" separate from China, but the fictive equivalence between "nation-states" in the Western sovereignty system also produced a different ambiguity—one in which Japan could become the superior translator of Western rational international law for a "less enlightened" Korea.[18] And in 1905, with the end of the Russo-Japanese War, Japan claimed Korea via the international language of treaties—in the Portsmouth Treaty, Russia ceded to recognize that Japan could "protect its interests in Korea," an agreement brokered by none other than President

Theodore Roosevelt, for which he received the Nobel Peace Prize. In a later meeting between Roosevelt's secretary of war, William Howard Taft, and the Japanese prime minister, Katsura Taro, on July 29, 1905, it was mutually agreed that the United States would not interfere in Japan's interests in Korea, and in turn, Japan would recognize US interests in the Philippines. By the end of 1905, again with the threat and presence of military forces, Japan achieved the Second Japan-Korea Agreement, which made Korea a Japanese protectorate and essentially "gave international legal precedent to Japan's control over Korea's foreign affairs."[19]

And in 1907, the doors of the Second Hague Convention remained closed. But the publicity generated by the three envoys was enough for the Japanese to force King Kojong to abdicate his throne to his son, Sunjong. The Korean military, disbanded by the Japanese, fought the Japanese troops in the streets of Seoul. On August 29, 1910, Sunjong gave up the throne. Japan formally annexed Korea as a colony in 1910.

During World War II, the framework of early twentieth-century civilizational discourse gave shape to the American vision and sense of what the postwar occupation was supposed to look like. At the Cairo Conference in 1943, Franklin Delano Roosevelt, Winston Churchill, and Chiang Kai-shek discussed what to do with the colony of Korea once Japan was defeated:

> Japan shall be stripped of all the islands in the Pacific which she has seized or occupied since the beginning of the First World War in 1914, and that all the territories Japan has stolen from the Chinese, such as Manchuria, Formosa & the Pescadores, shall be restored to the Republic of China. Japan will also be expelled from all other territories which she has taken by violence and greed. *The aforesaid three Great Powers, mindful of the enslavement of the people of Korea, are determined that in due course Korea shall become free and independent* (my emphasis).[20]

Korea had been singled out in Roosevelt, Churchill, and Chiang's overview of Japan's colonial holdings, and became the territory on which the Allied forces would demonstrate their moral claims to the postwar order.[21] And the interpretation of the clause "in due course Korea shall become free and independent" quickly took the shape of potential trusteeship under President Roosevelt. Thus, Korea entered the Allied-dominated conversation over the postwar global order via a longer conversation—the question of disposing the colonial possessions of an enemy power, one that had already been in motion with the League of Nations, "mandates" and the end of World War I.

The telos would be the United Nations and the United States, according to Roosevelt's vision—one that still relied on racial civilizational hierarchies and ideas about tutelage. In January 1944, when Roosevelt spoke with his Pacific War Council about his vision for the dismembering of the Japanese empire, he spoke of placing Korea under a trusteeship for a "forty year tutelage."[22] When Roosevelt later spoke with Stalin on the afternoon of February 8, 1945, at Yalta,

> He [Roosevelt] said he had in mind for Korea a trusteeship composed of a Soviet, an American and a Chinese representative. He said the only experience we had had in this matter was in the Philippines where it had taken about fifty years for the people to be prepared for self-government. He felt that in the case of Korea the period might be from twenty to thirty years. Marshal Stalin said the shorter the period the better.[23]

Korea had become part of the American genealogy of overseas military projects and interests—one that included the Philippine-American War and the previous negotiating with a different faltering empire—Spain—and its possessions. But in the policy vacuum left in the wake of FDR's death, the US Navy stepped in and brushed aside the idea of a trusteeship, arguing for the strategic importance of Korea militarily.

August 15, 1945—the day of the announcement of Japanese surrender to the Allied forces—heralded simultaneously the liberation of Korea from Japanese colonial rule and the arrival of the Cold War to the Korean peninsula. Late at night in Washington, DC, on August 14, in anticipation of the Japanese surrender, two US officials—Dean Rusk and Charles Bonesteel—were assigned the task of proposing a dividing line for the US and Soviet occupations on the Korean peninsula. With only a *National Geographic* map for reference, they could not "find a natural geographic line," and "saw instead the thirty-eighth parallel and decided to recommend that." This "choice of the thirty-eighth parallel, chosen by two tired colonels late at night," wrote Rusk in his memoir, "proved fateful."[24] With the Soviets accepting this line of division, the superpower binary dynamics of the early Cold War were put into motion on the Korean peninsula. Soon, the Korean peninsula was divided at the 38th parallel into two different foreign military occupations— with the Soviets in the north and the Americans in the south.

From September 1 to 5, 1945, three hundred thousand leaflets poured out from the sky over the southern part of the Korean peninsula for four straight days. The US commanding general, John Hodge, appointed by General Douglas MacArthur to direct the military occupation of Korea, had ordered the air force to distribute these leaflets in advance of the occupation forces' arrival on September 9. Addressed "To the People of Korea," the leaflet began,

> The armed forces of the United States will soon arrive in Korea for the purpose of receiving the surrender of the Japanese forces, enforcing the terms of surrender, and insuring the orderly administration and rehabilitation of the country. These missions will be carried out with a firm hand, but with a hand that will be guided by a nation whose long heritage of democracy has fostered a kindly feeling for peoples less fortunate. How well and how rapidly these tasks are carried out will depend on the Koreans themselves.[25]

But MacArthur did not feel that this message was enough of an introduction of the US military occupation to the Korean people and issued Proclamation Number Two on September 7, 1945. This time Mac-Arthur, identifying himself as the "Commander-in-Chief, United States Army Forces, Pacific," addressed the "People of Korea" in a tone that departed markedly from the previous proclamation that had fallen from the skies:

Any Person Who:
  Violates the provision of the Instrument of Surrender, or any proclamation, order, or directive given under the authority of the

Commander-in-Chief, United States Army Forces, Pacific, or does any act to the prejudice of good order or the life, safety, or security of the persons or property of the United States or its Allies, or does any act calculated to disturb public peace and order, or prevent the administration of justice, or willfully does any act hostile to the Allied forces, shall, upon conviction by a military Occupation Court, suffer death or such other punishment as the Court may determine.[26]

The line between the benevolence offered in Proclamation One and the death threatened in Proclamation Two became the line of division of more immediate urgency and importance to the Korean people than the 38th parallel. And according to these two proclamations, the award of benevolence or the punishment of death was dependent on the behavior of "the Koreans themselves." These proclamations were a twinned self-introduction of the nature of rule that would be enacted on the peninsula.

When US military personnel arrived on the peninsula on September 9, 1945, to commence the military occupation, this pair of proclamations was part of the slender file of documents given to them as potential guidance. "Each officer did receive a copy of the Cairo Declaration, of MacArthur's three proclamations to the Korean people, of the secret operational military government plan that had been hastily improvised by a joint-staff committee of the XXIV Corps and the Seventh Fleets, and of those dozen or more ordinances, general orders, and notices thus far printed by Military Government."[27] It was more pastiche than coherent policy making. And none of these papers addressed the most fundamental questions about the military occupation itself. Ernst Fraenkel, an influential jurist working for the US military government in Korea, summed it up succinctly: "Military occupation of a 'liberated country' is basically self-contradictory."[28]

The contradiction of "Korea" was at the crossroads between the genealogy of Western international law and the history of anticolonial claims to sovereignty. How did one "occupy" a former colony of a wartime "enemy" who had surrendered unconditionally? If the United States self-proclaimed to be both an occupier and a liberator, how did one carry out a military occupation for liberation? And because Korea was now a postcolony divided between two foreign military occupations, did the sovereign near future look like trusteeship, nation-statehood, or something else altogether?

According to Gregory Henderson, the US vice consul for USAMGIK, the first civilian officers who arrived in Korea had actually been trained for nine months for the Philippines, "with no more than a single hour's lecture on Korea."[29] Korea was the policy afterthought to Japan within the War Department, the Department of State, and even within the realm of the concurrent US occupations of Korea and Japan. For the initial group of "all professional soldiers and none with any training or experience in civil affairs" who arrived on the Korean peninsula to begin the occupation, the Cairo Declaration "provided the only statement of high policy available at the time, the single sentence: 'The aforesaid three great powers, mindful of the enslavement of the people of Korea, are determined that in *due course Korea shall become free and independent.*'"[30] Or in other words, as according to the official *History of the United States Armed Forces in Korea* (HUSAFIK), "Koreans were to be treated as liberated people, but liberation was to be given gradually."[31] The period of military occupation was to be one of granting, one of becoming, and one of suspension.

But there appeared to be a challenge to this project of bestowing and teaching proper liberation to the Koreans. "The 'natives' and their institutions form a completely separate world," wrote Ernst Fraenkel on January 24, 1946, after his first week in Korea on assignment. Fraenkel was a German socialist émigré jurist who had joined the USAMGIK to help construct the legal parameters of both the occupation and foundations for a possible Korean state. Having worked on the US military occupation legal structure for Germany after World War I, Fraenkel arrived at the Korean peninsula and immediately had a crisis of imagination. Korea was a "most primitive oriental society," even beyond Japan. "The streets are terribly dirty, the shops are so strange (to use a very polite term) that I did not dare to enter a single one and that I cannot imagine to do it in the future. The idea to eat in a Korean restaurant is phantastic." But it was not simply a case of a physical impossibility to enter this "completely separate world," it was also about comprehension, language, and translation. "I wonder whether it is possible to have any contacts with them, except a very small crust of intellectuals who have been educated in US, Europe or Japan," he wrote. "And now we try to do the job to govern these people of whom we know so little and whom we probably never will understand. We enact statutes and even a constitution, establish institutions which are wholly based on occidental thinking and apply ideas to the government of this country which are meaningful only in the framework of our tradition and civilization."[32] The problem, according to Fraenkel's logic, was not simply one of translation, but of the capacity of the Korean to comprehend the elements of basic governance.

At the 1907 Hague Convention, the delegates rendered Korea's status as a sovereign nation-state into an impossibility. In the first few months of the US military occupation of Korea in the mid-twentieth century, US officials began asserting that Koreans themselves were unable to imagine and comport themselves as fully sovereign subjects. The USAMGIK brought Fraenkel to Korea for "legal advising," reasoning that his expertise in German and US law would help the restructuring of the "Japanese empire's legal code, which ... had been based on German law."[33] Fraenkel arrived in Korea with a firm conviction that the United States provided the best mechanism through which to promulgate a "virulently anti-Communist collective democracy," the political project of his that had been cut off in the Weimar Republic but had been given new life by the New Deal state he had encountered in the United States as an émigré.[34] Fraenkel was someone who wholeheartedly participated in the US military occupation, with its goals of ensuring that Korea would become a firmly anti-Communist nation-state intertwined with US material and political interests. But Fraenkel's confessions of his confusion, disgust, and incomprehension in front of Korean society clearly laid out the deeper sociopolitical shifts happening over the twentieth century in the discourses undergirding imperial expansion and hegemony. US and Western powers were moving unevenly from the tropes of "civilization" to the markers of "governance" in how they racialized the global order. The language and logic used by the USAMGIK demonstrated this political and cultural shift in conceptualizing racial orders from the hierarchy of "mankind" differentiated along markers of phenotype to a differentiated plane of measuring capacities for "governance."

The Civilizing Mission, Improvised

On September 10, 1945, the Korean populace quickly made it known to the US occupation officials that they also had ideas about what the US military occupation should look like as they filled the streets of the capital city, Seoul, to protest the first decision announced by the US military occupation authorities: the "United States Army orders leaving temporarily in office Japanese overlords who have ruled the little empire for thirty-five years."[35] Demonstrations were extensive, and Associated Press journalists noted that the Koreans had "plastered walls with posters of protest"—the Koreans were speaking back to the US military forces through these writings that took up public space in the capital. When it was announced that the Japanese government would remain in office, Koreans claiming to be leaders of various political movements violently denounced the policy.[36] According to US intelligence reports, "Posters and pamphlets continue to appear in INCH'ON and SEOUL criticizing and denouncing the U.S. Army occupational policy in KOREA.... These writings are identified with different radical political parties associated with the Communistic group."[37]

Confronted by this public mass protest on the streets and walls of Korea, Lieutenant General John R. Hodge, the commander of the Twenty-Fourth US Army Corps, declared in a press conference, "In effect, *I am the Korean government* during the transition period" (italics added). Hodge's assertion that he was the sovereign—"the Korean government"—was an attempt to wrest away possible authority from the masses in the streets, but it also exposed an unsettled anxiety on the part of the US military authorities—such an utterance put forth the legitimate authority of the US Army as assumed, as a priori, but as the posters, parades, and clamoring press attested, authority was anything but assumed in this moment.[38]

In early October 1945, a little less than a month after the US military government arrived on the Korean peninsula, published copies of a pamphlet began circulating in the streets of Seoul, amid the escalating demonstrations by the Korean people regarding decisions made by the US Army Military Government in Korea (USAMGIK). This pamphlet, written in English and titled "Message to U.S.A. Citizens," caused a good deal of concern among intelligence agents of the USAMGIK, who were also in the middle of trying to divine exactly who kept on taking down the military government ordinances that had been plastered on the walls of the city. This handbill gave a few words of counsel to the new military government. "A few days ago," noted the handbill authors, "the Military Government of U.S. Army in Corea issued a decree that says, 'No gathering, no procession or parade should be held without permission of the government authority.' ... Do you think it is possible to build a new nation in democratic way without freedom of speech, without freedom of mass meeting without freedom of all political activities?"[39]

The authors of this pamphlet were members of the Committee of Preparation for Korean Independence, a recently organized national body that had emerged from the People's Committees formed at the local level in anticipation of and ever since the Japanese surrender of August 15, 1945. In preparation for the arrival of the US troops on September 9, 1945, this governing organization convened in the capital city of Seoul on September 6. With the representatives who had been elected in the provincial assemblies, the "delegates formed a national government with jurisdiction over all of Korea."[40] The People's Republic articulated and developed its platform based on five elements: (1) unification of different political groups, (2) a land distribution program in which current tenants could afford to buy their farms, (3) the purging of collaborators and Japanese from official positions, (4) extension of suffrage across the population, and (5) minimization of government monopoly. It was a platform on which to begin the restructuring of postwar liberated Korea.

Speaking as citizen (Korea) to citizen (USA), the Committee of the People's Republic insisted on a horizontal plane of relation to the US military government officials in their tone of address and offered a few lessons for the newly arrived occupation officials: "Let the Coreans govern themselves. Protect us, but do not try to rule over us. We know what is the best government for us." The committee did not oppose occupation in absolute terms, but they did maintain that the US occupation was to be a temporary phase. "The people's Republic of Korea needs your unlimited sympathy and help in her development. Your sympathy and your help will make an imperishable record in the glorious history of New Korea." US military occupation was a mere bounded event, within a longer history—a history quite literally embodied and enacted by the Korean person. It is important to note that the handbill did indeed position the US military as a supporter and aide in the liberation of Korea, and explicitly pointed to Lieutenant General Hodge by name and referred to Proclamation No. 1:

> In his first message, General Hodge declared that one of three missions of the armed forces of the United States in Corea is to "rehabilitate Korea." We took his message in gratitude and with respect because we believed in his commandership—the general of the nation of Washington, Lincoln, and Roosevelt.[41]

The central committee also took special care to position a particular equivalence between "Korea" and "America" by emphasizing a shared enmity against Japan: "You know Japanese, their ambitions, their cruelty and their treachery. However, if there is any people who have a deepest grudge against the Japanese, it is the Koreans who have lived with them for thirty six years."[42]

But the authors took this question of colonialism to another level by narrating an unbroken line of political will and subjectivity from the colonial period through the present—a narrative argument, essentially, against the idea that decolonization would require the United States and Western powers to teach "politics" to the decolonized Korean. Most importantly, the authors of the handbill laid out the interior world of the Korean:

> If any Corean remained mentally normal during the war, he was a fool. Coreans made themselves split personalities. They showed obedience in the presence of Japanese and they did just the opposite thing in reality. Without any munitions, revolutionists fought bravely in fields and in factories.

The "split personality" of the Korean was a conscious political performance, one that left intact the uninterrupted history of Korean sovereign agency. Political desire and historical agency were already the realm in which Koreans acted and made decisions. Perhaps most importantly, the committee, in asserting that the "mentally normal" Korean was a fool—which would conversely mean that insanity was actually a marker of calculated intelligence—was parlaying to the US military government that it would have severe limits in trying to "read" the Korean. There was no need for the United States military government to invent the Korean as a political subject.[43]

When Ernst Fraenkel first arrived in Seoul, he was greeted by English-language signs that declared, "We thank you for the liberation—but we want a Korean government, without trusteeship." It was an "absolutely orderly and peaceful" parade of "some hundred women and children who waved flags and cried and sang," but when he neared the parade, the "women and girls," thinking of him as a "big shot or a Russian (there [were] relatively few American civilians here)," vigorously waved their flags at him. They "told me in a 'Spechchor' what they expected me to do," wrote Fraenkel in a letter to his wife.[44]

In front of these parades, the circulating pamphlets, the countless demands and instructions from the Koreans on how occupation should be run—the commander of the United States Army Forces in Korea (USAFIK), Lieutenant General Hodge, could not deny the urgency of the demands: "The Koreans want their independence more than any one thing and want it now. This stems from the Allied promise of freedom and independence which is well known by every Korean without the qualifying phrase 'in due course.' I am told there are no Korean words expressing 'in due course.' "[45] By essentially reducing the demands for immediate independence by Koreans as an impossibility of translation, Hodge held that the Korean language itself was incapable of holding the more complex meaning of a deferred temporal process of indeterminate duration. *In due course*—the operative phrase of the Cairo Declaration that placed Korea within the "waiting room of history" along with other mandates, colonies, and trusteeships—had become a concept indicative of mature and enlightened political thinking—and, according to Hodge's logic, it was one external to the Korean person and history.[46]

And yet, as if it was attempting to make its own voice heard over the political debates and clamor in the public spaces, the US military projected its authority through a tremendous amount of paper—ordinances, proclamations, and published speeches. Distribution, however, turned out to be an entirely different issue than reception. A G-2 Intelligence Weekly Summary dated October 9, 1945, stated, "Civilians interviewed state that the proclamations issued by the US occupation forces reach only a few of the people. Some of these orders have been misunderstood because civilians are not able to either read or interpret the proclamations."[47] MacArthur had declared English to be the official language of the US occupation, adding the issue of translation to the mix. Without a reader, these pieces of paper distributed throughout the southern part of the peninsula became simply that—pieces of paper.

While young Korean women were lecturing Fraenkel in the streets of Seoul at the same time he was insisting that Koreans were incomprehensible and uncomprehending, the large Korean populace that extended across the peninsula was fomenting deep anxiety on the part of USAMGIK. "The population of Korea is almost wholly in the lower social scale," observed US military intelligence personnel in a weekly summary dated October 23, 1945. "It consists mainly of peasants and laborers whose lot has been bad from any standard. In any form of popular government this is the class of people who will swing an election. This is the class which every political party will woo and in which the radicals will find the most fertile ground."[48] Land, rice, and the question of distribution had been the central concerns of the conversation between Chang and the Russian and North Korean soldiers at the threshold of his home on the 38th parallel in April 1946. And like the vast majority of the Korean populace—much to the chagrin of USAMGIK and CIC—he had already taken the initiative in determining the terms of his livelihood.

In his work reflecting on the US military government's work, activities, and policies in the first year of occupation, Edward Grant Meade, himself a participant in the US military government, noted that there was indeed a "*de facto* government" on the Korean peninsula even before the arrival of the American army personnel in early September

1945.[49] This government was called the People's Republic of Korea (Chosŏn Inmin Konghwaguk), the very same organization that had authored the handbill addressed to the officials of USAMGIK in Seoul.

Earlier in 1945, anticipating Japanese surrender and Korean liberation, the governing Japanese officials looked for Koreans to contain order when the Japanese surrendered. Needing someone who held legitimacy in the eyes of the Korean peasant masses especially, the Japanese officials chose Lyuh Woo Hyun,[50] a centrist leftist with a deep history of involvement with the independence organizing and movement in Shanghai and also founder of the Korean Restoration Brotherhood, and he accepted the position.[51] Under Lyuh, the Committee of Preparation for Korean Independence coalesced into existence, each province creating its own committee. Koreans had formed People's Committees all throughout southern Korea. After August 15, 1945, members of the People's Committees, who would later become part of what would be called the People's Republic, had stepped in to help manage and organize the rice collection and food stock in the midst of Japanese officials fleeing the peninsula. "After the Koreans drove the Japanese police out [the KPR leaders] took over the rice collection machinery and were operating it successfully when the Americans arrived."[52] The question of land, rice, and distribution were not simply abstract mechanisms for state-building for the majority of Koreans—it was immediate and material. In 1945, the average caloric content of the Korean diet had dropped to between 1,000 and 1,800 calories a day from the prewar average of "approximately 2,077 a day," which was "little more than a slow starvation diet," according to the HUSAFIK.[53] When we look at the picture of land tenancy in 1945 provided by historian Bruce Cumings, we can see the problems underlying the difficulty in obtaining fundamental means of subsistence: "About 80 out of every 100 Korean farmers were tenants or semi-tenants." And this situation had resulted from the rapid increases in tenancy under Japanese colonial rule.[54] A decolonized Korea would need to address these fundamental issues, and the People's Committees had begun to do so.

In a "Memorandum to Public Safety Officer" dated November 7, 1945, an assistant public safety officer made the following observation regarding the People's Committee in his particular area of leftist Gokseong-gun and rightist Yeonggwang-gun:

> My further opinion is that the People's Committee in the more rural districts is well organized and has a large and influential membership ... they do not appear to be gangsters, hoodlums or [a] "bad element" organization, but on the contrary a representative group of Korean people.[55]

The fact that this assistant public safety officer had to insist that the members of the People's Committee in his region were not "gangsters" or "hoodlums" revealed how within the first two months of the US military's arrival on the peninsula, the higher-level officials held a suspicion of these mass, peasant-based political organizations. Meade himself addressed this characterization of the People's Committee directly in his book:

> Charges of radical tendencies leveled against many of the leaders can be easily substantiated, but they merit further explanation. The original heads of the movement were, for the most part, respected men of the community, who had little or no association with either the Japanese administration or the organized Korean underground movements.... The members of the underground, on the other hand, were acutely aware of the people's desires and attitudes and allowed their knowledge of the public mind to mold their politics. If the People's Republic exhibited radical tendencies, it only reflected with reasonable accuracy the views of the Korean majority.[56]

Meade quite pointedly remarked on the fact that many of the People's Committee leaders were men who did not have experiences prior to liberation that could be easily labeled as either "rightist" or "leftist."

But from their perch in Seoul, the USAMGIK could only comprehend the combination of peasant organization, land reform, and radical restructuring of on-the-ground police forces through the early Cold War lens of an anti-Communist narrative. The civilizing mission impulse of FDR, the League of Nations, and trusteeship was soon to be reconstituted via the anti-Communist mission of the Truman Doctrine, the United Nations, and the national security state. On October 10, 1945, US Major General Archibald Arnold, the military governor of occupied southern Korea, responded to the activities of the People's Republic—perhaps with the handbill specifically in mind—with his own statement in front of the Korean press: "Self-appointed 'officials' and 'police groups,' big (or little) conferences representing all the people, the (self-styled) government of the Republic of Korea, are entirely without any authority, power or reality. If the men who are arrogating to themselves such high-sounding titles are merely play-acting on a puppet stage with entertainment of questionable amusement value they must immediately pull down the curtain on the puppet show."[57] The political gathering or organizations of Koreans—and here, Arnold is specifically concerned with the Committee of the People's Republic of Korea—was not a canny, strategic performance. Indeed, in the eyes of Major General Arnold, it was only a mere farce, a pathetic mimicry, a false gesture. Political authenticity—or to quote Arnold, "authority, power, or reality"—lay with the US military government, and it was theirs to confer. The Koreans were not yet legally citizens, and Korea was not yet a nation-state.

On November 2, 1945, the US military attempted to further undermine the legitimacy of the People's Republic of Korea by publishing Ordinance No. 21, which announced that Japanese colonial laws and regulations were still "in full force and effect":

> Until further ordered, and except as previously repealed or abolished, all laws which were in force, regulations, orders, notices or other documents issued by any former government of Korea having the force of law on 9 August 1945 will continue in full force and effect until repealed by express order of the Military Government of Korea.[58]

The text of the ordinance specified what was being "suspended" during the state of emergency—and essentially, it was not Japanese colonial law or the force of law that was suspended or eradicated. What was suspended was any competing claim to the "force of law." Legitimacy was something to be granted by the American forces. Ordinance No. 21 was clearly an attempt to render the authority of the US military government as assumed—as the sovereign. In this early phase of the occupation, the US military government was not interested in creating a normative legal framework for state-building, but rather much more concerned about holding competing claims to the "force of law" in abeyance, as that became the object supposedly in the hands of the USAMGIK that would then be granted as Korea gained independence. On December 12, 1945, Hodge "outlawed the Republic," to use the words of Gregory Henderson.[59] And, as Henderson further wrote, "There was nothing to put in its place but armed authority."[60]

The CIC, the Informant, and Governance

On the streets of Seoul, in the villages of the countryside, and at the ports along the coasts, a small number of US Counterintelligence Corps agents began arriving to work for the US military occupation. On September 9, 1945, when agents of the 224th CIC Detachment arrived at the port of Inchon on the USS *Chilton*, they were coming from campaigns in Leyte and Okinawa. But despite this previous experience of US military and imperial projects in the Philippines and Japan, these agents of the "CIC had come to Korea without much preparation and with little idea of what to expect," according to the official military history of the CIC in US-occupied Korea—"No precedents for CIC from previous occupations were available as guides for action."[61]

If the proclamations deposited from the sky only a few days previous to the CIC agents' arrival had introduced "benevolence" and "death" as the parameters for the US military occupation, then the CIC agents were the ones who created and inscribed the formulas for applying either "benevolence" or "death" to the human landscape of occupied Korea. Donald Nichols, a CIC agent born in Hackensack, New Jersey, and trained in Karachi during World War II, arrived in Korea on June 29, 1946, as a special agent in the "K" Subdetachment of the 607th Counterintelligence Corps. Soon after arriving, he became the detachment commander of his "small three man unit."[62] And shortly thereafter, he noted that his "unit was really moving in 'high, very high' South Korean government circles. All doors were open to us."[63] Within the span of only a few months, the Counterintelligence Corps had become indispensable to USAMGIK. Captain Kenneth MacDougall, who became the chief intelligence advisor to the Korean Department of Internal Security, recalled that General Hodge had described the CIC as a "tower of strength."[64] In the absence of direct policy directives from the US State Department, Hodge turned to the CIC. "CIC's political coverage helped him make the decisions he had to make since his advisors seemed to offer little that was concrete along those lines," MacDougall stated. And accordingly, the CIC's influence was direct and not to be underestimated. As CIC agent William Tigue recalled, "Gen Hodge relyed [sic] a lot on CIC's political coverage. To some extent he was willing to back anyone that CIC recommended."[65]

The Counterintelligence Corps garnered an outsized authority within the US military occupation structure because it supposedly offered Hodge the ability to make the most important claim that an occupier who was also a liberator needed to state: The US military government knew the desires, intents, and actions of the Korean mass populace. As much as members of USAMGIK might have agreed with Fraenkel's observation that the " 'natives' and their institutions form a completely separate world," that world of activity was both the object of control and the source of much anxiety.[66] But the role and legacy of the CIC in Korea went beyond resolving anxieties about control when the CIC began providing the material for the crux of binary Cold War politics— defining who was an "enemy" or a "friend."

The USAMGIK faced a crisis essentially of its own making almost immediately after arrival. On October 5, 1945—the same date of publication as the handbill issued by the Central Committee of the People's Republic—the US military government published two different ordinances regarding land tenancy and the rice market. The first ordinance declared a "national emergency ... by reason of oppressive rents and interest rates payable under existing contracts by tenants of farm lands."[67] This ordinance's professed objective to declare a maximum ceiling on land rent costs was popular among the Korean tenant population, but the ordinance—and the "national emergency"—failed in practice due to the fact that it was landlords on the ground who were supporting the

US military government, and the US military had no effective means of regulating and enforcing the ordinance. The second ordinance—called General Notice No. 1—declared, "All laws and regulations having the force of law described below are hereby abolished to the end that Korea may have a free market in rice," and ended with disastrous consequences.[68]

US military intelligence noticed a change in the activities they usually reported from week to week. "Many people are out of work and are encountering some difficulty in obtaining food," stated a report dated October 9, 1945. "An increasing number of instances were reported of Koreans forcing Japanese employers and factory owners to pay bonuses and advance pay even though the plants are closed."[69] By the end of the month, US military intelligence reported "12 disturbances in widely scattered localities though S Korea." Korean laborers were beginning to demand that Japanese employers hand over ownership and control of businesses. "Force was used to obtain compliance with many of these demands," the report went on. "No organization of labor in general or of employees were caused by employees of individual plants and who are capitalizing on the defeat of Japan and the opportunity to put pressure on Japanese civilians who are being forced evacuate Korea."[70] Labor organizations were seemingly absent from these incidents—and US military intelligence conceded that these demands were indeed more spontaneous than meditated.

The effort to expel Japanese factory owners rapidly developed into the demand for the expulsion of all Japanese administrative officials and also policemen all over the southern half of the peninsula. For the period between October 23 and 30, 1945, "22 disturbances by political parties in widely scattered localities throughout S Korea were reported."[71] These disturbances were "directed against Japanese soldiers and civilians who are still in public positions, such as policemen, school teachers, local officials, etc.," and all were associated in some form with the Korean People's Republic. In Hadong, the Korean People's Republic moved to take over the local government and "refused to recognize the Military Government." As a seeming pattern emerged, the US military intelligence G-2 summary concluded, "It is believed that disturbances will continue in communities where Japanese or former Japanese collaborators are in office or are used as advisors by US Military Government."[72] Using the network of People's Committees already in place on the ground, the Korean populace had clearly decided to act on the structural change they wanted to see happen, which was the immediate replacement of markers of Japanese colonial sovereignty with local Korean authority. The Korean populace was not waiting for the US military to "grant" them their independence.

Confronted with a population that had apparently deemed the US military government as inadequate and insufficient for their demands for change, on October 30, 1945, the US occupation forces published Ordinance Number 19—and Section One was titled "Declaration of National Emergency." Significantly, the ordinance began with a reintroduction of the American forces to the Korean people, a move reminiscent of Proclamation Number 1: "After four long years of war, from which they emerged victorious, American Forces landed upon your shores the friends and protectors of the Korean people." The theme of the "benevolent sovereign" had reentered the frame. But the lengthy ordinance also very pointedly commented on "certain groups," which the authors of the ordinance portrayed as mercenary—the opposite of the "benevolent" US military government: "In addition, certain groups, with the sole idea of acquiring the wealth of the Korean people for themselves, have prevented labor from returning to employment, children from returning to school, and farmers from selling the produce of their lands. Such conditions," the ordinance continued, "have created within Korea an emergency." Following such a statement that essentially denied any agency or will on the part of the strikers and resisting farmers, the next sentence brought the benevolence front and center of its self-portrayal of the military government:

As all of the people know the American Nation is a powerful nation. Its people, however are gentle with the true gentleness that come only through an appreciation of their own good fortune and in their desire to protect others against adversity.[73]

And although the ordinance did not stipulate what the national emergency entailed, the ordinance declared that "rigid emergency controls are therefore hereby established, in order to prevent such conditions from existing which will harm the people."[74] The US military government declared yet another "state of emergency" in an attempt to create a strategic severance between any collective political organizing and widespread popular political recognition. This ordinance, in a sense, was a strategy to render the US military government as *relevant* to the Korean populace.

But Section Two of the ordinance brought the other element of the "state of emergency"—death—more squarely to the fore. An act that challenged the military government's authority was construed as an act that threatened the "People's Welfare"—and the three stipulated "unlawful acts" revealed the difficulty the military government had encountered in establishing legitimacy on the ground. The three "unlawful acts" encompassed an almost infinite range of actions—from language, physical action, to political intent. For example, the first unlawful act was "knowingly making any false statement orally or in writing to any member of or person acting under the authority of USAFIK or the Military Government"; the second unlawful act consisted of any "[attempt] to obstruct, or contravening any orders or announced program of the Military Government; and third, "directing or participating in acts of discipline, threats, coercion or any other form of intimidation of victimization (including boycotting) against any person cooperating in any form directly or indirectly with USAFIK or the Military Government of Korea."[75] In essence, the US military government was ordering the Korean populace to at least act and behave as if they had accepted the legitimate authority of their presence, while also broadening its power of oversight.

The US military government's preoccupation with controlling speech acts exposed its anxiety about the Korean population. The different types of documents issued by the US military government—such as the posted ordinances or the printed identity passes—were often torn down, forged, or challenged by Koreans, who often, in turn, printed their own publications or pamphlets. Six months later, on May 4, 1946, the US military government published Ordinance Number 72 titled "Offenses Against the Military Government." This nine-page ordinance outlined *eighty-two* specific behaviors considered "Offenses Against the

Military Government." It stated that the specificity with which these offenses were enumerated did not "[limit] the provisions of Proclamation Number 2," the proclamation issued by General MacArthur in the early days of the occupation that announced that those who committed acts "inimical" to the aims of the US military government would "suffer death or such other punishment as the Court may determine."[76] Ordinance Number 72 became the purveyor of the "state of emergency" framed by the threat of death.[77]

Twenty-seven of the eighty-two stipulations dealt with language, paper, and the performance of authority—such as slander, rumors, fraudulent documents, false statements, forged identity cards or any other type of permit pass, "concealing" papers from authorities, falsifying contracts, and even impersonation of military government personnel.[78] The "offenses" demonstrated the extent to which US military authority could be mimicked and to which it was fragile and still not established. This ordinance specifically attacked the political use of language in the public sphere, a provision under which the handbills of the Central Committee of the People's Republic no longer would be permissible. Number 22 stated,

> Acts or conduct in support of, or participating in the formation of, any organization or movement dissolved or declared illegal by, or contrary to the interests of, the occupying forces, including publication or circulation of matter printed or written in aid of any thereof or the possession thereof with intent to publish or circulate same, or the provocative display of flags, uniforms or insignia of any such organization or movement.[79]

Number 30 addressed "removing, obliterating, defacing or altering written, printed or typed matter posted by or under authority of Military Government"; number 31 forbade the publishing and distribution of material deemed "detrimental or disrespectful to the occupying forces or to the United Nations ... or any person acting under their authority," and also forbade the dissemination of rumors that "undermine the morale of the occupying forces."[80] Ordinance 72 conceded that the rumors circulated by Koreans could "undermine the morale of the occupying forces," an indication of the fractured, fragmented nature of the US military occupation itself.

The criminalization of these behaviors was also essentially the criminalization of the political left, primarily the People's Republic of Korea. More importantly, the criminalization of these Korean speech acts points to the lack of hegemony behind the spectacle of exceptional sovereign power. Instead, Koreans treated the printed laws and bureaucratic papers exactly as just that—paper. Even the US military was afraid of becoming ordinary, everyday, and mundane.

In turn, the criminalization of Korean leftist politics required the professionalization of the Counterintelligence Corps. The CIC interpreted and put into practice the notion of appropriate behavior between the benevolence and death that the US occupation offered. In other words, the CIC determined the parameters of death and benevolence for the southern part of the Korean peninsula, while inventing themselves in the process. The city streets of mass protest, the factory spaces of labor strikes, and the escalating confrontations between villagers and the police—these very same public spaces became the domain of the CIC. The protests, the strikes, and the violence were not attesting to either consent on the part of the Korean masses or to the legitimacy of the US military government on the ground. Between the focus on militarization and the professionalization of the CIC, the US military government concentrated its efforts on manufacturing evidence of a "liberated" democratic Korea via a state of emergency. The Counterintelligence Corps, perhaps more than other organizations—helped to control what a Korean public sphere looked like under the rubric of a "state of emergency." Who could speak, what could be spoken, and in what manner? As the People's Republic of Korea and then subsequently in quick succession other leftist and Communist-inspired organizations such as the South Korean Labor Party (SKLP) were deemed illegal and banned by the US military government, the CIC operated to undermine these organizations.

During the early Cold War, the US military's use of counterinsurgency and counterintelligence tactics for the objectives of regime change or the de-legitimation of a mass political movement formed already a key element in U.S. global projects of regime change or counterinsurgency, whether in the Philippines or in Latin America. But in the case of the US military occupation of Korea, the Counterintelligence Corps differed from other mobilizations of counterinsurgency in how public its operations were. Even though we may usually imagine CIC agents as working under cover, the annals of the CIC attest otherwise—"since CIC was outfitting its men in a uniform worn by no other organization, agents were open to compromise on all occasions."[81] And, "the distinctive uniform of CIC agents in Korea was only one factor contributing to the unsought notice given to CIC operations in Korea."[82] The Korean population was wary of the CIC, reluctant to talk freely with them because "many Koreans [believed] the CIC is the American counterpart of the Japanese Kempei Tai." As a result, CIC agents instead disguised themselves as "G-2 personnel, Office of Public Information personnel, members of the Political Advisory Group (PAG), or as novices who have developed a curiosity of and an interest in Korean politics," although it is difficult to say that Koreans would have necessarily trusted these uniforms or performances either.[83] General MacArthur had forbidden "fraternization" between the US military personnel and Korean civilians, but unfortunately, "the lonely and homesick young soldier will talk at length with any Korean who can speak English and who wants to talk with him."[84] Cautionary injunctions like "Don't Brag about your Last Case" to explicit capitalized directives like "GET OUT AND GET IT!!!" regarding the leftist organizations that had gone underground reveal a gamut of concerns over the CIC's professionalization and effectiveness in its own official monthly reports.[85] The Counterintelligence Corps found itself with a more immediate difficulty in carrying out operations—establishing its own legitimacy.

The CIC was a very public operation, and even its learning curve regarding what the CIC official history called the "peculiar situation in Korea" was on public display.[86] "CIC was well-known by the local populace.... At first CIC took a hand in manipulating local politics," Captain Kenneth MacDougall stated.[87] When the CIC first began its operations on the Korean peninsula in late 1945, the agents had been primarily responsible for "assembling all Japanese nationals preparatory to their repatriation; and maintaining law and order."[88] However, by the 1947 drafting of the permanent standard operating procedure (SOP) for the CIC, "the basic mission of Counter Intelligence Corps," which was "to assist in the maintenance of military security," had been "enlarged to require special investigative activity in both the Positive Intelligence and Counter Intelligence fields involving political groups and social organizations and the collection of information relating to adjacent areas to insure the successful completion of the over-all mission of the U.S. Forces in Korea to set up a democratic form of government."[89] The SOP signaled a significant development in the objectives of the CIC. The organization that had begun the first two months of the occupation engaged in activities similar to the other forces of the US military was now focused on the activities of "political groups and social organizations," which had become the CIC's sense of purpose.

This space of legitimatization and professionalization was the realm of "espionage." "Espionage" became the all-encompassing term for the supposed realities of the activities and individuals involved on the ground in Korea—and it would have a profound afterlife in the Korean War, as mobilized and identified by the CIC:

> In many respects, the armed conflict that broke out in Korea in June 1950 was simply a new phase of a war that had been going on silently, insidiously, for five years. In its earlier phases, this war made few headlines and drew little attention. But CIC agents in the Korean occupation had known the quiet struggle. It was a war of espionage.[90]

The "war of espionage" became the coalescing paradigm for the CIC, one that could focus a disparate group of amateurs into an efficient body of agents who could produce narratives useful for the military government.

For the very public CIC, comprised of primarily white male agents, creating a network to cover the "quiet struggle" would require Koreans. The CIC had to rely on Korean agents for "information" "because of the language barrier, and the customs of the Korean people, and the physical difference between the Oriental and the Caucasian." The professionalization of the Counterintelligence Corps was directly linked to the CIC's increasing dependence on Korean labor and networks. By the end of 1947, CIC had developed a network of "180 regular CIC informants," who were Korean nationals. Of the 180 informants, 150 were employed "to cover the subversive activities of the leftist Communist dominated and infiltrated organizations." Korean "nationals employed as interpreters, detectives, and undercover agents" often carried around "passes for identification purposes to entitle them entrance into the CIC office and to assure them immunity in cases where, on a special assigned task, they may be apprehended by the police for suspicious activities." The other thirty of the approximately 180 Korean agents worked within political parties. The CIC focused recruitment on civilians, since even the Korean police and other US military government organizations could not know the identity of the informants.[91] A report from an informant usually cost the CIC around 1,172 Korean won, or the equivalent to $1.18 on the "open market." However, the "outstanding informants were those who were developed through the painstaking effort of the Agent who guided the informant in his work."

The 1948 Annual Progress Report of the 971st CIC Detachment in Korea gave an "illustration of the development and use of an informant of CIC." Stating up front that this illustration was indeed "a factual case," the authors of the report described a twenty-six-year-old Korean man who arrived at one of the CIC offices in the provinces with a note from the CIC office in Seoul. The note said that this young Korean man had provided the Seoul office some valuable information, and "was on the way to the home of his father (he had no home of his own), and it would be appreciated if this office could be of any help in obtaining employment for the individual concerned." The CIC agents soon understood that this young man was a refugee from North Korea, but the man was "reluctant to discuss such things."[92]

The young man was born in the southern provinces but had left six years previously to work as a "crane operator in the employ of Japanese business interests" in Manchuria. In 1946, he attended a Chinese Communist Army Political College in Manchuria, and after graduation went to Pyongyang where he was "appointed a Lieutenant in the People's Army of North Korea." But when he "persistently declined to become a member of the North Korea Labor Party," he was imprisoned. He managed to escape, and with his wife, he returned to southern Korea.

The CIC at this point was at a critical juncture. In early 1947, the CIC considered "communist elements in South Korea ... to be completely crushed." However, the South Korean Labor Party, which had gone "completely underground," appeared to be the "predominant communist party in South Korea." The CIC "intimated to this refugee" that if he were able to infiltrate the SKLP, "he would find himself in a remunerative position." Pointing out how dangerous such an undertaking would be for himself, the refugee refused.[93]

However, the refugee could not find work easily and soon had to send his wife to live with his father, and he stayed in the capital of the province to work "as a common laborer." On "two or three more occasions," an agent from the CIC office reminded the refugee of the offer and opportunity of the SKLP assignment. Later that year, the refugee appeared at the CIC office and agreed to serve as an informant on the SKLP. Soon, the refugee was promoted to high positions within the SKLP. His "real identity is known only to his wife and CIC," stated the CIC report. "He was arrested and interrogated by the Police on three occasions, and was interrogated so severely on one of these occasions that it was necessary to have him attended by a physician." The CIC report authors focused on how they had been able to create an ideal "native" informant—one whose desire for survival was so enmeshed with the project the CIC had created that the informant's ultimate loyalty was unquestionable. No matter the informant's actual political beliefs, due to the kind of human relations the CIC required him to create and sustain, he behaved in a manner that was both predictable and reliable. It was this kind of ability—to create a subject who operated ideally in a state of emergency—that garnered the CIC perhaps credibility in Hodge's eyes.[94] And on August 13, 1947, according to Captain Kenneth MacDougall, the "CIC [raided] every Communist headquarters in sight. The Korean Police aided them." "It was a formal recognition of our largest enemy," MacDougall recalled.[95]

The CIC's extensive use of and reliance on informants were logical outgrowths of how CIC interrogators understood the mental capacities of Koreans. As CIC agent Joseph Farell noted, the CIC interrogator had to be "careful" in the "treatment of [Korean] people or they will soon take advantage of you." He explained,

> What must be taken into consideration about these Korean peoples is that they have been suppressed for over forty-five years, they are used to being treated and beaten like dogs by their own Korean CIC and police.... They have no sense of moral terpitude [*sic*] and will lie and steal without qualm, unless they are caught."[96]

Instead of reading the Korean's hesitation or resistance in "lying" as a possible bid for survival in negotiating multiple, simultaneous planes of exceptional sovereign claims on his or her personhood (namely, the Korean CIC and the American CIC), Farell read the Korean's "lying" as a symptom of an internalized colonialism, one that was not about structures or meaning but rather simple violence. The Korean remained in a closed system of meaning, unable to comprehend larger codes of civil society, like morality.

Theodore Griemann, a CIC agent during the occupation, explained the casual theorization he had made regarding colonialism and the psyche of the Korean person:

> There were few Koreans alive who remembered anything other than the Japanese dictatorship. They were not trained in any skills and that included the art of governing themselves. A very few were able to function at all if someone were not telling them what to do and how to do it. A democratic government or any government other than a dictatorship of some kind, would have brought chaos.[97]

Sovereign power, even when legally institutionalized, would have to be a continuous state of exception, according to this logic. The individual Korean, understood by Griemann as devoid of agency or judgment, could not participate in a democratic society, where language went hand in hand with rational, political thinking. Instead, violence would need to be the common denominator of expression and structure—after all,

General Hodge himself had dismissed the Korean language as being unable to translate or hold the meaning of the term "in due course" as written in the Cairo Declaration.

To use an informant was to bypass rules of law in governance, and the CIC legitimated this practice through a racialized understanding and theorization of the Korean person's interiority. The Korean, the CIC agents asserted, could not comprehend regular codes and modes of self-governance, and was incapable, without the guidance of the Americans, of being an autonomous subject. Earlier in the twentieth century, Japan had grabbed the imperative of self-representation for Korea on the international stage of nation-states—all in the interest of establishing Japan's arrival at the table with Western imperial powers by conducting a successful expansionist colonial enterprise. Korea was not capable of sovereign autonomy, according to Japan's argument. And between the use of military force and the shutting out of international recognition, Japan successfully performed a key move in colonization: to render the process of colonizing Korea as natural, inevitable, and sensible for the Western audience. For the CIC agents, Koreans were not capable of independent thought, and operated more on the level of habit and response—hence, the idea that Koreans were inherently prone to "chaos" and were unable to operate without the habitual confines of a colonial force. Working with Koreans half a century after the doors of the 1907 Hague Conventions remained closed to the three Korean emissaries, the CIC agents were naturalizing another structure of international governance based on the assumption that Koreans were incapable of truth and only responded to force: the state of emergency, which facilitated interventionist actions and not democratic processes.

The United States ensured that this structure of counterintelligence—which essentially functioned as a form of "governance" in South Korea—endured on the ground. The Republic of Korea and the United States were in a tight, intimate embrace via this intelligence network. And similar to how the US CIC molded the confines of power, threat, and money to guarantee the loyalty of the Korean informant and control over his actions, the US was attempting to establish such a relationship with the ROK. The United States may have granted "sovereignty" to the

ROK by supporting the controversial elections in 1948, but it helped create a permanent state of emergency on the peninsula, which would necessitate the military and political presence and intervention of the United States. The Republic of Korea Army CIC was officially institutionalized in 1949—"It is said that U.S. Army CIC officers had a hand in the initial organization and training of ROKA CIC.... Many of the officers served previously with the Japanese army in enlisted and warrant officer capacities. Therefore, their investigative methods are primarily based on a mixture of Japanese and American concepts." The US Counterintelligence Corps was, in fact, institutionalizing a war without end—and the Republic of Korea state founded in 1948 under Syngman Rhee was invested in using the state of emergency in order to assert sovereign power. Suh Hee-Kyung, a chief investigator for the Truth and Reconciliation Commission of Korea, notes the continuity between the pre- and post-1948 intelligence structures, as the Korean Defense Intelligence Unit—called the ROKA CIC in US military documents—"took charge of counter-communist activities from the 971st U.S. counter-Intelligence Corps."[98]

Even toward the official end of the occupation in 1948, CIC agent John Dilworth noted that the CIC's "reputation among the Koreans" was that "citizens continued to regard CIC as the highest organ of the occupation forces," even though "indigenous police were gradually given more and more authority by MG [military government]."[99] The Korean populace understood that the CIC's activities were indeed the most critical dimension of the "state of emergency" instituted under the US military government. Sovereignty in a state of exception here was not a singular, overdetermined kind of power over the subject; rather, it was variegated, with swiftly moving parts, in this US military occupation.

The "Police Action" and the State of Emergency

In late June 1950, when the US Eighth Army landed on the Korean peninsula under the banner of the United Nations, salvaged remnants from World War II appeared on Korean territory. The Truman administration doled out moral rhetoric about a fight against totalitarianism—along with rusted tanks, finicky guns, and repaired jeeps—to young soldiers who had either volunteered or been drafted under Truman's 1948 "Universal Military Training" executive order. Language, machines, and bodies had been repurposed with haste and an insistence for a new global war, the Cold War. In the villages, towns, and mountains of Korea, the US military ended up confronting not the expected specter of Cold War totalitarianism, but the afterlife of a US military occupation that had effectively never left the peninsula since its inception in 1945. Tying together the days of occupation with those of war was the thread of US military intelligence. By 1950, Koreans living on the peninsula were more fluent than newly arrived American soldiers in navigating what had become an everyday web of intelligence, violence, and surveillance. When US CIC agents arrived in Korea in 1950, the South Korean CIC was in full operation. And perhaps most telling of the extent of CIC's impact from the occupation days was that the Korean people feared both the Korean and American CIC. First Lieutenant Jack Sells of the 111th CIC Detachment commented, "The letters 'CIC' strike fear into the hearts of all Koreans, for Korean CIC is an utterly ruthless organization. American CIC is generally regarded in the same light."[100] Master Sergeant Joseph Gorman of the CIC noted the same: "CIC was very much feared. The Korean CIC and ROK police were also very much feared."[101]

Following the close of the first year of the Korean War in February 1951, the US Counterintelligence Corps made a surprising discovery in the southern city of Masan. "Thirty Korean Nationals [had been] posing as members of a G2 [US Army Intelligence] Office in Masan" and had been effectively running a "G-2 office" ever since the month of October in 1950. This group had taken over an abandoned fish warehouse in the city and had furnished the front door with a sign: "Branch Office, Namhang Commercial Company, Telephone Masan 19." Paper, uniforms, English-language writing, and a perfectly calibrated performance were all that was needed—with "false G2 passes, permits to wear military uniforms, and travel authority permits," the members would at times also disguise themselves as members of the CIC.[102] When questioned by the CIC on whether or not they knew about the G-2 office, the Masan police replied that "they believed that the organization was authorized by the United Nations forces."

The Masan G-2 case was a double-edged sword for the CIC regarding the legacies of US military intelligence work on the Korean peninsula. The case demonstrated that the US military had indeed created a sovereign, exceptional plane of activity and authority on the ground in Korea; at the same time, it also demonstrated that the Korean people did not necessarily consider it sacred or inviolable. The "thirty Korean Nationals" who had established a false US military intelligence local headquarters in the city of Masan were clearly familiar with the performance needed to establish a semblance of US sovereign authority on the Korean peninsula. The personal histories of the Koreans involved in the case demonstrate a longer history of engaging in the struggle over the political public sphere. One of the members, Kim Chi Kyu, illustrates the continuity from the late colonial period through 1951. Arrested on July 17, 1944, for "disturbing the peace," he was later released. In April 1946, after liberation, he joined the Masan branch of the Democratic Youth League and began working with organizing students at the Masan Commercial School, whom he led in a strike on October 7, 1946. Supposedly around June 30, 1950, he "posted street posters welcoming the North Korean People's Army (NKPA) and denouncing the American Far Eastern policy." He joined the NKPA and later returned to Masan to help establish the G-2 Office.[103]

The strategy of these Korean nationals to establish a G-2 office as a front to and facilitator of their activities is a testament to the type of sovereignty and "state of exception" the US military government established on the peninsula. Instead of positioning "espionage" within the rubrics of paranoia, suspicion, or even conspiracy, the brilliant performance of the Masan G-2 office reveals how "espionage" was a practice of sovereign exception, where espionage signaled a type of doubled, simultaneous act of reading and also performing on the part of sovereign exceptional power. Anthropologists Thomas Blom Hansen and Finn Stepputat call for us "to disentangle the notion of sovereign power from the state and to take a closer look at its constituent parts: on the one hand, the elusive 'secret' of sovereignty as a self-born, excessive, and violent will to rule; on the other hand, the human body and the irrepressible fact of 'bare life' as the site upon which sovereign violence always inscribes itself but also encounters the most stubborn resistance."[104] It was a "secret" that the Committee of the People's Republic of Korea—the authors of the pamphlet mentioned earlier—knew all too well, as their cannily "split personalities" navigated for a brief space in how sovereign exceptional power read the Korean body. The thirty Korean nationals involved in the Masan G-2 office case had also conducted a critical reading against the grain, exploiting exactly how they anticipated the United States military would misread the Korean—and itself.

It was apparent that the Korean people simply assumed that the US or UN forces would operate on a parallel plane of activity similar to how they had during the occupation, but as evidenced by this investigation case, this plane of activity did not inspire the complete fear or respect that the United States had assumed it was due. As the Truman administration was busy inventing the "Korean War" for the benefit of the global stage, the war over decolonization on the Korean peninsula had absolute continuity with the occupation itself. The "war of espionage" was indeed continuous from the US occupation period through the Korean War—and instead of the war operating over a boundary like the 38th parallel, this war was operating over individual Korean subjects. The US military intelligence agents and the leftist political organizations and networks encountered each other in a very familiar terrain—a "state of emergency" that was now called a "police action."

On the ground on the Korean peninsula, the Counterintelligence Corps had returned, and the approach of the CIC to the "war of espionage" and the navigations on the part of the Koreans revealed surprising continuity from the 1945 to 1947 period. In November 1950, on the Korean peninsula, the 704th Counterintelligence Corps continued their activities in the southern region of the peninsula. "The former and present area of responsibility," states the historical report, "is the territory within the arc of the perimeter formed by the following towns, Pohang-Dong, Kyongju, Taeju and Masan, with the headquarters organization located at Pusan." This area was the same region the CIC had covered during the US occupation of Korea—and its objectives seemed to present an uninterrupted continuation between the occupation period and the war: "The primary mission is the protection of the Port of Pusan and the entire area by all counterintelligence measures available and the detection of former and present South Korean Labor Party members within this area of responsibility."[105] The SKLP and the guerilla fighters were the same characters in the conflict over sovereignty and decolonization in the pre-1950 occupation era.

It was onto this stage that the "prisoner of war" entered. The "prisoner of war" was certainly a figure of warfare, a temporary category that would cease to exist supposedly once the war stopped. Prisoners of war were brought within this rubric, not as a new category per se, but rather as contiguous with the SKLP and the guerilla fighters: "Sub-Team #2, during the month of November 1950, continued to interrogate Prisoners of War, primarily to gain information of subversive activities, knowledge of atrocities or war crimes, locations, strength and armament of units of the North Korean Army and Guerilla Units. Worthwhile information has been secured by this team during the course of its activity with its present project." Another "Sub-Team" of the CIC, Number 4, was reported to have "maintained constant liaison with the Korean Law Enforcement Agencies, with the emphasis on the detection of subversive elements, such as South Korean Labor Party members and guerillas. Good liaison has been made by this team with the police."[106] The POWs of the Korean War must be understood and inflected through the prism of the political landscape as shaped by the policies, experiences, and violence of the US occupation period.

The prisoners of war the US soldiers did take belied the soldiers' expectations, as the longer history of US military occupation and relations with Korea entered their frame of war. Sergeant Joseph Vincent Lisiewski, a nineteen-year-old from New Jersey, had captured a total of six Korean prisoners of war, but he noted that "some went to school in the U.S.A., smoked U.S.A. cigarettes, spoke American."[107] A staff sergeant named Robert H. Moyer, who had enlisted in 1947 and had served in South Korea before the outbreak of the war, offered the following assessment: "Before the war, Koreans considered us as another occupier of their country. And after the elections in 1948, we were only permitted off post in groups of 3 or more, for safety reasons. They disliked us."[108] The "enemy" Korean smoked American cigarettes, and the "friend" Korean resented the American military presence. The US soldiers, a number of them also from farming families in the Midwest or South, expressed "compassion and pity" for the ROKA or KATUSA soldiers, calling them "poor farm boys who had no idea what was going on."[109]

With the US troops, the question of death for the potential prisoner of war was highly dependent on the tide of the battlefields. Robert William Burr, who joined the US Army on January 26, 1951, at twenty years of age, noted the following:

> I was present when a half a dozen prisoners upon capture [sic]. A platoon sergeant asked for volunteers to take them to the bottom of the hill, when he got no volunteers, he said he would take care of them himself. He shot them.[110]

Burr had been a part of two battles—Bloody Ridge and Heartbreak Ridge—that had resulted in devastating casualties for all sides. "One thing that will remain in my memory forever is the uphill struggle climbing hill 1179 (meters) which equates to over 3800 feet.... I think that was why the men were reluctant to take prisoners. They were so dogged tired that they were ready to drop in their tracks, without the added duty of taking prisoners to the bottom of the hill." And indeed, as Burr admitted, he did not see the Asian soldiers on a horizon of humanity. "At the time I would have felt worse if I were to run over someone's dog with my car. But now I can't help thinking that they were someone's son or brother or husband."

Eighteen-year-old Yi Mu-ho, who had crossed over the 38th parallel from the north before the war's outbreak in hopes of receiving refugee status in the south, had enlisted as an ROKA soldier, most probably in hopes of escaping the constant interrogation he had suffered at the hands of multiple policemen as a "refugee." After the Chinese pushed the US and UNC forces back to the 38th parallel, Yi and two other fellow ROKA soldiers asked the people of a local village to hide them.

FIGURE 1.2 Newcomers to the Pusan POW camp waiting for processing and distribution. October 15, 1950 (International Committee of the Red Cross Archives)

FIGURE 1.3 Newcomers to the Pusan POW camp waiting for processing and distribution. October 15, 1950 (International Committee of the Red Cross Archives)

The villagers agreed to do so, but only on the condition that Yi and the others dress in civilian clothing and put down their rifles. They agreed, but later when Yi and his friends approached US military troops who were nearby, they found it challenging to explain that they were indeed ROKA troops.[111] Soon, they found themselves marked as "POW," lost in a large crowd of surrendered Chinese soldiers.

In January 1951, the US Army decided to construct a camp to hold over 150,000 prisoners of war on Koje-do, a mountainous island off the southeastern shore of the Korean peninsula. The island was also home to a sizable population of Koreans, the majority of whom cultivated rice or fished as a livelihood. These peasants had also been, especially in the postliberation period, highly supportive of land reform, and the US military had marked Koje-do as a "leftist" territory that was sympathetic to Communists during the pre–Korean War occupation. When the US Army engineers decided on two valleys in the northeastern part of the island as the location for the camp, the Korean peasants protested the wholesale confiscation of their land, and US Army memos noted that the peasants often angrily wielded their farming tools dangerously in their protests. However, within record time, the US Army took over "1,260 Korean houses and buildings, as well as some 1,680 acres of land" for the camp's construction, and as International Committee of the Red Cross delegate Frederick Bieri would later report, "It is interesting to note that the Compounds are built on former paddy fields."[112] Soon, both the CIC and POW Yi Mu-ho would arrive at what became the largest POW camp constructed during the Korean War.

The operations of the Counterintelligence Corps charted out a long state of emergency on the Korean peninsula from the US occupation through the Korean War. The strategic suspension of law and the repeated declarations of emergency formed the bookends of benevolence and death, and the US military intelligence units such as the Counterintelligence Corps and the G-2 intelligence branch were the interpreters of what "emergency" would look like on the ground. Who deserved benevolence, and who deserved death? The US occupation—and its subsequent structural and discursive legacies through the war—essentially collapsed the parameters for political discourse in Korea by

FIGURE 1.4 Construction of new compounds in the Central Valley of Koje-do.
Note the proximity of residential dwellings. May 28, 1952
(National Archives and Records Administration)

distilling the question of power and the political into one that is the
relation between the sovereign and the individual. Not the state and
the citizen, nor the nation and the subject—but the sovereign and the
individual. The profound material question of the nation-state itself—
and the more immediate concerns surrounding the issues of land, rice,
and distribution—would be swept under the rug, with all eyes focused
on the meanings of the trilingual sign of the peasant farmer Chang Sung
Sum rather than on his interests in land distribution.

Meanwhile, international attention was focused on the unfolding
"police action" on the Korean peninsula. In June 1951, Ernst Fraenkel
gave an address to the German Academy for Politics in Berlin. At this
point, he had served multiple roles in the US occupation of Korea,
beginning with heading the "jurisprudential division of the Korean

ministry of justice," to helping write the constitution of the Republic of Korea, to serving as the "liaison officer for the American Supreme Command to the Korea Commission of the United Nations." The title of the talk was "Korea: A Turning Point in International Law?" He began this talk with the following reflection on the changing nature of warfare in the eyes of humankind:

> Over the course of this century, the Greek philosopher's observation that war is the father of all things has fallen into disrepute. In this age of nuclear war, we are more inclined to regard war as the destroyer of all values and goods. But—are these two statements in fact mutually exclusive? Or might it be that war, in its destruction, paves the way for the emergence of new values and systems that will be immune to the dangers and deficiencies of the old world that it so destroyed?

For Fraenkel, Korea was both an opportunity and a testing ground. The fire of warfare burned the political and legal landscape supposedly into a tabula rasa, one where a wholly new system could be erected. He articulated what he considered to be at stake in the "police action" on the distant Korean peninsula for his German audience: "The battle now being waged in Korea will be of decisive importance not only for the continued existence and efficacy of the United Nations—it will also define the character of our future international legal order."[113] The testing ground for this "future international legal order" soon became the figure of the prisoner of war in 1952.

2

The Prisoner of War

WHEN FREDERICK BIERI, an International Committee of the Red Cross delegate, visited the United Nations Command Camp #1 in May and June 1951, he noted, "Koje-Do ... is very hilly.... Lovely landscapes. Healthy surroundings." Koje-do was a mountainous island, and the United States military had decided to construct a camp in two valleys, with mountains surrounding the camp except for one side that opened to land that stretched to the water's edge. The camp was still under construction. "Hundreds of thousands of stones have been, and are still being carried by POW by hand from the seashore and from the hills, into the building areas," reported Bieri.[1] Back in February of that year, the US military hurriedly began transferring prisoners of war from the southern port city of Pusan to Koje Island, and because the US military needed to send all available troops to the front lines, the prisoners themselves built the camp. Even the official report written up by the US military on the construction of the camp stated that "the first POW's were detailed to seeing fenceposts and stringing barbed wire for their own confinement."[2]

The United Nations Command Camp #1 on Koje Island eventually would come to hold over 170,000 prisoners of war behind its barbed wire fences. The camp would become, in the words of ICRC delegate Bieri, "the largest POW camp ever run in accordance with the Geneva Conventions."[3] A posted abbreviated copy of the 1949 Geneva Conventions on the Treatment of Prisoners of War was placed in the center of each compound in the camp. Bieri noted one particular request of the POWs, voiced during two meetings he had held on June 5, 1951, one with all of the spokesmen from Enclosure No. 6 and another meeting with the spokesmen from Enclosures No. 7 and 8 on the same day. "Issue of more copies per compound of the Geneva Convention (POW) Extract in Korean," Bieri noted in his report. "The one copy displayed in each Compound is not sufficient." And the delegate added a remark following the request: "The POWs are very interested in the Convention, which is quite new to them."[4] However, it turned out that it was the Korean POW that was "quite new" to the conventions, and not the other way around—the Korean POWs, whether anti-Communist or Communist, held and mobilized an awareness of the profound stakes involved in the application of the 1949 Geneva Conventions.

In 1950, when the official outbreak of the Korean War occurred, the International Committee of the Red Cross (ICRC) quickly moved to establish communication with all parties involved in the war. But the entities that had entered the conflict on the Korean peninsula were not the idealized sovereign nation-state entities that the Geneva Conventions had traditionally envisioned in war: the recently formed United Nations had entered the conflict as a belligerent, the Korean peninsula was still divided, the northern Democratic People's Republic of Korea was not recognized as a sovereign entity by either the United Nations or the United States, and the United States was a former military occupier on the Korean peninsula. And none of the parties involved had directly ratified the 1949 Conventions. Within the first few weeks of the conflict, the ICRC had received the pledges from the United Nations, United States, the Democratic People's Republic of Korea, and also the Republic of Korea, that they would uphold the "principle" of the 1949 Geneva Conventions. But what was the "principle" of the 1949 Geneva Conventions?

This very question soon preoccupied a core group of people working under the Truman administration. On April 4, 1951—only a few months after the opening of the POW camp on Koje Island—President Harry Truman issued an executive directive for the creation of the Psychological Strategy Board (PSB) "for the formulation and promulgation, as guidance to the departments and agencies responsible for psychological operations, of over-all national psychological objectives, policies and programs, and for the coordination and evaluation of the national psychological effort."[5] Or as Raymond Allen, director of the PSB, once stated, the PSB was to "combine with the forces of military and economic strength in the free world a systematic U.S. psychological effort under a single strategy," enabling the United States to "put to work something more powerful than dollars and weapons—the power of ideas."[6] The Korean War, as it proved to be the needed catalyst to enact NSC-68 into reality, also became the first testing ground for the PSB to demonstrate its efficacy by demonstrating what psychological warfare could look like and what it meant for the Cold War.

On November 16, 1950, the senior staff of the NSC issued an interim report on the "United States Courses of Action with Respect to Korea," recommending "a political course of action" if UN forces were forced to "retire" from Korea.[7] Although Chinese forces, along with the KPA, did not succeed in pushing the UN forces out of Korea, this "political course" eventually took the form of armistice meetings, first at Kaesong and then at Panmunjom located near the 38th parallel. Over the course of the summer in 1951, members of the newly formed Psychological Strategy Board focused on the figure of the prisoner of war as a potentially useful fulcrum on which to turn the "political course" of the war. The POWs on the Korean peninsula, at the beginning of 1951, were primarily a logistical headache for the US military, as the POWs themselves strung up the barbed wire that enclosed their compounds on Koje Island. On October 9, 1951, the Psychological Strategy Board issued a "Status of POW Policy Review." Within the year, the PSB formulated the "voluntary repatriation proposal" that Admiral Libby placed on the armistice negotiations table at Panmunjom on January 3, 1952. The prisoner of war became a figure of policy making during the Korean War—and perhaps more importantly, a figure of Cold War psychological warfare.

For the Psychological Strategy Board, the figure of the prisoner of war was not simply the accidental object of its focus. It would be through the POW that the PSB would attempt to grasp the imperatives over defining what kind of war the Korean War was. "We are living in an apocalyptic period of 'no peace and no war,'" declared Raymond Allen. "This is a paradox arising out of the confused and contradictory relations between sovereign states, some of which refuse to behave according to the rules of civilized international relations which they helped to write."[8] The Korean War, in the view of the US officials, was an opportunity to have the US be the arbiter of these "civilized international relations" in the post-1945 era, especially as the issue of sovereign recognition was fraught at the armistice table and the United Nations. The PSB had a political mandate essentially to instruct the American public on how the nature of war itself had changed, and thus why a vigorous reinvention of the terms, reach, and purposes of psychological warfare was needed. Although often delegated to the footnotes of histories of the Korean War as being mere propaganda, the POW repatriation controversy gained such explosive traction in the policy debates because those involved understood that what was at stake was the actual meaning, character, and rationale for the war. There was a concern over how the Korean War would become a template for future conflicts, especially given the demands for sovereign recognition from postcolonial societies.

The creation of the Psychological Strategy Board indicated the particular historical conjuncture within which the Truman administration was attempting to position itself on the world stage. The war-weary and war-wary public in the face of a staggering number of military US casualties, the horror of the atomic bomb, and the threat of World War III—all of these specters of war and death were implicated in the actions of the Truman administration. Wartime death—both past and present—was proving to be a complicated issue for the administration. Within a similar vein to the ICRC's concerns with the legacies of World War II, the Truman administration also did not want the public to consider the Korean War as a potential "World War III." Instead, the Korean War had to become the global "state of emergency"—thus legitimating US intervention—that effectively deferred "World War III," a nuclear showdown with Russia. However, a "state of emergency" that was quickly resulting in staggering numbers of casualties—both military and civilian—was becoming harder and harder to sustain. Thus, the "prisoner of war" debate became the new site on which to manufacture consent, where the stakes in the conflict were rendered "apolitical" and "moral." As Truman would announce in May 1952, the prisoner of war repatriation issue was one about a divide between "freedom" and "slavery."

However, the POWs in UNC Camp #1 on Koje Island did not remain simple figures abstracted into moral universalisms. In a US military study conducted during the war, titled "The Oriental Communist Prisoner of War: A Study from the Intelligence Viewpoint," the writer states, "The United States Army has never had to deal with this type of prisoner before.... He has taken unto himself many duties and missions to perform to further the interest of his fatherland. He has not stopped fighting just because he is a prisoner of war. He continued his fight with all the zeal and patriotism he had on the fighting line."[9] The Korean prisoners of war—whether Communist or anti-Communist—understood and insisted that the stakes of the war revolved around the questions of sovereignty and decolonization. While the Psychological Strategy Board and the National Security Council fashioned a different kind of "warfare" for the American public via an abstracted figure of the "Oriental" prisoner of war, the prisoners of war themselves were asking a different question. What did postcolonial sovereignty look like, and who could claim it in the midst of this "police action"?

During the very same month of August when the PSB formulated its proposal for voluntary POW repatriation, an incident—later numbered as Case #64—took place at UNC Camp #1. It was August 15, 1951, and Liberation Day had come to the prisoner of war camp on the island of Koje. At 2130 hours, when the sunlight was beginning to recede, strains of singing could be heard. US Army Lieutenant Colonel Cary S. Tucker was in his quarters at the time: "Due perhaps to the direction of the wind it appeared to me to come from outside the enclosure to be similar to the songs sung by the ROK (Republic of Korea) when marching." Prisoner of war Suh Chung Man was in the Admissions and Dispositions office of Compound Number 3, where he worked as an interpreter, when he heard the singing. He realized that it was coming from the nearby POW women's compound, and he recognized the songs: "First I heard Korean folk songs being sung and then the songs of North Koreans and Chinese were mixed in." Fifty women

POWs had gathered in the common open ground of their compound, singing. The singing carried over to other compounds—POW Lee Cheul Soo, the chief of labor and POW police in Compound 6, heard the singing begin in Compound 4, then spread to Compound 3, and then to his compound.

Members of the Republic of Korea Army soon arrived at Lieutenant Colonel Tucker's quarters and told him that the "songs were recognized as Communist." Quickly driving out through between the compounds, Tucker and a Colonel Kauffman reached the top of a hill located southeast of Compound 6, POW Lee's compound: "Between the crest of the hill and the guard tower at the southeast corner of Compound #6 Colonel Kauffman had the car stop and we all got out to listen to the singing, trying to place the focal point. While we were standing there[,] there was a shot fired."[10] Eight prisoners of war were killed and twenty-one injured by gunfire from ROKA soldiers shooting from outside the compound barbed-wire fence. The subsequent inquiry conducted by the camp administration into the deaths of the POWs became "Case #64."

In the papers of Case #64 lies a transcript of the US military investigation board's questioning of prisoner of war Yun Kyung Koo, a young man who was originally from south of the 38th parallel, about why he participated in the singing. He replied,

> I sang North Korean President's song, General Kim and Young Democrats. I learned these songs when I was with the North Korean Army. I heard many singing outside so I joined in the singing.... The 15th of August is Liberation Day for the Korean people and we celebrate this day with any means available.[11]

Yun was the only prisoner of war brought to the investigation board who talked openly about his participation in the singing—and it was Yun who insisted on bringing the question of "liberation" into the space of the investigation board's inquiry. According to Yun, "liberation"—and nothing less—was still at stake.

Within the span of one year after the events of Case #64, the figure of the prisoner of war became the central focus of the armistice negotiations at Panmunjom, stirring up so much controversy between the delegates of the UNC, China, and DPRK that the fighting on the battlefields raged on indefinitely into the future as the signing of the ceasefire was deferred again and again.

The Path to Koje Island

Surrender never guaranteed life. This unpredictable calculus between life and death in the moment of surrender was on the mind of Taik Song Jeung and the eighteen other soldiers of the Korean People's Army as they retreated south from the fighting at Inchon. It was September 1950, and the military success of General Douglas MacArthur's landing at Inchon had turned the tides of battle. Soon, they came upon what Taik recalled was "an American camp," and two "brave men" among their group volunteered to scout out the camp.

Ingeniously, the two men communicated with the American troops they met using "sign language," and very strategically, they made the Americans understand that the number of KPA soldiers with them who wanted to surrender was "several hundred." With this quick sleight of hand, these two men transformed the precarious moment of surrender into a significant event of potential wartime honor for the American soldiers. Instead of allowing the American soldiers to weigh the worth of their lives, the two men directed their attention to their own increased value as measured by the number of surrendered—and alive—Korean soldiers. The American soldiers quickly went to find their commander, a lieutenant colonel in the Quartermaster Corps.

"Fortunately that group was not Infantry," commented Taik Song Jeung. Again, in the calculus of warfare, it was good fortune for the retreating KPA soldiers to have happened upon the Quartermaster Corps who were responsible for the supply lines to support troops on the battlefields. Troops from the infantry might not have been so eager to take the KPA soldiers as prisoners of war, especially in the midst of escalated fighting after the Inchon landing.

The lieutenant colonel came to meet the nineteen KPA soldiers with a Korean civilian who had been working with the American soldiers.

With the Korean civilian serving as a translator, Taik explained to the US lieutenant colonel that his group of KPA soldiers were, in fact, only nineteen and not "at least 400." Although disappointed, the US lieutenant colonel accepted their surrender, and the KPA soldiers gave him their weapons. The strategy to entice the US lieutenant colonel with the promise of a windfall of a mass surrender had worked.

On September 27, 1950, the Joint Chiefs of Staff authorized General MacArthur to cross the 38th parallel, transforming the focus of the war from containment to rollback. For the American soldiers, they had been promised to be back home by Thanksgiving. And Taik marveled at how different the American troops seemed to be from the Koreans, who felt "desperate" in the fighting. During "break time" from the front lines, the American troops tuned the dials of their walkie-talkies to pick up music, and to Taik it "looked like they were having a picnic at that time."

Things changed yet again for the nineteen KPA prisoners when they were handed over to the First Marine Regiment. Initially, the prisoners were tasked with carrying the ammunition, food, and water for the regiment, but once the marines trusted them, they gave the KPA prisoners combat camouflage uniforms. Taik and his cohort became scouts for the marines. The marines sent these nineteen Korean prisoners of war to search "for the enemy if they were still hiding in the villages" ahead of the marines.

After twenty days with the marines, the commander called in Taik and told him, "You people are being sent to the Korean army." According to Taik, he and his fellow former KPA soldiers were eager to join the southern ROK Army to fight against the north. But instead, Taik and the eighteen other soldiers found themselves in a prison. And in a prison located in Inchon, nonetheless—the very place they had fled initially.[12] The war had changed again. By November 6, MacArthur was sending reports to Truman about the large numbers of Chinese Communist forces crossing over the Yalu River into Korea. The aim of the war was to shift yet again. "As I look back," Dean Acheson wrote in his memoir, *Present at the Creation*, "the critical period stands out as the three weeks from October 26 to November 17," a period after which

General MacArthur would state on November 28: "We face an entirely new war."[13]

In this "entirely new war," Taik and his fellow KPA prisoners were all rendered suspicious, and all possibly the enemy. In the prison, Taik witnessed many "prisoners die of malnutrition." "The UN side didn't expect so many prisoners and didn't have enough food," Taik said. The sheer numbers of the POW population presented an immediate, unanticipated problem to the US military. The numbers of Korean prisoners of war coming under US military custody increased exponentially week to week, month to month. At the end of August 1950, before the Inchon landing operation, a total of 1,745 Korean POWs were under US custody. By the end of September, the number had jumped to 10,819; the end of October saw a total of 62,678; November saw 98,143; and December's total tallied up to 137,118.[14] In total, the number

FIGURE 2.1 "Marines of the Fifth Marine Regiment strip and examine Prisoners of war."
May 29, 1951, by Sergeant John Babyak (National Archives and Records Administration)

of POWs under US military custody for the duration of the Korean War reached 170,000, and Taik Song Jeung became part of that statistical population.

Until the Inchon landing, ROKA and UNC soldiers had gathered and processed the POWs in prisons that had been used through the Japanese colonial era and US occupation, such as the prisons in Mapo in central Seoul and Suwon to the south of Seoul. But with the Chinese Communist forces pushing back the United Nations Command to the 38th parallel, the US military began transferring POWs southward to a temporary camp in the southwestern port city of Pusan. Beginning in February 1951, the US Army began to bring the prisoners of war to Koje Island.

The camp on Koje Island—massive in scale and in population—would become the first large-scale application of the 1949 Geneva Conventions, and the US military would be first and foremost responsible for the application, being that the United States was the head of the UN forces, under which the ROK Army was included. A total of 170,000 prisoners, US soldiers, Korean Augmentation to the US Army (KATUSA) and ROKA members, and Korean civilian workers composed the camp population. In the pages of the Geneva Conventions, the POW camp was a site where military personnel retained rank, were grouped together with their companies, battalions, and such, and held elections regarding representatives. In other words, the vulnerable human subject configured by European humanitarian discourse— the POW—was protected by the semblance of the state. In the light of Western laws of war, Camp #1 was to be a reflection of the order of the nation-state system, where the norms of sovereignty would protect the POW individual. The logistical template was laid out, a seemingly straightforward rubric.

On July 29, 1951, at UNC Camp #1, the prisoners of war themselves brought to the fore the stakes involved in marking the POW body regarding sovereign claims to power. The prisoners of war in Compound 76—primarily POWs from north of the 38th parallel on the Korean peninsula—had begun to gather at the barbed-wire fence surrounding their compound. It was a strange sight—a few of them were dressed in their newly issued bright red uniforms, but the rest of the prisoners were naked.

These Korean POWs were staging a protest against their new uniforms. Until that point, prisoners of war wore old military fatigues or handoffs from the US military. In an effort to make escape more difficult, the US military decided to hand out red uniforms. There was anxiety among the POW camp administrators regarding the civilian population surrounding the camp—a POW could escape to the surrounding villages and easily appear like a local civilian.

The POWs began to gather at the fence an hour after finishing their supper. Soon, a few of the prisoners took off their uniforms, wrapped them around a rock or two, and threw the package over the fence into the next compound, Number 77. "We cannot wear this kind of clothing," cried out the POWs.

Members of the ROKA Thirty-Third Battalion had surrounded the compound. Words were exchanged, and the POWs insisted on refusing to wear the uniforms. A scuffle ensued. Some POWs threw stones, and some of the ROKA soldiers opened fire. Three POWs were killed and four injured. The US military investigation board concluded in its case file that the shooting was indeed "justified."[15]

The Korean prisoners of war in Compound 76 had been protesting on behalf of the Korean POWs in the camp. They contended that under Japanese colonialism, prisoners who were sentenced to death were assigned the red-colored uniforms in prison. The prisoners' refusal to wear the red uniforms was not simply a sign of their obdurate refusal to recognize the authority of the US military—it was also an act that insisted on the US military's recognition of their own histories, experiences, and understandings of conflict and war. The Korean prisoners of war were refusing to be marked as criminals.

The decision of the hundreds of prisoners of war to stand naked in protest, without their red uniforms, and the subsequent shootings, laid bare the vulnerability of these prisoners. The 1949 Geneva Conventions on the Treatment of Prisoners of War were a constant presence in the camp, and as it was supposed to mediate the encounter between Oh Sehŭi and the ROKA soldier at the opening of this book, the Conventions were to also mediate the different encounters within the camp—whether between prisoners of war themselves, prisoners and sentries, or prisoners and the administrative powers. The "red uniform" incident in its entirety, from the protest at the barbed-wire fence to the finished drafts of the investigation board's conclusion, simultaneously exposed the Geneva Conventions' assumption underlying its script of proper POW treatment while also challenging the ability of the US military to carry out its role as the detaining power according to Western standards.

At the Koje Camp, the following provision, Article 121, would hold a particular significance:

Article 121: Prisoners Killed or Injured in Special Circumstances

Every death or serious injury of a prisoner of war caused or suspected to have been caused by a sentry, another prisoner of war, or any other person, as well as any death the cause of which is unknown, shall be immediately followed by an official enquiry by the Detaining Power.[16]

An examination of the over three hundred incident case files on the instances of death or injury in the Koje-do camp reveals an entire political economy of violence, ranging from suicide, escape attempts, hunger strikes, and interrogation procedures created by the POWs themselves.[17] These files, complete with transcripts of interrogation and testimony statements, provide material from which to glean the shifting sociopolitical landscape in the camp.

Early administrative memos from the POW camp on Koje-do indicated both frustration and anxiety over the categorization of the POW. Even the most basic administrative task—the identifying and marking of the POWs—was difficult. A memo detailing instructions on the proper processing of prisoners of war dated from February 20, 1951, and in the instructions lay the following rather straightforward process for creating the identification tags for the prisoners of war:

As soon as possible after capture and, in any case, as soon as prisoners of war come into military police channels, prisoner of war tags, UN AGO Form #3, will be prepared. In addition to the data shown on the form, the prisoners' name will be written on the form, if possible in both Korean (or Chinese) and English characters, to provide a means of identification since enemy prisoners of war have not, in general, been provided with identification by their own forces. Thereafter, each prisoner of war will be required to keep this tag on his person, at all times, until he is issued a permanent identification tag carrying his internment number.[18]

However, in a memo addressed to the Office of the Provost Marshal General regarding the handling of prisoners of war dated over a year later than the previous memo, the tone and concern regarding POW administration had changed quite considerably.

Prisoners of war or Civilian Internees are furnished with identification tags of metal, however, this serves no purpose for the metal is used by the prisoners for other purposes.... Another ... difficulty [is] resolving the Chinese or Korean characters into anglicized names. The oriental prisoners of war interchange their names, forget their internment serial number, or deliberately change them, etc., therefore, any attempt at identification by other than fingerprinting has been abandoned as impractical.[19]

The camp administration's frustration with how the POWs were subverting the administration's bureaucratic surveillance—and also authority—is clear in the above quoted memorandum.

As the camp began to be put together with barbed wire, stones, and tarp, the prisoners of war created an administrative quandary for the US military. When POW Yi Chong-gyu arrived at Koje Island, he was assigned to Compound 91—the camp was expanding constantly during the year, and new compounds running through the 80s and the 90s were in construction. The camp he encountered on arrival was in constant flux and reorganization. Each compound held tens of thousands of POWs or civilian internees (CIs), and because of the demand for military personnel at the front, there was a dearth of US military personnel assigned to Koje-do.[20] In fact, a report dated January 3, 1952, stated that "189 US personnel were charged with the supervision of

FIGURE 2.2 "A communist woman leader, aged 20, formerly a student in Pusan, Korea, admits upon being questioned in the ROK Capitol Division POW Stockade, Kurije, Korea, having been communist before the attack in June 1950." December 13, 1951, by Corporal Paul E. Stout (National Archives and Records Administration)

37,000 prisoners."[21] As a result, ROKA soldiers and KATUSA personnel were usually the ones who performed perimeter guard duty, while US military personnel would occasionally perform a head count and other administrative duties. The lines of authority within the Koje-do POW camp were neither evident nor stable.

The prisoners of war themselves were a motley population—some had come from as far away as Uzbekistan, others from Manchuria, and still others from both north and south of the 38th parallel. Yi Chong-gyu, for example, arrived at United Nations Command Camp Number 1 in late 1951 and became a part of this POW population. Many prisoners of war had family in the south, and Yi recalled that during his time in the camp at Pusan, a prisoner of war would receive food daily from his

FIGURE 2.3 "A Communist POW acts as barber for newly arrived prisoners of war
at the U.S. Army POW Processing Compound, Korea." November 27, 1951,
by Corporal William E. Newman (National Archives and Records Administration)

elderly father, who visited the camp every day. The prewar occupations
of the prisoners were as far-ranging as their hometowns. Although a
good percentage of the POWs reported their previous occupation as
"laborer," other positions such as teacher, railroad conductor, merchant,
journalist, student, doctor, and nurse were offered as background information.[22] Female soldiers and nurses, who had joined the KPA, as
well as female guerilla fighters, were in their own compounds. In his reports, inspector Bieri discussed the infants and children living with their
mothers in the camps. Yi Chong-gyu had even mentioned that in his
compound at Koje-do, three generations of one family were present—
the grandfather, father, and son.

In March 1951, approximately 50,000 prisoners of war were claiming
that they had been residents of Korea south of the 38th parallel before

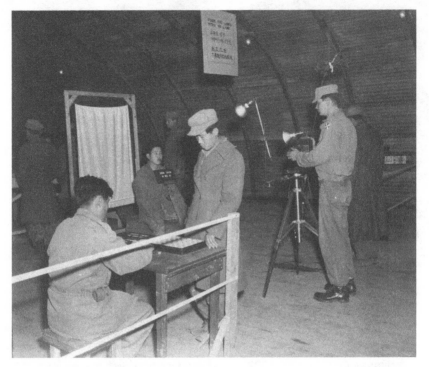

FIGURE 2.4 Identification photo step of POW processing at Koje-do, Korea. December 10, 1951, by Corporal C. E. Halbert (National Archives and Records Administration)

the outbreak of the war and had been forcibly drafted into the KPA. As later stated during the meetings at Panmunjom, the US Army had captured persons of a wide-ranging circumstances—guerrillas and Communist sympathizers. Some had been "taken into custody as a security measure," and still others had become prisoners of war "through the confusion of war."[23] Soon, the category of "civilian internees" [CI] was made available to the camp population, and the US military and the ROKA initiated a screening process to sift through the claimants. The civilian internees and prisoners of war from "South Korea" were assigned to compounds marked with numbers in the 60s, and those from "North Korea" were accordingly assigned to the compounds marked with digits in the 70s.

But even after being designated as "civilian internees," much conflict continued. Oh Se-hŭi, who became one of these "civilian internees," described five different categories of people who were in his compound:

1. Civilians who were unable to flee during the KPA southern advancement, and then were subsequently drafted by or joined the KPA or the Chinhandae.
2. Civilians who had been forcibly drafted by the KPA, fought against the ROKA, and then subsequently became POWs.
3. ROKA soldiers who were captured by the KPA, became POWs under the KPA, and then were captured again by the US military when they crossed the 38th parallel.
4. ROKA soldiers who had either defected or became stragglers and were regarded as KPA soldiers because of language miscommunication.
5. Civilians who had either purposefully or mistakenly joined the lines of POWs being marched by the US forces. Or civilians who had been suspected of being spies, and thus arrested.[24]

Civilians from both north and south of the 38th parallel, along with a large population of ROKA soldiers, composed this category—an unexpected population to find behind the barbed-wire fence of a POW camp. The US military practice of summarily rounding up civilians or all captured soldiers had shaped a significant portion of the POW population—and the character of the still ensuing civil war did also. Among the members of the Korean People's Army from the DPRK who had also become POWs, whether through capture or surrender, were people—both men and women—who had been born on either side of the 38th parallel. Certain members of the KPA had received military and insurgency training in China during the anticolonial movement, while members of the ROKA had been trained under the US military during the occupation years, and some members had been a part of the Japanese imperial army even before then.

The category of "prisoner of war" or "civilian internee" was a bureaucratic category of warfare that did not reflect the on-the-ground experiences of the prisoners of war. One former POW, Ko Yeong-gyun, titled his memoir *Facing Death* and structured his narrative of his wartime experience around sixteen moments of near-death experiences, beginning with his entrance into a temporary camp and ending with a confrontation in the Koje camp.[25] Each moment of confronting death results from an encounter with new people, whether it be DPRK soldiers or ROKA soldiers, or even other POWs. The question of, "What are you?" was not asking the prisoner of war to narrate him or herself, but rather signaling the beginning of a process that the soldier or policeman would execute in order to determine exactly "what" a potential prisoner of war was. When the ROKA soldier ripped up the UN leaflet in front of Oh Se-hŭi, the soldier was rejecting any claims the United Nations or United States would have on the conflict itself, an assertion of his own representation of state power on the ground. The US- or UN-led conflict of intervention was not to have any bearing on the encounter between the ROKA soldier and Oh Se-hŭi—only the civil war, a conflict that had its origins in the Japanese colonial period and its escalation during US military occupation, could be the legitimate template in which Oh Se-hŭi could become visible.

The prisoner of war Yi Chong-gyu's experience of becoming a prisoner of war illustrates this working of the state. At the outbreak of the war, sixteen-year-old Yi Chong-gyu was hiding with his older brother from the Korean People's Army, not wanting to be drafted. His family held a firm reputation as Christians in the community and owned a sizable piece of land, larger than most other farming families. Finally, on August 10, 1950, they decided they could no longer continue hiding. Yi was drafted, received ten days of training, and then was sent south.

> I walked all the way down from the north as a soldier in the Korean People's Army. On the night of General MacArthur's Inchon landing I was on a mountain close to where the Imjin and Han Rivers meet ... , Two large naval ships were shelling bombs all through the night, lighting up the northern skies. The bombs seemed like chunks of fire.[26]

The landing at Inchon would prove to be a military turning point. Faced with hundreds of US marine units and a naval flotilla, Yi and others in his KPA unit began a fast retreat northward. Among his fellow soldiers were a few men from Yi's hometown, and eventually he made a pact with one of them to desert the Korean People's Army and find their way back to their hometown; both were certain that only death awaited them if they continued to march north in those conditions. They left one night and began making their way back to Sŏhaedong. They trekked over mountainous terrain, only pausing to dig out radishes left over in the earth for their food.

As they neared their hometown, soldiers from the Republic of Korea Army captured them. Holding his hands up, Yi Chong-gyu repeated over and over that he was a Christian and not a Communist. The ROKA soldiers, somewhat skeptical, took him aside for interrogation and asked him to recite the Lord's Prayer. He did. Yi became a POW.

The prisoners of war that the ROKA soldiers took in were essentially prisoners of war who were not prisoners of war—that is to say, if one seemed to be a fervent enlistee in the Korean People's Army of the DPRK, then certain death would have been waiting. In the cases of Yi Chong-gyu, Oh Se-hŭi, and also Ko Yeong-gyun, the ROKA soldiers granted them the privileged status of "prisoner of war" because they seemed to be in a third category aside from the two states engaged in civil war. Their humanity—or at least recognition of being worthy for another moment of life—stemmed from their appearance as a "civilian," in the case of Oh Se-hŭi, or appearance as a "refugee," in the case of Christian Yi Chong-gyu. The utterance of the Lord's Prayer or the presence of long hair became a shorthand in a time of continued mass violence of reading a person's relationship to the state, and to the violence itself—a moment that reveals what anthropologists Fernando Coronil and Julie Skurski have described as when "individual biography and collective history seem momentarily united, as history and the body become each other's terrains."[27] And indeed, the Korean War had engendered such a moment when "the territoriality of nations and the corporeality of people become privileged mediums for reorganizing the body politic and for forcibly controlling the movement of persons and ideas within the nation's material and cultural space."

The Psychological Strategy Board

The massive mobilization of the public, labor, and finance that the "police action" of the Korean War catalyzed in the United States laid the grounds for those in Washington, DC, to execute their visions of the post-1945 world order. The architects of the National Security Council Paper 68—with its narrative of the Manichaean struggle between the Soviet Union and the United States holding up the outline for a kind of state apparatus of increased militarization and psychological warfare—knew that the American public and Congress might not be so inclined to approve the incredible increase in expenditures and taxation needed to put this kind of plan into action. In his history of the CIA, John Prados notes a key shift: "Suddenly the Korean War made concrete all the previous belly-thinking about peacetime/wartime distinctions in psychological warfare."[28] Noting that President Harry Truman retained a "deep presidential interest" in psychological warfare, Prados tracks an arc from Truman's initial directive that "started the CIA on its road to covert operations" to Truman's decision to establish the Psychological Strategy Board in 1951.[29] Within a year, the PSB commanded "a budget two and a half times bigger than of the NSC staff itself," and had become "the largest element of the National Security machinery."[30] The PSB members would be the undersecretary of state, the deputy secretary of defense, the director of Central Intelligence, and any other head or representative of a department or agency as deemed necessary by the board. In addition, a representative from the Joint Chiefs of Staff would sit as a military adviser. As part of the PSB's duties, the members would report to the National Security Council regarding its evaluations of "national psychological operations," according to Truman's executive order.

The term "psychological warfare" itself had been a more recently created label for a set of practices that the US military had been using for different ends throughout the past few decades. Psychological warfare during World War II was one conceived primarily around the idea of "information" in order to influence individual opinion.[31] The Psychological Strategy Board was the first fully institutionalized oversight structure for psychological warfare, and it continued the earlier objectives of "explaining" American liberalism to the broader global public. But by the time Truman had issued the executive directive for the creation of the Psychological Strategy Board, a marked shift in the attitudes about the importance of psychological warfare had taken place. Indeed, propaganda—or psychological warfare—appeared to be kind of a "frontier" of American expansionism. In a study he conducted on US government interest in social science research in the years after 1945, Henry Loomis commented, "the support of research in the social sciences by the US government, for use in political warfare, is a new but growing phenomena.... After the war, the atmosphere must have been similar to the opening of the Oklahoma territory to the settlers—each agency dashed in to stake out as large a claim as possible to the most fertile territory visible."[32] The possibilities were vast, and there was a sense of the ability to capture the mutability of human interiority, will, and desire.

As a new "frontier" for US ambitions and conquest, psychological warfare seemed to be the perfect site filled with latent potential, an ideal arena in which to forge the weapons for what US officials were insisting was a new kind of war. The writings of Raymond Allen, the second director of the Psychological Strategy Board, framed the epistemological crisis in warfare as follows:

> The development of the modern totalitarian state has introduced new methods of waging war. Although the basic principles of war remain unchanged, the introduction of new methods has altered the application of those principles and has necessitated new organizational arrangements in government.... U.S. measures of international security now acknowledge the reality of continued "war in peacetime." ... International relationships are dominated today by the constant actions, and inter-actions, of powerful psychological, political-subversive, economic, and military forces.[33]

As Allen had stated in a lecture titled "Psychological-Political Strategy Re-examined" delivered at the National War College in February 1952, "[An] essential feature of the World Struggle is that all the old lines of distinction get blurred and we have to talk more and more with hyphenation—politico-economic, politico-military, etc."[34] The putative distinction between wartime and peacetime was no longer applicable, and warfare itself would necessarily operate in a kind of interdisciplinary manner, where the economic was political, and the social was military.

And such a paradigm shift in the conduct and conceptualization of warfare demanded a new object or target for such a conflict. In May 1952, the PSB gave a report assessing the current state of US psychological strategy and gave two very important recommendations. First, the PSB encouraged the US military and government to go beyond the "battle for men's minds" and to "conceive of psychological operations as counter-offensive actions directed toward the satisfaction of fundamental urges, requirements, and desires of individuals, groups, and even entire societies." Second, the PSB insisted on a pivotal role postwar Japan could play in the East Asian region: "The degree of success of U.S. policy in resolving the problem of Japan's place in the region and the world at large, in the face of the extension of the Kremlin's power, will determine to a large degree the future of the Far East."[35]

The Psychological Strategy Board, beginning in August 1951, already began focusing on the POW repatriation issue as a way to fashion such a conduct of war that would prove the efficacy of PsyWar in a struggle over geopolitical control in the East Asia region. In 1951, the US military and government no longer claimed that rollback was the aim, and the war moved to a more explicitly political and ideological terrain. In the "entirely new war" of the post-MacArthur period, the dynamics that would determine the war seemed to be contained to the tables and tents at Kaesong and later Panmunjom—the villages at the 38th parallel where the armistice talks took place. The figure of the prisoner of war became emblematic of this type of war, where the terrain was ideology and politics, not territory. Although militarily the war was now one of containment, rollback was still operating—this time over people and their "psyches."

On October 9, 1951, the Psychological Strategy Board issued a "Status of POW Policy Review," stating that the PSB, "after an exhaustive study of the various legal and psychological aspects of the problem," was now "endeavoring to secure working-level inter-Departmental and Agency (State, Defense, CIA) agreement" on the issue of POW repatriation. The Joint Chiefs of Staff supported some form of voluntary repatriation, where POWs could elect whether or not they wanted to repatriate to China or North Korea; the secretary of state narrowed the possible POW population eligible for nonrepatriation and stated that only ROK personnel forcibly drafted into the Korean People's Army of the DPRK should not be sent north of the 38th parallel; and the secretary of defense, fearing that any alteration of the repatriation principle would result in jeopardizing the welfare of US POWs, advised against voluntary repatriation.[36]

The PSB saw the following advantages to the policy of voluntary POW repatriation: "1) It would reinforce the principle of United Nations asylum from tyranny. 2) The effectiveness of future United States psychological warfare programs would be enhanced by the adoption of this policy."[37] More specifically, the PSB hoped that the policy would encourage future defections from Communist armies, especially from the Chinese Communist Forces. Moreover, the proposal placed the Korean War squarely within the parameters of the "war of wills" that Allen had characterized. The POW of the Korean War would become a figure of the Cold War—an individual abstracted from history who would freely make a choice between "Communism and anti-Communism," and based on his or her fundamental humanity would choose the free-market democracy espoused by the United States.

In a December 18, 1951, memo to fellow PSB staff member Tracy Barnes, Palmer Putnam offered a few suggestions regarding resolving the legal issues surrounding POW repatriation:

2. Why not announce to the world that prisoners of war unwilling to return to the political control of the armies from which they were captured shall be regarded as political refugees who will be given sanctuary?

3. Why could not the International Red Cross, or some similar nonpartisan group, accept the responsibility for interviewing each prisoner and establishing the truth of his personal wish?

4. Why does this not solve the problem of forced repatriation
   of prisoners of war, while at the same time conforming to the
   intent, at least, of the Geneva Convention?[38]

Under this rubric, the post-1945 international nation-state order as managed by the United States, sanctioned by the United Nations, and looked after by the International Committee of the Red Cross would claim a moral legitimacy—and the POW would be its perfect subject, a person deserving of sanctuary within Western international humanitarian norms.

The POW repatriation issues struck at the heart of a larger project the PSB began to articulate for the US government on a global scale—how the "innate" desires and will of those under Communist rule would seek and "choose" American democracy instead. The Korean POW repatriation issue had larger consequences though when we take into consideration the 38th parallel, the arbitrary line drawn by the US military colonels in August 1945. A divided Korea had been destined, according to the 1943 Cairo Conference, to become the first official experiment in "trusteeship" under the newly formed United Nations—the north occupied by the USSR, and the south occupied by the United States. "Trusteeship," of course, was a new rendering of President Woodrow Wilson's "mandate," a program of tutelage for former colonies under the auspices of an international community of nation-states.[39] "Trusteeship" on the Korean peninsula soon gave way to a Cold War divided military occupation by the time the US military arrived in 1945. The US military and the United Nations set up the 1948 elections that resulted in President Syngman Rhee, a man unpopular with the vast majority of Koreans. However, it was not the legitimacy of Rhee's regime per se that was preoccupying and concerning the US policy officials during the Korean War—it was the issue of a proper subject of decolonization under US guidance. Indeed, in the face of the Soviet Union and the formally decolonizing world, the United States needed to present a subject it had successfully "decolonized," and to demonstrate that the Koreans had willingly participated in and desired the particular system of governance put forth by the United States.

The PSB's voluntary repatriation proposal had as its main concern the continuing de-recognition of North Korea as a sovereign state, where the individual would renounce the state's sovereign claims over him or herself. In the state's stead, the post-1945 international nation-state order as managed by the United States, sanctioned by the United Nations, and regulated by the ICRC would lay a claim on knowing the subjective desires of the individual POW. Rendered stateless, the POW who chose not to repatriate would be under the sovereign auspices of an international system. By January 2, 1952, the US delegates at Panmunjom had placed the demand for voluntary repatriation on the armistice negotiating table.

Such a PsyWar strategy worked well with the "Over-all Strategic Concept for our Psychological Operations" which the PSB drafted in May 1952. In this strategic framework, in order to launch effective counteroffensives to Moscow, the PSB insisted that "the objectives must be translated into effective propaganda and repeatedly proclaimed to humanity in terms the people can understand." For example, the PSB urged the United States to no longer use the language of "containment," and instead "[espouse] 'liberation.'" Or to drop the "Made in America" labels used in aid programs, and instead use tags that stated, "Peace Partnership of Free Humanity." And such emphasis on being on the side of those fighting anticolonial struggles for liberation would also emerge hand in hand with the "[quiet] speeding up [the] material rearmament" of the United States. Most critically, the PSB reminded government officials that "the free world—and ultimately the peoples not free—will welcome American leadership, just in the degree that we are genuinely and humbly seeking to help all humanity."[40]

With the specter of the atomic bomb after 1945 and the horrors of mass violence in the aftermath of World War II, the United States and the decolonizing world was facing a shift in the language and conduct of warfare, a change that had been in place well before 1945—a shift noted by German jurist Carl Schmitt in his work *The Nomos of the Earth*, which was published in 1950, the same year of the outbreak of the Korean War. The universal moralism espoused by the ICRC and as observed by Carl Schmitt in *Nomos* "would bring into existence—in fact allow only the existence of—wars on behalf of humanity, wars in which enemies would enjoy no protection, wars that would necessarily be total." The United States, in Schmitt's judgment, would be the harbinger of this new type of war and empire, articulated and enacted along lines of "intervention," "which was not confined to new states and governments in the traditional sense of the praxis of European law."[41] The emphasis on a moral universalism as the framing for the war had an uncanny resonance with the "war over humanity" that Carl Schmitt had predicted would become the hegemonic form of war in the post-1945 world.

In the years immediately following the end of World War II, the question of repatriation loomed large on the global stage, especially regarding prisoners of war. In Europe, there were approximately fifteen million people under the category of "Displaced Person" (DP), and POWs fell under this rubric. The mass mobilization that had taken place during the war now transformed into the tides of returning soldiers and civilians—as the apparatus of both empire and military were dismantled or reconfigured. In early 1952, when President Truman declared that the United States would not engage in what he dubbed "forced repatriation," he was making a moral reference to the US decision to repatriate, under the conditions agreed at Yalta with Stalin, tens of thousands of Cossacks who had fought with Nazi Germany, but who had previously fought against the Bolsheviks. News later spread that on arrival in the Soviet Union, these repatriated Cossacks were funneled into the gulag system under Stalin.

But such a framing of the Truman administration's turn to the figure of the POW during the Korean War was fundamentally imprecise and inaccurate. The more relevant context for the prisoner of war issue's relevance was the European colonial powers' struggle in their colonies after World War II, whether the French in Algeria or the British in Kenya. As historian Sibylle Schiepers notes, "while it is commonly assumed that the treatment of prisoners depends on the nature of the war in question, this equation sometimes also works the other way around."[42] And in the wars of decolonization that marked the latter half of the twentieth century, whether regarding the National Liberation Front (FLN) in Algeria or the Mau Mau in Kenya, "granting POW status to prisoners in those wars was often perceived as acknowledging the political legitimacy of their cause."[43] The question of sovereign recognition and US ambitions in the Asia-Pacific once again converged on the question of Korea in the post-1945 years.

In fact, the PSB's proposal of voluntary repatriation was a literal reversal of the US delegate's position on repatriation only less than two years earlier at the 1949 Geneva Conventions. On Thursday, April 21 1949, when Mr. Max Petitpierre, the head of the Swiss Federal Political Department, made the opening welcome speech for the gathering of delegates from sixty-four nations for the Geneva Conventions, he laid out what type of work was in front of them: "The Convention of 1864, first conceived by Henry Dunant, a citizen of Geneva, has come to form part, as it were, of the spiritual heritage of mankind. It is one of the steps mankind has climbed in its endeavors to raise the standard of civilization."[44]

The conventions had come together primarily in the interest of one particular category—the wounded and the sick. But soon another figure of war would incite a great deal of debate and energy—at a level far surpassing the other categories of "civilians" or the "wounded and the sick." As historian Geoffrey Best has written, "The 1949 POW Convention, so much enlarged beyond the 1929 bridgehead, was made up of 143 articles and five annexes.... None of the three other Conventions possessed as concentrated a character or invited such concentrated attention. Its spotlight focused on just one actor, the POW, and one crowded stage, the POW camp."[45] The prisoner of war had taken such central importance at the conventions because of the very basic questions of state legitimacy the figure of the POW evoked and revealed.

The UK delegate argued that some of the POWs still under the United Kingdom's care did not want to repatriate to the USSR. On June 23, 1949, the delegate from Austria proposed such an amendment that would allow the prisoners of war to choose whether or not to repatriate at the war's end, but a large majority promptly rejected it.

General Sklyarov (USSR) feared that a prisoner of war might not be able to express himself with complete freedom when he was in captivity. Furthermore, this new provision might give rise to the exercise of undue pressure on the part of the Detaining Power. General Parker (USA) shared that opinion.[46]

At stake was the state's sovereign claim on its citizen-individuals. The focus on the individual—and its attendant implications for state sovereignty—at the 1949 Geneva Conventions became the later focus of the PSB in formulating voluntary repatriation. If the twentieth century witnessed the institutionalization of warfare, then the 1949 Geneva Conventions and the debates over the POW during the Korean War evidenced a shift in conceptions of the "individual" as a way to regulate state behavior. In 1958, an extensive commentary on the 1949 Geneva Conventions—a nine-hundred-page undertaking, was published under the editorship of Jean Pictet, who was the director for General Affairs of the ICRC, and it offered the following perspective:

> The individual is considered in his own right. The State is not the only subject of law, and this step forward by the Geneva Conventions constitutes an important advance in the present-day international law.[47]

Thus, the PSB's proposal for voluntary repatriation was not, in the strictest sense, a reversal of the previous stance in 1949. It was a different claim on the individual as a way to shape the most basic relationship over sovereignty—that between the state and the individual. US military psychological warfare tactics and the international laws of war espoused by the ICRC may appear like unlikely bedmates, but during the Korean War, the struggle over the prisoner of war and the subsequent application of the 1949 Geneva Conventions demonstrated how the terrain of warfare had shifted to a subject that both PsyWar and the ICRC had in common as their focus: the individual human subject.

The POW repatriation proposal was a strategy offered by the PSB in the interests of larger US ambitions to shape the East Asian region.

In the 1951 San Francisco Conference on the Peace Treaty with Japan, President Harry Truman extolled the American project of teaching the Japanese former empire how to be a proper nation-state within the Eurocentric system: "For a new Japan had grown up in a relatively short space of time.... Continued deprivation of their sovereignty, continued repression of their ability to assume their own tasks, would force the Japanese people to reverse the constructive direction in which their energies had been gaining momentum."[48] Absent from this conference were the two Koreas, since the question of sovereignty—a resonant echo with 1907—for either state was unresolved. At stake for the United States in the San Francisco Conference was the strategic dismantling of the Japanese empire—literally about marking the sovereignty of territory—that would serve US Cold War interests.

Korea was a critical crux to the US Cold War restructuring of the Asia-Pacific. Members of Truman's Psychological Strategy Board formulated "Operation Take Off" regarding the Korean armistice talks, concerned that the possible "breakoff of negotiations" would spur a "period of alarm and spiritual depression," and thus the "peoples of the world will be psychologically vulnerable."[49] As a way to buoy public investment in and enthusiasm for the Korean War, the PSB created the "voluntary repatriation" proposal. The figure of the prisoner of war was to provide a new way for the American public to understand the stakes in the war. The United States was involved in the war on the Korean peninsula in order to enable individuals to exercise choice and "free will."

The Truman administration invented a new kind of interrogation room—the repatriation screening interrogation room. The Korean and Chinese POWs under UNC custody would be free to "choose" whether or not they wanted to return to their homeland, and the US military interrogation room, as both the US delegate and the Truman administration insisted, would be a space of "free will," where individual desires and not totalitarian forces were expressed.[50] Truman had declared Japan a successful project of US tutelage. The choice of the Korean War POW would be further evidence of the fundamental appeal of US-mandated projects of democracy on the global stage.

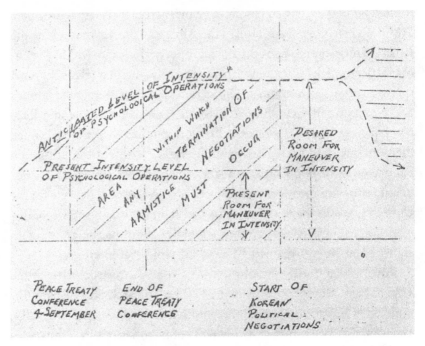

FIGURE 2.5 Chart created by the Psychological Strategy Board to demonstrate the potential flux in public support for US objectives in the Pacific Far East surrounding the Korean armistice meetings, the San Francisco Peace Treaty Conference, and the Korean political negotiations. The proposal for the POW voluntary repatriation was aimed at sustaining high public support as the Peace Treaty conference ended.
(National Archives and Records Administration)

The United States put forth the prisoner of war as the crux for US military involvement on the Korean peninsula. The Korean peasant had been abstracted into a universalized liberal individual, as the notion of defending humanity came to the fore as the moral impetus for war. Sovereign recognition, decolonizing imperatives, or state interests—including those of the United States—none of these elements were placed on the table regarding how the American public should imagine the US military intervention abroad. But Korea had played a critical role for the United States' own ambitions regarding expansion in Asia in the early twentieth century and also regarding a strategic military network in the Asia Pacific during the Cold War. Korea had been the object of negotiation regarding the Japanese empire at each historical conjuncture. And in 1951, the stipulations of the peace treaty with Japan granted the United States the ability to create its own "defense perimeter" via the allocation and variegated legal status of different territories that had been under Japanese colonial rule. On the individual figure of the prisoner of war, the United States had pinned its global and also hemispheric ambitions of structuring a vast military network that would serve what President Truman termed a "shield which protects men from the paralysis of fear," and without such a shield, in "the Pacific as in other parts of the world, social and economic progress is impossible."[51]

But the POW did not remain a simple discursive figure of war. Dean Acheson would devote a few pages of his memoir to the "POW problem." "By mid-April a disconcerting report came in from General Ridgeway.... Again in March twelve prisoners were killed. General Ridgeway now reported that 37,000 prisoners in seven of the seventeen compounds could not be screened without the use of force."[52] The POW was laying claim to determining the application of the 1949 Geneva Conventions, and the three wars of civil war, Cold War "hot war," and anti-imperial revolution were present in the camp. The war over the Korean War was on both sides of the barbed-wire fence.

The War in UNC Camp #1

The Geneva Conventions of 1949 on the Treatment of Prisoners of War operated on the assumption that prisoners of war were essentially vulnerable persons and was invested in creating a normative understanding that taking a person prisoner rather than his or her life was a marker of advanced civilization. In fact, according to the conventions, the measure of any society's civilization was revealed on the body of the prisoner of war—how the detaining power clothed, fed, and sheltered the body; how the detaining power marked, administered, and transported the POW body; and how the detaining power guarded, surveyed, and knew the POW body.[53] But these standards were most intimately revealed in the very moments they were transgressed, mocked, or resisted—as in the case of the red uniform uprising.

Violence in the camp did not initially trouble the US military camp authorities. Of the 102 incident cases during the first year of the Koje camp operation, the average time between the date of the incident and the file date of the investigation was between four to nine months. Among these 102 incident cases, twenty-eight of them specifically dealt with cases of injuries and/or death within the POW compounds. The narrative of the on-the-ground experience in the camps these incident case files offer unsettles a basic ideological narrative that was mobilized by the anti-Communist ROK government and the US government in their stance toward communist Koreans in both the battlefield and the negotiating table: the Korean Communist prisoner of war was a fanatic, an ideologue who employed violent means in order to achieve totalitarian or fascist compliance from others. However, only four of the twenty-eight cases involved Communist "perpetrators," which means that it is the anti-Communist cases that provide a broader sense of the violent stakes in the camp.

A major incident the anti-Communist POWs instigated occurred on March 13, 1952. Over sixty ROKA soldiers who were serving as guards on Koje were summoned and instructed by an ROKA captain to escort a "parade" of three hundred POWs at around nine thirty in the morning. One of the ROKA guards in his later testimony stated, "I was surprised because the PWs were carrying the South Korean and UN flag.... I was at the head of the parade with a South Korean Flag detail of six men and myself." The parade began "200 yards from compound 92" and was slated to pass specifically by the compound, a Communist Korean POW area. As they passed the compound, words were thrown, and soon the situation had escalated. UN military personnel soon arrived to join the ROKA personnel, and someone shot rounds into the compound. At the end of the parade, twelve POWs were dead and twenty-eight were injured.[54]

The "parade" incident on March 13, 1952, was exceptional only in its explicitness. The claiming of legitimacy and sovereignty, signaled by the pairing of the ROK and UN flags, was demonstrated by a collective group of POWs, in a space outside of the barbed wire of their compound. In the months preceding the parade, much of the assertion of the ROK nation-state was occurring within the compound, often in the tent of the compound monitor, in the form of interrogation and beating. From April 18, 1951, until March 13, 1952, the US military opened twenty-six case files for the investigation into POW deaths resulting from beatings inside the primarily anti-Communist-dominated compounds. Although often the case files investigate the causes of only one POW death, a number of cases involve as many as fifteen deaths, or nineteen injured POWs. Beating and interrogation took place after the transfer of a POW into a new compound, which accounted for the clustering of incidents around specific dates. On September 17, 1951, around four in the afternoon, seven prisoner of war guards in Compound 83 severely beat newcomer Choi Hyun Hyo, who later stated, "The guards had asked me if I was Christian and when I replied 'no,' they beat [me] about one hundred times with pick handles." Lee Yun Jun, a witness to the beating, said that Choi "was beaten because he was a communist and he had killed other anti-communist prisoners at compound Number 78; he had been transferred from that compound to 83."[55] Surveillance was in place.

In the March 13, 1952, incident of the POW "parade," the Communist Korean prisoners of war began shouting insults at the passing POWs and ROKA soldiers. And for the year preceding the incident, the Communist Korean POWs hurled verbal insults constantly through the barbed-wire fence at the ROKA soldiers and military police. The fact that these incidents consistently ended with at least one POW shot by an ROKA soldier merits a closer analysis of the dynamics and meanings of insults, how the form of insults evolved over time, the power these insults displayed, and the violence and reprisals these insults provoked in these moments.

At approximately 6:15 P.M. on April 10, 1952, at Compound 95, PFC (private first class) Lim Chai Kwan, a member of the Thirty-Third Korean Military Police Battalion, shot and wounded a prisoner of war while on guard duty. The narrative of the full incident begins about a half an hour earlier. A prisoner of war had shut himself inside the compound latrine, which was located at the corner of the compound area near the fence. Sergeant Robert J. Mackenzie, part of the 551st MP Escort

Guard Company, was making his rounds when he saw three ROK guards standing in a group at the corner of Compound 95. "I stopped to see why they were not walking their posts. They were perimeter guards. There was a PW in the latrine, a stone latrine with a tin roof right outside the fence of Compound 95, and from what I gathered he was giving the ROKs a bad time.... He had a megaphone inside." Another soldier (Louis D. Raines, PFC, 551st MOP EG Company) said that he had heard that the PW had "been shouting to the ROK through one of these tin deals that makes your voice louder, calling him all kinds of names about the ROK Army and the UN Army, swearing at him."[56]

Eun Jin Sik, a POW questioned by the board, stated that the POW had in fact been, "in the toilet, on the way back. He was talking to this guard about Geneva conference, and this guard didn't want to hear, and they shot him." "What did he say about the Geneva Conference?" asked the board. "The 95 compound, POW's all very bad, so they didn't distribute the rations equally like the other compounds, so we demanded that we want equal distribution of the rations."[57] The POW in the latrine holding a megaphone was accusing the ROKA soldiers of withholding the full ration distribution that was allotted to his compound simply because his compound was a firmly Communist one.

According to Lim's testimony, "The prisoners talked to us, all Korean ROK soldiers, and bad words, and then meantime, throw the stones to us. If I let them do that way, I will be punished by the law of Department of Defense of Republic of Korea, so finally I shoot."[58] A much earlier case needs to be looked at briefly in order to appreciate the full import of Lim's statement. In an earlier case where another ROKA guard shot a POW for insulting him, Captain Lee Byong Wha, who had been in command of the ROKA guards at the POW camps, gave the following testimony at 1500 hours on February 13, 1952:

> In the past I received the following order: If a PW attempts to escape to yell "Chung-Jee" [sic] (chŏngji) three (3) times before firing the weapon. But if the PW continues to escape the weapon may be fired.
>
> I misinterpreted the orders to read as follows: In case a PW attempts to escape from the compound, commit a disturbance in the

compound, attempts a riot, insults or threatens the guards or resists
or disobeys the guards the guard may fire his weapon for the purpose of killing.[59]

According to Lee's statement, the acts of escape, rioting, and insulting
carry the same equivalence in terms of punishable crimes. But what
did an insult transgress that rendered it possibly the equivalent of an
act like rioting, or an escape attempt? Lim's claim that he would have
faced punishment if he allowed the POW to continue to insult him
suggests that for the South Korean state, insults were equivalent to a
riot, an act of rebellion, endangering national security.

On June 18, 1951, the North Korean officers in Compound 72 staged
a hunger strike. However, in order to make the members of the investigation board appreciate the full import of these North Korean POW
officers' refusal to eat, Major Carroll Cooper, one of the top camp officials on Koje-do, vented his frustration with this particular group of
POWs by narrating a string of refusals on the POWs' part in the past.
According to the Geneva Conventions, as officers, they did not have
to labor because enlisted men would undertake the work for them.
However, the North Korean officers had refused and protested against
enlisted men working for them and insisted that they would do the
labor themselves. Then, according to Cooper, the POW officers were
strategically refusing to maintain their compound areas. "Prisoners
were refusing to observe even the basic requirements of sanitation, be
defecation and urinating on the ground, even though adequate recep-
tacles were provided, and throwing trash and garbage on the ground."

On June 18, 1951, at 1000 hours, Captain Robert R. Armstrong, who
had been assigned as the supervisor for Compound 72 on June 8, 1951,
gathered all of the senior officers for a meeting where he stated that
their living quarters would be inspected on a daily basis.

On June 18, I made an inspection of the entire compound. The Chinese area was well within the desired standard. The North Korean
officers area was in a deplorable condition. The senior officers were
called into the compound CP at which time they were told of the

condition and that there would be another inspection at 1800 hours, the same day. They were also told that no one would be served the supper meal until after the inspection.[60]

According to Armstrong, when he returned at 1800 hours, prisoners in one of the three subcompounds had blatantly refused to put their compound into order. Armstrong issued the order that the POWs in subcompounds 3 would not receive food until they complied with his orders. "At about 2030 hours, Master Sergeant Kahl, compound commander, reported to me that all the North Korean officers had refused to touch their food and would remain on a hunger strike until subcompound 3 had been fed."

The US military came to see the hunger strike as the most provocative of actions taken by the POWs, and soon violent measures were taken by the US and ROKA military personnel. On the morning of the nineteenth, the POWs still refused to touch their food. The US and ROKA soldiers were greeted with military songs accompanied by the beating on cans. As Sergeant Armendo Poretta moved into the compound, he was greeted with stones—and a POW had reportedly attempted to assault him with a "heavy chain." Soon, more stones were thrown—Poretta got out of the compound and manned a machine gun. There was gunfire, and eleven prisoners of war were injured, seven of them dead on arrival at the camp hospital.

The case file also contains the transcript of an exchange with Lee Hak Ku, a senior colonel of the KPA, which reveals a rather differently inflected narrative of the instigating moment of the June 18 incident:

> On 18 June 1951, the prisoners were supposed to have cigarettes distribution. Some of the prisoners of 2d Battalion hung some laundry on the barbed wire which is prohibited. When American M/Sgt saw it he took the laundry away with him. This was the prisoner's fault so we did not ask to get the laundry back, but since it was cigarette distribution day they requested their cigarettes.[61]

Senior Colonel Lee noted that the supposedly flagrant acts of defiance were perhaps more minor acts of transgression. For example, the sup-

posedly unkempt subcompound only had a water can indoors, instead
of outdoors, which then resulted in the punishment of withholding food.
Keeping his testimony rather evenhanded, Lee appeared to strive to
illustrate the severe disjuncture between the resulting death under the
gunfire and the simple misdemeanors that the POWs committed.

Yet, the investigation board would again conclude, similarly to the
red uniform uprising case, that the violence had been "justified" because it prevented a possible riot and escape attempt. Cooper concluded
his testimony with three "facts":

1. Since arriving in this Enclosure these Prisoners have resisted
   in every way possible the efforts of the protecting personnel to
   provide adequate facilities for them.
2. Their desire to work was only a method by which they felt they
   could make demands upon and receive concessions from the
   protecting power. These demands were always to their advantage, and never to advantage of all concerned.
3. Their false promises indicate that they were stalling for time, in
   order to bring discredit, and criticism upon the United States
   Government.[62]

Carroll's frustration with the prisoners of war in Compound 72 stemmed
from the fact that they did not accept the care or treatment of the US
military. In essence, the POWs refused not only to play their role as
the prisoner of war but also to allow the US military to play its role as
the detaining power, according to the script of the 1949 Geneva Conventions. The POWs' refusals were multiple: the refusal to keep the
compound clean, the refusal to allow enlisted men to labor for them,
the refusal to work efficiently and quickly, and the refusal to eat. Again,
the body of the prisoner of war was at the center of the discussion—
and the prisoners of war were strategically not allowing the US military to take care of their bodies in terms of shelter, exercise, and nour-
ishment. And the punishment for not accepting their roles as POWs
was a possible death.

In a sense, the prisoners of war could only render their protest—
and thus political position—visible via the use of their bodies. The US

military constantly harped on the fact that it was the Korean Communist POW, not the Chinese Communist POW, who would create the most trouble for the administration. In fact, among the over three hundred incident case files investigating acts of violence to and among POWs in the camp, over 96 percent of the cases involve Korean prisoners of war, both anti-Communist and Communist, not the Chinese prisoners of war. In demonstrating resistance by making their bodies vulnerable to possible violence, the Korean POWs marked their bodies as political, demonstrating that they had something at stake that

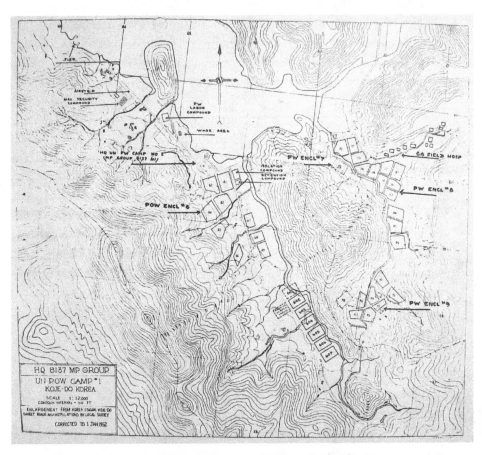

FIGURE 2.6 Map of UN POW Camp #1, Koje-do, Korea. Corrected to January 1, 1952
(National Archives and Records Administration)

FIGURE 2.7 Photograph of Compound #62, Enclosure #6 at UNC Camp #1.
December 23, 1951, by Agent Donald Sinclair, 20th MP CID
(National Archives and Records Administration)

the Chinese POWs did not. That something was the meaning of the
war itself. The Korean POWs were refusing the United States' claims
to a universal moralism by disallowing the fulfillment of a detaining
power's duties—and in turn, they were critiquing the United States'
professed moral reasons for its involvement in the war.

February 12, 1952

On February 12, 1952, a memo from Panmunjom pushing for the preliminary screening of prisoners of war arrived at the Koje camp. There
had been a previous round of repatriation interrogation in late December 1951, but a few compounds had successfully prevented the interrogation teams from passing through the gates to their compound.

Compound 62 had been one of those groups—it housed 5,600 civilian internees (CI), people who had been formerly classified as "prisoners of war" but whose status was changed to "civilian internee" when they argued that they had been civilians, not military personnel. Compound 62 civilian internees were self-professed Korean Communists and had rejected the notion of voluntary repatriation.

On February 18, US and ROKA military interrogation teams accompanied by 850 US troops from the Third Battalion of the 27th Infantry arrived at Compound 62 at 5:30 A.M. It was before daybreak, and the compound sat in darkness, save for three corner areas illuminated by the fence lights. The arrival at the compound before daybreak was a part of the strategy to take the 5,600 civilian internees living in large tents within the compound area by surprise. The received orders stated that the military personnel must take control of the compound, line up the civilian internees for breakfast, and conduct them to the latrines afterward. Then according to the testimony of Lieutenant Colonel Norman Edwards, the orders explicitly instructed, "When breakfast is finished and everything is ready, conduct the polling team to each area and begin polling.... Keep the CI's squatting or lying down."[63]

However, the plan did not unfold as anticipated. By 9:00 A.M., one US Army enlisted man was killed, fifty-five civilian internees killed, four US Army enlisted men wounded, and 140 civilian internees wounded—of whom twenty-two later died of the inflicted wounds. Alerted to the presence of US military troops surrounding the compound, the CI's met the troops with homemade cudgels, barbed-wire flails, and hundreds of stones. The majority of POWs died from wounds inflicted from the concussion grenades. The large number of casualties raised the question of why the US military had been so insistent.

Lieutenant Colonel Edwards gave the professed goal of the mission as he understood it: "To give each CI [civilian internee] the right to freely express his desire for a rescreening, which meant that when he was rescreened, he could indicate whether or not he wanted to go to North Korea or South Korea."[64] The bounded space of the polling areas was to facilitate the CI to "freely express his desire." But the mobilization of military troops necessary in order to construct the space signaled how the "freedom" of the polling area was made by the threat of mass violence by the troops' presence. The patent juxtaposition of the bureaucratic space for the expression of liberal individual choice and the mobilization of military troops in order to construct it certainly threatened to be a contradiction of sorts, and it became the central focus of the subsequent investigation.

According to Lieutenant Colonel Hartlet F. Dame, the US troops have been instructed to "present overwhelming force in such a manner that prisoners would be discouraged from any overt act, and particularly discouraged from attack against troops being used."[65] The investigation board continued this line of logic in the conclusion section of the case file: "That the civilian internees deliberately attacked UN military personnel in the face of overwhelming firepower capabilities." "Overwhelming force" became the presentation of a rational state power in the narrative of the investigation case. The POWs had not recognized this rational display of power and thus forfeited their claims to protection of life.

But a particular interaction destabilized this presentation of "overwhelming force" as the characteristic of a "rational state." Colonel Maurice Fitzgerald, the camp commander of the Koje-do camp, appeared before the investigation board. The following exchange transpired between the board and Fitzgerald regarding the use of force:

Q: Am I correct in my conception of compound 62 as being in
   effect enemy held territory?
A: No, we can go into Compound 62 any time to do anything we
   want.
Q: Without force?
A: It means, to do what we want. Is open to adjustment at anytime.
   We might do without force. We have the capabilities of doing
   what we want.
Q: I didn't mean that. I am not questioning the capabilities at all.
   My point is that would require force to enter the compound?

A: Based on their prior conduct, their sections, their implied
  intentions and threats, it is reasonable to assume that we would
  have to use force.[66]

Fitzgerald, the camp commander during this incident, hesitated and
hedged on the question of the necessity of force. If force was used, then
it was clear that the civilian internees had neither consented to nor
recognized the authority of the United States as a protecting power.
The use of force threatened the actual professed goal of the "mission."

When President Truman announced three months later on May 7,
1952, "The United Nations Command has observed the most extreme
care in separating those prisoners who have said they could forcibly
oppose return to Communist control," he demonstrated why the bureaucratic interrogation room was so attractive to a nation-state insistent on disavowing its own imperial ambitions.[67] Just as "overwhelming force" was a rational display of power, the bureaucratic interrogation
room of the simple "yes" or "no" was a rational display of governance.
For the Korean POW to resist "overwhelming force" or even entry into
the repatriation interrogation room, the POW was placing him or herself outside the bounds of a legible humanity. Following such logic, the
US military investigation could conclude that the POWs had brought
the mass violence on themselves, and President Truman could unequivocally claim that the US military had "observed the most extreme care"
in questioning the POWs.

Immediately after this incident at Compound 62, the US military
decided to discipline Colonel Maurice Fitzgerald by assigning him to
the oversight of certain Communist compounds at the Koje camp.
Brigadier General Francis Dodd soon arrived at the island of Koje to
assume the responsibilities of camp commander of UNC Camp #1.
But the issues concerning the uses of force and bureaucracy in creating
the POW subject would remain. What type of individual was the prisoner of war supposed to be?

The stakes involved in the question of voluntary repatriation were
high both at the tables of Panmunjom and behind the barbed-wire
fence on Koje Island. As the Psychological Strategy Board's proposal

FIGURE 2.8 The official caption to this photograph incorrectly refers to these POWs as Chinese. The caption notes, "Recent outbursts of violence resulted in the death of many prisoners," a comment most probably in reference to the February 1952 incident with no mention of US and ROKA responsibility for prisoner deaths or injuries. The most prominent sign in this photograph is written in both Korean and English. The Korean Communist prisoners had written a bilingual sign for their audience: "Stop Instantly Brutal Threat, Menace, Insult, Torture, Injailment [sic], & Atrocity Against the PWs of North Korea People's Army!" All other signs are written in Korean. March 5, 1952, by G. Dimitri Boria (National Archives and Records Administration)

and the three different wars on the ground in Korea converged on the figure of the prisoner of war, the prisoner of war him/herself would make demands on the international community, in turn. At this point in the story, the Korean prisoner of war was afforded perhaps the most visibility on the global stage than at any other previous point in the Korean War; however, this was also the point where the "fanatic Oriental Communist" prisoner of war would begin to appear in the bureaucratic annals of the US military and government. In the struggle over defining the "prisoner of war," the United States had taken a definitive turn—the

FIGURE 2.9 "On Koje Do, Korea, a guard stands by his 30 cal light machine gun as prisoners
in Compound #62 put on a demonstration." Note that this is the same compound as the one
involved in the February 18 incident. The signs on the fences are all written in English.
One sign reads, "Let Us See the Commander of UN POW Camp." Dated May 27, 1952,
by Private First Class Irwin Feinstein (National Archives and Record Administration)

"Oriental Communist prisoner of war" was to be a "fanatic," one devoid of rational thinking, and certainly devoid of any claims to the
political.

But the Korean Communist prisoner of war would use the very
structures of bureaucracy and language outlined in this chapter, as they
laid literal claim to their own sense of sovereignty in the shifting conflict over the meanings of decolonization. The prisoners of war were
later about to have a personal conference with the head of the UNC
Camp #1 on Koje Island. And it would be on their terms.

3

The Interrogator

IN LOOKING BACK on his experience as a drafted interrogator for the US military during the Korean War, Sam Miyamoto recalled that Korean Communist prisoners of war would, almost without fail, spit on the interrogation room floor before entering. However, when they arrived at his interrogation room, they would instead want to ask him a question. Indeed, there was one particular question the Korean POWs all seemed to want to ask Miyamoto. The Korean prisoners of war wanted to learn about the internment camps that the US government had created for the Japanese American population during World War II after Pearl Harbor. The exchange, in Miyamoto's words, unfolded as follows:

> Well, they know that I was in a concentration camp in America during World War II, and they said, "You know, if I was in a concentration camp, I won't be in the army here. I won't be fighting under the U.S. Army." [And] I told him the truth. I said, "I'm here because I was ordered to come here. I didn't come here by choice. I was ordered to join the army and I was ordered to study the Korean language, and I was ordered to come here and talk to you about this."[1]

"I told him the truth," the seventy-year-old Sam Miyamoto said in reflecting on his experiences as an interrogator during an oral history interview he gave in February 2008. It was an extraordinary gesture—a former interrogator in reflections on interrogations he had conducted over a half century before was insisting that he had told the "truth" to the prisoners of war in his interrogation room.

In November 1950, second-generation Japanese American Sam Miyamoto found himself on the Korean peninsula, after having been drafted by the US military to work as a POW interrogator. The US military reasoned that since Korea had been a colony of Japan, interrogators could use Japanese to communicate with Korean POWs, even though many Koreans refused in practice. The Japanese American had been the object of bureaucratic rule and surveillance during World War II, but in the Korean War, the Japanese American interrogator became the small military bureaucrat in the role of the POW interrogator, responsible for assessing the "reliability" of the Korean POW. During the Korean War, in the face of a severe dearth of translators, the US military drafted and recruited Japanese Americans to serve as interrogators and translators for the war. Approximately four thousand Japanese Americans were in the Korean War serving in some linguistic capacity in the US military.[2] The majority of them had spent their adolescence in the internment camps of World War II, behind barbed wire.

The US military's reliance on Japanese American translators and interrogators was expressly recognized in a hearing held by the US Subcommittee on Korean War Atrocities, a subsidiary of the larger Permanent Subcommittee on Investigations headed by Senator Joseph McCarthy. On December 4, 1953, Colonel James M. Hanley, the former head of the War Crimes Division, expounded on the process of interrogation used to guarantee the veracity of the reports and cases filed by his Judge Advocate General (JAG) teams:

> You might be interested in how we interrogated these prisoners. We used Koreans, of course, to carry on the preliminary interrogations of the prisoners, and in the case of the Chinese used the Chinese or at least Chinese-speaking Koreans. Some of the work, interrogation, was done by American Nisei, speaking Japanese, with the Koreans who understood and spoke Japanese, many of whom did.[3]

Hanley emphasized that in order to verify the accuracy of the information given, the protocol required that the POWs "swear to them before an American officer in all cases, or subsequently getting the document translated into English. Those documents were sworn to in the native tongue of the prisoner so he had an opportunity to read it and know exactly what he signed." For Hanley, the procedural bureaucratic nature of the process was clearly fundamental to the presentation of the interrogation room as a site that would, in turn, produce "objective truth" or "information." Distortion—as in all possible human variable elements—was supposedly eliminated through the checks and balances of bureaucracy. During the war, the US military interrogation room was being heralded as exemplary of the transparency, compassion, and objectivity the liberal US-led international community espoused.

But the interrogation room looked nothing like what Colonel Hanley asserted in front of the House Subcommittee in 1953. The US military interrogation room had its own history, one embedded in a longer temporality of multiple imperial projects across the Pacific. Miyamoto's "truth" was one of a man who had been made a subject of multiple projects of empire—namely, Japanese and American imperial ambitions. But Miyamoto's insistence that he had told the "truth" was also his insistence that he had made a choice. Miyamoto's own life story framed the Korean War within a series of different "state of emergency" policies fashioned and mobilized by the United States. Born in California, Sam Miyamoto was fourteen years old when Roosevelt's "Day of Infamy" occurred and his family subsequently sent to the internment camp in Poston, Arizona. Within less than a year, Miyamoto and his family found themselves aboard the SS *Gripsholm* as parties to a POW/hostage exchange, where Japanese nationals and Japanese Americans were exchanged for white American businessmen, journalists, and missionaries. On arrival at the port at Yokohama, Japan, Miyamoto's own strangely rendered "statelessness" would take yet another twist—because his parents had not registered his birth in Japan, he was therefore not recognized as a citizen in Japan. Unable to attend Japanese schools and struggling to survive in a war-devastated Japan, Miyamoto left his family to try to make his own way, and eventually came to Tokyo. A witness to the US military firebombing of Tokyo and later to the postatomic landscape of Hiroshima, Miyamoto was an American citizen legally, but was essentially a

FIGURE 3.1 and Figure 3.2 Photos of Sam Shigeru Miyamoto

stateless person, an enemy alien to two different empires. In 1949, after attending Christian missionary-run schools in Japan, Miyamoto enrolled at the University of California, Los Angeles (UCLA) but wanted to pursue studies in law, which at that time were only offered at UC Berkeley. While he was waiting for his transfer he was not officially enrolled in the system, and that was when the US military drafted him for the Korean War. Within a few months, Miyamoto found himself on the Korean peninsula with instructions to interrogate Korean prisoners of war.

The events of August 1945 catalyzed a different configuration on the trans-Pacific political stage. After 1945, the former Japanese colony of Korea was to become a nation-state through US military occupation, Japan would be a former empire domesticated into a nation-state by the United States, and the United States would emerge as a hegemonic power that had disavowed its own imperial ambitions. As Miyamoto stated during his interview, "You had to know history to survive." When the United States sent Sam Miyamoto to East Asia—for the second time—in November 1950 as a POW interrogator, Miyamoto's situation appeared to have been reversed—he was now the ally, not the enemy; the surveillant, not the surveilled. The laws of citizenship and not the laws of prisoners of war were the ones now applied to Miyamoto's actions and movements. But Miyamoto's arrivals—in 1943 and 1950—signaled not so much as a reversal in fortune as it did a shift in the global order. The US reinvention of the meaning of race for Miyamoto's personhood reflected a reconfiguring of the relationship between the state and the subject for the post-1945 order.

When the Korean War broke out in 1950, the Truman administration found itself in a peculiar quandary. In front of a war-weary public, President Harry Truman needed to find a way to present the involvement of the US military in the violent conflict on the Korean peninsula in a manner that would simultaneously appease anxieties over another situation of total warfare and mobilize public consensus over the moral impetus of the Cold War. The war, Truman stated, was a "police action." The Korean War was to be the first of the US wars of intervention waged under the aegis of NSC-68 and the desire for US global hegemony.

The fundamental argument for the viability of US military involvement in Korea revolved around a new characterization of military action: the US military had the capacity and the humanity to wage precise warfare. Much as the atomic bomb was supposedly a strategic technology that targeted specific populations, and thus, in the cold calculus of war, saved the lives of innumerable American soldiers, in the Korean War, the interrogation room emerged as the technology of precise warfare that would limit both the loss of human lives and the extent of the violence. The notion of precise warfare was seductive in this moment of a solidifying containment policy—the interrogation room became a node for the ideology of the Cold War.

Bureaucracy played a central role in this story of rendering the interrogation room as a site of precise warfare. The idea that the interrogation room could itself be a rational space for the production of information was the critical characterization the US government put forth. The US military interrogation room, in contrast with the interrogation rooms of the past that were cloaked in darkness, secrecy, and violence, was now supposedly an idealized site of regulated and willing exchange between the interrogator and the interrogated prisoner. How did one determine whether or not the information gathered during interrogation was reliable? How did one calibrate interrogation to induce the interrogated prisoner to give information willingly? The experiences of interrogators like Miyamoto during the Korean War break open the US military interrogation rooms' claim to objective authority by exposing how the interrogator's claims to accuracy is proportionate not to the quantity of information extracted but rather to the quality of the interrogated's will to provide that information. The person of the Nisei Japanese American as the military interrogator became integral to the idea of precise warfare in the Korean War. The US military assumed that the demonstration of the inclusion of Japanese Americans into the national project of US warfare would serve as persuasive evidence to the "Oriental" prisoners of war that they should embrace the benevolence of the United States.

As a POW interrogator, Sam Miyamoto was to embody the universalizing mission of the United States—his supposed desire for assimilation would leave the integrity of the United States as a nation-state intact, even in the face of the recent history of mass internment.[4] And desire on the part of the decolonized Korean POW and the Chinese POW would enable the critical disavowal of imperial ambitions on which the United States insisted—if others demonstrated their wish to belong to the US-defined liberal order, then the United States was not imposing an imperial design on the globe. Desire, however, was not a predictable variable in the interrogation room. Miyamoto's interrogation room pointed to a Korean War embedded in the struggles over the nation-state system in the post-1945 era. Spitting for the Korean Communist POW was not simply an act of refusing the authority of the US military; it was also a refusal of the United States' own insistence that the project of decolonization was complete on the Korean peninsula with the regime it had installed in the south. When Sam Miyamoto told the Korean Communist POW his "truth," he was also insisting on a small measure of recognition of his own history. The work of translation extended past linguistic mechanics and into the multiple, fractured histories of negotiating the demands of US liberalism and race-making within a trans-Pacific frame. Instead of the intimacies of diplomats and state officials often found in mainstream narratives of the early Cold War, here the relationships within the interrogation room come to the fore, and they, in turn, reveal the intimate (and indispensable) relationships between language and war-making, race and historical memory, and bureaucracy and violence.

The presence of defiance and reluctance in Miyamoto's interrogation room revealed not only how the subject-making was a twofold project, involving both the interrogator and the interrogatee, but also how both people were negotiating shifts of "personhood"—moving from colonial subject to national citizen, or, in case of Miyamoto, from enemy alien to citizen-soldier. In essence, the story here is of the making of both the interrogator and the interrogated prisoner of war in the Korean War. The story of making the interrogator begins in the sugarcane fields of Hawai'i at the turn of the century, through the "Day of Infamy" and the internment camps, through the battlefields and POW camps of the Korean War.

A Hostage Exchange to Herald the "War"

On December 8, 1941, President Franklin Delano Roosevelt stood in front of the US Congress and delivered a speech that would herald the entrance of the United States into World War II. "Yesterday, December 7, 1941—a date which will live in infamy—the United States of America was suddenly and deliberately attacked by naval and air forces of the Empire of Japan." He ended the speech with a request: "I ask that the Congress declare that since the unprovoked and dastardly attack by Japan on Sunday, December 7th, a state of war has existed by the United States and Japanese Empire."[5]

"War" was most immediately heralded by two actions taken by the US government in December 1941: the arrest of over two thousand Japanese Americans in the United States and the sending of a letter to Japan regarding a potential exchange of US civilians in the Japanese empire for Japanese nationals and Japanese American citizens in the United States. Agents from the Federal Bureau of Investigation (FBI) came directly to the homes of Japanese American families, and the arrests of two thousand Japanese American men affected the families of young adolescents like Toro Isobe and Sam Miyamoto. On December 7, 1941, Toro Isobe was fourteen years old. Born in San Francisco, Toro had moved with his parents to Los Angeles in 1939 to seek work during the Great Depression. His father found employment managing a small hotel called the Victorian Hotel, and they leased a small residential unit in the hotel itself. "On the night of December 7th, the FBI came and took my father away, so mother was left by herself with four kids."[6] Sam Miyamoto remembered the visit of the FBI to his family home also: "I still recall two FBI agents who came to our home on February 19, 1942 with sirens piercing the small farming community in Imperial Valley. It was frightening. My father was stunned." Miyamoto's father showed the FBI his passport to prove that he was a legal immigrant. In response, the FBI stated that they "were not questioning his loyalty, rather they were rounding up the community leaders." The FBI took Miyamoto's father away and froze the family's bank account. "Financial ruin and fear of an uncertain future for the family finally took its toll on my father. When Dad joined the family in July of 43, all his hair had turned white, and suddenly he looked old beaten and withdrawn. He showed pain when I told him we lost everything; the farm, equipment, car, home, truck, and all our personal belongings."[7]

By June 27, 1942, the infamous Public Proclamation No. 8 was posted on the walls and telephone poles of different communities all throughout the military zones:

The present situation within these military areas requires as a matter of military necessity that persons of Japanese ancestry who have been evacuated from certain regions within Military Areas Nos. 1 and 2 shall be removed to Relocation Centers for their relocation, maintenance and supervision and that such Relocation Centers be designated as War Relocation Project Areas and that appropriate restrictions with respect to the rights of all such persons of Japanese ancestry, both alien and non-alien, so evacuated to such Relocation Centers and of all other persons to enter, remain in, or leave such areas be promulgated.[8]

For the next three years, over 120,000 Japanese Americans would be forcibly removed by the US government into internment camps located in sites as various as Heart Mountain, Wyoming, and Poston, Arizona. "Although two thirds of the internees were American citizens, they were incarcerated without any charge, trial, or evidence against them."[9] Most of this study's cohort was shuttled through the Santa Anita racetrack camp eventually, and then was sent to camps scattered all over the United States: Manzanar in California; Jerome, Arkansas; Gila River near Phoenix, Arizona; Rohwer, Arkansas; Poston, Arizona; Heart Mountain, Wyoming. Arnold Yoshizawa, twelve years old at the time, was living in the Boyle Heights neighborhood of Los Angeles—he was sent to Manzanar. Robert Shiroishi, an eleven-year-old growing up in Long Beach, was shuttled with his family through Santa Anita and finally to Jerome, Arkansas.[10]

Another displacement would soon take place within the Japanese American communities, and Sam Miyamoto along with members of his immediate family would find themselves on yet another list. The names of all the members of the Miyamoto family appear within the pages of a different US government list dated September 2, 1943. Sam Shigeru Miyamoto at age fifteen, along with his parents and three siblings, found himself on a sailing list with a simple title: "Japanese Embarked for Second Voyage of Gripsholm."[11] They became part of a "hostage exchange" between the United States and Japan.

For the Miyamoto family, another document in addition to the Executive Orders, Proclamations, and the Constitution would be brought to bear—or held in abeyance—onto their experience: the 1929 Geneva Conventions on Prisoners of War. A different calculus in determining the proper subjecthood for people like the Miyamoto family came to the fore—and this time it was a certain formulation of sovereignty. In other words, there was yet another project of "military law" and "military necessity" being worked through the Japanese American population.

On December 8, 1941, the same day as President Roosevelt's "Day in Infamy" speech, the US government transmitted through the Swiss minister in Tokyo its initial proposal for the treatment and eventual exchange of Japanese government officials in return for American government officials. In 1942, according to US naval intelligence calculations, there were approximately 3,000 US citizens in the Far East, of whom 1,000 to 1,500 were missionaries. The Japanese military in its large sweep down from Manchuria to the south of the Asian continent—to Singapore and the Philippines—had taken prisoner these 3,000

American citizens.[12] Businessmen, journalists, and missionaries composed most of this "hostage" population—they were the "nonofficials." And they were the locus of the US government's concern.

On December 10, 1941, Japanese officials in Tokyo received the US proposal to exchange nonofficial American citizens who were within the reach of the Japanese empire, especially Manchuria, along with government officials. But one question remained: under which legal precedent or rubric would the exchange take place? On December 17, 1941, Max Huber, president of the International Red Cross, "answered a Japanese inquiry on this very point: 'We think that [the] fact Japan is not party [to the] 1929 conventions relative to war prisoners does not prevent carrying out above-mentioned scheme provided reciprocity agreed upon by parties of war or provided these parties declare themselves prepared apply de facto provisions contained in 1929 war prisoners convention.' "[13] As both the Japanese and US governments agreed to follow the provisions of the 1929 Geneva Conventions, the phrase "reciprocity" soon became a critical principle for much of the negotiations to follow.[14]

Soon members of the US Department of State were becoming upset over the treatment of "Americans" by the Japanese. BL (most possibly Breckinridge Long, the assistant secretary of state) wrote in a memo, "It has come repeatedly to my notice, and for sometime I have had the intention of recording the thought that according to the terms of our exchange agreement with Japan the whole affair was to be on a reciprocal basis."[15]

The Japanese military had sequestered American citizens into certain sections of cities, or camp-like areas. However, the anxiety provided a moment of reflection on the "reciprocal" aspect of the exchange, and members of the Department of State acknowledged that American actions with Japanese Americans had undermined a possible case for protest against Japan's sequestering of American citizens in camps:

February 16, 1943
    SD [special division] does not feel that this Government is in a position at this time to protest the mass internment of American na-

tionals on the basis of the four reasons outlined by the Swiss in Bern's 1028, February 13.

One: Many Japanese were moved to relocation centers before camps were completed.

Two: The aged and infirm and sick, as well as pregnant women and small children, were moved by trains and buses to relocation centers.

Three: Many Japanese were removed from their homes on only a few hours notice.

Four: Many of the relocation centers to which Japanese were removed are in remote inaccessible areas.

No reasons have been given by the Japanese for the mass internment of American nationals in and near Shanghai. It can be assumed that if we were to protest that action the Japanese would be justified in replying that this Government has already taken similar action in regard to Japanese nationals, which is true.[16]

The significance of the various interpretations, frustrations, and preoccupations with "reciprocity" on the part of the Special Division of the Department of State lies in the longer history of the United States and Japan negotiating their imperial ambitions with each other. This concern over "reciprocity," I contend, demonstrates another set of stakes involved in the "hostage exchange" with Japan.

The conflict over political recognition—or to put it more directly, the position of Japan within white, Eurocentric systems of imperial hegemony, namely, British and American—was one that had its own history. Scholar Bruce Cumings has charted what he termed the "archaeology of Japan in the twentieth-century world-system," where he analyzes how Japanese officials and diplomats had to negotiate with both Britain and the United States in their claims for hegemony in Asia, ambitions that were supported and encouraged by the two Western states as long as Japan remained "Number Two," to further borrow from Cumings's terminology.[17] Japan, in the opinions of prominent Anglo Americans, was uniquely positioned to extend the "civilizing mission" and "enlighten" the other areas of Asia, such as China and Korea. The

Taft-Katsura agreement of 1905 made the stipulation that Japan would be able to claim Korea as a colony, only if Japan would not impede American efforts in the Philippines. As Japan increased in ambition, expansion, and control over the Asian region, the fiction of equal nation-state actors or nation-bound entities came to the fore in the treaties in which Japan participated. Attempting to use leverage to claim itself as a recognized power with the Euro-American sphere of influence, Japan put forth a series of proposals, most importantly the racial equality clause for the Treaty of Versailles. But the proposal set forth by an Asian empire shone too much light on the inherent contradictions of Euro-American imperialism and colonial systems. The racial equality clause was not adopted—and Japan also found itself negotiating the Gentleman's Agreement with the United States in the face of the Asian exclusion act, which followed from the earlier anti-Chinese immigration era in the United States.[18]

In addition to the realm of migration and labor, war and sovereignty became also the arena in which questions of recognition and subjecthood were negotiated between Japan and the United States. The most notable was the Stimson Doctrine in 1931. On September 18, 1931, Japanese imperial forces moved to occupy cities and towns in southern Manchuria. Over the next two months, members of the US State Department debated over the proper stance to take vis-à-vis Japan. The most immediate concern—besides US access to markets and materials in China—was the breach of the Kellogg-Briand Pact. A resolution to the issue came in the form of a note written and sent by Secretary of State Henry Stimson—later to be known as the Stimson Doctrine—stating that the United States would not, in fact, recognize the territories the Japanese acquired in Manchuria. The fiction of the nation-state system was asserted in this moment of nonrecognition, and the Stimson Doctrine drove home the point that Japan was not to be an empire on a par with the Western nations.

Within the much longer history of treaty-making and exchanges between the United States and Japan, this particular "hostage" exchange would present an age-old dilemma in a new light: how does the United

States engage in a hostage exchange with an enemy it does not want to recognize as its equal? The language of "reciprocity" became critical to the dialogue over the exchange, laying bare the fiction of the equality of sovereign nation-states. According to scholar Bruce Elleman on the stance of Japanese officials over the hostage exchange: "In the midst of World War II, the Japanese negotiators were determined not to allow any inequalities between enemies. To make matters worse, at the beginning of the war there were many more American officials and ordinary citizens being detained by Japan than there were Japanese officials and citizens being held in custody by the United States. This made a truly 'reciprocal' exchange very difficult."[19] The calculus of the politics of recognition—each nation-state being an equal actor on the world stage—was also the calculus determining the logistics of the hostage exchange: one Japanese subject for every American citizen.

But who was a "Japanese" subject, and who was an "American" citizen? And what happens when one does not have enough "Japanese subjects" to exchange? The international language of treaties and warfare had officially become the framework that bound the exchange—and the language of "prisoners of war" had been adopted for application to the exchange of official and nonofficial civilians. In this moment, the Japanese American was being interpolated not simply by one state, but rather by the politics of recognition; the Japanese American was not firmly a citizen of a state, but rather a subject of two empires, on whom the conflict over political recognition would play out.

The Japanese government had already given a list to the United States of different Japanese nationals residing in the United States whom they deemed as acceptable "reciprocal" exchanges with the American citizens in its custody. The list-making was fraught with difficulties. In a telegram dated May 18 to Bern, the Special Division stated: "United States Government thus confirms that it expects to repatriate upon the contemplated voyages of the *Gripsholm* (numbering possibly three) all Japanese internees or detainees or other Japanese nationals expressing desire for repatriation whether that desire is first expressed by the individual or by the Spanish Embassy in charge of Japanese interests."[20]

Here, it is crucial to note that the US government was now beginning to turn to find Japanese nationals and Japanese Americans detainees who were not on the list sent by the Japanese government.

The Japanese American internees did not respond as the US Department of State had anticipated. According to a Department of State Special Division document titled "Individuals Named by the Japanese Government for Repatriation Who Have Refused to Go to Japan," 3,101 of those individuals had refused repatriation. Another fifty-six had refused to respond to the question regarding repatriation altogether. In response to these large numbers of repatriation rejections—and those who had refused to take the survey—George Brandt of the Special Division wrote that the Japanese individuals might reconsider repatriation once they realize that "their emperor" had requested their repatriation, since they were, as he noted, an "obedient race."[21]

But "obedience" and "loyalty" would not map out according to the expectations of those in the Department of State. In the fall of 1942, two different agendas between the War Department and the War Relocation Authority converged, and together they developed "a massive registration campaign that utilized not only background checks but also self-professions through questionnaires establishing loyalty and willingness to defend the country."[22] In its push toward total war, the US War Department needed more bodies for the military, whether in the battlefields or in support elsewhere. The Japanese American population soon came into consideration as a source of available labor. At the same time, the War Relocation Authority needed to prepare for future leaves and resettlement plans of the internees, as the US government needed internees for a domestic labor shortage also.

Two questions in particular from the questionnaire are well known for their controversial testing for "loyalty." The following version was given to citizen adult males in the camps:

(27) Are you willing to serve in the armed forces of the United States on combat duty, wherever ordered?

(28) Will you swear unqualified allegiance to the United States of America and faithfully defend the United States from any or

all attack by foreign or domestic forces, and forswear any
form of allegiance or obedience to the Japanese emperor,
or any other foreign government, power, or organization?[23]

Scholar Takashi Fujitani importantly notes that this "political ritual" of
registration combined with the questionnaires marked a difference
from the "original assumption behind the evacuation, which was that
the Japanese were like animals without subjectivity." In this ritual of
list-making, the US officials needed to think of the "internees as free
subjects making rational decisions" in order to make those who volunteered for military service viable participants in US society.[24] The US
"fully recognized the right of an individual to live as a citizen," Fujitani
writes, "only if that individual vowed that he or she would volunteer
to die as a soldier."[25] A notable dissonance and tension arose between
the assumption by the State Department that the Issei (first-generation)
internees would soon reconsider repatriation since they were an "obedient race" and the program offered by the WRA to the Nisei internees
to refashion themselves as Americans through choice. This contem-
poraneous duality of a more biological racism alongside a liberal racial
self-fashioning would endure, and it framed the racializing of the national security state that emerged in the postwar era. The burden fell
on the individual to render his or her desires transparent to the state.
And more critically, either choice, as Fujitani points out, exacted a kind
of death: inclusion into the American body politic meant the volun-
teering of literal death in exchange for the possibility of social, civil life,
while supposed willful self-exclusion meant that the person chose to
remain disposable in terms of both physical and social life. And the
internees themselves understood this calculus intimately when confronted with these kinds of questionnaires. What kind of life was possible? What would one need to grieve? Which choice would make
one's life literally precarious and in what ways, to what degree?

According to Bruce Elleman, the infamous loyalty questionnaire
was one method the US Department of State employed to find more
willing "repatriates" among the Japanese Americans. But in the end
"only 4 Japanese from the relocation centers were included on the first

exchange in 1942, while 314 others were included in the 1943 exchange."[26] The loyalty questionnaire had supposedly produced "a total of 20,161 Japanese citizens and American citizens of Japanese ancestry [who] offered to participate in the official U.S.-Japanese exchange program by returning to Japan." Of this group, over fifteen thousand ultimately decided to remain in the United States at the war's end—and the Japanese government, in its insistence on "reciprocity," rejected the exchange of primarily working-class Japanese nationals for the American officials in its care. On the other hand, as already noted, 3,101 of the Japanese and Japanese American citizens requested by the Japanese government refused "repatriation." "Loyalty" and "obedience" were clearly not the ideologies framing this choice of "repatriation." And yet, the constant reassessment, the constant list-making of the loyal versus disloyal, continued.

The project of racial liberalism had taken on many different forms.[27] But the constant list-making and recategorizing was also at the heart of the Japanese American internment project, and this obsessive activity itself demands our attention. The violent assertion of US imperial power over bodies through this list-making was a display of US sovereign power. The US state was demonstrating that it could render people stateless over and over in differently inflected ways. In front of the conflict over political recognition with the competing expansionist empire of Japan, the US exercised its sovereign power through its ability to manufacture statelessness, rather than via the conferring of subjecthood. The US attempted to undermine the arrival of Japan on the world stage of empires by asserting the US racial order ultimately with these projects of statelessness. For Japanese nationals and Japanese Americans, the politics of recognition was never an abstraction.

The Choice of an "Enemy Alien" between Two Empires

In September 1942, armed guards arrived at the Poston camp to escort the people who were to be exchanged on the SS *Gripsholm*. "It was not an adventure which I either desired or volunteered for," said Sam Miyamoto. On arriving in New York, a few protested and refused to board the ship, but according to Miyamoto, "those who refused were told that they would be tied and loaded on the ship with the baggage to be shipped to India." Eventually, everyone boarded, and the SS *Gripsholm* left New York.

> We sailed south hugging the South Pole in view of the magnificent large icebergs. Avoiding the war, we finally approached India. We were hypnotized by the beauty and mystic calmness of the Indian Ocean—sometimes when I see a beautify [*sic*] sunset, I am haunted by the memory of one Japanese American who jumped overboard into the Indian Ocean—what was he thinking? Was he a romanticist or was he grieving?

The choice to "repatriate" was one that was fraught with the unknown. For Sam Miyamoto, a young fifteen-year-old Japanese American who did not speak Japanese, going to Japan was unimaginable. And although we cannot answer Miyamoto's question of what the Japanese American man who had thrown himself overboard into the Indian Ocean was thinking, we can delve further into inquiring what this "choice" of pseudo-repatriation entailed for the nonofficial Issei and Nisei Japanese Americans.

Among the many lists of Japanese Americans in the Special Division archives is a series of excerpts from and summaries of letters sent between Japanese American family members, especially those families residing in Hawai'i whose fathers had been taken to US mainland camps for closer surveillance. A close reading of the excerpted letters demonstrates that the choice of whether or not to go to Japan as the Special Division was encouraging was debated in terms of family reunions and imaginings of what the postwar world would like.[28] Questions of loyalty, nationalism, and the Japanese empire were absent, at least from the excerpts. Instead, the question on the table for these families was: What kind of life would be possible for the Japanese American after the war, and where?

Fort Sill, Oklahoma, held many of these Japanese American men from Hawai'i's communities, and the letters addressed to the men interned at Fort Sill illuminate how these families were attempting to use "repatriation" as a possible way to reunite the family. Hirayoki Okaji from Hawai'i wrote to Toyomi Okaji in Fort Sill, Oklahoma: "clothing ready to be packed for trip to Japan, mother could go too. Sanehiro and I could remain here, we can always have any amount of cash sent to you." A T. Shoda from Maui wrote to Mr. Seichi Shoda: "If you go we might as well follow, if possible," an implication that the family would join Shoda in Japan, if necessary. The Special Division noted that in the letter from Mrs. Yasu Hino of Hilo, Hawai'i, to the Reverend S. Hino, "Writer says that her friends are assured that they are to be sent to Japan, and requests her husband to take steps to secure her evacuation to Japan." Yoshinao Kokuzo also of Hilo, Hawai'i, may have been one of Mrs. Hino's friends—the Special Division noted that in her letter to the Reverend Zenkai Kokuzo at Fort Sill, the "writer looks forward with complete assurance to her return to Japan and eventual reunion with husband."[29]

Anticipating and imagining the postwar era was a crucial part of the decision-making process. Toraichi Uyeda in Camp Livingston wrote a very revealing letter to Mrs. Masaye Uyeda in Honolulu: according to the summary done by the Special Division, "Husband tells wife why he wishes to be repatriated. Has aged mother and son in Japan and can return more quickly from Japan to the Islands than from U.S. to the Islands, after the war." Others noted the current treatment of Japanese Americans within the United States. T. Sekiguchi in the WCCA Center in Pinedale, California, wrote to a Mr. B. A. Ploe in Canada: "Dissatisfied with treatment received in Assembly Center American-born does not like to be treated as alien." Sekiguchi's letter was condemned, but other letters echoed similar sentiments, expressing wariness about the postwar future for Japanese Americans in Hawai'i or the United States. Mr. Hoshida in Lordsburg, New Mexico, wrote to Mrs. Tamae Hoshida in Hawai'i: "We'll have very little opportunities left in Hawaii after the war and believe will be better to start over in Japan."

Miyamoto did not know exactly why his father had decided to bring the family to Japan, but it is clear that the question of "repatriation" was a crucial moment in the transnational imaginary of the Japanese American community. And transnational for these Japanese Americans was not about "transcending" the national, as Eiichiro Azuma has asserted in his scholarship—the transnational was an important element of the Japanese American communities' strategies for negotiating their place within the competing "politics of recognition" on the global geopolitical stage.[30] For the Japanese Americans, the "politics of recognition" had already been playing out in terms of a particular claim to personhood—labor.

In his noted work, *The Issei*, historian Yuji Ichioka stated, "Japanese American history is labor history," and this frame of labor is crucial to our story as we follow the lives of the young Japanese Americans through the postwar era.[31] Their own family histories spanned an era that is significant in the policy changes rendered—from the Chinese Exclusion Act of 1882, the 1907 Gentlemen's Agreement, through the 1913 Alien Land Act, the 1924 Immigration Act, and the 1931 Stimson Doctrine. The displacement of Japanese Americans via internment camps and the "hostage exchange" fit within a longer history of negotiated migration and labor.

The story of labor begins with sugarcane, steel, lumber, and fish along the Pacific. The sugarcane plantations established by white American settler colonists in the US colony of Hawai'i, the expanding railroad system in the American West, and the fishing and lumber industries in the northwestern states were often the initial labor markets available to Japanese at the turn of the century. The parents of Thomas and Harry Tanaka, two brothers who were born in 1927, had come to Hawai'i from their home in Fukuoka, Japan, to work in the sugarcane fields.[32] The railroad companies had relied heavily on Chinese laborers, but with the Chinese Exclusion Act of 1882, some Japanese migrant laborers began filling the ranks, as did Howard Okada's grandfather: "You know the Santa Fe railroad that goes down to LA? He worked on that. Like a lot of Chinese laborers did."[33] Roy Shiraga's father and Jim Yanagihara's father both went north. Shiraga's father arrived in San Francisco in 1905 at the age of sixteen, but after the Great Earthquake in 1906, went north to work as a lumberjack in the mills of Oregon and Washington, later working on the northern railroads. Yanagihara's father first worked in the fishing industry in Seattle and later settled in Imperial Valley, in southern California, similar to Okada's grandfather.[34]

In 1907, in an attempt to extricate and exceptionalize Japan in the face of the 1882 Chinese Exclusion Act, the "Gentlemen's Agreement" was reached between the United States and Japan, allowing for the travel of Japanese students and diplomats to the United States with the understanding that Japan would prevent further immigration to the United States. In 1908 a shift in the strategies of the Issei would be heralded: they were already residing in the United States—and they changed from being a primarily labor-contracting source of labor to inhabiting what scholar Eiichiro Azuma has called a "settler colonist" identity.[35] The Issei became permanent settlers as a way to counter the anti-Japanese and anti-Asian movement in the United States, and agriculture in turn became the primary strategy.

The decision to move to southern California became a common one among the first-generation Japanese Americans. Cultivating "niche crops that white farmers tended to neglect—such as asparagus, berries, celery, onions, potatoes, and cantaloupes," Japanese Americans were able to create a living.[36] Okada's father cultivated strawberries and vegetables outside of Fresno; Roy Matsuzaki's parents worked on a strawberry farm, and in the winter, they grew cucumbers; Katsuya "Kats" Nakatani's father had a stall in the Ninth Street City Market in Los Angeles, where he would sell produce, primarily cabbage, grown by the other farmers who lived around them.[37]

But this period was quickly followed by a series of legal actions that further disenfranchised the Japanese American communities. California's first Alien Land Act was enacted in 1913, and it declared that "aliens ineligible for citizenship" were limited to land leases of up to three years, and all ownership by "aliens" was banned.[38] The period between the 1913 California Alien Land Act and the 1924 Immigration Act was one characterized by multiple legal challenges by the Japanese American community, all concurrent with the rapid adoption of similar Alien Land Acts in Arizona (1921), Oregon, Idaho, and Montana (1923). The legal challenges garnered the most attention with the historic case,

Ozawa v. U.S., but in 1922 the Supreme Court decided to uphold the continuation of denying naturalizable citizenship to Japanese Americans. Historian Azuma characterizes the 1920s as a moment for significant change in the strategies of the Issei in the United States: "While most Issei chose to stay, many immigrants rejected lives under the command of another race. In order to break away from such social conditioning, they left the United States for their homeland, or for third countries, where they believed they could remain 'the people of a first-class nation.' "[39] During the years 1923 and 1924, the US census reported the highest rates of Japanese farmers leaving the United States.

Although George Taniguchi's father was on the very last boat from Japan to the United States in 1924, he would later take his family to Brazil. Taniguchi's father had been a student, and therefore was allowed under the Gentlemen's Agreement to immigrate to the United States, but the 1924 Immigration Act prevented any further emigration from Asia. Faced with the legal racism in the United States, Taniguchi's father decided to find work with a Japanese construction company as an engineer in Brazil—another site for Japanese settler colonists within the hemisphere.[40] From Brazil, they would later sail for Japan on the eve of the world war. Other families moved to settle in places such as Mexico or Manchuria, the latter being the latest acquisition of the Japanese empire in 1931.[41]

Families had begun discussing possibly moving away from the United States—Katsuya Nakatani recalled that his parents thought about moving to Japan, since they could not buy land in the United States.[42] The Alien Land Act influenced the parents of George Tsuda, a Japanese American who had grown up around Salinas, California, and whose grandfather had come to the United States sometime before 1910 to work on the railroad and eventually moved back to Japan. In 1937, due to the war between Japan and China, Tsuda remembered the growing anti-Japanese sentiment.[43] Tsuda's father also had other thoughts about their family's future in the United States. According to Nakatani, his father wanted "to be paid for the work we do around the farm. He felt that [this] family value needed to be instilled. I also believed that the lease was up on the farm, and the owner wanted a bigger share. These consideration[s] help my folks decide to go back to Japan, at least temporarily." At age thirteen, Tsuda and his family boarded the *Taiyo Maru*, a Japanese passenger ship, at San Francisco on February 3, 1938.

The diaspora present in the Americas and Japan also shaped the population aboard the later SS *Gripsholm*—Peru, Panama/Costa Rica, Mexico, Cuba, Ecuador, El Salvador, Honduras, Nicaragua, and Bolivia were among the places of residence for those aboard the exchange ship. After the SS *Gripsholm* departed from New York on September 2, 1943, it made a few more stops—at Rio de Janeiro, Brazil, and Montevideo, Uruguay, to pick up more passengers—and at Port Elizabeth, South Africa, to replenish supplies. The destination for the SS *Gripsholm* was actually Goa, the one location in south Asia that was under Portuguese colonial rule, and thus deemed neutral territory. Mormugao, Goa, was to be the site of the exchange. The exchange took place on October 20, 1943. The passengers from both the *Teia Maru*, the ship from Yokohama, and the SS *Gripsholm*, the ship from New York City, had disembarked onto the shore. "During the exchange, passengers of both ships ... walked past each other in a line and boarded the other ship."[44] One "Japanese" subject for each "American" subject.

Labor History Meets the US Military

When Sam Miyamoto and his family disembarked at the port of Yokohama in Japan, Miyamoto's family began their travels to his father's hometown village. But the food shortage was severe, and Sam Miyamoto decided to leave his family to ease the burden of feeding yet another mouth. He set off for Tokyo, telling his parents that he would return once he had made a life for himself. In Tokyo, Miyamoto witnessed the US firebombing of the almost completely wooden-structure Tokyo, and there he also discovered that because he was not a Japanese citizen, he could not attend any schools or use any of the public hospitals.[45] A Catholic missionary school became his refuge, where in exchange for English lessons, he received shelter, food, and an education. But when he heard that the United States had dropped the atomic bomb on Hi-

roshima, Sam Miyamoto and his older brother decided to leave Tokyo
to witness Hiroshima themselves:

> In August of '45, America dropped the atomic bomb. It is very diffi-
> cult to find holiness in this ugly war; especially when you witness
> the aftermath of the atomic bomb.... I wanted to see Hiroshima. I
> arrived at the outskirts by train and walked into the city. There was
> total destruction of the city by the atomic blast as far as I could
> see.... Sometimes I still have nightmares of this hideous "living
> hell." Of those who survived the initial blast, their bodies were dis-
> figured and burnt beyond any form of medical help. They survived
> only to suffer and die a few days later. I learned the hard way that the
> screams and fears of a suffering victim are the same in any language.
> It is ironic that 45 years after my visit to Hiroshima, I became ill with
> a brain tumor the size of a lemon. Was it the radiation from the
> atomic bomb or just a coincidence?[46]

Sam Miyamoto was sixteen years old when he "wanted to see Hiroshima." Traveling by train with his older brother from Tokyo to Hiroshima, Sam moved through a landscape devastated by the fire-bombing
and warfare. One may wonder why two Nisei Americans felt compelled to witness the aftermath of Hiroshima directly. But if we linger in
Hiroshima and look around, we would realize that Miyamoto's presence
was neither unexpected or a necessarily a contradiction. The interstices
of empire between the US and Japan were present in Hiroshima and
other prefectures of Japan also.

Hiroshima, on the day of the bombing, held its own populations that
complicated both Truman's lens of Hiroshima as the "enemy population" and Japan's own lens of proper subjects of empire. In Hiroshima
and Nagasaki, among the victims of the "total destruction" were "as
many as twenty-thousand conscripted Korean workers," laborers from
the Japanese colony of Korea, annexed in 1910. "One or two dozen Caucasian American prisoners of war" were also in Hiroshima. But there
is a final population statistic still to be taken into account—"probably
three thousand U.S. citizens of Japanese background were residing" in

Hiroshima, according to scholar John Dower, at the time of the atomic bombing. And at least one of them, a young woman named Judy (Aya) Enseki, had arrived in Japan via the SS *Gripsholm*, the very vessel that had taken Miyamoto and his family to Goa.[47]

Enseki was born in Delano, California, the fifth of eight children in a farming family. After Roosevelt's "Day of Infamy," Enseki found herself at the Manzanar Relocation Center, where she gave birth to a child. Her husband, also a Nisei, renounced his American citizenship and decided to "repatriate" to a Japan that neither of them had known very well. Once they arrived in Hiroshima, her husband was soon drafted by the Japanese Imperial Army, and the Soviets took him prisoner in Manchuria.

Judy Enseki described her experience in wartime Japan as being like a "fish out of water." Like many other Nisei Japanese Americans in US-occupied Japan, she later turned to the postwar US occupation forces as a possible way to make a living and to return to the United States. "There were many opportunities available as interpreters for older Nisei who still remembered English. Enseki left Hiroshima on a special occupation train for Tokyo," writes scholar Rinjiro Sodei.[48] And indeed, General Headquarters was aware of the utility of these Nisei individuals and families for the US occupation. On May 8, 1946, GHQ "ordered the Japanese government to compile and submit to American authorities lists of all Japanese Americans residing in Japan during the war, those who had obtained Japanese citizenship, and those who had served in the Japanese military or government institutions." The GHQ would determine not only who would be eligible to work for the US occupation but also who would be eligible to cross the Pacific one more time—to the United States.[49]

The year 1948, according to a history of southern California Japanese published that year, the highest number of Nisei came from US-occupied Japan to southern California.[50] But in 1948, the United States' treatment of Japanese Americans had taken a marked turn. And the memory of Japanese internment had been cast differently by another story of Japanese American involvement in World War II, where through military heroism and sacrifice, Japanese Americans had demonstrated both loyalty and assimilation into the American nation.

On June 5, 1948, the *Los Angeles Times* and *Washington Post* published articles detailing a funeral for two Nisei soldiers in Arlington National Cemetery, their respective headlines announcing, "Arlington Honor Paid to Two Heroic Nisei" and "Tribute Paid to Nisei Heroes." The articles focused on the loyalty of these two Japanese American soldiers. The *Los Angeles Times* reported,

> The Army buried two Japanese-American soldiers in Arlington National Cemetery today with a general's graveside declaration that "they proved their loyalty and devotion beyond all question."
>
> The two privates were Fumitake Nagato of near-by Arlington, Va., and Saburo Tanamachi of San Benito, Tex....
>
> Gen. Jacob L. Devers, chief of Army Field Forces and one of several high-ranking officers who paid final honors to the two Nisei, said:
>
> "There is one supreme final test of loyalty to one's native land. This test is readiness and willingness to fight for, and, if need be, to die for one's country. These Americans and their fellows passed that test with colors flying."[51]

With the Nisei soldiers, their military deaths did not signal a continuation of the "unfinished task" of battling totalitarianism on and beyond the WWII battlefields; rather, their deaths proved their adherence to such American ideals. The battlefield was the "one supreme final test" for the Japanese American soldiers, a place where "they proved themselves to be 'Americans first class.'" according to General Devers. Within the media portrayal and official military speeches, the "test" was not about the Nisei soldiers defeating German troops in the Vosges Mountains; instead, the ultimate "test" was whether or not they could sacrifice themselves "for one's country." The accomplishment of the soldiers was an isolated, internal one, where they proved their desire to be assimilated into the abstract ideal of "Americanness." The experience of internment, however, was not recognized.

The politics of visibility had a particular relevance to the shifting racial formations around Japanese Americans. The constructedness of racial ideologies would be blasted into high relief as the US government employed a host of shifting characterizations of the "Oriental" to buttress the projects of Japanese American internment camps; postwar occupation of Japan, Korea, and the Philippines; and the manufacturing of a racially harmonious US society for the "world." The Japanese American soon became the model figure for the successful assimilation and internalization of American values—a discourse of liberal individualism was mobilized in order to focus attention on the dynamism of American democracy, rather than the dynamism of racial hierarchical orders.[52]

On July 20, 1948, the *New York Times* reported, "President Truman started the draft today with a proclamation requiring 9,500,000 youths to register during seventeen designated days of August and September." With Proclamation 2799, President Truman had effectively begun the increased militarization of the US global presence, later articulated in NSC 68. The Cold War had become the rallying cry for rapid militarization within the United States, as President Truman delineated a global drama between two binary forces: anti-Communism versus Communism.

But for the Japanese American young men who had spent their adolescence in the internment camps of World War II, the draft meant something altogether different. Education and family ended up being the most important factors affecting how they rationalized participating in the US military. For example, Arnold Yoshizawa had settled in Chicago after getting out of Manzanar. Still unsure about college, Yoshizawa was working two jobs—one as a shipping clerk and the other with a Christmas tree light company. Another Nisei named Tom Honda, who had been in Manzanar with him, had helped him get these jobs. Yoshizawa recalled that his sister had dared him to join the army:

> The next morning I go down there and they told me if I sign up for three years they'll send me to any part of the world the Army has people. I could go to Germany, I could go to France, Puerto Rico at

that time, Persian Gulf, Japan—Oooooh. What if I go to Japan and find grandpa? I said, "Oh. Japan."[53]

For Jim Yanagihara, enlisting in the US Army was a strategic move: "I got the draft notice, but didn't want to do two years and five years of reserve time."[54] Yanagihara simply enlisted. Even Roy Shiraga, who had enlisted in the US Army a year before Truman's 1948 proclamation, had not signed up for the US Army with the growing Cold War in mind. In 1947, Roy Shiraga graduated from high school in Washington State. "My parents wanted me to go to college, but I didn't have any money," Shiraga recalled. He had planned to work on the Great Northern Railroad, similar to his father, who was dismissed from his railroad job after Pearl Harbor. But Shiraga soon had a conversation with a Nisei World War II veteran, Spady Koyama, who was also a friend of the family. Koyama encouraged Shiraga to join the army, "because he said you could pick any school you want and they'll send you there." On August 4, Shiraga enlisted.

"As I recall I signed up for photography school. I wanted to be a photographer," Shiraga said. But during the tenth week of basic training, Shiraga and another Nisei enlistee were sent to the Presidio of Monterey, in California, for a test. "This lieutenant comes in and he made a little speech, said that you're going to take this test. He handed out a page that was all in English and he says write in Japanese." The other Nisei in the room

> wrote down his name, rank, and serial number. Then he put it aside. He picked up a magazine as I recall. I said hey, aren't you going to take that exam? He says, hell no, I don't want to go over there. I said, oh, I don't either. I want to go to photography school. So I did the same thing.[55]

The lieutenant came back twice, but each time, the papers in front of Shiraga and the other Nisei were blank. Afterward, they were both sent to basic training, and at the end of the thirteenth week of training, both Shiraga and the other young man received their assignments. They were both going to the Presidio of Monterey for language training.[56]

Arnold Yoshizawa was also sent to the Presidio of Monterey for language training. If at all possible, the US Army attempted to funnel Japanese American enlistees and draftees into the language programs; the US occupations of Japan and Korea demanded a large corps of translators, interpreters, and interrogators. Most of the Japanese American men did indeed find themselves at the language school in the Presidio of Monterey—and those who passed the intensive language training then usually found themselves shipped to Camp Zama in Japan, where they received further training and began their work with the Allied Translator and Interpreter Service (ATIS). Yoshizawa, in his own words, "flunked" out of the Presidio language school and moved to the engineering corps in the army.[57] Roy Shiraga, on the other hand, explained that he was sent to the Presidio language school and eventually was assigned to go to Hokkaido, Japan, where his older sister, Ayako, lived.

> She was an interpreter. She was thirteen when she went back to Japan but she maintained her English with her brother George.... Every weekend I used to go into town and talk to her. She used to be an interpreter for the officers of the 7th Division, 31st Infantry Regiment because they found out she could talk both English and Japanese.[58]

The year 1950, before the outbreak of the Korean War, found the Japanese American communities on both sides of the Pacific profoundly altered by the experience of World War II. Language, the US military, and citizenship became the triangulated matrix in which young Japanese American men found the means to make claims on their futures within the United States and Japan. Their labor, though, would be used in ways they may have been familiar with already: truth itself had a racial hierarchy.[59]

The Choice of an "Oriental" in an Interrogation Room

On June 26, 1950, when President Harry Truman announced that the United States would not tolerate the "act of aggression" of the Democratic People's Republic of Korea, the nature of war had changed considerably since FDR's "Day of Infamy" speech in 1942. In 1948, the year

Miyamoto had left Japan for the University of California, Los Angeles (UCLA), the United States had made a crucial decision regarding its occupation of the Korean peninsula south of the 38th parallel. The United States, unable to find a majority population of Koreans who were willing to accept a US-dictated government, moved to hold elections in the southern part of the peninsula. With the northern half of the peninsula also having held elections, two governments soon were claiming sovereignty over the entire peninsula. The United States and the United Nations only recognized the southern Republic of Korea as a legitimate sovereign body.

Stimson's doctrine of nonrecognition had come into play again. Previously, the United States had been insistent on perceiving Japan as a nation, not an empire (although one can note that being a "nation" is not mutually exclusive of being an "empire"). But now, a former colony of Japan was on the map, one divided by the 38th parallel. How did one enter war with an entity one did not recognize? Previously, the question revolved around repatriation and putative "citizenship." Now, the question would revolve around repatriation and the figure of the "prisoner of war." And the Japanese American interrogator would be the key figure in facilitating and mediating this particular alchemy of sovereign power in this era of formal decolonization.

In effect, as the Korean War escalated on the peninsula, and the US Army scrambled to find translators and interrogators, a new geography had been mapped for the drafted and enlisted Japanese Americans. From the language school at the Presidio of Monterey to Camp Zama in Japan to G-2 headquarters in Pusan, Korea, yet another mapping of US empire had become the frame for the movements of this cohort of Japanese Americans. And in 1950, Miyamoto found himself back yet again in East Asia—first in Japan, and then later in Korea. Another war that involved the United States and East Asia had determined his life trajectory. But there was a critical difference between the time he had arrived in Yokohama in 1944 and when he arrived in Pusan in 1950. The Japanese Americans in this particular cohort who became a part of the US military in1950 were almost all drafted—and almost all had undergone internment. Howard Okada, who had been born in Fresno,

California, and later sent with his family to the camp in Jerome, Arkansas, was drafted in November 1950.[60] Jim Yanagihara, born in San Diego, California, and sent to the camp in Poston, Arizona, remembered receiving his draft notice on his nineteenth birthday—November 30, 1950.[61] The United States brought Katsuya Nakatani to Maryland in November 1950—and one of the first things he was obligated to do was an FBI test that consisted of a thorough self-history narrative. "They wanted to know what I've been doing my whole life," recalled Nakatani. "And then my father's too—they want to know his history. And my grandfather." During his class time, one of his superiors brought him out of the classroom and asked him pointedly about the information he had provided. The exchange that followed challenged Nakatani's superior's understanding of what had happened during World War II, as Nakatani explicitly brought up the "concentration camps" in which the United States had incarcerated him:

> An officer said, "Where were you from 1942 to 1945?" And I said, "I was in prison." And he said, "What were you charged for?" And I said, "I don't know." He said, "Soldier, you don't say I don't know to the officer. What were you charged for?" Again I said, "I don't know. I don't know. I've never been charged for anything." ... Then they asked me, "Where was this?" "Arkansas." ... "Arkansas?" I said, "Yeah, Arkansas." "Arkansas State Penitentiary?" I said, no.... I finally told them that it was an American concentration camp. And he got mad. He said, "Soldier, we have no such thing in this country." ... And I said, "Well, you call it whatever you want to. Well, that's what it is."[62]

Nakatani was summarily tossed into the stockade for insubordination, but his "insubordination" made it clear that this generation of Japanese Americans were bringing their experiences and memories of a previous war in the trans-Pacific into the Korean War. How would this generation negotiate their experiences with internment and the hostage exchange within the interrogation room, the battlefield, and the administration offices of a war the United States was waging on the territory of a former Japanese colony?

How to Interrogate an "Oriental"

Japanese American interrogators and translators worked in all aspects of US military work, ranging from the diplomatic to the bureaucratic, from the battlefield to the field offices. Primarily though, Japanese American interrogators worked with the Allied Translator and Interpreter Service (ATIS), Military Intelligence Service (MIS), and Interrogation of Prisoner of War teams (IPW). The language of "military necessity"—earlier encountered in the form of internment and a hostage exchange—returned to the lives of these Japanese American young men in the form of "information"—the purpose of interrogation was to procure "information." However, despite the seemingly straightforward depiction of the bureaucratic processes of garnering and verifying information provided by Colonel Hanley in front of the House Subcommittee, procuring and verifying "information" from a Korean prisoner of war was not a simple straightforward bureaucratic procedure. According to a widely circulated US military pamphlet on interrogating "Orientals," a certain cultural finesse was necessary. Interrogation was performance, although the question of "for whom?" remains to be answered.

Interrogation training for the Korean War drew extensively on previous experiences—not from the US occupation of Korea, but rather from the Asia-Pacific Wars. One particular lecture given by Lieutenant Commander Samuel C. Bartlett Jr., a US Naval Reserve interpreter who had been present at the Japanese surrender at Iwo Jima, gained considerable traction and circulation within the Military Intelligence Service sections. The lecture had most probably been given by Bartlett to the interrogators working in US-occupied Japan, but due to the multiple copies of the lectures—the original lecture draft with Bartlett's notes in the margins as well as the distillation of Bartlett's lecture into an illustrated pamphlet for easier consumption—present in the files of the ATIS and MIS archives for the period of the Korean War, one can surmise that this lecture also had relevance in the interrogation training of those deployed to Korea.[63]

At the heart of Bartlett's lecture, titled "Some Aspects of Interrogation of Oriental POWs," was a template for the process of procuring "information" from an "Oriental" prisoner of war. Mr. Jack Alberti, an interrogator who had worked with German POWs, specifically in terms of submarine warfare, was scheduled to talk with the class later in April. Deferring to Alberti's expertise, Bartlett prefaced his lecture by saying that his comments would simply supplement those of Alberti.

The first part of Bartlett's lecture was a lesson in how the interrogator must conceive of the interrogation process, and the process hinged on the successful objectification of the POW as a receptacle of information. He then delineated what he considered to be a few differences between Alberti's experiences and "ours," meaning that Alberti had interrogated Europeans, not "Orientals." The "purpose of POW explanation," which Bartlett noted "hardly needs to be said," was "to obtain information which the POW has and which we need." "While the process is not always quite so simple," began Bartlett's notes, "it may be likened to a drink out of a coconut—cut the top off with a machetti [sic] and pour it out. There are six steps even in this simple process: 1. Get coconut, 2. Make sure there is milk in it, 3. Cut it open, 4. Remove milk, 5. Taste milk for potability, 6. Give it to the thirsty party."

US military history in the Pacific during World War II affected the construction of the interrogation room at the most fundamental level—in the conceptualization of the process and the "target" himself. In the collapsing of the coconut (a symbol of the tropical landscape, void of people and rendered ready for conquest) and the "Oriental" mind (the Japanese POW), Bartlett had, in fact, offered to the interrogators working in US-occupied Japan and later the Korean War an analogy of racial violence. Through the language of "paradise" and "conquest," Bartlett offered a characterization of interrogation as a standardized relationship between two subjectivities. What I argue though is that the interrogation training and manuals for the soon-to-be-interrogators did not so much theorize the mind of the interrogated as much as it presented a certain subjectivity for the interrogator to inhabit. In the end, the interrogation training was not so concerned with the "Oriental" as it was with controlling and shaping the agency and subjectivity of the US military interrogator. Interrogation training was about subject-making—making the interrogator.

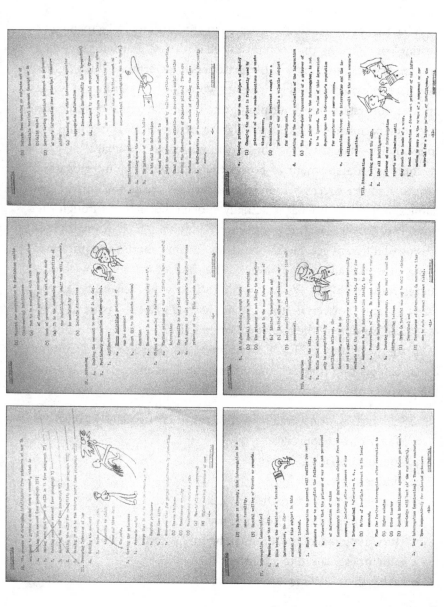

FIGURES 3.3–3.8 Pages from a pamphlet based on a lecture by Lieutenant Commander Samuel C. Bartlett Jr. (National Archives and Records Administration)

What makes an interrogator, according to Bartlett? In "Screening or Testing" or "Shaking the coconut to see if it's dry," Bartlett suggests a preliminary examination of "ALL" prisoners to determine which POWs may have information and which ones would be most willing to "yield up his information." In determining the latter, Bartlett states that the interrogator must evaluate the "Nature of the POW," meaning his "personality—Security, tractability—intelligence—language."

There is an assessment of power that occurs in the interrogation room—and the successful interrogator would create the correct dynamics, not through what is actually spoken, but rather through the unspoken. Bartlett's lecture—although highly simplified through a collapsing of different geo-racial ideologies and imaginaries—is primarily about how to read and hide intent. The interrogator must be able to successfully "read" the POW, be able to assess the "reliability" of the POW, be able to ascertain the "intent" of the POW. The issue of judgment is at the core of the interrogation practice.

In the next step, called "Conditioning the Prisoner" or "Cutting open the coconut," Bartlett mentions eight different methods to start the prisoner of war talking.[64]

1. Self-starters, or naturally talkative prisoners frequently occur.
2. Matter-of-fact approach
3. Rough approach
4. Kindness approach
5. Combination or alternate approach
6. Appeals to pride of prisoner of war
7. The willingness of most human beings to correct mistakes can sometimes be used to advantage
8. Saving the POW's face

For "self-starters," Bartlett cautions the interrogators-in-training about "plants," POWs who are purposefully giving incorrect information in order to mislead the US military.

The other "approaches" are primarily templates or scripts for the interrogator to follow to direct the POW's attention away from the interrogator's intent or objective. For example, in the "matter-of-fact approach," Bartlett suggests beginning the session with a seemingly purely bureaucratic matter, such as the filling out of forms or simply obtaining very basic information from the prisoner of war. The bureaucratic approach—or the "matter-of-fact" approach—seems to set the stage for an emotionally detached encounter, one where the interrogator is not a subjective person, but rather simply carrying out orders. In the "kindness approach," medical care, food, water, cigarettes are all part of a possible exchange—but Bartlett cautions that "the prisoner of war should be made to realize (by indirect suggestion) that any favors he receives come from the hands of the interrogator (any pup wags his tail for the hands that feed him)." Upending the expectations that the POW has of the interrogation is key to a few of the approaches recommended by Bartlett—a strategic disorientation of what the interrogator's expectations might be. In the "combination or alternate approach," Bartlett recommends for the interrogator to switch between two or more different methods of interrogation, or to literally alternate the interrogation with another interrogator. The last two aspects—"Appeals to pride of prisoner of war" and "The willingness of most human beings to correct mistakes"—are methods that intend to give authority to the POW in a particular strategic moment, the illusion of choice in a sense.

Further theorizing on the "coconut" itself—or the Oriental POW—can be found in other supplemental documents on interrogation within the archive on training and education. In a document titled "Techniques of Interrogating Orientals," the author states that the techniques discussed in the document "will be mainly concerned with the Japanese, since much of our experience during World War II has been concerned with this particular group of 'Orientals.' "[65] Indeed, "an interrogator must first understand the background of the particular people with whom he is dealing, and, most important, the racial psychology of the people in order for him to understand the behavior pattern of his subject which will, therefore, result in a successful interrogation."

"Many Orientals," stated the document, "believe themselves to be inferior to Americans and are easily kept in their proper places as prisoners." During World War II, there were three different configurations of interrogation teams:

  a. An American who spoke Japanese interrogated PW's.
  b. A Nisei (American-born Japanese) soldier interrogated PW's.
  c. A Nisei interpreted for an officer interrogator.

In reflecting on the relative effectiveness of these different configurations, the author concludes that "(a) was considered to be the best.... When the Nisei interrogated the Japanese PW, a psychological advantage had been lost to a degree, in that the average Oriental feels inferior to an American (Caucasian) and when a Nisei confronted the PW, this advantage was lost, and they were on an equal footing."[66] What is striking about the document is the racial ideology that frames the subjectivity of the Japanese "Oriental"—the author insists on how the Japanese Oriental essentially has no sense of agency due to a low intelligence level: "The average intelligence of Orientals is lower than that of Caucasians, and the illiteracy rate precludes any possibility of a high standard of intelligence being achieved for some time to come. The knowledge of the average Oriental will therefore amount to little more than what he has seen or has been told." The "average Oriental," according to this document, would give only naive, straightforward answers, and yet a racialized hierarchy of labor would be instituted to insure the accuracy of the "truth" provided.

The Babel of Interrogation

In October 1952, the second year of protracted fighting in the Korean War, Associated Press journalist John Fujii followed an interrogation team of the Military Intelligence Service onto the battlefields. "There is a babel of tongues on this much fought over ridge—a babel of Chinese dialects, Korean, Japanese and one soft Louisiana drawl," he began his article. The Louisiana drawl belonged to Lieutenant Henry J. Picard, "who [headed] a frontline interrogation team the Allies have whipped into shape to question prisoners." The team functioned as follows:

Four languages are employed on each operation by the interrogation team.

Prisoners are interrogated in their native dialects by Hsiao Shu-len,
a Chinese civilian, and Yun Bong Chun, a former Korean policeman.

Their findings are written in English.

Lieutenant Picard, who learned fluent Korean in a U.S. Army
Language school, and his assistant First Lt. Thomas Shiratsuki, a
Nisei from Salinas, Calif., who speaks fluent Japanese and English,
translate the English into Korean for officers.

It sounds like a cumbersome way of doing things but the team
functions smoothly with Pvt. Kenjiro Fred Wakugawa, another Nisei,
of Honolulu, acting as a sort of jack of all trades.[67]

In fact, there were even more people involved in this "babel" of interrogation: when the Chinese prisoners of war began speaking quickly,
"South Korean Lieutenant Pak Chan Be, who was born in China and
educated in Japan, explained the proceedings in Japanese to Lieutenant
Shiratsuki and in Korean or English to Lieutenant Picard."

Officials in the Military Intelligence Service of the US military
stated that they did not want the article to be published because it
mentioned the names of the interrogators, and Fujii's article never actually made it to press.[68] But perhaps Fujii's article also threatened the
US military's integrity in that it exposed the tremendous labor and contingent variables in creating the performative authority of US military
intelligence. In the interrogation scene provided by John Fujii's AP article that had been censored and therefore never published, six different people were involved in the interrogation of Chinese prisoners of
war after a battle on the Korean peninsula, resulting in an interrogation
report written simply in English. And language—the supposed medium for communication—was itself mediated by the negotiations and
imaginations of all six people present. The histories of US occupation,
Japanese American diasporas, and racial templates for interrogation
from World War II were all present in this one team, who would then
produce a single document of "military information," or intelligence.

But perhaps the single most important variable to the integrity of the information was Lieutenant Henry J. Picard from Louisiana, trained in Korean by the US Army. The racialized labor hierarchy of producing "truth" in the US military intelligence bureaucratic structure became clearly evident in this scene. Picard, the final overseer of the interrogation, heads this team, consisting of "middlemen," such as the "jack of all trades" Wakugawa. The Nisei, although perhaps now "loyal" and considered more "reliable" than the Korean, still operated within the checks and balances of a white superior. And indeed, during World War II and the Korean War, officers of interrogation teams and divisions, who primarily "checked" and "evaluated" interrogation reports, were white, while those conducting interrogations and writing the reports were Korean civilians or Japanese American interrogators.

Let us now return to Sam Miyamoto, after he completed his language training both at Presidio and Camp Zama. Schooled in basic Korean, Miyamoto had now also become fluent in Japanese, thanks to the experience under the hostage exchange. With three languages—and a fraught relationship with each one of them—Sam Miyamoto began his work on the Korean peninsula as an interrogator of Korean prisoners of war.

"You had to know history to survive," remarked Miyamoto in his interview as he reflected on his experiences living between the United States, Japan, and Korea. History, to Miyamoto, was an awareness of the relationships between different states. And because of his insistence on this type of historical consciousness, language was the first and foremost concern of Sam Miyamoto in his interrogation room. Interrogators would usually commit a crucial mistake, according to Miyamoto, by launching into Japanese immediately with the Korean POW. "Most of the well-educated [Korean] people they know Japanese because a lot of them went to universities in Japan," said Miyamoto in his interview. "They speak Japanese but if you just went out and asked them from the direct start, 'Do you speak Japanese?,' they would say no." Speaking from the perspective of the Korean prisoner of war who would have been sitting across from him, Miyamoto continued, "For five years now, we've been speaking the Korean language, we were no longer part of Japan, so why would you expect me to speak Japanese, and we're not going do it." For Koreans, 1945 had been the year of liberation from Japanese colonialism, and in 1950, Miyamoto was navigating between the years of liberation and the years of colonialism in the choice of language to use in the interrogation room.[69]

Miyamoto was able to converse in Korean due to Korean language courses at the US Army language school, but he was still not completely comfortable conducting an interrogation in Korean. He recounted his usual method for beginning an introduction; with the POW in front of him, Miyamoto would call out over his shoulder to a fellow Japanese American serviceman in Japanese purposefully:

> I call out in Japanese, "There's coffee and donuts, so can you bring us some coffee and donuts? And put a lot of sugar and cream in. Coffee for him, and make mine black." And we were just talking Japanese so that the prisoner would know that I speak Japanese.

Then, he strategically would begin speaking in Korean:

> And I would ask [the prisoner], "Would you like another donut?" And I call out again [to my friend], "Hey, bring a couple more doughnuts. Maybe he can take one back to his friends." Then I would go up and then offer a cigarette. I say something like, "중국어를 모르겠습니까? [Spraken] Deutsch? Francais?" And then I would think to myself in Japanese [out loud]: "But I know that all the educated Korean people they speak two or three different languages so I wonder what other languages he speaks." And then I would say something like, "Do you speak a little Japanese?" And he would say, "Oh yeah, I speak Japanese." And then from there you pick it up and that doesn't hurt their sensitivity.

Reflecting on the other Japanese American servicemen who had also served as interrogators during the Korean War, Miyamoto claimed a certain exceptionalism in terms of his experience. His own experience—and those of his brother, Archie—resulted in experiencing discrimination not only from the US government but also from the Japanese government. "And so we understand what other people had to go

through, so we understand their sensitivity," said Miyamoto. Miyamoto attributed the moments when other Japanese Americans encountered resistant Korean POWs during interrogation to the Japanese
Americans' own ignorance of the histories—or "sensitivities"—of the
Korean POW.

Miyamoto's interrogation room was essentially created by a strategic performance on Miyamoto's part—a performance of his own language skills, a performance that was also contingent on the presence of
another Japanese American. He had created a situation where the prisoner of war could feel that he "knew" more than the interrogator. It is
a situation that differed, perhaps, in one crucial way from the "cutting
open the coconut" interrogation room illustrated by Bartlett. Miyamoto was offering the interrogated prisoner of war a seeming *choice* of
language in which the interrogation would be conducted.

Miyamoto recognized that his interrogation methods and process
were different from those used at the front lines of battle during wartime. Those on the front line were "asking different questions." His preoccupations were different from the Interrogation of Prisoner of War
teams (IPW) who followed combat units, similar to the team described
in Fujii's AP article: "Because people like me, I don't care how many
soldiers were up in the hill over there with him. I mean, if you're on
the frontline and you're shooting in the frontline, you want to know
how many people are up there because your life is at stake." He then
described the interrogation done by the ATIS interrogation teams, who
primarily interrogated POWs in order to gain information and maps of
areas in China and North Korea: "If a war breaks out with China, because MacArthur wanted to sort of encourage to go into China, we got
to know where all the targets are. So there are different questions there."

This section examines the different interrogation rooms—the IPW,
ATIS, MIS, and the repatriation interrogation room—of the Korean
War through the experiences and bureaucratic records left by this
cohort of Japanese American interrogators. Although, as Miyamoto's
statement has demonstrated, we often think that the type of information needed shapes, or is, the purpose of the interrogation, this section
will take a different conceptual approach. In an attempt to destabilize

our assumptions about interrogation and its embedded aims, I demonstrate how persuasion was actually at the heart of the interrogation pushed to the fore by the US government. In other words, the Japanese American interrogator often had the task of "persuading" the "Oriental" POW of accepting and inhabiting a specific positionality vis-à-vis the United States. The most high-profile interrogation room during the Korean War was the repatriation interrogation room, and this section will locate this interrogation room within a genealogy not simply of "military necessity" but rather of subject-making.

Miyamoto, even before setting foot in his own interrogation room, would find out the military rank of the prisoner of war before the interview. For example, if the POW was a second lieutenant, he would put the markings of a first lieutenant rank on himself. In his words: "if you're a second lieutenant and some private or corporal questioned you, I mean that's an insult for me. I had a picture here of Tojo and he was asked 'When did you finally realize that Japan lost the war?' and he said, 'When I was in Sugama Prison when the Japanese American soldier came up and simply told me to come.'" There were multiple genealogies for the interrogation rooms set up by the Japanese American interrogators, ones that Bartlett's lecture did not encompass.

Mamoru "Steve" Yokoyama was one of the Japanese American interrogators who were assigned to Hideki Tojo in Sugama Prison. In 1943, Mamoru "Steve" Yokoyama, born and raised on Maui, was eighteen years old. And instead of finishing high school, Yokoyama decided to enlist in the US Army, since at that time, the US government had decided to recruit Japanese Americans for the military. Although he was initially brought into the army as a possible replacement for the 442nd, Yokoyama recalled his motivations for enlistment differently: "And the reason why I wanted it was, it would fulfill all my dreams. I got my shoes; I never had shoes. I never had pants. I mean I would wear my brothers' pants or something, my brother's shoes. We never had anything good and then all of sudden we had army chow!" Yokoyama recalled that it was during basic training when officials began testing the Japanese Americans for their proficiency in the Japanese language. The US Army sent Yokoyama to Camp Savage in Minnesota for language training—and soon, Yokoyama was being flown out to Australia.[70]

At the war's end, Yokoyama was sent to be an interrogator at Sugamo Prison in Japan. The man to whom he was assigned was Hideki Tojo, a general in the Japanese Imperial Army and Prime Minister of Japan for much of World War II. "Nice guy, I mean he acts nice when we interrogate him and stuff," recalled Yokoyama.

> We had to see him about five times because we needed him to be the bad guy that caused all the problems for the officers below him. And he would smile and say this or that, but he would never take the blame for any . . . what we needed from him was to say . . . "Hey look, I take responsibility and by doing so, you guys lay off all the higher generals. They weren't the guys that decided all those rules and those kinds of things that they had to do." . . . As for the information that I needed to get from him, it wasn't necessarily military strategies or anything, it was a question of "Can you take the blame so that all these lower class guys don't get hanged?" He said, "No."[71]

Yokoyama's interrogation was not one of military information, but rather one of persuasion. His interrogations began in a manner reminiscent of Miyamoto's: "[Let's] have a chat, won't you sit down? You give him a cigarette and give him an extra pack and you smoke and he smokes. That [was] the beginning of the end for him. Because there's nothing he can do other than to say, 'Hey, thank you for being polite to me, I'm an officer.'" Yokoyama's experience as an interrogator of Tojo is significant for our analysis of Korean War interrogation because it points to a different end point of interrogation than merely "information." Rather, Yokoyama was attempting to persuade Tojo to inhabit a particular subjectivity, one where American legal "disciplining" of the Japanese military imperial ambitions also reflected a larger project of disciplining the empire of Japan into a nation-state entity determined by the United States. If Tojo had taken responsibility and blame for the war crimes, the United States would have been able to state more effectively that it had meted out "justice." Persuasion, not information, was the basis of the "military necessity" in this form of interrogation.

"Reliability" as a category to be assessed by the interrogator also had its own history in the US occupation of Japan. Many Japanese American interrogators within the US Army worked primarily on screening Japanese repatriates from the Asia-Pacific Wars—and most of the repatriates were former prisoners of war from Russia. George Taniguchi was one of these interrogators. "Reliability is a factor when we analyze the information we get," he remarked, and for him "reliability" was defined along Cold War ideological lines. Describing some of the Japanese repatriates as "brainwashed," Taniguchi noted, "We were talking with them just for 'information,' not there to convert them out of communist thinking. [But] we would make a notation on the report that the guy was left-leaning," said Taniguchi.[72] The notation of a POW's possible leftist sympathies was a marker of the "reliability of the information." And indeed, Taniguchi's standard of "reliability" inflected with Cold War ideology had a legacy in the Korean War also, as the question of whether or not an "Oriental" was capable of rendering the truth would converge with a concern over "communism" and individual "agency."[73]

George Tsuda also had been an interrogator working with ATIS in interrogating the repatriated Japanese POWs—both Tsuda and Taniguchi were deployed to Korea to work with the front-line IPW teams. As Tsuda recalled, "Right after the Inchon landing, they needed some translators. So they threw me in, and when I got to Pusan, there was a sergeant waiting for me. And they put me on a bus that ran on the rail. They took me to the outskirts of Tongnae." From there he was moved close to the Chosin Reservoir. There were many, many Korean prisoners of war. As Taniguchi also remembered from his experience in a POW compound located in Ascom City near Inchon right after the Inchon landing, "The marines were bringing in thousands of prisoners of war. Of course, this was right after the Inchon landing, so they were surrendering by the thousands."[74] At this point, interrogators such as Tsuda and Taniguchi were primarily responsible for registering the prisoners of war, taking down names and assigning serial numbers.

But these prisoners of war were also considered a source of "information." And according to Tsuda, when he was working at the Tenth

Corps Headquarters near Tongnae, he worked with a Korean inter-preter while talking with the prisoners of war. Often, the POWs came to them in groups of twenty or thirty. The immediate task at hand was to divide those who might have "information" from those who might not have "information."[75]

> When there's a whole bunch of them, then you have to immediately separate them. And the way they do it is look at them—he looks smart; if he looks dumb; or if he looks clean-shaven; or after you talk with them, maybe he seems smart. There could be as many as three hundred.

But, as Tsuda recalled, the challenge "was the guy who knows, and you're pretty sure that he knows, but he won't speak up."

> You try to let them relax. Give them a cigarette or candy. [chuckles] It's a sort of bribing. It doesn't matter if it takes thirty minutes or an hour. You talk about the family, where his hometown is. Things like that. And gradually, you see if you can go into key parts. But you can't take too long ... because there are too many of them.

Regarding what he meant by "key parts," Tsuda explained that the higher command would give them the questions, the agenda. The "hakujin" (meaning a white non-Japanese person in this context) officer would tell Tsuda and his colleagues which questions to ask. Interestingly, one question that Tsuda remembers being of high priority was asking the prisoners of war "what they thought about colored troops." "I think that what they wanted to hear was that they weren't too good of a fighter. But a lot of them said that, 'They're black, and it's the first time I see them, so I'm afraid.' And then the lieutenant said [to me], 'You sure they said this?' In other words, he doesn't like the answer."

Tsuda's recollection of this particular "key part" is revealing because it illuminates two important aspects of interrogation: the racialized hi-erarchy and the role of interrogation as "feedback" on the performance of the US military. The military "information," although encompassing questions such as numbers, types of weapons, and identification of higher command members, also included a crucial aspect—the prisoners of war were to provide feedback on the effectiveness of different military tactics the US military employed. What kind of "image" and "performance" was the United States hoping to portray and enact in front of the Korean and Chinese soldiers?

But the performance and image of the United States in the US military interrogation room could be at times precarious, and Taniguchi expressed particular frustrations regarding the dearth of qualified translators with whom to work. When the US military began taking in Chinese prisoners of war, no one was prepared in Taniguchi's unit to interrogate the POWs. Quickly, they looked for available Mandarin speakers in the local, surrounding villages. According to Taniguchi, they were only able to locate two men: one was a "skinny, old guy" named "Mr. Wong." He was sixty-five years old, and spoke Chinese, Korean, and some Japanese. "The other guy was sixty-years-old," said Taniguchi. "He could only speak Korean and Chinese." Using yet another interrogator who could speak Korean and Japanese, Taniguchi showed different pictures of Russian weapons to the two elders and explained how they were going to be asking prisoners of war if they had used or seen any such weapons.[76] And as a group of four, much like the team of six in Fujii's article, they began interrogating Chinese prisoners of war.

Race and War in the Interrogation Room

"I told him the truth," said Sam Miyamoto during his reflections on his work as an interrogator of POWs during the Korean War. Miyamoto had told the Korean POW that he had been drafted, that he was only acting under orders, that he had not chosen to be an interrogator. In essence, Miyamoto was attempting to carve out space for his own autonomy in the interrogation room, a space where the subject-making project also included him. The "truth," although perhaps not of structural consequence in the interrogation room, held significance because of Miyamoto's insistence that his own history and experience were not erased in the US military interrogation room.

The interrogation room was to produce an interrogator and the interrogated POW—two differently inflected subjects of US empire. But as the case with encounters in Sam Miyamoto's interrogation room, consent was not always assumed or given. Instead, through this close history of the interrogation room and the Japanese American interrogators, a different story about war, states of emergency, and military necessity emerged, where the United States rendered "statelessness" strategically in their program of "repatriation." As the reordering of power between the rising empire of the United States and the collapsing empire of Japan occurred, this cohort of Japanese American young men had become one of the sites for this reassignment of racialization, subjecthood, and labor.

To consider Miyamoto's "truth" is to consider the history of the acts—the spitting, the reluctance, the negotiation—elided from the final product of the clean, typed interrogation report written in English, with only the names of the interrogators and translators as evidence of any human exchange in the document's making. If, as Giorgio Agamben has written, "language is the sovereign who, in a permanent state of exception, declares that there is nothing outside of language and that language is always beyond itself," the US military interrogation room was precisely located on this edge of language's presupposed power.[77] In other words, we can see that sovereign power lay in how the reader would take the interrogation report at face value. Taking the neatness of the narrative for granted was accepting the bounds inscribed by the state—to read only this, and not that. To consider the experiences of the Japanese American interrogator, and subsequently what he considered possible, necessary, or expendable in the interrogation room, is to read the interrogation report radically differently because the labor of the Japanese American interrogator was essential for the production of the straightforward, bureaucratic narratives. Paying attention to war becomes a much more urgent and encompassing task when we begin with Miyamoto's story.

PART II

Humanity Interrogated

4

Koje Island

ON MAY 7, 1952—in a twist of events that journalist Murray Schumach of the *New York Times* would later describe as "the strangest episode of the Korean War"[1]—a group of Korean Communist prisoners of war "kidnapped" US camp commander Brigadier General Francis Dodd of the Koje-do POW camp, the largest US-controlled camp during the Korean War. The POW spokesman for Compound 76, Joo Tek Woon, had placed multiple, repeated requests to meet with Dodd, and that afternoon, Dodd finally agreed to meet with Joo. They met at the main gate of the compound, the barbed-wire fence between them. One of the prisoners of war from the compound served as a translator. The list of topics to be discussed was lengthy, ranging from mundane complaints about camp logistics to the larger issue of voluntary repatriation screening. The gate opened during the meeting to let a large truck carrying several tons' worth of tents through. One of the POWs, Song Mo Jin, a large man of considerable strength, walked slowly through the gate, waited until Dodd put away the piece of wood he was whittling, stretched his arms as he pretended to yawn, and then grabbed Dodd. The POWs literally carried Dodd into the compound, closing the barbed-wire fence behind him. Soon, the POWs unfurled a large sign, approximately twenty-five feet long and three feet wide, over the main compound building. The following message in English had been painted on the banner: "We have captured Dodd. He will not be harmed if PW problems are resolved. If you shoot, his life will be in danger."[2]

On Saturday morning, May 10, tanks began arriving to the island by ship. A heavy rain was pouring down, and at least twenty Patton and Sherman tanks filed down the muddy roads toward Compound 76. The US Army had explicitly forbidden the presence of any media on the island, but one journalist—Sanford L. Zalburg—had managed to get onto the island by the graces of a Korean fisherman and his twenty-foot boat, traveling four hours through the "rain-swept seas" from the town of Chinhae on the peninsula to the island of Koje. Approaching the island at two thirty in the morning on Saturday, he described the island as such:

> From miles out you could see Koje's prison camps. The island is large, but the prison camps are concentrated in one section.
>
> We landed at a village.... A mile or so on either side of the village strings of lights blazed over the prison enclosures and the guards quarters and camp. Blue-gray colored light poured down into the enclosures from searchlights on the mountainside....
>
> Koje Island compounds are heavily barbed wired, with two high wire fences surrounding each plot. At night the lights blaze down. In the corners of the compounds are three story high guard houses where machine guns are mounted.[3]

Army jeeps manned by armed military personnel were patrolling the entire length of the coast surrounding the camp, and armed foot patrols could be seen also. To Zalburg's eyes, Koje Island had become a military fortress, or in the words of Icle Davis of the 156th Military Police Detachment, Koje was an "Alcatraz" for the Korean War.[4]

Before being escorted off the island with a scolding by the US Army, Zalburg was able to talk with a few of the US infantry officers on the island. One infantry officer who had been on duty at Compound 76 during Dodd's captivity told Zalburg that "he could see Dodd plainly. The General's clothes were freshly washed, he said. Dodd was about 100 yards away and surrounded by a great mass of Communists. None of the Reds laid a hand on Dodd."[5] The juxtaposition between the seeming order and calm within Compound 76 and the demonstration of sheer force by the over twenty armed US tanks moving steadily toward Compound 76 was the scene that greeted Zalburg on that Saturday morning.

Rumors of the POWs' capture of Dodd and finally a brief press release by the US Army sent the US press into a frenzy. The front page of the *Los Angeles Times* on May 9, 1952, blared: 8TH ARMY ORDERED TO FREE GENERAL HELD BY RED POWS. By and large, the reaction was one of disbelief. "Sensational," "bizarre," "incredible," and "fantastic"—a vocabulary of the unbelievable, the ungraspable, was mobilized by the editorial desks and the journalists who had the task of reporting the event to the American public.[6] Each newspaper and each statement issued by the US Army echoed the similar sentiment—why had the POWs kidnapped the camp commander? Every newspaper stressed that the POWs had made a rather unusual request: "It was disclosed that the Communists had asked for 1,000 sheets of paper [presumably writing paper] and that this already had been sent to the island.... The purpose was not clear but the requisite order was issued by General Colson."[7] By the next day on May 10, the *Atlanta Daily World* was calling the kidnapping "a bizarre episode."[8]

At the press conference General van Fleet held with the media, Lieutenant Colonel James McNamara, van Fleet's public relations officer, described the situation as such: "The Communists are talking with General Dodd. Apparently they are trying to get as much as they can. General Dodd is apparently holding out and talking to them. It is a one-day Panmunjom."[9] Even the US Army personnel on the island of Koje were not clear on what the demands of the POWs were. According to Zalburg, "one officer said that the Communists 'keep making demands, sort of like at Panmunjom.'"[10] The cluster of tents at the village of Panmunjom where the armistice negotiations were taking place had become a shorthand for a certain type of negotiating. And indeed, the corollary between the activities within Compound 76 on Koje-do and the negotiations in the tents at Panmunjom signaled a set of stakes in the conflict that challenged the bounds of the imagination of the US mainstream press.

The term "prisoner of war," in this historical moment, did not merely describe a category of wartime status. During the Korean War, the figure of the prisoner of war became central to explaining the meaning of the conflict itself, whether it be anti-imperial resistance, anti-Communist Cold War conflict, or a civil war. This story moves between the negotiating tents at Panmunjom to Compound 76 at United Nations Command Camp #1 on the island of Koje. A close reading and microhistorical study of the Panmunjom negotiations over POWs and the Dodd incident itself reveal that the conversation and conflict effectively revolved around the structural legacies of the 1945 division of Korea at the 38th parallel and the subsequent foreign occupations on the peninsula by the United States and the Soviet Union. The stakes were about the meanings of effective postcolonial liberation and sovereignty as the legitimacy of the 1948 elections held in the north and south respectively was forced onto the table of war by both the POWs at Koje and the negotiators at Panmunjom.

However, diplomats and policy makers fashioned the figure of the prisoner of war as central to the moral discourse underpinning the Cold War. On May 7, 1952, in the pressroom of the White House, perhaps no less than twelve hours after the kidnapping on Koje Island, President Harry Truman made a statement regarding the ongoing armistice talks in Korea. "There shall not be a forced repatriation of prisoners of war—as the Communists have insisted," he announced. "To agree to forced repatriation would be unthinkable. It would be repugnant to the fundamental moral and humanitarian principles which underlie our action in Korea.... We will not buy an armistice by turning over human beings for slaughter or slavery."[11] The prisoner of war was, essentially, a propaganda item on the negotiating table inside the tents at the village of Panmunjom. But the controversy surrounding the voluntary repatriation issue signaled a more fundamental problem than a simple claim to morality in the post–World War II global order.

The cease-fire negotiations had begun on July 10, 1951, and by the end of the year, all parties had agreed on the location of the cease-fire line near the 38th parallel. A single item of debate—Agenda Item 4, which concerned the matter of prisoners of war—was still on the table. However, on January 2, 1952, US delegates presented a new demand— voluntary repatriation. The Chinese and North Korean delegates pointed out that the 1949 Geneva Conventions on the Treatment of Prisoners of War required mandatory repatriation.

The Dodd kidnapping revealed how the Korean War was a conflict that the Geneva Conventions had not anticipated. A postcolonial civil war in a nation divided at the 38th parallel by the occupying United States at the moment of liberation from Japanese colonialism, the Korean War had begun less than a year after the 1949 Geneva Conventions had drafted new "laws of war." The United Nations and the United States did not recognize the Democratic People's Republic of Korea (DPRK) as a sovereign state, and the United Nations had entered the conflict as a belligerent. Such a situation tested a core assumption—that the "military" and the "political" could be divided—of the 1949 Geneva Conventions, which still essentially regarded warfare as a conflict occurring between two nation-states. The prescriptions of the 1949 Geneva Conventions did not encompass the very real geopolitical shifts of the decolonizing world, and Korea would prove to be the first, direct challenge to the "international community." As the United States and the United Nations sat down at Panmunjom with representatives from the Democratic People's Republic of Korea, the situation brought into stark relief that high-level negotiations were about to take place with an entity the United States and the United Nations did not recognize, calling into question the assumptions about the laws of war. With the applicability of international laws of war called into question, the Korean prisoner of war represented the site on which resolution or conflict would proceed.[12] The kidnapping of Dodd and the subsequent US military response revealed a moment when the POWs themselves, the US military, and the Panmunjom negotiators attempted to claim the definition of the POW.

In the days following Dodd's release, the US Army launched the longest investigation of a POW-related incident conducted during the Korean War, resulting in a case file that stretches to almost five hundred pages of interrogation transcripts and statements.[13] During Dodd's questioning, the US military focused initially on attempting to delineate the use of force by the POWs in capturing Dodd; however, Dodd could not provide a satisfying answer about the violent nature of the prisoners of war themselves. "The only thing broken was my fountain pen," he asserted.[14] At 9:30 P.M. on May 10, three days after the initial capture, the POWs of Compound 76 escorted Dodd to the main gate, received a written receipt for his release, and allowed Dodd to walk out of the compound. The POWs had released him on the condition that the US and UN military recognize the organization—named "The Korean People's Army and Chinese Volunteer Army Prisoners of War Representatives"—they had formed during their time with Dodd. When one pauses to consider these details in view of the request for the thousand sheets of writing paper, one can clearly see that this was indeed no ordinary kidnapping situation.

In a memo dated May 13, 1952, the POW Command of the US Army instructed the following to new camp commander Haydon Boatner: "Upon assuming command ..., your missions are to secure and maintain uncontested control of Prisoners of War and Civilian Internees under United Nations control wherever located."[15] The POWs of Compound 76 continued to refuse the entry of US and ROKA military personnel into the compound after Dodd's release. On June 10, 1952, Boatner ordered US military troops and paratroopers to storm Compound 76 using tanks, tear gas grenades, and flamethrowers. That day, the death count was thirty-four prisoners of war and one US soldier, and "uncontested control" became the official policy for POW camp administration.[16]

The story of the Dodd kidnapping was the story of the invention of different strategies of war and diplomacy—but the site of invention was neither the battlefield nor the negotiating table with career diplomats and politicians. Instead, the questions of sovereignty, decolonization, and self-determination were played out in the POW camp on Koje Island and the tents at Panmunjom. The strategies were not about bombs per se or technological advances, but rather about the interrogation room, the negotiating table, and wartime bureaucracy. The POWs' demand for one thousand sheets of writing paper and Truman's demand for voluntary repatriation were part of the same story.

The prisoners of war themselves did indeed have a sense of the larger international system in which they were embroiled. Sometime earlier in 1952, the International Committee of the Red Cross received a letter from a Korean prisoner of war at the UNC Camp #1 on the island of Koje. It was Senior Colonel Lee Hak Ku, and the letter was written in English, dated "29 December 1951," and addressed "To the Delegate of the International Committee of Red Cross."[17] "Honorable Delegate," he began, "I wish you are healthy and happy, on behalf of all P.W.s, including officers and E.M.S., who are being kept in detention by American forces at Kojedo." He was writing to protest the voluntary repatriation interrogation screening that was being conducted by the US military in the POW camp, even though the issue had not yet been resolved at the Panmunjom meetings. Lee presented himself as a representative of the POWs and then continued by reminding the ICRC of its own responsibility toward the POWs. Referring to the 1949 Geneva Conventions, he appealed to the humanitarian mission of the ICRC: "At the same time I hope that our request to you ... would be fulfilled satisfactorily by you and your Committee's endeavor, whose mission is to carry out its just and sacred duties along with other humanistic problems entrusted by all the mankind of the world." To put it simply, the Korean POWs were not rejecting wholesale the notion of "humanity" as a political entity—they were rejecting the United States' attempt to confer it on them. Lee revealed his knowledge of the Panmunjom proceedings—and an awareness of how politically linked the tents at both Panmunjom and Koje-do were to each other with the figure of the prisoner of war at the core of these discussions. Included with Lee's letter was a message for General Nam Il, the North Korean negotiator at Panmunjom. The US Army had removed the message, but Lee had clearly thought of the ICRC as a meditating factor, all the while with an eye to intervene in the negotiations underway at Panmunjom. Lee would become a central figure in the Dodd incident on May 7, 1952.

The Dodd Incident

Compound 76 in the Koje-do POW camp was located in the maximum-security area. On May 7, 1952, Brigadier General Dodd went to the compound to negotiate the entry of US interrogation teams to conduct preliminary repatriation screening. Holding a population of 6,418 prisoners of war, Compound 76 had already given a bit of grief to the administrative officials of the camp regarding voluntary repatriation screening, having persistently refused the entry of screening interrogation teams into the compound. Dodd was hoping to at least have the POWs agree to submit to fingerprint identification, since the POWs had made it a practice to give false names, swap ID numbers, and multiple other acts to undermine the bureaucratic oversight.[18]

At 2:00 P.M. on May 7, Dodd was listening to the list of requests and complaints compiled by Joo Tek Woon through the barbed-wire fence. A group of approximately six prisoners of war had gathered for the meeting.[19] Although Joo could communicate sufficiently in English, one of the other POWs from the compound was serving as the official translator. The topics of discussion ranged from arranging weekly compound spokesmen meetings to material requests such as socks, raincoats, and toothbrushes. According to the statement of General Raven, who had stood beside Dodd, prior to the kidnapping, Joo had repeatedly invited Dodd inside the compound: "Please come inside the compound where we can resolve all the problems at a desk," and "please come inside and we will sit down and resolve our problems as gentlemen." At around 3:00 P.M., a work detail passed through the gate, and the POWs seized Dodd and carried him into their compound. Kim Chang Mo, who was the compound monitor for Compound 76, had instructed their chief compound clerk, O Seong Kwon, to paint a banner with the following English message: "We capture Dodd. We guarantee his safety if there is shooting, such a brutal action then his life is danger [sic]." The banner unfurled from the compound's main building after Dodd disappeared into the compound.

Once inside the compound, Joo Tek Woon made an extraordinary gesture toward Dodd. In his interrogation transcript, Joo, the spokesman for Compound 76 who had ordered Dodd's capture, recollected that after they had carried Dodd into the Compound, "I then … told the General … that we were sorry that we had captured him against his will, and that we would guarantee his safety and not harm him." Without the barbed-wire fence between them, the terms and meanings of the roles of camp commander and prisoner of war could have been dramatically altered. With the camp commander behind the barbed-wire fence, Joo's apology set a rather unexpected tone for Dodd's duration in Compound 76. Joo's statement, I suggest, revealed that it was crucial to establish that Dodd was still a camp commander, and the POWs were still prisoners of war.

What was at stake in this incident was the definition of the prisoner of war as a political subject. After Dodd's capture, Joo immediately began negotiating with the authorities through the barbed-wire fence, stating that representatives from the other Communist compounds must be brought to Compound 76 in order to have a meeting with Dodd. In hopes of negotiating this point, the US Army brought the senior colonel of the DPRK Army, Lee Hak Ku, to the main gate—who, in the words of Colonel William H. Craig, was "the most influential officer PW." But on arrival at the compound, Lee simply stated: "it would be impossible to hold a meeting with a barbed wire fence separating us, therefore it would be necessary to enter the compound."[20]

O Seong Kwon, the twenty-two-year-old POW clerk in Compound 76 who had also translated the appropriate words for the sign announcing Dodd's capture, went with Captains Havilland and Carroll to each compound in the maximum-security section. He spoke with the spokesman and commander of each compound, telling them about the successful capture of Dodd, "and that a meeting would be held with the General in Compound #76, and that they should all come." Kwon and the two US captains went to Compounds 96, 95, 607, 605, and then 66 and 62, bringing two representatives from each compound.[21]

The group of Communist prisoners of war ultimately charged later with "mutiny" by the US Army numbered thirty-four POWs, three of whom were young women and the rest of whom were men. But another important detail of this infamous cohort of prisoners of war is that a total of ten POWs out of thirty-four Korean POWs had been born in South Korea. They patently did not fit the later narrative of the US press and military of "fanatic communist North Koreans." The ages of the prisoners of war ranged from nineteen to thirty-seven—all of them had been born during Japanese colonial rule. These prisoners of war were a particular group among the rest of the POW population. It was most probable that many of the prisoners who had participated in the kidnapping—all of whom were spokesmen and women for the other POW compounds—had a certain level of experience in anticolonial resistance movements.

The personal history of Lee Hak Ku, a critical POW figure in the Dodd incident and a senior colonel with the Korean People's Army, followed these historical shifts, according to the reports of the multiple US interrogations he had undergone. Lee was born in north Hamgyŏng—the northernmost province of the Korean peninsula, right on the border with Manchuria. After graduating from school, he had supposedly farmed for one year and then taught Japanese at a local primary school. However, the chronology of his life shifted markedly at the moment of liberation from Japan. From August 1945 to August 1946, he was "employed by the North Korean People's Government Ministry of Interior as Chief of Public Security (Police) Section in Myongch'on." In August 1946, he "enlisted in the Peace Preservation Corps at Nanam," and he had also been a member of the North Korean Democratic Youth League as well as the North Korean Labor Party.[22]

Manchuria, also an area that had been under Japanese colonial rule, figured as an important dimension to the geopolitical experiences of these POWs. In the extensive investigation report on the Dodd incident, a prisoner of war named "Liu I," who had served as an interpreter for the two Chinese POW representatives, appears in the interrogation records. In his interrogation report, the space reserved for noting whether the POW was "SK" (South Korean) or "NK" (North Korean) held an explanatory phrase: "Born in South Korea, citizen of China, Chinese Korean." The presence of two Chinese Communist representatives in a group of predominantly Korean POWs was a significant act of recognizing the history of the Korean anticolonial resistance movement in China—and the larger vision of international anti-imperial struggle.[23]

Eventually, all the representatives from other Communist compounds arrived at #76. After multiple meetings with Dodd within the main compound tent, they moved to the Civilian Information and Education (CIE) building—the largest structure in each compound designed for teaching US democracy and English to POWs, but now had been transformed into the site for POW organizational activity unanticipated by the US Army. According to Dodd: "We were up on the stage of the platform; I would say there were about a dozen persons on the stage, and down in the chairs facing the stage, down on the lower level, there were three or four rows of persons."[24] The POWs collectively formed the "Korean Peoples Army and Chinese Volunteers Prisoners of War Representatives Association." Sitting at a desk on the stage above the members, Dodd signed a note recognizing this representative organization. This act of writing by Dodd was central to the project of the POWs—and it was clear that in order for the POWs to claim a redefinition of the POW as a political subject that they would need to transform—but also still require—the authority of the camp commander.

Just as the space of the CIE building had been transformed into a diplomatic meeting hall, other spaces that Dodd occupied were similarly altered. After the meeting, the POWs escorted Dodd to a room that had been prepared for him: "rice mats on the floor and blankets on top of the rice mats, a wooden bunk, table, three chairs and rack on which to hang my clothes." As Senior Colonel Lee Hak Ku remarked in his interrogation: there were always two guards outside of the room, but they were there to "maintain the prestige" of Dodd. His meals were delivered through the barbed-wire fence, the POWs noted in their interrogations—perhaps to help ease Dodd's ulcerated stomach, they did not give him their POW rations. But also, perhaps eating the POW rations would have also challenged Dodd's hold onto his own authority as camp commander. A performance of North Korean songs and plays had been planned that evening in the CIE building—and Brigadier General Dodd was a guest at this performance.[25]

FIGURE 4.1 Members of the Korean People's Army and Chinese Volunteers Prisoners of War
Representatives Association (National Archives and Records Administration)

JANG JUN WON
63NK 89339
IN COMPOUD 76
2 JULY 52

HAN KYUNG SUN
63NK 29203
IN COMPOUND 76
5 JULY 52

SUN JIN KWAN
ISN 63NK 700101
IN COMP 76
19 JUNE 52

CHANG CHAI SHIH
ISN 63NK 730050
IN COMP 76
22 JUNE 52

PAK CHANG HWA
6 N63NK 34121
IN COMPOUND 76
8 JULY 52

CHOI IN HO
ISN 63NK 50759
IN COMPOUND 76
19 JULY 52

CHEON TAE SEONG
6 N63NK 48193
IN COMPOUND 76
7 JULY 52

CHANG SUL BONG
ISN 63NK 71069
IN COMPOUND 76
5 JULY 52

PAK JAE DOO
63NK 29163
IN COMPOUND 76
4 JULY 52

KIM NAM SWOO
63NK 21318
IN COMPOUND 76
3 JULY 52

CHE KYUNG IL
ISN 63NK 32543
IN COMPOUND 76
25 JULY 52

KIM TAE HOON
ISN 63NK 135086
IN COMPOUND 76
25 JULY 52

LEE EUNG CHUL
ISN 63NK 66685
IN COMPOUND 76
25 JULY 52

FOO CHOO HEONG
ISN 63NK 713183
IN COMP 76
19 JUNE 52

LIU I
ISN 63NK 701790
IN COMP 76
24 JUNE 52

JEONG SOON IL
ISN 63NK 127735
IN COMPOUND 76
15 JULY 52

KIM UI HAN
ISN 63NK 10763
IN COMPOUND 76
6 AUGUST 52

LIM KYEON JAE
ISN 63NK 139203
IN COMPOUND 76
6 AUGUST 52

63NK 201 814

FIGURE 4.2 Brigadier General Francis T. Dodd. March 12, 1952
(National Archives and Records Administration)

The next morning, the POWs had arranged a certain morning routine—or ritual perhaps—for Brigadier General Dodd. In the five-hundred-page expanse of the investigation case file, there is a particular interrogation of a POW who was not directly involved with the kidnapping or the creation of the POW representative body—An Jong Un, a POW who served as the compound doctor. He gave the following testimony during his interrogation:

Q: What knowledge do you have concerning the seizure of General DODD?

A: An unidentified POW came to the dispensary and requested
that I accompany him to a tent near the mess hall in 3rd Bn area
to treat General Dodd. Enroute to the tent I met Lee Hak Ku and
he asked what I was doing. When I explained that I was going to
treat the General, LEE stated, that is fine, go ahead. Upon arrival
at the tent, General DODD was taking a bath in a metal tub made
from an oil drum. About three (3) PW monitors were washing
the General's body.... When the General had finished bathing I
examined his finger and knees and observed they were healing.
The Interpreter told me the General had a cough when he woke
that morning, so I listened to his heart beat and examined his
chest. He appeared to be in good condition.... In leaving, the
General gave me a pack of cigarettes.[26]

The spectacle of Dodd being bathed by three POWs and then the
careful medical attention Dodd received toed a line between the assertion of a complete surveillance over his body and also the offer of special services to an elite guest. Dodd was unmistakably a prisoner under
the care of his captors, who were prisoners of war. Yet, there was no
reversal of a binary hierarchy of power between a POW camp commander and the POW. The POWs did not replace Dodd in his position
as camp commander. Instead, the POWs carefully marked Dodd's body
and the space of the compound itself to establish and assert Dodd's
authority—which they explicitly made contingent on their own authority as a collective of representatives for the POW camp.

FIGURE 4.3 Prisoner of war An Jong Un, the compound
doctor who examined Dodd (National Archives and
Records Administration)

On May 8, the POWs gave Dodd the most important document of the incident: a list of eleven functions and demands of the POW representative organization. Item 7 on the list was the most revealing: "In order to secure the business of this institute, we request four tents, ten desks, twenty chairs, one hundred K. T. paper and two hundred dozens of pencils, three hundred bottles of ink and two hundred stencil paper and one mimeograph." The organization wanted to create their own archive, their own bureaucratic overseeing function, of the POW. When we ponder the meaning of such a demand and look at the very first item on their list of organizational functions, we can see how this move toward establishing the means of an archive on the POW was also a move toward claiming a legitimate sovereignty: "1) We organize the representatives of PW's association by total PWs of Korean Peoples Army and Chinese People's Candidates that are confined in Koje Island." In his interrogation, Joo stated that after Lee Hak Ku was elected president of the PW representative association, he effectively "became the commander of all PW Compounds in the UN POW Camp #1."[27]

The bureaucracy they would create would approach the POW as the subject of a state, not simply a wartime category. The single, most important demand the POW organization made was the cessation of US military repatriation screening, claiming that the United States was forcing subjects of the DPRK to renounce the state's sovereign claims over them. Using their position as prisoners of war, these representatives in turn forced the international community to ask what type of political collective body the DPRK was—and to argue that it was a legitimate state.

In an effort to lessen, or triage, the damage from the capture of Dodd, the US military sent in General Colson to become the camp commander of Koje. Colson's duty was to announce to the POWs on his arrival that Dodd was no longer in command, and therefore all negotiations with him would be null and void. Colson delivered the following message via loudspeaker and writing to the members of Compound 76 at five minutes after midnight, the night of Dodd's capture:

At about 1500 hours of 7 May certain PW of Compound 76, maliciously attacked Brigadier General Francis T. Dodd, then CG of this

Camp and Lt Colonel W. R. Raven, CO of Enclosure Number 7. General Dodd against his violent opposition was forcibly carried into Compound 76 where he is now held a prisoner. Such an action is contrary to all the principles of the Geneva Convention. I am the new CG of this Camp and as such I am authorized by the rules of the Geneva Convention to order you to immediately release General Dodd and permit him to return safely. I do hereby order that you release him unharmed.[28]

Dodd was not released. Instead, altogether twelve messages were sent through the barbed-wire fence to the new camp command. A message sent to the US command on May 10, signed by Lee Hak Ku on behalf of the POW representative organization, provides a crucial frame through which to understand the functions of the organization they had created. "This Representative Group announce once again that the unwilling detention of Brig. Gen. Dodd, US Army, your predecessor by this Representative Group is the legal leading measure for the protection of lives and personal rights of our POWs who have been intimidated by unjust management handled by your authorities having decreased the authority of Geneva Convention and nullified the said Convention by the illegal management of POWs and the violence against the POWs."[29] The invocation of the Geneva Convention in this exchange message makes a very crucial discursive move: it unhinges the authority of the United States from the moral authority of international humanitarian law by stating that the United States was not synonymous with the international order.

Lee ended the message by writing, "I announce that American Brigadier General Dodd is, as he has reported, in utterly safe condition, being protected from all danger and there is not even the smallest change in his sanitary or mental condition could be seen. He is discussing with us in most usual condition. Your health and new result of practicing Geneva Convention is hoped for. Representing the representatives group of KPA and Chinese volunteer Troop PW by the approval of the then CG of PW Camp. Signed Lee, Hak Koo."[30] The POWs were not necessarily either surprised or perturbed by the change in command. They shifted their bureaucratic strategies in their negotiations—all

statements regarding past events of violence, and such, that had occurred under Dodd's command would be verified by Dodd's signature,
and those statements regarding the future entitlements and functions
of the POW representative organization would be signed by Colson.

On May 10, 1952, both Dodd and Colson had marked their signatures on the corresponding statements. On Dodd's release, the US military, in turn, immediately demoted both of them. It was the fact that
they had signed their signatures on documents written up by POWs
attesting to violence in the camps among multiple other items that led
to the quick demise of both of these men's military careers. Their signatures were the acts of transgression.

From inside Compound #76, the diplomatic and the bureaucratic
took precedence over other kinds of activities. The members of the

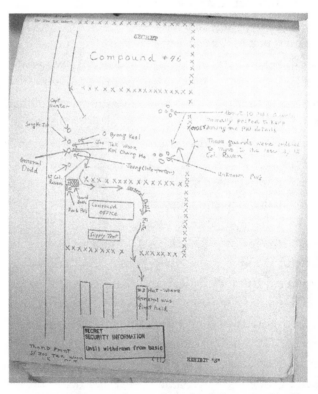

FIGURE 4.4 Schematic drawing done of the kidnapping of Dodd
(National Archives and Records Administration)

FIGURE 4.5 POW compounds involved in the Dodd kidnapping case
(National Archives and Records Administration)

Korean People's Army and Chinese Volunteers Prisoners of War Representatives Association brought the issue of political recognition to the fore. Statements were written in English, and the POWs were careful to ensure that Dodd was not physically harmed. Evidence of physical coercion would nullify Dodd's act of signing the given statements. The medical attention, the evening entertainment, and the meeting with the POW representatives—all of these activities and gestures were calibrated to a fine pitch, and they demonstrated how attuned the POWs were to the symbolic elements that they needed to assemble in order to legitimate their more material demands.

The Korean POWs were essentially reenacting the sovereign claims of their state—the Democratic People's Republic of Korea—over their own selves, using the Geneva Conventions as the framework and General Dodd as the medium for their claims. They demanded to be recognized as prisoners of war of a sovereign nation-state. Indeed, the Dodd kidnapping touched on a not entirely resolved issue at the 1949 Geneva Conventions about the category of the "prisoner of war." Delegates at the Conventions argued to extend the Geneva protections to "long-term resistance movements," and notably the British delegate resisted this extension. "The British, driven by imperial self-interest, were looking forward to an era of colonial policing and national liberation movements," and they "wanted to avoid creating protective rights for anticolonial nationalists."[31] This extension of protections was eventually enumerated in the Conventions, but it was clear that in era of national liberation movements, the granting of wartime status categories like "prisoner of war" would go hand in hand with the issue of sovereign recognition in the post-1945 nation-state system. In the negotiation tents at Panmunjom, one would assume that the debate over the prisoner of war category would focus primarily on whose interpretation of the 1949 Geneva Conventions prevailed. But instead, another unresolved issue reared its head. The negotiators debated not only POW repatriation, but also the meaning of the 38th parallel.

Negotiations without Recognition

The meetings at Panmunjom began on October 25, 1951, a single day after nine two-and-a-half-ton trucks moved material and tents to the site, where forty men labored to erect the conference tents, complete with lighting, flooring, and heating.[32] In his memoir, titled *How to Negotiate with Communists*, Admiral Charles Turner Joy, the chief negotiator for the United Nations Command, uses a consistent phrase— "stage setting"—to describe much of the negotiating that took place in the tent.[33] The negotiations at Panmunjom revolved around the ritual gestures of sovereignty—and revealed the performative aspect of the meetings. The politics of recognition were deeply embedded in the negotiations themselves. The United States and the United Nations did not recognize the sovereignty of the Democratic People's Republic of Korea, and yet the rituals of negotiation implied conditions of equality—the foundation of the sovereign nation-state order was based on the notion of equality, and each nation-state was an individual actor within a larger community of states. As anthropologists John Kelly and Martha Kaplan have furthered, "what is novel about modern nationalism is not political self-consciousness, but the world *system* of nation-states," a system that became "real ... with the construction of the United Nations."[34] How would the United States and the United Nations negotiate with North Korea and China without granting them recognition as a sovereign nation? In an effort to sidestep this morass, the United States decided to delegate the task of negotiating to the "military commanders in the field" rather than career diplomats or politicians.[35] Thus, the tents were ostensibly a site that could effectively partition the "military" from the "political."

However, there was one negotiating tent at Panmunjom that repeatedly could not finesse effectively the discursive construction of a separation between the "military" and the "political."[36] The meetings of the subcommittee on Item 4 on the negotiation agenda—prisoners of war repatriation—began on December 11, 1951. The negotiators representing the Democratic People's Republic of Korea and China respectively were Major General Lee Sang Cho and Colonel Tsai Cheng-wen, two men described by the official US Army history of the Panmunjom talks as the "enemy['s] two ablest negotiators." Seated across the negotiating table were Rear Admiral Ruthven E. Libby, whom the very same history described as "a fiery sea dog with salty tongue," and Colonel George W. Hickman Jr., who "provided added balance to the UNC team."[37] Each team had brought their own staff, interpreters, and stenographers.[38] The time was 1300 hours, and Major General Lee said, "Let's begin the talks."[39]

The first major debate revolved around the issue of "civilian internees."[40] Major General Lee repeatedly put forth the argument that to simply sift through the POW population to determine who had been where vis-à-vis the 38th parallel before the outbreak of war was not a valid way to determine who belonged to which state. "Can people who are not prisoners of war be made prisoners of war by this conference?," he asked. "That is not possible.... I was myself a person of South Korean origin, but you know, and the other people of the world know, that I am not a person of your army but a loyal General of the Democratic People's Republic of Korea."[41]

In response, Libby insisted on creating what he called "a clear distinction between politics and law, between a political question and a legal question." Invoking the "law of nations," Libby asserted that the people in question regarding "civilian internee" status were for a "fact," "citizens of the Republic of Korea," and thus "they have certain rights guaranteed to them by the laws of that country and they have certain responsibilities to their country." In this negotiating tent, one would expect that the discussion would have primarily revolved around the 1949 Geneva Conventions, but the quick turn in the conversations and arguments soon exposed the central stakes of the discussion. To talk about the prisoner of war was to discuss the claims a state could make on its subjects—and, more importantly, which states were considered legitimate within the post-1945 world order.[42]

In essence, the talks surrounding Agenda Item 4 at Panmunjom revealed that five years after the division of Korea, it was still not clear what type of border the 38th parallel should be. Born under the hands of "two tired colonels working late at night" at the Pentagon in Washington, DC, on August 10, 1945, the 38th parallel did not follow any geographical or cultural division—rather, the latitudinal line of the 38th parallel had served as the division between two foreign occupations of Korea—the United States' and the Soviets'.[43] For Koreans, the 38th parallel was entirely an artificial division. Under Japanese colonial rule, the experience of being a subject of empire exceeded any territorial state bounds. Koreans were factory laborers in Manchuria or sugarcane workers in Hawai'i, while others built political Korean governments-in-exile in Shanghai and multiple anticolonial military training outfits throughout the Manchurian-Korean border, the Korean peninsula, and in Hawai'i.[44] The prisoners of war in the camp on Koje-do reflected the migrations forced by Japanese colonial policies and also by Stalin's deportation policies during the late 1930s due to perceptions that Koreans, still colonized by Japan, could serve as enemy spies.

In the year 1950, five years after liberation, the question of the 38th parallel had not been resolved. And the Korean War itself presented a true quandary to all involved. On one hand, if the war were a civil war, the 38th parallel would simply be a vestige of foreign occupation since it did not have a longer historical meaning to the politics and communities in Korea. If the war were a war of rollback, somewhat similarly the 38th parallel would not signify territorial sovereignty. On the other hand, if the war were an anti-Communist war of containment, the 38th parallel would have been solidified as sovereign border, albeit selectively, since the United States and United Nations did not want to grant political recognition of the DRPK's sovereignty. And yet on another level, if the war were a war of national liberation, the 38th parallel would primarily only have meaning as an imperial gesture. In the negotiating tents at Panmunjom, the question of the 38th parallel and the war would have to be resolved over the prisoners of war.

Lee asserted the legitimate sovereign claims of the DPRK over the Korean peninsula by returning to the elections of 1948:

> If you talk about the so-called citizenship or nationality of these people we are talking about, as I have said, it is a complicated question. You should remember the name of our Republic is the Democratic People's Republic of Korea and when the Democratic People's Republic was born, it was born as a result of an election which showed the will of the entire people of Korea, including the South Koreans.[45]

The putative division between the "military" and the "political" fell apart in the negotiating tent because the debate addressed the very core of "sovereignty" in the post-1945 era—what type of military action rendered a state legitimate in the decolonizing world? Did the military government of the US Army render a decolonized state legitimate? Or did a history of anticolonial military resistance impart legitimacy in terms of the relationship between the people and the state?

It became clear that the subsequent naming of these respective states was another aspect of the sovereignty and recognition issue. "You made reference to 'Syngman Rhee's government,'" said Libby to Lee on the meeting on December 27. "By this reference I assume you meant the government of the Republic of Korea, ... since there is only one recognized government in Korea.... For the purpose of this conference it is sufficient that our side pays you the courtesy of referring to your government by the name you prefer—the Democratic People's Republic of Korea. We do this out of common courtesy and in deference to your wishes, and not because we recognize any such government in fact."[46]

And then on January 2, 1952, Rear Admiral Libby put another issue on the table: voluntary repatriation of the prisoners of war. The issue of repatriation pushed the negotiations to another level of debate over the nature of nation-states in the post-1945 world. On January 26, 1952, Libby was the one who commenced the day's talks. Addressing General Lee, he said, "In closing yesterday your side stated that it is proper to talk about north and south Koreans and about the areas north and south of the military demarcation line in order to avoid any political discussion.... These negotiations are being conducted within a certain political framework. We cannot, and will not, as you suggest, close our eyes to these facts," Libby asserted.

> The Republic of Korea is a sovereign state. It exists. It exists as a result of the free will of hundreds of thousands of Koreans. By their act of creating this state, the residents of the area south of the 38th Parallel made themselves nationals of that state.... This is not politics. This law. This is fact. However unpleasant this fact may be to you, it remains a fact.[47]

In response, Lee addressed the question of an individual's will vis-à-vis the state. He said, "It is impossible to arbitrarily classify the Korean people in accordance with their northern or southern national designation.... Because in Korea there are two forces which differ from each other in nature: on the one side, there is the Revolutionary People's Army which represents the interests of the people; on the other side, there is a reactionary army." He continued:

> All those prisoners of war whom we captured from your army we do not classify into whites or blacks; nor do we instigate the negro to oppose the whites, and we have not canceled their military designation.... We do not raise the question of whether those Americans should go to England or Africa after the war. That is a question of electing one's political standpoint. We do not ask them to do so, and we don't find it necessary either."[48]

At this juncture in the negotiations, the question of POW repatriation had pushed both Libby and Lee to betray a specific tension in the construction of the nation-state in the post-1945 world—the contradiction of the "military" and the "political" in the formation of a state. The legitimacy of military participation, for both the DPRK and the United States, was founded on the assumption of consent and choice on the part of the participants themselves, whether Korean revolutionaries or African American soldiers. And yet, Lee attempted to undermine this notion by pointing out that the participation did not necessarily indicate a putative identity between the subjectivity of the person and the political agendas of the state.

Libby took this opportunity to push the discursive logic further: "The position taken by your side has two basic themes which are so diametrically opposed to each other that the inclusion of both in the same proposal cannot, in our view, be defended on any grounds of logic or reason. These themes are: 'freedom of choice' and its opposite 'forced repatriation.'"[49] And he went on to state, "So far as the individuals themselves are concerned, the United Nations Command proposal is a bill of rights."[50] The debate over the prisoners of war repatriation exposed that the negotiations were more than a struggle over whose interpretation of "international law" would be valid—this was a conflict over who could lay claim to knowing the subjectivity, the desires of the "prisoners of war" amid competing notions of citizenship, human rights, and sovereignty in the post-1945 era of formal decolonization. The debate continued in the interrogation rooms at UNC Camp #1, where the POWs involved in the Dodd kidnapping again invoked the 1949 Geneva Conventions, and the US military attempted to charge the POW representative organization with "mutiny."

Interrogation without Recognition

The administrative summary to the US Army investigation file on the May 7, 1952, "kidnapping" of Brigadier General Francis Dodd contained a peculiar turn of phrase: "When Dodd was released he was in good physical condition and there is no doubt that his captors treated him

well, in fact, to the point of being patronizing."[51] The usual straightforward chronological telling of the case file's events paused, and an "in
fact" created a rupture large enough for a comment, a slight aside—
and suddenly, it was evident that there was something in this case file
that could not be contained by the bureaucratic language of the US
Army. Case #33 of the Dodd kidnapping was the sole case where the
United States Army brought charges of "mutiny" against prisoners of
war. The labor involved in the investigation and preparation for pros-
ecution was evident, but in the end, as the file was prepared for the
archive, the administrative summary insisted on noting that the prisoners of war were "patronizing." The amount of effort the US Army
exerted to address a "mutiny" committed by "patronizing" prisoners of
war raises a simple question: what political/psychological boundaries
had these Korean Communist prisoners of war transgressed in taking
the American commander of the POW camp prisoner? What was the
mutiny?

The 29th Military Police (MP) Criminal Investigation Detachment
(CID) of the US Army began its investigation into the Dodd incident
on May 29, 1952. The investigation did not end until August 7 of that
year, with the investigation officially declared "closed" on August 25,
1952. Two separate cases, Cases #32 and #33, were filed by the United
Nations against the prisoners of war who had been involved in the kidnapping. Case #32 involved the six prisoners of war who were present
at the meeting at the barbed-wire fence with Brigadier General Dodd:
Joo Tek Woon, Kim Chang Mo, O Seong Kwon, O Byong Keol, and
Song Mo Jin. Case #33 also included Joo and Kim but expanded its list
of accused to the POWs who were in the POW representative organization. The official charges, according to the case file summary, read as
follows:

> The defendants in Case #32 are charged with unlawfully striking
> Brig Gen Francis T. Dodd, a member of the United Nations Com-
> mand, on 7 May 1952 at UNC PW Camp #1, Koje-do, Korea. The
> twenty five (25) defendants in Case #33 are charged with mutiny in
> their joint refusal to release Gen Dodd in accord with a lawful order

given them by Brig Gen Charles W. Colson, Gen Dodd's successor as Commanding General of UNC PW Camp #1.... Included among the defendants in #33 are two (2) former members of the Chinese Volunteer Army. All other defendants are Korean.[52]

The phrases "unlawfully striking" and "joint refusal to release Gen Dodd in accord with a lawful order" clearly attempted to stress the characterization of these POWs' actions as outside the bounds of the law. But when Dodd's own interrogation revealed that the result of the physical kidnapping had been minor scratches and a broken fountain pen, one can question why the authorities had insisted on using "unlawful striking" as the characterizing phrase of the incident. And the act of "mutiny" occurred not necessarily in the moment of bringing Dodd behind the barbed-wire fence of Compound 76 but rather at the moment of refusing to recognize the authority of Colson's demand to release Dodd. To undermine the authority invested in the signatures of Dodd and Colson on the documents recognizing the POW representative organization, the US military criminal investigation team had to de-invest the political content of the POWs' demands by criminalizing the POWs. The investigation report was one particular process to criminalize the prisoners of war in order to nullify the other actions of the two brigadier generals, Dodd and Colson.

Rather significantly, the investigation case file revealed an important aspect of the investigation: there are twenty-eight transcripts of interrogations with prisoners of war who had been involved in some way with the incident, while all US military personnel involved submitted narrative statements. The only other interrogation transcript was the questioning of General Dodd after the incident, while he was stationed at Pusan. The interrogation transcripts show the template of questions and the priorities the CID held during the investigation, and more specifically, they reveal that the main concern of the CID agents was the representative organization the POWs had created.

The investigating CID members had to demonstrate the premeditated nature of the kidnapping while also eliding the broader political and organizational aspects of the POWs' activities. The kidnapping had to be a criminal act, not a political one. There was one particular question that the CID agents would ask only the POWs directly involved in the POW representative organization. The question was essentially twofold: "Q: Have you read the rules for governing PW's as prescribed by the Geneva Convention?," which was followed by, "Q: Did you, *as a member of the association*, know that you were holding General Dodd against his will and in violation of the Geneva Convention?" (my italics).

The answers the prisoners of war gave in response to the first question were almost unequivocally "yes"—or they would specify which parts of the Convention they were familiar with. The responses to the second question, without exception, all held to the claim that ultimately the POWs had not violated the Geneva Conventions and that the capture of Dodd had been simply a necessity because they could not otherwise have a meeting with him. For example, four female Korean prisoners of war had been members of the KPA and Chinese People's Volunteers Army (CPVA) PW Representative Association—all of whom were from Compound #80 in Enclosure 8, the all-female compound. Pak Soo Pok, a twenty-year-old woman from South Korea who had joined the North Korean Army as a nurse, stated in her interrogation on June 10, 1952: "I, as a member of the committee, disregarded the Geneva Convention laws governing Prisoners of War because I felt that we were right in detaining General DODD." Kim Jong Sook, the twenty-two-year-old spokesman for Compound #80, declared, "I as a member of the association felt that I was right in helping to detain General Dodd." And Kim Jong Ja, the twenty-one-year-old commander of Compound #80 from South Korea, stated, "I thought we were right in holding General DODD and that we were not violating the Geneva Convention Laws." These POWs offered the same rationale as the others accused in the case: the circumstances surrounding the Dodd incident were extraordinary, and the conditions in the camp previous to the incident had rendered the kidnapping necessary. The Geneva Conventions, according to the POWs, did not hold in the circumstances due to particular violations of the Conventions committed already by the US military and the supporting ROKA soldiers within the camp.

Or as POW representative Sun Jin Kwan stated, "I felt that our demands were legal."[53]

On June 25, 1952, the CID agents brought in Lee Hak Ku for interrogation. The usual question was put forth: "Q: Did you, as a member of the association know that you were holding General Dodd in violation of the Geneva Convention?" Lee's response was brief: "A: I do not care to answer this question." Lee's apparent refusal—and perhaps "patronizing" attitude—to recognize any obligation toward the US authority in the interrogation room later prompted the writers of the investigation case file to brand him as a leader of the "fanatical" POWs.

Lee's responses during the investigation's interrogation must be understood within his extensive experience with the US military bureaucracy, having gone through multiple interrogations. A senior colonel in the Korean People's Army, Lee had been a highly valued POW under US custody. However, his intake interrogation report noted an unexpected surrender on Lee's part soon after MacArthur's landing at Inchon in mid-September 1950:

> PW surrendered to US troops on his own volition....
>
> PW left his unit in the mountains (south of TABUDONG) and approached the American lines at night. He approached two American soldiers sleeping on a roadside, and roused them by gently shaking them; and they brought him in as a PW.
>
> PW was disgusted with the Communist doctrine and system and consequently surrendered.[54]

In the follow-up interrogation on September 25, 1950, the interrogator, a Sergeant Hayashi from ATIS, characterized Lee Hak Ku "as intelligent and very cooperative." He made the following notes on Lee during the interrogation:

> No attempts were made at evasion and answers were given without hesitation. Although PW at one time was in position of great responsibility in the NKPA, he did not show any signs of being a Communist. PW is of a higher than average caliber, and, from all indications, highly ambitious.... Reliability—good.[55]

The element framing both of these character assessments of Lee was his position vis-à-vis Communism—his disgust with Communism enabled the first interrogator to portray Lee as "gently shaking" awake two US soldiers, his potential threat neutralized and evacuated. Lee's aspirational desires—"highly ambitious"—rendered him "of a higher than average caliber." Lee would come to the attention of President Truman less than a year later through a mailing dated May 3, 1951, sent by Major General Frank E. Lowe.

Lee Hak Ku gave the following personal timeline: Born in "HOI-Dong" on January 18, 1921, he then graduated primary school in 1936, and then farmed "at place of birth." He then taught Japanese in his hometown during 1937, after which he attended Honam Primary School, and later passed the National Teachers Examination. He became a Japanese teacher at Yanghwa Primary School, and supposedly on the day of interrogation Lee still carried a valid teacher's certification of his appointment at Yanghwa. After liberation from Japanese colonialism in 1945, Lee Hak Ku was "employed by the North Korean People's Government Ministry of Interior as Chief of Public Security (Police) Section, MYONGCH'ON." He then would become a member of three critical organizations: the Peace Preservation Corps at Nanam, the NK Democratic Youth League, and the North Korean Labor Party.

In light of Lee's personal timeline, the comment that Lee "did not show any signs of being a Communist" raised the simple question of exactly what a "Communist" would show or demonstrate. In fact, if we continue to follow the paper trail of Lee's interrogation reports, we come upon the report sent by Frank E. Lowe, the above-mentioned major general in the US Army, to President Harry Truman. The introductory letter reads as follows:

Dear Mr. President,
    Colonel Lee Hak Ku, as of 6 October 1950 and since that time as far as I know, the highest ranking NOK officer captured as well as those voluntarily surrendering.

Attached hereto is a copy of his interrogation which is both interesting and significant. I believe that overall it is as significant today
as it was on 6 October 1950.

Yours faithfully,

Frank E. Lowe

Lowe had attached a narrative of the interrogation that an interrogator
named Edward L. Bowles had conducted with Lee on "Friday, 22nd of
September, in the detention area at Pusan." It was a day after Lee's initial intake interrogation report, and two days before the later tactical
interrogation report. "The man answered my questions forthrightly
and willingly so far as I could observe," wrote Bowles. "I had the im-
pression that he was an able person." As for the actual process of interrogation, Bowles briefly mentioned that there was a translator of some
sort—"The interpreter seemed unusually able in his translations"—
and attributed the fluency of the translation to Lee's character. "[He]
gave one the feeling that he is precise not only in his manner of speech
but his thinking."

Interestingly, Bowles began his conversation, at least according to
the provided narrative, with a question about the North Koreans. "Several times during the interrogation I questioned the prisoner as to what
it was that caused the North Koreans to fight with such fever. His answers pointed consistently to the conclusion that the soldiers, at least,
believed that they were fighting for the unification of Korea without
Russia." The issue of the Russians clearly loomed large for Bowles—
the discussion soon turned again to the Russians:

> I ... asked why is was that the North Koreans were not given more
> aircraft by the Russians. He stated quickly that it was because the
> North Koreans had no pilots for the aircraft. I then asked why if the
> Russians sent guns, tanks, munitions, and radar and communica-
> tions equipment, they did not send pilots. He explained that this was
> different. He made this statement as if it had aroused an intense feel-
> ing in him. I tried to develop the subject further, and he went on to
> explain that equipment was a "thing," whereas the pilot was a "man,"

and that the Russians were concerned with United Nations action (he actually referred to the United Nations as such). He went on to say that the Russians were worried about world opinion.

It was a moment in the narrative where Lee Hak Ku supposedly becomes impassioned—and it is a moment that seems to indicate that Lee was not the passive "Oriental" Bowles imagined. He was insisting on explicating the Russians' actions even within a US military interrogation room.

In his letter to President Truman accompanying a copy of Bowles's narrative, Lowe asserted that the interrogation was "both interesting and significant" and went so far as to say, "I believe that overall it is as significant today as it was on 6 October 1950." Similar to Hanley's characterization of the interrogation room, Bowles's interrogation room—and the success of the interrogation—was dependent on the seeming transparency of two major aspects: language and the intent of Lee Hak Ku. Language, according to Lowe's report, was not an issue—and the translator, who had most probably been either a Korean civilian translator or a Japanese American interrogator/translator, was rendered immediately invisible. Indeed, even the complex bureaucracy and multiple interrogations surrounding Lee Hak Ku's surrender were hidden—the intake interrogation done by MIS, the reports filed by ATIS, the tactical interrogation done by the Advanced Allied Translator and Interpreter Section (ADVATIS). But the omission of these multiple types of interrogation was perhaps significant in itself—each type of interrogation was conducted with the objective of extracting a specific type of information. But what type of "information" was being produced supposedly in Bowles's interrogation?

Lowe sent the interrogation memorandum to President Truman to demonstrate how US interrogators were putatively able to discern and gain insight into the "North Korean mind." The ability to note and judge Lee Hak Ku's character was on full display in the three-page typed narrative written by Bowles. There was also an element of spectacle present in the narrative as we watch vicariously through Bowles the particular physical gestures and verbal emphases Lee supposedly made during the interrogation. Bowles's parenthetical notation that Lee had actually noted the United Nations by name juxtaposed with observations of Lee's emotional reactions conveyed the positionality of the interrogator all too well—detached, the interrogator noted with some surprise that Lee was aware of the United Nations, and also paid attention to his physical gestures, often characterizing them as somewhat naive. Lee Hak Ku was supposedly a rather intelligent, but ultimately unsophisticated and naive "Oriental."

Lee Hak Ku was very consciously insisting on the agency and autonomy of the North Korean army and state—throughout the interrogation, Lee reiterated his belief that the North Korean soldiers were fighting on behalf of unification, not because of Russia. After his time in the detention center in Pusan, the US Army made Lee Hak Ku a "prisoner of war." Lee later became the lightning rod for much of the US Army's frustration with Korean Communist prisoners of war, as they refused to participate in US military interrogation. Later, the US military would characterize Lee as an "Oriental Communist fanatic," a man with no regard for human life—and Lowe's letter to Truman was most probably quietly disregarded. The desires of an empire were much too vulnerable in the interrogation room—and the desire to claim knowledge over Lee Hak Ku was all too exposed in Bowles's interrogation narrative. But even in the archival, bureaucratic record of the US military, Lee Hak Ku's insistence opened up the possibility for recognizing the agency of Korean Communist POWs in the interrogation room. The "Oriental" who was being read by the US military was also aware of the different projects taking place.

Bowles's interrogation was a portrait of an anti-Communist Korean, to convey to President Truman what manner of "man"—and what kind of human intelligence substance—the United States was involved with in both war and occupation. And perhaps there was even a measure of reassurance in the sending of Bowles's interrogation narrative to Truman by Lowe—it was reassurance that the United States could indeed render transparent the will and desires of the Korean, and, more importantly, that the Korean would render himself willingly as a transparent subject in front of the United States. In the Dodd investigation files, and the subsequent US media outlets, Lee would fill a necessary role in the script the US military needed to delegitimatize the claims the POW representative organization made. Lee Hak Ku would become the "fanatic Oriental Communist prisoner of war" *par excellence* in the narratives of the US military archival records, a critical obscuring of the politics expressed by Lee.

When we consider scholar Elaine Scarry's assertion in her book on torture, *The Body in Pain*, that "the relative ease or difficulty with which any given phenomenon can be *verbally represented* also influences the ease or difficulty with which that phenomenon comes to be *politically represented*,"[56] and take another look at the investigation files on the Dodd incident, what initially may have simply seemed to be a "strange event" was, in fact, a political gesture—one that reveals the high stakes of articulation, visibility, and power in the prisoner of war camps of the Korean War. And the arrival of Brigadier General Haydon Boatner would articulate these stakes with tanks, paratroopers, and flamethrowers.

The "New Regime"

An internally circulated US Army history titled "The Handling of Prisoners of War during the Korean War" dubbed the arrival of Boatner at Koje as "The New Regime," a welcome change supposedly from the previous bungling of Dodd.[57] In his own unpublished memoir typescript, Boatner made the following bold statement: "Well, then, just what if anything was the weakest element in our prisoner of war methods in Korea? In my opinion, the greatest weakness stems from our inability to cope with the Oriental."[58] Boatner prided himself on having been the commanding general of troops in Burma during the Asia-Pacific Wars. Fluent in Mandarin, he recollected many moments where he surprised the POWs on Koje with his linguistic knowledge. The June 10, 1952, storming of Compound 76 with tanks, flamethrowers, and even paratroopers would be hailed as a success by the US military.

In the memoir, Boatner recalls the morning of June 10. Boatner had constructed new, smaller compounds under US Army directives to split the Communist compounds into more "manageable," smaller groups.

"I took Colonel Lee [Hak Ku] over to the site of the new compounds so he could see them for himself. Then I gave him orders written in Korean, Chinese and English to assemble all prisoners in the open area in the center of his compound, No. 76, in groups of 100, to be marched under armed escort to the new compounds. I told him if his men moved orderly no one would be hurt, but that if they resisted force would be used and any resulting casualties would be his responsibility and due to his own disobedience of my legal orders."

After dismissing Lee and sending him back into Compound 76, Boatner allotted thirty minutes to wait before entering the compound. Then, according to Boatner, "fifteen minutes after the announced time for our entrance, our troops cut holes in the wire and the tanks entered followed by flame throwers and then the paratroopers."

Boatner then stood at a command post on an adjacent hill so he could observe the operation. He noticed homemade "Molotov cocktails" being thrown at the oncoming tanks. In the later investigation interrogations of the POWs, it became clear that the POWs had been preparing for some sort of conflict—the US troops were surprised to find that the POWs had somehow made gas masks in the event that gas grenades would be launched. The operation had lasted four hours. "What a gruesome sight it was!" exclaimed Boatner in the memoir. "A battlefield in every respect. Entrenchments, wounded, dead, burning buildings and tests [tents] with a few human hands, legs or feet here and there."[59]

The former policy of "overwhelming force" had found new expression under Boatner's command. But even after the June 10, 1952 incident, the highest levels of US military command were still not content with the situation of "uncontested control" in the POW camps under US Army control. On closer examination, the policy of "uncontested control" no longer means the demonstration of "overwhelming force," but the complete eradication of resistance that was not only physical but also symbolic.

The Dodd incident reveals a process of fashioning the Korean Communist POW into an ideological figure—or more specifically, a "fanatic"—a phrase used extensively by US military personnel to describe the Communist POWs in both their statements for the case file and administrative memos passed from higher command to the camps. "Uncontested control" would become the central official policy for the camps, and Boatner's decision to storm Compound 76 on June 10 and the resulting deaths were clearly in line with the new objective of pre-empting the issue of consent on the part of POWs. I contend that we can view the policy of "uncontested control" as the other side of the coin of "voluntary repatriation"—both depoliticized the Korean prisoner of war and demonstrated the prerogative of the United States to define a normative POW subjectivity for the post-1945 order, and thus the power to define the relationship between the international order, the state, and the individual.

On August 4, 1952, in a statement to all POWs that was posted in the compounds, Boatner gave this summary of the Dodd incident: "The last two months have been a critical period in this Prisoner of War Camp. Many difficulties were caused by the kidnapping of General Dodd and other acts of mutiny and defiance by Prisoners of War. Those were criminal acts which were caused by stupid, selfish and politically motivated self-appointed leaders, who act as compound representatives." In contrast, he offered the following template of the normative POW: "Each Prisoner of War must remember that he has surrendered and is a prisoner of war under the custody and command of the Camp Commander, acting for the Detaining Power. Each prisoner must do his duty as a soldier, and do nothing illegal. He must obey orders and comply with the policy of the Camp Commander. Do these things promptly and in good spirits and you will be more contented."[60] A proper POW must be a content one—and more importantly, a subject of the camp itself rather than an outside state.

The longest clause of Boatner's statement to the POWs that invoked the Geneva Conventions repeated this sentiment that POWs cannot claim a subjecthood outside of the camp's confines:

> The Geneva Convention states: "In all places where there are Prisoners of War, except in those where there are officers, the prisoners shall freely elect by secret ballot, every six months, and also in case

of vacancies, prisoner representatives entrusted with representing them before the military authorities, the Protesting Powers, the International Committee of the Red Cross and other organizations which may assist them.... Every representative must be approved by the Detaining Power before he has the right to commence his duties...." You will see, therefore, that your representatives can be removed by your Camp Commander. I want him to serve you for the well-being of the POW's in accordance with my orders and policies. If he does not, I will remove him from his responsibility and call upon you to elect another representative.[61]

Representation and the cessation of forced repatriation screening were the two most important demands the POW representative organization made. As both the US government and the Korean Communist prisoners of war understood, at stake in the interrogation process was the question of what type of political subjectivity would be legitimate within the post-1945 international nation-state system. Clearly, if the US military could demonstrate that an overwhelming number of Communist combatants and civilians desired nonrepatriation, the US interpretation of the Geneva Conventions' humanitarian intentions would take precedence at the negotiating table. But more importantly, the POWs understood that the repatriation interrogation held up only one particular template for subjectivity—the internee would need to narrate him/herself as a "human," a subject devoid of claims to collective subjectivities, such as citizenship, nationalism, or a Communist revolution. If we take Carl Schmitt's statement, "War is the existential negation of the enemy," we can see how the voluntary repatriation policy was, in fact, creating a different discursive violence—by focusing on the individual, the US essentially "negated" the claims to sovereignty made by North Korea.[62] But the discursive violence was not directly committed by the United States, but rather by the POW individual him/herself.

On August 16, 1952, Mark Clark, the commander of the United Nation Command, sent a memo to the head of the Korean Communications Zone (KCOMZ), which was the military branch in charge of the

POW Command. The top figure of the US Army was concerned about the situation on Koje:

> A review of reference messages as well as previous reports from your headquarters show continued incidents, ranging from what appear to be minor incidents to mass demonstrations and open defiance of the camp authority, many of which have resulted in deaths, serious injuries, and intolerable affronts to camp authority.... I assume you are familiar with my previous directives to seize and maintain un-contested control of all POW installations....
>
> 2. If proper control is being exercised it is incomprehensible to me how prisoners could have in their possession Red Flags for demonstrations, or how they could seize a member from the security forces and force him to eat a POW ration. The continued complete dependence on use of Tear Gas from compound perimeters for putting down demonstrations is also a manifestation of weak control. This can never be substitute for immediate intervention within the compounds by an adequate group of guard personnel authorized to use such forceful means as necessary.
>
> 3. I do not intend to tolerate the conditions which have resulted in the disorders in UNC POW Camps and which have proved embarrassing and harmful to our position in the Eyes of the Free World. The adverse effect on the Armistice negotiations at Panmunjom is obvious.[63]

The "Eyes of the Free World" were now on the infamous Koje camp. But what exactly did the Koje camp need to demonstrate for the "Eyes of the Free World"? Clark's memo revealed much more about the shifting tactics of the POWs than about how "uncontested control" was to be achieved. The POWs continued to insist on waving signs of their sovereign state, and the forcing of a US soldier to eat a POW ration seemed to be a demonstration of tactics of humiliation. In the face of Boatner's shift in the use of "overwhelming force," the POWs in turn seem to have understood the stakes involved in maintaining a situation of conflict with the US military on the island.

The Aftermath of the Dodd Incident

On May 13, 1952, *New York Times* journalist Murray Schumach gave a narrative on what had happened behind the barbed-wire fence at Compound 76—Brigadier General Dodd had finally given a statement at a press conference in Korea: "General Dodd nervously read to correspondents an account of his experiences in the compound with 6,000 Communists. In a deep voice that quavered a few times, the burly, gray-haired general started with the Communist ruse that brought him to the gates of the compound." In this long article, Schumach quoted directly from Dodd in describing his treatment by the POWs—"During my entire stay in the compound," Schumach quoted Dodd as saying, "I was treated with the utmost respect and courtesy, and my personal needs were looked out for. The demands made by the P.O.W.'s are inconsequential, and the concessions granted by the camp authorities were of minor importance."[64]

Dodd was attempting to minimize the significance of the kidnapping —and, most importantly—the consequences of his signature on multiple documents the POWs had presented to him. And the US military, both in terms of military investigation and military force, had begun to work toward resolving the problem of the kidnapping event. But the attention had already been garnered. In his "Confidential Report Concerning the Real Crisis in the Relationship between the Detaining Power and the Prisoner of War in South Korea" dated May 27, 1952, ICRC delegate Georg Hoffmann stated, "The capture of an American general by the prisoners of war of Koje-do created a sensation throughout the world and suddenly brought mass attention to the precarious situation in Kojedo."[65] Hoffmann then provided the following analysis of the reasons behind the turmoil and conflict on the island of Koje:

The Korean war, although an object of international politics, is also a civil war, and nonetheless a civil war where the conflicting adversarial ideologies do not strictly lie within specific region, such as, for example, the "war of Sonderbund" or the "war of succession" in

America. In the past, the larger centers of communism were in southern Korea, where much more of the population as a whole resided than in the northern half of the country.[66]

The kidnapping of Dodd had sparked a discussion on the international stage about the meaning and character of the Korean War.

But back on the Korean peninsula, the Korean newspapers were reporting the event to their Korean readership. On May 16, 1952, *Dong-A Ilbo* ran an editorial titled, "The Meaning of the Dodd Incident."[67] The editorial began with none of the disbelief, surprise, and outrage expressed in the US media outlets. "The implications of the event are various," the editorial began. "And if one examines the possible objectives of the kidnapping of the camp commander by the prisoners of war, it is not difficult to discern the myriad significance and meanings of the event." Rather than using "bizarre" or "fantastic" to describe the event, the editors of *Dong-A Ilbo* used the word "performance." The kidnapping had been a performance, very similar to the performances enacted by the North Korean negotiators at Panmunjom, according to the editors. In positioning "democracy" and "communism" as antithetical to each other, the editors moved to a vocabulary of "performance," of empty gestures, to delegitimate the political claims of the Korean Communist prisoners of war, and to strengthen anti-Communism as the concrete stronghold for democracy. As Harry Truman stepped down and Dwight Eisenhower became the president of the United States, the Korean anti-Communist POWs made their own appeals for political visibility to the US government.

5

Below the 38th Parallel

BETWEEN BARBED WIRE AND BLOOD

AT THE STROKE OF MIDNIGHT on June 18, 1953, near the city of Pusan, Lieutenant Colonel Sung Yong-Chang and his task force of Korean military police (MP) began "to cut the barbed-wire fences" of United Nations Camp Number 9. They were under instructions to cut a "space of four square meters" at each corner of the camp. Six other Korean MPs quickly surrounded and disarmed two American guards and had to place another American guard "inside the water tank to prevent him from making screams." At fifteen minutes past midnight, Sung declared the following to the prisoners who had already received instructions earlier in the day about the mass escape:

> I have been ordered by the Commanding General of the Joint Provost Marshal Command to occupy this POW camp temporarily and release all of you anti-Communist prisoners![1]

At UNC Camp 6 near Nonsan, two hours later at 2:00 A.M., "all the outdoor lights went out." A light drizzle was falling. The Korean POWs from two of the three compounds escaped through the breaks made in the barbed-wire fences by the ROKA troops. In the morning, the US colonel who was the camp commander ordered a thorough search, but there was "no trace of the fugitives." As Brigadier General Song Hyo-Soon of the Republic of Korea Army mused in his memoir, "The

American soldiers who took part in the search said to one another in disbelief: 'They must have wings!'"[2]

By daybreak, over 25,000 prisoners of war had escaped from United Nations Command POW camps located on the mainland Korean peninsula. President Syngman Rhee issued a public statement that morning: "According to the Geneva Convention and also to the principles of human rights," began Rhee, "the anti-communist Korean war prisoners should have been released long before this." Noting that the pending armistice being negotiated at Panmunjom would "lead to a serious consequence," Rhee announced that he had ordered on his "own responsibility the release of the anti-communist Korean prisoners on this day, June 18th, 1953." In one sentence, Rhee refused to explain himself: "The reason I did this without full consultation with the United Nations Command and other authorities concerned is too obvious to explain."[3]

When the National Security Council met that very same day, President Dwight Eisenhower had to delay the meeting for forty-five minutes as he drafted a message to Rhee. All other items on that day's agenda were deferred, so the focus could be on the POW crisis at hand. When the NSC meeting commenced, Eisenhower "invited any suggestions from the members of the Council as to how to handle this terrible situation."[4] The possibility of an armistice now seemed to be in jeopardy. The POW break posed an existential problem: On the Cold War geopolitical chessboard, Korea was a pawn between the two archenemies of the Soviet Union and the United States; yet, on the Korean War battlefield of psychological warfare, the prisoner of war was the pawn. Thus, when Rhee removed approximately 25,000 anti-Communist Korean POWs from the equation, it created an uproar for the US government, who maintained that Rhee did not comprehend the rules or the stakes of the game at hand. But what was the game?

The members of the NSC were concerned that the Communists would see this incident as evidence that the United States "could not even control the ROK": "Rhee had broken his word, and the President pointed out that our national self-respect was involved in what had happened." Regarding allies of the United States involved on the Korean peninsula, the minutes of the NSC meeting recorded that Harold Stassen "suggested that we tell the British that our Rhee is like their Mossadegh—they would certainly understand that." The members agreed that Eisenhower needed to tell Rhee "bluntly . . . that if he would not agree to behave himself in the future we had no alternative but to make other arrangements in Korea."[5]

As Stassen's use of "our Rhee" indicated, the Syngman Rhee–led Republic of Korea was understood to be a project of the United States. Sovereignty was delineated along an axis that clearly aligned the US-ROK relationship along the fraught precedent of European imperial powers and "their" territories. Between the United States and the Republic of Korea, sovereignty became a strange disappearing act. The very structure of command ensured this. The Republic of Korea Army was under the command of the United Nations, which was headed by the United States military. As a result, the United Nations Command represented the Republic of Korea at the Panmunjom armistice meetings. Rhee was not even a recognized player in the chess game.

The NSC was busy with crisis management over the image of the United States as the result of Rhee's deliberate move to act in seeming defiance of US instructions. And indeed, if the very head of state the United States had put into power on the southern half of the Korean peninsula was challenging the legitimacy of US authority over the conduct of warfare, then the claim that the United States was acting on behalf of the best interests of the Korean people was certainly undermined. Between Rhee's assertion of his own national reach as the legitimate sovereign and the NSC's concern over this very public affront to US ambitions for global hegemony, the drama of political figures on the international political stage certainly could affect the negotiations at Panmunjom.

While international attention fixated on the machinations of these politicians, another plan was unfolding smoothly on the ground once the POWs left behind the barbed wire fences of the UNC-controlled camps. Korean policemen were ready with clothes and identity cards for the released POWs. And although these POWs were essentially refugees once outside of the barbed-wire fence, they were quickly drafted into the Republic of Korea Army. From POW to refugee to soldier—the passage was swift and almost seamless.

These Korean POWs did not simply vanish into thin air. The barbed-wire fences did not demarcate an entire separation between society outside and inside the camps; indeed, the orchestration of the simultaneous mass release across the different anti-Communist POW camps on the peninsula required careful collaboration between the ROKA and anti-Communist POW youth groups within the camps. An important component to the mass release of 25,000 Korean anti-Communist POWs was an established youth group called the Anti-Communist Youth League (ACYL), organized by POWs in each compound of these camps. When the US military authorities questioned a POW named Kim Hak Joon at UNC Camp 7 located in Masan about the mass breakout, Kim stated, "To tell the truth, there was no plan to escape in PW organization before. All the compounds were instructed to escape at 0200 hours, 18th by Headquarters, ACYL in Compound 'A' Enclosure #2 at 2130, 17th June." What became clear in these instructions is that the Republic of Korea Army and the ACYL worked closely together, and that the ROKA had passed on instructions to the ACYL leaders in order to organize the breakout.[6]

The POW camps, when viewed through the lens of the Korean youth groups, were a new iteration of an infrastructure of violence and surveillance established on the ground during the US occupation period. The story of the anti-Communist Korean prisoners of war—and the kinds of interrogation sites they created within the POW camps—was a story about state-building, one that was fundamentally also intertwined with the larger mechanisms of US military intervention. The rightist youth groups were critical and integral to both the operations of the US military Counterintelligence Corps (CIC) and the establishment of the Republic of Korea Army from 1945 through 1950. Youth groups on the southern half of the Korean peninsula were a key feature of the postliberation political landscape. Members were young men roughly between the ages of eighteen and thirty-five.

"An age of youth groups came to Korea," wrote US official Gregory Henderson about the occupation in a later analysis of Korean politics, titled *Korea: The Politics of the Vortex.*[7] The first youth groups established in the wake of August 1945 were leftist and had formed the grounds for the Peace Preservation Corps. In Seoul, approximately two thousand youths had joined groups, and over one hundred forty groups were working across the southern peninsula.[8] Soon, practically every political party organized a "youth auxiliary," and youth organized in urban and rural areas, working at times intimately with the police or helping farmers with agricultural labor. The US military government became an embedded player in this landscape as it soon issued ordinances that rendered leftist organizations such as youth groups illegal, while the US military governor John Hodge helped fund and support the creation of the rightist Korean National Youth Association (KNYA) in October 1946. Henderson noted how the USAMGIK "set about secretly to form a national youth association backed by some five million dollars in official funds, American Army equipment, and an American lieutenant colonel as training advisor."[9] Yi Pŏmsŏk, a fervent follower of Generalissimo Chiang Kai-shek, became the head of the KNY, and he instituted the framework he had learned from his time as a guerilla fighter, student of military affairs in Germany, and a company commander in the Kuomintang (KMT) Military Academy in Hangchou, modeling the KNY in the fashion of the "Blue Shirts," a paramilitary youth group with whom he had worked closely, and the fascist youth groups he had admired in Germany and Italy. With his slogan of "nation first, state first" ("*minjok chisang, kukka chisang*"), Yi was soon the head of one of the most powerful organizations in South Korea. The phenomenon of rightist youth groups in Korea was certainly a part of a global pedagogy of state discipline, national aesthetic, and militarization of the everyday.[10] And it was this kind of anti-Communist fascist mass organization that emerged as one of the most important elements of a claim over the monopoly of violence in post-1945 Korea, alongside the Korea Constabulary and the later establishment of the Republic of Korea Army.

Youth groups proliferated within the POW camps of the Korean War, most notably the rightist Anti-Communist Youth League (ACYL). And the POWs within the camps had not created these youth groups in a vacuum—the Republic of Korea Army was literally also within the barbed-wire fences, since those who had been part of the ROKA, then taken prisoner by the Chinese or North Korean troops, and then finally taken in as prisoner by the US-led UNC were a part of the POW population. Another sociopolitical dynamic from the pre-1950 period also informed the consolidation and participation in these anti-Communist youth groups—anti-Communist refugees from north of the 38th parallel, who were arguing that they were wrongly being held as prisoners of war when they wanted to fight as soldiers with the ROKA and the US military.

Scholars have tracked the relationships between the founding of anti-Communist youth groups, the establishment of the Korean Constabulary, and the start of the Republic of Korea Army during the prewar years. But a vital relationship has remained embedded in the background, and it is a relationship that emerges when we read the labor and politics of these anti-Communist youth groups backward from the POW camps of the Korean War through the extensive violence and surveillance practiced during the occupation period. One particular youth group stood out in Henderson's retrospective account: "Seoul's tough Northwest Youth Association of P'yŏngan-do refugees was used to quell rebellion in Cheju-do, becoming notorious there for its cruel use of bamboo staves."[11] It was this exact youth group that became central to the operations of the US military intelligence network created by the Counterintelligence Corps. The youth groups were a critical hinge between the state that formed during the early Rhee regime and the covert intelligence network that was essential to the US military and political operations on the peninsula. Installed within the UNC POW camp network during the Korean War was a US military intelligence group that had been highly influential and powerful during the occupation period: the Counterintelligence Corps (CIC). In 1952, at the same time that the anti-Communist POW camps were being created on the Korean peninsular mainland, the US military decided to assign the CIC to POW camps in order to support the "detection of treason, sedition, subversive activity, and disaffection, and the detection and prevention of enemy espionage and sabotage." It was the CIC agent who interrogated the POW on his or her arrival in order to "make an initial segregation." The information they needed to determine regarding each POW included the POW's "political adherence, and desire to be repatriated or not."[12]

From its inception in the southern half of Korea, the US Counterintelligence Corps had to rely on Korean agents for "information" "because of the language barrier, and the customs of the Korean people, and the physical difference between the Oriental and the Caucasian."[13] The professionalization of the Counterintelligence Corps was directly linked to the CIC's increasing dependence on Korean labor and networks. For the very public CIC, comprised of primarily white male agents, creating a viable network of surveillance would require Koreans. And the members of the North West Young Men's Association were the pivotal fulcrum which made this work possible.

The undeniable continuity of such an infrastructure of labor, surveillance, and militarism has been systematically obscured from historical memory because of the US continuous disavowal of its support of violence in order to maintain the image of a successful "anti-Communist" project in the East Asian region. As this chapter will make clear, the United States military and government used these youth groups, and the violence was not merely an inconvenience, but indeed integral to the US project of occupation and subsequent war. At the heart of this project then is a core mechanism of the US military and government: the simultaneous exploitation of violence, while also employing ideas about the "Oriental" race to disavow the US role in manufacturing such an infrastructure across the peninsula. Certain kinds of violence, the US contended, was not only necessary but also actually the only form of state discipline the Korean could understand. From CIC interrogators' discussions about what a Korean could understand about truth to the NSC's discussion about how to properly domesticate Rhee— these racialized understandings and formulations about rational thinking and truth telling undergirded the US project of a permanent state of exception across the peninsula.

The other side of the racial coin of US militarized logic was the racial element of South Korean anti-Communist fascism. What did an anti-Communist politics look like, and what kind of subject did it demand?

The archive of the relationship between Korean youth groups and the US Counterintelligence Corps spans the occupation years and the Korean War. The practices of interrogation spanned tattooing, list-making, essay-writing, and the blood petition. But more importantly, tracing the development of these interrogation practices also is tracking the development of an intimate structural relationship between the Korean youth groups and US counterintelligence. And, remarkably, it was a tenuous—but highly flexible—discourse on race that enabled a fraught, but productive, relationship between the interests of the US counterintelligence community and the labor of the postcolonial Korean youth, with the former heavily invested in maintaining the symbolic and material economy of the latter.

The Restructuring of Empire

Twenty-six-year-old Gregory Henderson arrived in Seoul in mid-July in 1948 to serve as vice consul for the United States. He arrived right before the UN-sponsored presidential elections were held on July 20. In his later recollections, he wrote, "Pre-war Seoul combined incomparable intimacy and excitement, almost like some early love affair with someone at dusk whose nature one could only guess through the touch enchanted." Noting that "[lines] between civilians and military were not drawn as they are today," he considered members of the Korean Constabulary or Services as his "playfellows." After all, he wrote, "We were the same age and were graduates of the same war; the fact that we happened to have been on different sides made little difference even though that day's Korean officers were inwardly proud that they had been good Japanese officers and that hardly one of all those who had served Japan had ever been unfaithful to her."[14] Henderson had served in the Marine Corps as a Japanese-language interpreter in World War II, and he met his "first Koreans" who were the "forced labor" for the Japanese troops in a naval base located in the city of Calapan in the Philippines.[15] Henderson's sense of intimacy in prewar Seoul was not simply one of scale—he described Seoul as a "village of a little under a million souls where you soon knew almost every player"—but one where military experience in World War II's total warfare, whether American or Japanese, was the common ground for relating.

The prewar Seoul that Henderson sketched out in his recollections was one where two critical projects were happening simultaneously. The first was the reconfiguration of the American total warfare system, created and mobilized during World War II, into a system consisting of military bases and occupation, as well as free market opportunities. On the Korean peninsula, this American structural reinvention went hand in hand with the postcolonial reconfiguration of the Japanese imperial military and the consequent vast transnational apparatus that had been in place to support it; this included factory laborers, military volunteers or conscripts, policemen, and Korean "comfort women" throughout the empire. The post-1945 demobilization of the Japanese Imperial Army was a strategic remobilizing of the conscription of young men into militarized service.

Park Ki Byung, who had been a student in Japan and later became a soldier in the Kwantung Army in Manchuria, remembered the period after liberation as being one with a "shortage of food," with "so many people evacuating from the north, and so many Korean soldiers." Twenty-eight years old in 1945, Park vividly remembered the repatriation of both the Korean men demobilized from the Japanese Imperial Army and the mining laborers and other civilians who had been forced to go or taken to Japan. And perhaps very significantly, Park remembered that it was around November 5, when the US Army ordered that "any former officers, regardless of their background—Japanese Army, Manchurian, or Chinese—were to register so they could form the Korean Army."[16] Korean veterans from the Soviet Army arrived. Three thousand Korean members of the Korean Restoration Army, who had been working under Chiang Kai-shek's Kuomintang, came to the peninsula. These Korean fighters had already been "trained by a detachment of the American military mission to the Nationalist army," or had been involved with the US Office of Strategic Services (OSS) missions during World War II.[17]

Another "transnational circuit" of the US military empire crossed over the Korean peninsula via the arrival of Lieutenant Colonel Russell D.

Barros in September 1945. Having worked as an officer with Filipino guerrillas in Luzon during 1944, Barros was soon given the task to set up an "indigenous security force." Scholar Simeon Man has noted that the Korean National Constabulary, established in January 1946 by Lieutenant General John Reed Hodge, was "similar to the one formed at the start of the US colonial rule of the Philippines," an entity formed to ensure "internal security."[18] Hodge soon put Barros in charge of the Korean Constabulary, and a twenty-seven-year-old captain of infantry named James H. Hausman became the adviser. Considered the historical "father of the modern Korean army," the young Hausman took on the project of creating the Constabulary, which served as the basis on which to develop the Republic of Korea Army. Notably, in the first round of officer recruitment, almost all had been veterans of the Japanese army, many of whom were graduates of either the Imperial Japanese Military Academy in Tokyo or the Manchukuo army's military academy. And according to military historian Allan Millett, this recruitment practice extended in 1947 to "another source of new officers: the growing flood of refugees from the Soviet occupied zone," who were again "veterans of Japanese service and 'class enemies' of the North Korean Communists; they tended to be Christians, educated, and middle-class."[19] The Constabulary was a group of elite military officers who were staunchly anti-Communist.

But according to Hausman himself, the Constabulary did not hold the monopoly on power over "internal security." Certainly, the Constabulary was in tension with the Korean National Police, but it was also part of the larger anti-Communist network in the southern half of the Korean peninsula. The youth groups were undeniably important. "In the early days of U.S. military government, along with the usual departments of government, we formed a Department of National Youth. It was established even before the Department of National Defense.... It was budgeted and had control of all the youth groups," said Hausman. As the head of the Department of National Youth, Yi Pŏmsŏk was " a very powerful man, potentially, at least."[20] A structural readjustment of the Japanese empire's "total war" expansionist military into a US-hegemonic anti-Communist national security state turned on the sheer labor of the youth of Korea. The youth of Korea—young men coming of age or demobilized from the Japanese imperial warfare apparatus—were the target population for the ambitions of both the US military government and the competing Korean political parties on the peninsula.

Sociologist Dong-choon Kim notes that as the popular People's Republic and the Peace Committees established extensive local youth groups in preparation for and after liberation in August 1945, "some Koreans who had collaborated" with the Japanese colonial state such as "bureaucrats, policemen, military officers, businessmen and intellectuals ... looked for political groups by which they could be saved from possible imprisonment or punishment." Formed in conjunction with the arrival of US military occupation forces on the peninsula, the Korean Democratic Party (Hanguk Minju-Dang) emerged as the conservative party with its own explicit proclamation to remove the People's Republic and the Preparation Committees. As members of the professional class and college graduates (with 47 percent having studied in Japan and 27 percent having studied in the United States), the KDP became the party to whom Japanese businessmen and landlords turned to protect their business and property interests.[21] In his analysis of anti-Communism in South Korea, Kim contextualizes this postwar elite within a longer trajectory of anti-Communism on the peninsula, originating in the 1920s under Japanese colonial rule. In front of the Korean working class with the growth of Communism on the peninsula after the 1917 Russian Revolution, the Christian middle class and the landed Korean elite were in line with the anti-Communism of the Japanese imperial power, which was also invested in "safeguarding the principles of private property."[22] In the immediate postliberation moment, creating rightist youth groups became one way for these elites to challenge the network and local authority of the People's Republic, and to counter the demands on the ground of Koreans for the redistribution of land and the change of people in positions ranging from local police to the larger national bureaucracies. The KDP had support from the US Army in this endeavor. In a report to the Department of State in June 1947, the headquarters of the US Army Forces in Korea singled out the "youth of Korea" as being "the largest and most promising population group among which real democratic ideals can be developed." The authors of the report noted a "new organization known as 'Korean National Youth,' open to membership by men of 18 to 30 has been formed under the leadership of a prominent Korean general," and that the US "Military Government has provided this organization with finances, supplies, and an American adviser."[23]

In Gregory Henderson's Seoul of 1948, other political "lines" besides those of "American" and "Korean" also had not yet hardened. "One was not quite so abruptly communist or anti-communist then," he commented. "There was middle ground. All of the officers personally knew those who had either chosen the other side or leaned in some way toward it. Nor had they always disliked them." In an attempt to provide his American audience some analogy to the situation, he described the "Southern way of life" as being "a little more on the collaborating side while the North was steelier, more Spartan, more hardbitten, more ideological and less yielding and opportunistic."[24] North and South were less binary and more dimensional in Henderson's portrayal of his circles in 1948 Seoul. This kind of flexible mapping of the political onto Koreans did not deny familiarity, history, or agency. But this kind of intimate cartography was also in tension with and embedded in a setting that was being organized via mass violence. And Korean rightist youth groups, who operated as paramilitary extensions of the state by 1948, were essential to creating the contours and fault lines on this terrain.

The Long Arc of the CIC, the NWYMA, and Anti-Communism

The US Counterintelligence Corps was the organization that determined the lines between "Communist" and "anti-Communist" for the US military from the occupation period through the Korean War. During the occupation, the CIC garnered a great deal of power by providing lists of Korean "Communists" and a narrative of what it called the "war of espionage" on the US-occupied south of the peninsula.

General Hodge relied on the claims the CIC made on knowing which Koreans were unreliable Communists. "Nothing in the three years of the Occupation so shook Americans at all levels as the autumn uprisings of 1946," scholar Bruce Cumings has commented. And indeed, at the Joint Korean-American Conference called by General John Hodge and Major General A. E. Brown to allow "Koreans [to] present to the US authorities for discussion and consideration the major problems confronting the Korean people," a major agenda item was "The Causes and Background of the October Riots and the Anti-Police Feeling." The CIC was asked help prepare a report for G-2 Colonel John N. Robinson, who would then present it at the conference. In essence, the CIC had been given the assignment and responsibility for gleaning a narrative significance—a discernible pattern—and thus an explanation for the autumn uprisings. The title of the report succinctly conveyed the CIC's conclusions about the uprisings: "Case Against the Communist Party, Disrupting the Peace of South Korea." "Based upon investigation of the riot and disturbances incidents as they occurred, it was evident that the riots were not spontaneous reaction of the people, but were planned political moves led and agitated by political leaders and henchmen.... [I]t was necessary to show that the Communist Party, itself, through a long series of mis-education, propaganda, and false incidents, had fomented and guided the physical violence against police and civil elements of South Korea."[25]

Members of the Korean Communist Party had indeed been organizers and leaders of certain parts of the uprising, but local people's committees and labor and peasant unions provided the majority of the leadership. The "Communist enemy," as painted by the CIC, was a puppet of the Soviets, smaller Communist cells who received instruction from either Pyongyang or Moscow.[26] Cumings, in his analysis of the Autumn Harvest uprisings, notes that the uprisings themselves did not occur simultaneously but rather in waves as "one rebellion touched off another in contiguous areas." "The evidence suggests," Cumings writes, "that South Chŏlla peasants rose up not because of Communist agitation, but because of deep grievances arising from land conditions and relations, grain collection inequities, and the local interlocking of landlord, government official, and policeman."[27] The project of making the "Communist enemy" was a denial of indigenous claims and grievances and the possibility of a local form and application of Communism. And it was not simply a project of finding and making the "Communist enemy"—it was also a project of knowledge claims. The CIC, in this 1946 report, had asserted its abilities to discern, understand, and narrate the political landscape of US occupied Korea. In other words, the CIC "knew" the Korean better than the Korean herself.

Developing this "knowledge" was highly mediated. The CIC gathered and read both people and paper—interrogation and the constant translation of handbills, posters, and leaflets were at the center of the CIC operation. However, one needs to go one step further in examining the CIC and ask the question of how the CIC found people and paper to analyze. The North West Young Men's Association, an organization comprised of young men who had crossed over the 38th parallel to the south, became the critical element in the daily operations of the CIC. These young men, among whom many came from the landed class in North Korea, created one of the most extreme rightist youth groups in Korea.

Two elements that would facilitate the operations and activities of only eighty-nine agents in twenty-one field offices to cover the entire southern half of the Korean peninsula were in short supply: interpreters and paper. Native Korean interpreters were "motivated by strictly mercenary impulses and could not be trusted to any great extent," while second-generation Korean and Japanese Americans numbered at most at twelve. Paper also was in short supply—"Paper, an essential for any intelligence agency was particularly scarce. The USAFIK supply people did not seem to understand why a CIC District Office needed more paper than the orderly room of an infantry company."[28]

But the Korean population was wary of the CIC, reluctant to talk freely with them:

> Many Koreans believe the CIC is the American counterpart of the Japanese Kempei Tai, and, as a result of this misunderstanding, CIC agents find it advantageous to represent themselves as G-2 person-

nel, Office of Public Information personnel, members of the Political Advisory Group (PAG), or as novices who have developed a curiosity of and an interest in Korean politics.[29]

The Counterintelligence Corps found itself with a more immediate difficulty in carrying out operations—establishing its own legitimacy. And even though we may usually imagine CIC agents as working discreetly undercover, the annals of the CIC attest otherwise—"since CIC was outfitting its men in a uniform worn by no other organization, agents were open to compromise on all occasions."[30] And, "the distinctive uniform of CIC agents in Korea was only one factor contributing to the unsought notice given to CIC operations in Korea."[31] As mentioned earlier, the CIC was actually a very public operation, and not the clandestine operation one would assume of a Counterintelligence Corps. In the first place, the CIC's objectives and mission resonated with the Korean population—but not in the way that CIC had hoped.[32]

As a result, the CIC had to rely on Korean agents for their "information." The "total authorized strength" of the CIC was 126 agents, but in September 1946, the number of agents only came to eighty-nine.[33] But a combination of eighty-nine CIC American agents with a minimum of 180 Korean informants would not necessarily provide the type of coverage that the CIC wanted to claim. The CIC also developed a network that depended on paid agents of various sorts, youth organizations, and the interrogation of refugees who were picked up by this section when they entered South Korea.[34] Over 1946 and 1947, the element that became central to the CIC operations was the "Use of Youth organizations." The CIC weekly report for June 19, 1947, noted that rightist organizations had set up their own "networks of agents and their own intelligence section for the purpose of working against Communism," and the "most valuable of these organizations was one made up of individuals who, themselves, had fled from the Communist Police State, North Korea"—the North West Young Men's Association (NWYMA).[35] In his memoir on his activities as a CIC official in Korea, Donald Nichols commented that he recruited primarily from "refugees and deserters from the N.K. military and civilian populace."[36]

The NWYMA, according to the CIC, had "complete coverage of each district" in the city of Seoul and had men stationed in each section: "they know almost all of the people in their areas; they know when new persons move in or others move out, and they know the reasons for this moving. They become acquainted with the activities of almost every individual in their area and are able to report on anything suspicious."[37] The surveillance system set up by the NWYMA became crucial to the CIC's claims to knowing what was happening on the ground. The NWYMA—as well as the other rightist youth groups the CIC used—enabled the CIC to maintain and develop an exceptional reach. In this way, the CIC carved out its own niche within the military government apparatus through its claims on superior knowledge of on-the-ground Korean political activities.

Soon, however, a revealing tension developed between the CIC and the NWYMA over the use of violence in a state of emergency, or, what theorists call the realm of exceptional sovereignty. The tension was not over the escalating violence increasingly employed by the NWYMA all over the southern peninsula; rather, the tension was created around the question of jurisdiction over police actions on the ground. By 1946 the CIC "had all the prerogatives of a police agency, including search and arrest."[38] As its history notes, these "police prerogatives and functions … endowed [the CIC] with power never intended for a confidential investigative organization." In fact, in retrospect, former CIC agents "described the 971st as a rough and ready outfit that probably interpreted this unusual power too liberally, and have stated that, especially early in the occupation, operations were too 'high, wide, and handsome."[39] Or as William J. Tigue, another CIC agent in Korea during the occupation, noted, "For the early months of the occupation, CIC was God In Korea as far as the police and the general populace were concerned."[40]

However, within less than a year, by the end of 1947, the CIC had a problem on their hands. The NWYMA was refusing to be merely an instrument of procuring, gathering, and purveying "information." In fact, it turns out that the NWYMA was purveying violence in greatly escalating volume. In the CIC report titled "Statistical Analysis of Terrorism, 1947," the tally of the different acts of terrorism reported was as follows:

Rightists instigated—223
Leftist—74
Neutral—5
Unknown—203
Total: 505
Killed—90
Injured—1100[41]

In this report, the NWYMA emerged as one of the rightist organizations most involved in the violence—construed as "terrorism"—noted across the southern half of the peninsula. "Numerous reports of the Terroristic activities of the North West Association have reached this office during the past weeks," stated the CIC report dated April 23, 1947.[42] "Numerous reports on terrorism were received from almost every office. In Taegu, Taejon and Ongjin the North West Youth Association seemed particularly on the rampage," a report from May 22, 1947, stated.[43] By August 28, 1947, the CIC report revealed an escalation in the situation in the area of Kangnun, where the NWYMA's "acts of terrorism [were] innumerable" in their "fight for control and complete extinction of the leftists. The rightists [were] believed to be capable of much more trouble in this area than the leftists, and in some instances they may even resist American personnel."[44]

What becomes apparent through these detailed accounts of the NWYMA is that its violence did not pose a problem to the CIC; rather, what the CIC found troubling were the moments when the NWYMA usurped the police actions of the CIC and refused to be only a conduit of information. "Lectured on his responsibility for the activities" of the NWYMA in the area encompassing Taegu, Taejon, and Ongjin, by CIC agents, one NWYMA leader "pleaded that his group were mostly boys and really not bad boys at that."[45] Lecturing, reprimanding, and warning were the extent of the CIC's commentary on the NWYMA's activities and violence, commentary prompted only when the violence suggested the organization's assumption of certain sovereign, surveillance powers. For example, the CIC had been preparing a raid to "apprehend three visitors from North Korea only to find that the North West Association had beat CIC to the punch and had abducted these men." The CIC prepared a meeting with the leader to make NWYMA "understand that they have no powers along this line."[46]

The transgression lay, then, not in the acts of violence, but rather in excessive claims to authority by Koreans: the kidnappings, the threats, the wielding of death. While these transgressions merited the label "terrorism" by the CIC report writers, villagers—and even policemen—began to take matters into their own hands. Under constant harsh criticism from leftists for essentially facilitating rightist violence/terrorism, the Korean police, according to May 1947 CIC reports, began implementing a different policy toward youth groups. Arrests were made and troublesome members relocated. In one town, the "NWYA [sic] were ordered out of town by the Police and in another many members of the NWYA were placed aboard a train and shipped from the province; place the burden on someone else—you know."[47] In late August, reports from Pohong indicated that leftists had sent a petition to "General Hodge asking for the abolishment of the Northwest Young Men's Association and other terrorist youth groups."[48] This request was never acted on; only once in 1947 was a rightist youth group dissolved by order of the US military government, and it was not the NWYMA. With the CIC and the US military government condoning the violence, Korean villagers began to undertake measures for their own security. In Taejon, after "approximately 29 members of the Northwest Youth Assn, some of whom were armed, had attacked a small village in their area the villagers gathered together and drove the youths away." The youths took shelter in a police box in the village, and the villagers surrounded the police station. As the NWYMA members began throwing stones, the villagers threw some stones also; soon the "police fired into the crowd—killing three villagers."[49]

The NWYMA, the CIC observed, had "increased faster and become of more significance than any other rightist youth group" by early 1947.[50] In a report dated September 11, 1947, the CIC noted another trend concerning the NWYMA: "Terrorism by the right wing, for the most part,

continue [*sic*] merrily on its way. An apparent all out attempt to eradicate the leftists is under way." Observing that the police in these situations "were either afraid to act against this society or were in complete
accord with their actions," the CIC confirmed that the NWYMA's activities were often condoned or supported by the police.[51]

Physical violence was deemed a necessary tool in interrogation. Donald Nichols, who became the commander of the "K" Subdetachment
in the 607th CIC, felt that by 1948 he "had become an expert interrogator with a real feel for asking the right questions at the right time." But,
he wrote in his memoir, "on many occasions, I had to accept the methods used during interrogation by our Allies.... I had to maintain an air
of detachment—even approval."[52] "As an example," he wrote, "many
times I have seen a person tied prone on his back on a table or bench,
arms and legs tied down, the victim's head arched in such a position
that his chin jutted upward, his face covered with a soaking wet wash
cloth." With each breath, the victim would take water into his lungs.
"Results: slow drowning and much pain. The victim told the interrogator anything he wanted to hear—false, or otherwise."[53] There was one
particular situation that Nichols wrote he would "never be able to
erase" from his memory. Members of the ROKA had tied a man up to a
"wooden cross, his arms outstretched." They wrapped a "thin copper
wire" around one finger of each hand and connected the wire to a "hand
cranked field telephone." Once the "sergeant began cranking," Nichols
recalled, "the victim began to scream the answers we were seeking."[54]

The "terrorism" of the NWYMA was neither an aberration nor even
a contained strategy. The NWYMA was an integral part of the func-
tioning of the CIC and the fundamental basis for its legitimacy. The
CIC's operations and presence were visible and public, well known to
those on the ground, and thus the NWYMA's integrated partnership
with the CIC was also public. Indeed, the members of the NWYMA
exploited their authority derived from operating as extensions of the
CIC in their own activities. This relationship formed between the CIC
and the NWYMA was emblematic of the politics sanctioned, envisioned,
and enforced by the US military government. For James Hausman, this
kind of governance through force was the point, not an accident:

We had no illusions about forming a true democracy. Benevolent dictatorship would do for starters. We hoped this would eventually progress into some form of democracy. Communism was outlawed. The police relentlessly sought out the communists.[55]

And in 1948, the fist of this "benevolent dictatorship" would be formed as the following organizations came to work closely together, when "all intelligence agencies, Korean and American, shifted their focus to combating the Communists."[56] Hausman's Korean Constabulary, the USAFIK G-2, the US 971st CIC Detachment, the Korean National Police, and the NWYMA were among the "disciplining" forces sent to Cheju-do, setting off what scholar Su-kyoung Hwang calls "one of the most violent events in twentieth-century Korean history."[57]

On April 3, 1948, 350 socialist Koreans began an uprising on Cheju Island, and their actions touched off a general insurrection against the police and the repressive policies and measures established under the US military government. Branding those involved in the uprising as "Communists," the US military government and Syngman Rhee deployed massive force onto the island's population. The narrative the CIC offered in 1946 was mobilized again as the official narratives of the uprising characterized the local rebels as "Communists" involved in a war of espionage. However, even the US military reports themselves complicated this story, and one report noted that the majority of people who were involved in the South Korean Labor Party (SKLP) did not have "any real understanding of, or desire to join the Communistic movement." For the most part, they were "ignorant, uneducated farmers and fishermen whose livelihood had been profoundly disturbed by the war and the post-war difficulties," and the report concluded that the SKLP must have "offered them increased economic security."[58] But the escalation of violence was stunning. Chalmers Johnson notes that the "Northwest Youth League" was "by far the most ruthless of Rhee's agents," "a paramilitary vigilante organization ... whom the U.S. Army tolerated with full knowledge of their reputation for brutality."[59] With the police, the Constabulary, and multiple rightist youth groups engaged in a "purge" operation on the island, what began as a revolt of three hundred rebels transformed into the state-sanctioned massacre and killing of "thirty to eighty thousand islanders."[60]

Accounts and histories of the Cheju-do uprising almost always note the brutality of the NWYMA's violent tactics. But it is also important to note how these rightist youth groups were not simply vehicles for "rabidly anti-Communist" members, but also political organizations through which members could gain power. For example, one of the rightist organizations called the Korea Democratic Young Men's Association (KDYA) was led by a young man named Kim Du-hwan, who later "readily" admitted to the murder of two leftists and the torture of other leftists of the SKLP. Kim eventually became Rhee's personal bodyguard and a member of the National Assembly in the 1960s.[61] Rather than labeling the violence employed by the NWYMA as an irrational use of force, I argue that these very brutal, very public acts of violence were integral to the anti-Communist politics practiced and developed on the southern half of the Korean peninsula in the post-1945 era. In other words, the NWYMA's practice and mobilization of violence were a part of the everyday political landscape created under the USAMGIK-supported regime.

The work of the CIC generated a critical paper archive for the US occupation and also the US military during the Korean War. For example, during the war Nichols's CIC detachment "submitted from 600 to almost 1000 intelligence reports <u>each month</u> from information collected from agents, prisoners-of-war, refugees, defectors and other sources and contacts."[62] Members of the NWYMA and other rightist youth groups were essential for the culling and gathering of the information to write up the reports. And even more importantly, the CIC used the NWYMA and other Korean contacts to draw up the black, gray, and white lists used by the USAMGIK, the Rhee regime, and the US military. These lists consisted of names of people. Those on the black list were considered to be enemy threats to security; the gray list held names of people who could serve as possible sources of information or skills, but their loyalty or "security" was unconfirmed; on the white list were those considered favorably disposed to the United States. According to internal CIC documents, the "Army CIC detachment compiled and maintained target lists and white, black, and grey lists." When the CIC returned to the Korean peninsula in 1950, they drew on these lists again, and they updated them through "1) Interrogation of captured enemy Agents, refugees, PW's, civilians; 2) Screening of reports from South Korean Police, South Korean Army CIC, and anti-Communist youth organizations of both North and South Korea."[63] These lists were not politically neutral pieces of information. These lists circulated within an already established practice of archiving.

Hausman related his understanding of the Korean process on the ground for investigating someone's political and personal background:

> They also have a record of punishment and of the offense, etc., but unlike in America, that follows a man to his grave. That will be on police records, it will be transferred to his province when he goes back home and everything, and for the rest of his life the police will have a dossier on him for whatever it is. It doesn't matter how trivial it is or how important.[64]

And in police recruitment, Hausman noted that the Korean methods of background checks involved "police records, local files from the man's village," and the recruiters would "talk to the village elders, who could vouch for a given family many generations back."[65] Hausman characterized the violent techniques of the Constabulary as a way people used to try to circumvent the paper archive:

> A man is brought in and ... whoever does the disciplining—he will say to him, "Do you want this punishment or do you want this punishment?" Well, he knows the back and the guts are going to hurt like hell, but it's going to go away in a few days—the marks and everything else, so a lot of them take the back and the guts.... The commander calls in the man and asks him if he wants his punishment recorded, or, take several thumps in the stomach with the baseball bat.[66]

Much as how the police files were a constant presence in people's lives, where a person would have to negotiate for the rest of their lives the mark of one past encounter with the police, these black, gray, and white lists had material consequences and afterlives for the Korean populace even beyond the US occupation and the Korean War. Using these lists over and over again, officials held a calculus between life and death over the populace, a strict mapping of how violence and governance would apply to social relations.

But the sheer volume of the CIC reports, the lists of Communists, and the mass violence projected a fantasy of certainty. These lists, however, derived their power from their inherent instability. Names could be added at any point, especially to the black list. Names could move from one list to another. The figure of the "native" agent, especially a member of the NWYMA, was also seen as potentially unstable in his self-declared political affiliations. As members of the NWYMA charted out for the CIC who was a "Communist" and who was an "anti-Communist," the status of the NWYMA members was also still precarious because it was difficult to do the background check on refugees' kinship and village ties. Donald Nichols recalled that he had a problem with the "elimination of dangerous or untrustworthy agents, for example, certain double … agents." The "methods to accomplish this job" were about literally disposing of the agent: "bail him out in a paper-packed chute; dump him off the back of a boat, in the nude, at high speed; give him false information plants—and let the enemy do it for you."[67]

The politics of anti-Communism on the Korean peninsula required an inherent instability. To mark oneself as an anti-Communist, one needed to mark someone else as a Communist, and because suspicion was the essential political practice of anti-Communism, this gesture would have to be enacted ritually again and again to ensure and reassure others of one's own anti-Communist standing. These politics of suspicion demonstrate the workings of what theorist Paik Nak-Chung has termed the "division system" on the Korean peninsula, where the "division" of the Korean peninsula has proven to be socially productive and generative of an everyday life. It is not simply a case of needing an enemy, where the "Communist North" needs the "Anti-Communist South," and vice versa. Rather, in this "division system," every action and imagining of either the North or the South involves the dyadic conjuring of the other. "A *system*," writes Paik, "signifies a social reality that to a considerable extent has taken root, for better or worse, in the everyday lives of the people living under that *system*."[68] With every gesture that insisted on the impossible divide from the Communist, the anti-Communist Korean was, in fact, revealing a deep intimate dependence on the figure of the Communist in constituting an anti-Communist personhood.

The high stakes of this everyday politics continued temporally into the Korean War and spatially into the POW camps. To become a POW under UNC custody meant becoming immediately suspicious in the eyes of others. The POW status was a social stigma, where the suspicion of Communism was marked on the POW. And everyone understood that if the war ended, this stigma of having been a POW during the war would attach itself to the person for the foreseeable future within South Korean society. For the ROKA soldiers who had been prisoners under the KPA and then became prisoners under the United Nations Command when the KPA troops either surrendered to or were defeated by the US military, this mark of the "POW" status was not a temporary concern. It was going to be a matter of life or death, both physically and socially.

And the CIC was again a structuring organization of who became a POW and also maintaining their own agents within the POW camp compounds. The CIC created the pipeline on the Korean peninsula that moved refugees into POW camps, changing their status fluidly from one to the other. "We cannot tell which side they are working for just by looking at them," asserted the standard operating procedures (SOP) manual for the CIC in 1952. In describing a "typical day of operations" for a CIC detachment, the manual authors wrote, "Early in the morning we will receive at least one and sometimes more, truck loads of Koreans. These Koreans come under several categories. They are farmers, they are prostitutes, they are houseboys, shoeshine boys, businessmen, black marketeers and other Koreans who are considered refugees." Picked up by "Military Police, by UN Security Police, by National Police, and by individuals, units and members of the 1st Marine Division," these refugees came to the CIC for screening. "Screening a person can take anywhere from 10 minutes to 10 days and sometimes longer. This screening is done through interrogation, records check, etc. The interrogation is done by Agents of the CIC. An interpreter is used for the interrogation."[69] As the manual noted: "whenever CIC Agents had a reasonable suspicion that an individual was a saboteur or espionage Agent or guerrilla, the man was classified a PW and sent to the rear." Explaining this common practice, the manual noted, "The alternative was to release the suspects; and any activity by infiltrees cost UN Force lives and cut troop faith in CIC."[70]

To render the vast majority of the Korean population as suspicious ultimately was not a useful tactic for the CIC. To garner some kind of legitimacy, the CIC had to demonstrate that their agents were capable and had the necessary skills to differentiate between an anti-Communist and a Communist Korean. What was absent from the standard operating procedures outlining the process of interrogation was the actual infrastructure of intelligence already created by both the CIC and anti-Communist youth groups on the Korean peninsula ever since 1945. When the US CIC had arrived on the Korean peninsula during wartime mobilization, they in fact had remobilized the vast networks they had already put into place during the occupation years:

Informants were recruited from among the following groups:

1. South Korean police.
2. Suspected enemy agents.
3. Captured confessed enemy agents.
4. Refugees.
5. Missionaries.
6. Ex-employees of the post–WWII Korean Occupation CIC and other US Army units.
7. Anti-Communist Youth Groups. These were utilized profitably both in North Korea and South Korea.
8. Anti-Communist "Self Protection Groups." These were unpaid informants....
9. The indigenous employee ranks of the unit or place to be covered. Labor foremen were recruited to cover labor gangs. Such informants were utilized among the native workers at division headquarters, regiment and battalion....
10. Indigenous newspapermen.[71]

According to Captain Samuel E. Walton Jr., the operations officer for the 181st CIC detachment, "[whenever] an area was entered, immediate attempts were made to contact the heads of the rightist groups."[72] Or as First Lieutenant Arnold J. Lapiner noted, "The Greater Korea Anti-Communist League furnished the names of local Communists and collaborators; and also provided personnel for the hazardous mission of locating guerilla groups."[73] In this sense, the CIC's presence in the POW camps was both new and old; it was both autonomous and a product of already-existing social collaborations.

Youth, Race, and the Pedagogy of Violence

Just as the NWYMA became critical to the operations of the CIC during the occupation, the Anti-Communist Youth League came to play a similar role with regard to the US military during the Korean War. The Civilian Information and Education (CIE) division of the US military was a program operated by the Psychological Warfare section of the US military. The CIE, as part of its attempt to infiltrate everyday Korean social spaces within the POW camps, encouraged the formation of different types of youth groups, such as the "Students National Defense League" or the "Korean Youth Association." These groups, according to an internal military publication, were "to provide the framework whereby security might be maintained 'so that the common POW had nothing to worry about.'"[74] These youth groups later were subsumed into the overall organization of the ACYL, the formation of which had been encouraged by the Republic of Korea Army. In other words, the ACYL functioned as a proxy in many ways for the anti-Communist Korean state via ROKA and the US military organizations such as the CIE.

In an interview with the Psychological Warfare Section, a prisoner of war at Koje-do, who appeared in the report only by the name of "Lee," recounted his experiences negotiating and navigating the political landscape of the anti-Communist youth groups before his internment in the POW camp. He was born and raised in North Korea, but soon after liberation, he took up residence in Seoul to attend university.

Recalling May 10, 1948, the day of the "first big election in South Korea," Lee stated, "The government mobilized youth groups at election places. If men refused to vote for the right people, they were beaten up.... I saw goon squads all around with sticks at election time.... [There] was an atmosphere of terror all around there. Most of the youth of South Korea belonged to Rhee's party. All parties used youth organizations. They were organized in schools."[75]

As a student, he recalled how the "Rhee government put terrorists in the schools, not to study, but to keep surveillance on all other students.... Anyone talking about politics would be sure to be regarded as a communist." Characterizing the young men in these groups as "ignorant, strong-arm boys," Lee noted that they had beaten him up for refusing to sign a statement attesting to the innocence of students who had been arrested for the murder of a professor.

Considering himself as someone who was "yearning for national unity and constructive action," Lee then joined "gladly" the North Korean army in 1950. And then as a South Korean civilian internee in both Pusan and on Koje-do, Lee again experienced "anti-Communist terror." Soon, he joined the Communist group within his POW compound.[76]

The seeming omnipresence of the anti-Communist youth groups in the prewar period as described by Lee was the manifestation of a national project supported by the US military and consolidated by Rhee. By the end of 1947, one of the major Korean youth groups founded during US occupation—the Korean National Youth Association (KNYA)—claimed 1.5 million members. As a report from the US political adviser, Joseph Jacobs, in Seoul to the secretary of state noted, "No inquiry is needed, however, to justify the conclusion that an organization of 1,500,000 members will be incomparably the largest semi-military unit in South. It is too late to suggest that KNYA be disbanded."[77] Very quickly after the UN-sponsored elections in the south, Syngman Rhee announced on October 29, 1948, that he would centralize all youth groups. At the National Assembly in December 1948, another announcement was made: "All youth organizations in the country should be disbanded and a 'corps for the protection of the fatherland' should be formed."[78] When the Korean War officially broke out in June

1950, the Korean youth group had become a fundamental organizing unit for the ROK state.

The youth groups—in addition to their patent utility as paramilitary extensions of political groups, the US military, or the Korean state—were supposed to represent the future of the nation. In December 1948, in a meeting with Captain Sihn, who had just been appointed home minister by recently selected President Syngman Rhee, Bertel Kuniholm, the US first secretary in Korea, discussed the Korean youth with Sihn:

> Sihn feels that all of the major political effort must be made upon Korean youth. He believes that many of the older generation, excepting those who lived in exile, have been so badly treated and bludgeoned into docility by the over-bearing Japanese, as to render them unfit for the responsibilities of government. Only those who have lived abroad have maintained their self-respect and dignity, and can be counted upon to have the proper attitude, he feels. What he believes is essential for the future of the Government is the development of character, and a deep respect for the law.[79]

The youth of Korea were not only supposed to be the raw material for state-building, but the youth were also supposed to be evidence of the political potential of postliberation Korea. For Sihn, the youth represented a generational consciousness supposedly not habituated to colonialism. The rightist youth groups were thus to become a primary element in the project of state-building at the level of society in the southern half of the Korean peninsula. And they became a critical part of the infrastructure in the US-controlled POW camps of the Korean War.

At meetings of the Korean National Assembly in 1951, the issue of youth groups in the POW camps was already on the table. According to reports from the field, there were at least 5,511 prisoners of war who were from the north and declared themselves to be anti-Communist. Anti-Communist youth groups were already formed at UNC Camp #1 at Koje Island, and they were requesting that Syngman Rhee act to release them from POW status. One particular group led by a POW named Lee Kwang Soon had sent a petition to Syngman Rhee, along with the Republic of Korea flag drawn in blood.

In May 1951, the anti-Communist South Koreans in Compound 65 organized a "branch of the Daihan Youth Corps, a South Korean youth organization." The mission of the Daihan Youth Corps extended those exercised during the prewar period: "members of the corps were to: drill their minds and bodies in order to become defenders of the South Korean nation; work for the unification of Korea, and purge all subversives and work for world peace." And "at the compound level, the top leadership had operating bureaus—training, mobilization, intelligence, culture, propaganda, inspection, and organization."[80] The Anti-Communist Youth Association (or League) was a youth group created by North Korean anti-Communist POWs. Like the Daihan Youth Corps, the unification of Korea was among its expressed missions, as well as training the POWs to serve in the ROKA. In order to become a member, a young rightist POW would need to swear "with blood to fight against the Communists," as well as "pass an investigation of their personal backgrounds," and "secure two persons who would guarantee their loyalty."[81]

During the summer of 1952, the Psychological Warfare section interviewed twenty-four POW anti-Communist leaders selected for a study of the efficacy of the Civilian Information and Education (CIE) programs installed in the POW camps. CIE program developers descended on the POW camps in late 1951 with an eye to frame them as self-contained spaces for experimentation, like laboratories or classrooms. They proposed to study, examine, and mold the POWs in these controlled environments. CIE's programming reflected the prerogative of the US Psychological Strategy Board. In the camps, under CIE organization, films were shown, elections were held, group discussions were facilitated, and camp newspapers were published. But during the interviews, all twenty-four POW leaders insisted that there was an even more important and essential detail that the US military was not grasping: each and every one of the twenty-four Korean POWs stated that they should not be classified as a "prisoner of war."[82]

He was not supposed to be a prisoner of war, insisted thirty-two-year-old Sin Jong Kyun in his interview. Described by his interviewers as "very dignified" and "self assured," Sin was recognized as a leader of the Anti-Communist Young Men's Party (or League).[83] According to Sin's testimony, at the outbreak of the war, Sin was working for the 704 and 705 Criminal Investigation detachments of the US military in Seoul. A "certain enlisted man in the American Army ... cheated [Sin] out of three months' salary," stated Sin. Told to go down to headquarters to pick up his pay, Sin found himself put into the POW pipeline by this US military official in order "to conceal his crime." Sin was also concerned about his life after release from the camps: "I am still afraid that when I am released from the compound, I will be treated as an ex-PW. Because I was classified as a PW, it will be always be in my personal history and some people who do not know very much about my past will think ill of me."[84]

For Sin, being a POW was not simply a temporary wartime status. It was instead a kind of stigma, a political marking. In his interview, he demurred that he was not necessarily political, and instead claimed a more intellectual identity. "He read about 450 books per year," noted the interviewers. "He read mostly philosophy books, no political books." But Sin's seemingly exceptional background turns out to have shared a common set of characteristics with the majority of the other twenty-four anti-Communist POW leaders. These leaders were usually Christian, intellectuals, and/or from the Korean middle class; the majority of them had gone on to higher education at universities in Japan in the preliberation period. Sin himself had been born in the northern province of "Han Kyung Nam Do," and he had attended Waseda University in Japan in 1940, under colonial rule, to study philosophy. Within two years he received a master's degree and teaching certification from the Ministry of Education in Japan. He worked as a lecturer in psychology at National Ham Heung Medical College in the north, but after liberation in 1945, he headed south, where he eventually worked as the chief editor for the *Student*, which was, in his words, "a magazine for the enlightenment" of the youth. He was soon well-established enough that he ran for political office as a representative of the Ch'ŏngju area on the Korean Education Association ticket. Sin's involvement with the US military intelligence network as well as postliberation rightist youth movements pointed to an intertwined political landscape that far exceeded the confines of the barbed-wire fences of the POW camps on the Korean peninsula.

The Civilian Information and Education (CIE) and the Psychological Warfare sections of the US military both worked very closely with the ACYL. Indeed, the US military condoned the majority of the physical beatings and interrogations the anti-Communist youth groups administered on fellow prisoners of war. Violence was, as usual, not the main issue. Even so, a Psychological Warfare section report on the results of interviews with twenty-four POW ACYL leaders did express discontent with one particular finding:

> The anti-communist leaders seem so eager to establish their own role in the creation of the anti-communist phalanx that they tend to minimize, or even deny, the contributions of CIE toward their success in the internal political struggle. What these leaders regret is that CIE (and the Camp Command generally) did not take an active physical part in destroying the communist groups, that is this sense its position was, to the leaders, "too neutral."[85]

Here, according to the report, the ACYL leaders were critical of the CIE for their lack of action against Communists. ACYL leaders wished to eradicate such elements completely. One difficulty, then, as is clear from this report, was that the ACYL leaders, although anti-Communist, did not willingly express gratitude for the "benevolence" of US military activities. That is, the rightist leaders wished to assert a claim to a political subjectivity, or at least a political activity, that was not completely constrained by the policies and agendas of the United States. This claim presented a challenge to US hegemony.

The CIE program, with its basis on the Boy Scouts and a Deweyan approach to education, was geared toward molding what they took to be pliant, willing, and naive Korean postcolonial subjects into a version of American civic liberal citizens. This kind of imperial pedagogy abstracted the prisoner of war into a universalized subject, a type of postcolonial Everyman, who desired and needed US liberal structures and ideologies. It was about reproducing via education and training a blueprint of a subject by instilling a particular code of values that would then inform behavior. And at the heart of the program, like many of the American education projects abroad in Asia during the Cold War, was the assumption that if one could train the Asian to behave in a certain manner—an idealized "American" manner—then surely his political consciousness would develop and follow (American) suit. The Asian subject would learn to renarrate himself, embed his life trajectory into a larger American global and local story about liberal freedom and the desirability of free market capitalism.[86]

Literacy became central to the CIE project. The POWs wrote essays on given topics, and these essays were collected and then translated by the CIE as a measure of the effect of the CIE program. For example, according to a memo issued by the "Evaluation Branch" of the CIE on January 17, 1952, in "the first weeks of January 1952 about 4,000 essays written on Instructional Unit 13, North Korea under Communism, were submitted to 1st Lt. Ross Sheldon by prisoners in compound #94." CIE translators, most likely Korean civilians hired by the US military, assessed and summarized what they considered to be the patterns and categories of responses. For this batch of essays, the translators noted that half of the essays "agree with the content of the lecture," one-third complained of a "lack of detailed information on South Korea" in order to compare with North Korea, one-fifth were not "willing to express their thoughts," fearing repatriation to North Korea, and "a few" of the POWs "wrote typical communist essays."[87]

Indeed, the Korean POWs demonstrated in their essays an agile grasp of the tropes of US exceptionalism and insisted emphatically on the utility—rather than the superiority—of US practices of selfhood. In an essay titled "The New Life," Korean POW Lee Jae Bok of Compound 82 at Koje-do UNC Camp #1 posed the question: "What is the meaning of new life?" The archival remnant of this essay exists only in English translation, and not the original Korean, but the essay still conveys its central arc. "Is new life only concerned with the individual citizen? Or on the other hand, is it concerned with social and political life?" Lee then stated, "If this theme is limited to the war-damaged Korean people, then we should discuss the Korean youth who are wandering about in darkness without any destination." He turned to the crisis of the individual in modern society, writing, "Although each individual pursues happiness and freedom, the only life he gets is vacant. Truly all individual citizens of today have encountered a crisis in individual liberty and happiness." He goes on to paint a portrait of the Cold War, where "the reds cannot stand long before the power of scientific civilization in a free world. Is it not a bright light shining from a far place across the Pacific Ocean?" Encouraging Koreans to "step forward" toward the "justice and morality in the brilliant light from the bright land," Lee counseled Koreans to "look into their own thoughts with sagacious inward eyes and calmly criticize all the facts in their surroundings." He concludes with: "The new life that we long for will be obtained only through bloody war."[88]

POW Lee Jae Bok's identification of a "new life" construed that newness as a historical rupture from the colonial period. There is, hence, a dual aspect to his essay: first, he lays out the familiar enlightenment/civilization trope of moving from darkness to light, with the United States standing as the "beacon" of light shining across the Pacific to Korea. Second, he also identifies "new life" as stemming not from the individual alone, but rather from an appropriately understood "social and political life." The collective—or the embodiment of the "nation"—was to be represented by the "Korean youth." If the individual were to strive toward meaning without being a part of a collective, the resulting life would be "vacant." And although he instructed fellow Koreans to move toward the "light" of American civilization, ultimately he counseled them to "look into their own thoughts," and asserted that the final horizon of "new life ... will be obtained only through bloody war." In this sense, we can see that anti-Communist Korean POWs did not accept the United States as the ultimate benefactor of democracy. Rather, true democracy, according to this notion of the racial nation, was internal and latent in the Korean person. And such a concept reflected certain fundamentals of "Ilminchuŭi" (One People Principle), as promulgated by Syngman Rhee. As An Hosang, South Korea's first minister of education, had explained, there were three types of democracy: capitalist, Communist, and Ilminchuŭi democracy. According to the findings of the scholar Ou-Byung Chae, "An argued that because capitalism and communism are factional and materialist, an alternative nationalist ideology should be unanimous and based on Korean values and traditions, which were suggested in the concepts of the family state and moral politics."[89] Also, keeping in mind that Yi Pŏmsŏk had molded Korean paramilitary youth groups in the template of the "Blue Shirts," we can see how the prisoner's exhortation of "new life" possibly reflected the "new life" promulgated by the Blue Shirt faction. Maggie Clinton argues that the "men who orchestrated the purge and the ensuing White Terror" in Shanghai considered themselves as "vanguards of the future." Importantly, being counterrevolutionary did not mean the absence of "world-transformative impulses" for these nationalists in their ambition "to introduce capitalist forms of production evenly throughout China's vast territory (while understanding themselves as anticapitalist) and in [the] assumption that doing so required the total transformation of Chinese social life."[90] The Korean anti-Communist prisoners of war, through a fascist nationalist language of self- and nation-making, were claiming to already be agents of history and of the nation's future.

On the ground, the CIE was frustrated with the POW leaders because they considered the CIE to be their instrument for educating the POW population, and not the other way around. The report writers noted that the ACYL leaders emphasized in their interviews "that CIE by itself could not be trusted to wean intransigent communists away from their faith; genuine and appropriate anti-communist education was given by the leaders themselves." These leaders conducted what they called "special classes" to convert whomever they identified as Communists in their compounds. While the CIE interviewers expressed much frustration and hand-wringing over the fact that "the Western-liberal 'democracy' which CIE taught did not completely replace the most passionate and direct doctrine of the prisoners themselves," they were actually misrecognizing a project that had been in place for far longer between the US military and the Republic of Korea government.[91]

The twenty-four anti-Communist POW leaders understood that the critical and essential axis of political recognition did not lie with the

CIE. Sin's own insistence that the US military had incorrectly categorized him as a POW underscored his concern that the stigma attached to having been a POW would stay with him even beyond the barbedwire fences of the camp. The precariousness of being a POW stemmed from the more fundamental fact that no category—whether refugee, POW, anti-Communist, Communist—was stable. During the US occupation, basic questions about proper citizenship in a period of political emergency arose repeatedly: as there was no US-recognized Korean state until 1948, the Korean, according to the US military and government, was not yet a citizen. If this was true, then what was the Korean? How did one know? At the same time as the category of the citizen was not yet legally instantiated during the occupation, the figure of the refugee loomed large during the occupation period and all the way through the war years. In a time of massive displacement and in a time when the state itself was in doubt, how did one know who was who?

Polygraphs and Blood Writing

On June 11, 1952, four young Korean men were brought in for interrogation by David A. Levin of the Seventh CIC Detachment, and then later members of the 208th CIC Detachment continued the interrogation. Twenty-two or twenty-three years of age, these four men—Shin Hyun Uk, Kwan Tae Yong, Pak Song Won, and Im Sang Yung—were now prisoners of war, but they belonged to a specific subset of prisoners whom the CIC was keenly interested in interrogating. These four men had been members of the southern Republic of Korea Army who had been taken prisoner by the northern Korean People's Army or the Chinese Command Forces at different points between October 1950 and January 1951. On March 15, 1952, all four men were part of a group of POWs moved to a two-story school building in Pyongyang that had been painted with the letters "PW" on the roof. Almost two months later on May 7, 1952, a guard asked for twenty volunteers to collect bricks on a labor detail. This was the moment for their escape. They managed to cross over the Taedong River, passed through Sadong-ri, crossed over Namgang River, and once they went beyond the "outskirts of Inchon," they were in the mountains. They "traveled along mountain trails to avoid being recaptured. They judged the direction by the sunrise each morning and lived on the food they could steal from isolated houses in the mountains." And in early June, these four men surrendered themselves to members of the Thirteenth Engineer Battalion of the Seventh Infantry Division of the US Army.[92]

Eventually, after a series of interrogations by the CIC and most probably also the ROKA, these prisoners soon found themselves at the UNC Camp #1 on Koje Island. Although the CIC categorized all four men as "prisoners of war," the disparate backgrounds of the men mapped out experiences both pre- and post-1945 that demonstrated the transition from the demands of the colonial state to the US occupation. Shin, who had been born in Kyŏngsang Pukto province, "went to Japan with his family in 1942 or 1943 and lived in Fukuoka where his father was employed as a miner." In Japan, Shin received six years of primary school education, and then after liberation he and his family returned to their previous home in Korea in 1946. On the CIC record, Shin recalled June 1, 1948, as the date he joined the ROKA, "which at the time was a constabulary force," and he stayed with the transitioning forces all through until he was captured on November 26, 1951, at Yongwon.

Twenty-four-year-old Im Sang Yung was also from the same province. At fifteen, he went to Seoul, where he worked in a laundry for two years. He then came home and worked as a farmer for a year. After this, he then went to Kunchon where he worked in a brass factory for three years. And on July 12, 1950, he was drafted into the ROKA. With twenty days of training, he was then sent into the battlefields—and on January 6, 1951, he was captured by Chinese Communist Forces. It was as a POW that Im met the three other Korean prisoners from his province. "Since they were all in the same [POW] platoon, they became close friends."[93]

Im had met Pak Song Won when they were both POWs assigned to repairing the "bomb damage" at the Milim Air Field. Im had claimed to the CIC agents that he was "a very strong rightist," but it seemed to Pak that he "was interrogated more than the others" by the North Koreans.

"Pak was accused of being an officer, spreading propaganda among the PW, having belonged to rightist political groups in South Korea, and being the son of a rich man."[94] And judging from other details in his interrogation report, the class background of Pak seems to differ from his POW friends. For example, at a certain point, the Home Ministry Security Police had Pak sign "PW repatriation papers, both in Kanji and Korean." And although the other POWs had come from rural areas of Kyŏngsang Pukto province, Pak gave Seoul as his place of residence.[95]

The young men the CIC interrogated gave stories about lives that traversed the Korean colonial diaspora in Japan, the movement between the rural and the urban, and a range of class backgrounds. The North Korean interrogators had clearly also probed into their backgrounds in order to ascertain the possible political beliefs or affiliations that each ROKA soldier held. And despite the insistence of Im and Pak on their rightist politics, the CIC interrogators—through all of the repeated interrogations—labeled all four young men with "U" in their evaluations, meaning "Communist affiliation unknown." Putting the four young men in the pipeline for further interrogation by either the US Army or the ROKA, the CIC ensured that these young men joined the ranks of refugees and other ordinary Koreans who had been funneled to the UNC Camp #1 on Koje-do.

But the CIC interrogators themselves expressed a frustration with interrogating Koreans. The assignment of "U" practically to all Koreans interrogated was the result of the Koreans' assumed incapacity to tell the truth, and not the result of the CIC interrogator's inability to comprehend and assess the Koreans' narrative. As Lieutenant Colonel Verne O. Jackson of the 210th CIC Detachment commented in his exit interview from service during the war, "It was very difficult to interrogate Koreans. They lied repeatedly." Neither threats nor bribes seemed to work—"It was very difficult to break these people."[96] Or as Second Lieutenant Joseph Farell of the 116th CIC Detachment stated regarding the ROK military personnel who were working with them, "To describe the average mentality of the South Korean ROK, you would have to take into consideration the fact that they have been suppressed for many years, therefore, they have very little initiative ... I would judge the average ROK as being that of at least a seven year old boy."[97] The Korean was inscrutable, lying, unbreakable, immature, underdeveloped, still mentally colonized. The Korean, in sum, was incoherent. The issue of "truth," in the eyes of the US military, was ultimately less about language than about racial bodies. As the former CIC interrogators asserted, the Korean was supposedly still mentally colonized and therefore could only understand signs of violence, whether in the form of threats, beatings, or killings. Was the Korean racially capable of telling the "truth," or at least differentiating between the "truth" and a "lie"?

During the Korean War, the US military experimented with the use of polygraph machines—lie detectors—on Korean translators and interpreters who worked for US military intelligence. Ultimately, the US military hoped to use the polygraph machines to sort through the exponentially growing population of Korean prisoners of war in custody, so as to determine who was a Communist and who was reliably anti-Communist. According to a report titled "Military Application of Polygraph Technique" written by George W. Haney in early 1951, the operators of the polygraph machines posed a series of questions to twenty-five "Korean Nationals" who had been working as interpreters or translators for the US military. These were intended as experiments to test for the polygraph's utility and accuracy in the particular context for which they were now being readied for use. For example, the fifth question asked was, "Did you have something to eat today?," which was followed by "Are you now a member of any Communist organization?" In the report's summary of the experiment's findings, Haney stated that "the Korean National does not present any special or different problem of interpretation" for the administration of the polygraph. In other words, Haney concluded, "it seems clear that Korean Nationals react as definitely and positively as do persons of the white race." The "pressure changes in systolic blood pressure and changes in respiratory activity" that were the telltale signs of "emotions aroused during attempts at deception" were also predictably absent or present for the Korean body, similar to the Caucasian body.[98]

The capacity for truth-telling—and thus, rational and moral thinking—as well as its measurement had been raised as questions of racial embodiment. The polygraph experiments and the institutionalization of the CIC's "war of espionage" on the ground thus exposed a foundational ideology undergirding both the continued criminalization of the Korean left and the dependence on the Korean ultra-rightist youth groups during the war. The Korean national, according to the CIC's "war of espionage," could only comprehend, react, and act within a state of emergency, where martial law was the normative everyday structure. The presence of a civil war between two nation-states created under foreign military occupation only five years previously in 1945 was not a historical contradiction or problem. The problem was whether or not US hegemony over determining the parameters of a continued state of exception in Korea to continue Cold War objectives was established and recognized by the Korean population.

When a group of sociologists from the Psychological Warfare section of the Human Resources Research Office (HUMRRO) at George Washington University arrived at UNC Camp #1 in early 1953, they found the Oriental POW still puzzling. The US Army had commissioned this study because the "behavior of these soldiers, initially as combat fighters and then as prisoners of war, was so substantially different from what was expected that it was labeled 'unprecedented' and 'strange.' "[99] What struck these sociologists was the use of physical violence by the Korean prisoners within their compounds:

> Brutality was widely employed by both factions. The Communist organizations, however, seem for the most part to have used violence for definite purposes and as part of their over-all plan of total control. Anti-Communists, on the other hand, often adopted violence emotionally, out of fear or a desire for revenge but without an accompanying propaganda strategy, so that they gave many PW's the impression that they were more cruel, even sadistic.[100]

Indeed, one of the South Korean prisoners of war they interviewed had decided to repatriate to North Korea due to his experiences with the anti-Communist youth groups in Compounds 64 and 84. The sociologists described Min, "a South Korean engineering student," as having been "decisively alienated from his former loyalties." They quoted Min

stating, "In August, 1951, I made up my mind that [if given the opportu-
nity] I would be a repatriate for North Korea. The anti-Communist
leaders ignored the fact that the lot of all PW's was the same and should
be shared equally. The American authorities seemed to ignore what
was going on. If they knew, I feel that was very immoral on their part....
[In the spring of 1952] the Communist leaders gained control of the
revolt, and the Communist leaders attracted the PW's because they
set up a fair system."[101] Much as how Gregory Henderson had characterized the NWYMA as thugs and honchos during the US occupation
period, the US sociologists saw the violent tactics used by the anti-
Communist POWs as being sheer expressions of rage or revenge, a
form of immature passion and not political expression. But on closer
examination and tracking of the cases of anti-Communist POW violence within UNC Camp #1, a similar kind of form and logic unfolded
in each case.

    In UNC Camp #1 on Koje Island, around midafternoon of October
15, 1951, Suk Chang Joo, a POW supervisor for Tent #4 in Compound
#91, brought in POW Jeon Yong Ko to his tent for interrogation. Jeon
was a recent transfer from Compound #90, which was the maximum-
security compound in the camp. Two other people were waiting in
Suk's tent for Jeon; they were Yang Jung Ok, who was a member of the
ROKA Military Police Battalion, and Kim Kyo Whang, who was the
chief POW supervisor of the compound. They wanted to know why
Jeon had been placed in the maximum-security compound. "I asked
about his former Compound, why he had been in detention, and all
about his character," Suk stated later for an investigation affidavit. According to Jeon, in his former compound, a group of POWs had attempted a Communist-inspired riot. "Then the Compound Monitors
beat me on the face a few times," said Jeon for the investigation. Yang,
the ROKA military policeman, told the story differently, saying that
Jeon "resented" the questioning, and "refused to tell the whole story."
"At that time," said Yang, "I slapped him about three (3) times. The
POW supervisor struck him in the face also." Jeon supposedly then
began speaking.

After this interrogation, Jeon was released back to his tent for head count and supper. But again, in the tent, a group of fellow prisoners of war gathered, and as one of them said, "we tried to find out about the prisoner's character." It turned out that Jeon was wearing his jacket inside out because on his jacket was written these words in Korean: "A Murderer, This Man Should Be Killed." When the POWs eventually found out about the riot that had occurred in Jeon's former compound, they began beating him. As one of the POWs stated, "All prisoners in my tent resented him because we, seventy-two (72) prisoners, are all ROKA army stragglers." At a certain point, Jeon escaped and ran to the barbed-wire fence at the compound's perimeter. He had climbed over the first inner fence, and then a ROKA guard caught him as he began ascending the second and final fence.[102]

As Jeon's story illustrates, to be a POW was to be ambiguous, and ambiguity was politically dangerous. The anti-Communist Korean POWs very much understood the symbolic public significance of the CIE compound within their camps. It was the space for education, and it was a communal public space. The performance of a shorthand way of marking oneself politically by marking someone else publicly came to the fore in the interrogation rooms created within the POW compounds by the anti-Communist POWs themselves, usually working alongside the ROKA soldiers stationed at the camp. On December 23, 1951, a large-scale riot erupted in Compound #62 in Enclosure #6 on Koje Island. According to the statement of US Major Oliver L. Case, he had transferred seventy men from Compound #63, who were known anti-Communists, into Compound #62, which was dominated by Communists, "in [an] attempt to improve conditions therein." The conditions that developed, which Case must have anticipated, involved the POW Lee Byung Jin, who was a college-educated leader in the Boy Scouts within the camp and a fervent anti-Communist. Lee rounded up 124 Communist POWs for interrogation in the monitor's tent, and then placed 100 other POWs in the compound jail. Kim Han Jong, a twenty-three-year-old farmer, testified that he, along with others, were taken by the newly introduced anti-Communist POWs to the CIE

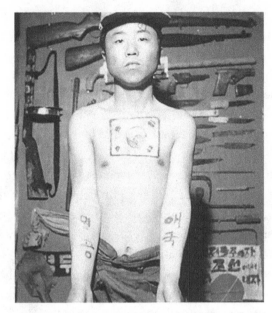

FIGURE 5.1 The Republic of Korea national flag, as well
as the phrases "Patriotism" (*right*) and "Rid of Communists" (*left*) tattooed on arms of a Korean prisoner of war.
(National Archives and Records Administration)

school. "There we were searched and made to lay face down. Then each
man was called up to the stage, where he was beaten again."[103]

Within a few months, the Korean anti-Communist prisoners of war
had developed a further shorthand for political marking: tattooing. The
practice of tattooing was similar and resonant with the interrogation
techniques, which were in themselves highly public and always demonstrated on the body. And the tattooing was also within the same political genre as the blood petitions. It was not a simple branding of one's
body, like a marking of belonging. Rather, it was sign that one was willing to believe that the anti-Communist state would be the ultimate future. As the POW Sin mentioned his concern about how he would be
marked as a POW in the future even after he had left the barbed-wire
fence behind, all of the prisoners of war were embroiled in a political
struggle about the *future* beyond the barbed-wire fence. To accept or

create a tattoo, something that would be that permanent, was a personal declaration of political commitment.

The challenge facing the rightist, anti-Communist prisoners of war in their aim to present themselves as politically viable subjects was that, in the eyes of the CIC and US military, all Koreans were suspicious. Those markers of identity, personal history, and self-narrative that had operated in the past to distinguish categories of people were no longer sufficient or deemed reliable. Language was not stable. Regarding survival and viability in South Korean society, these self-declared anti-Communist POWs understood that survival depended on the demonstration of their ability to read who was or was not a Communist. The ambiguity of being a refugee or a prisoner of war was actually something that applied to everyone, in a sense, under the Rhee regime. Everyone was under possible suspicion, and to be an anti-Communist was to demonstrate—over and over—one's own political position by identifying Communists.

Alongside the tattooing and the public beatings, anti-Communist Korean POW youth groups organized to write and send a prolific amount of blood petitions to figureheads within the Republic of Korea state or the US military. One particular blood petition lies in the vault of the National Archives in Maryland, quarantined away from the massive amounts of bureaucratic documents the US military produced but in the presence of all that is "uncategorizable" within the archive of US empire—such as Jackie O.'s blood-stained Chanel suit. Meticulously written in Korean and translated into English by the POWs themselves, three sets of petitions, all dated May 10, 1953, were addressed respectively to President Eisenhower, General Mark Clark, and Lieutenant General Harrison. This blood petition brings to the fore the political claims and subjectivities of the Korean youth groups at the center of multiply interrelated discourses of the time: race, nationalism, sovereignty, and empire. And because the blood petition raises the simple question of, what does blood do to text, and what does text, in turn, do to blood, the issues of Korean youth groups and politics cannot remain simply at the abstract level of discourse, nor at the brute level of inchoate violence. By making the body an undeniable presence, the blood petition enables us to address the shared, central concern of rightist Korean political groups and the US military: interrogation. The practices of interrogation were overtly concerned with the body of the Korean subject—the body became the medium through which to determine and extract the "truth."

For the text of the petitions, the POWs used a sharp, dark pencil, meticulously forming the Korean and English characters. For signatures, the POWs used their own pierced fingers. Blood was a vital medium in facilitating the self-presentation of the petition.

The petition requested the release of ACYL members from the POW camps—and thus from the category of "prisoners of war"—so they might fight against Communist Koreans on the battlefield. Beginning the petition with an excoriation of Stalin as the "son of a worthless shoe repairer," the petition writers lament the misrecognition of themselves as "prisoners of war":

> Our sad fortunes is that today still double fence weight heavy on us and fall asleep with detention and get disappointment at surrounding when we wake up, moreover, why and how comes we are punished as a guiltlessness and vexatious PW?[104]

At Panmunjom, there had been discussion on the part of the US Army about releasing the anti-Communist Korean prisoners of war in South Korea proper.

> We make a petition by our own warm blood. Dearest Your Excellency! Even though these bloods are not worthwhile to see and a little quantity but it is an expression of our real determination Sir. It is our crying that give us an opportunity of releasing just like what Your Excellency said. It is our real sincerity.[105]

"Real determination" and "real sincerity" were communicated in the medium of blood, where the blood would more transparently and directly convey the true intentions and sentiments than any language or text. In the end, it was the blood that mattered most.

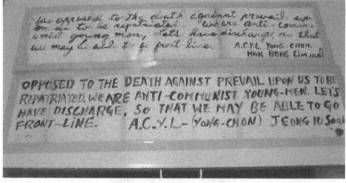

FIGURES 5.2 to 5.4 Blood petition written by ACYL members from Yŏngch'ŏn Camp
(National Archives and Records Administration)

In these petitions, the members of the ACYL insisted on their political will by framing their commitment in terms of their willingness to die for their state. Of course, this is yet another potential spilling of blood:

> Estimate the tremble recollection of long time from five years we, the all members of Anti-Communist Young Men who are would opposed against the Reds, have been fighting continuously and how many times was it go over the point of death?[106]

Blood reinforced the collapsing of the intention, desire, and body into a "sincere subject," where the willingness and ability to shed blood in the now or in the future expressed "real determination." However fractured the English, here, translation, in a sense, was circumvented by the medium: because of the blood text there was no denying or misrecognizing the intent of the prisoners of war.

Each of the proclaimed demands of the prisoners of war was positioned between two types of "death": that of the anti-Communist Korean prisoner of war and that of the Communist Korean. Here, the two deaths were juxtaposed in a hierarchy of ethics, where the stalled Panmunjom negotiations are set side by side with the urgency of the eradication of "the reds':

> 1. We opposed to the death against prevail upon us to be repatriated which is under negotiation at cease-fire talks at Pan-Moon Jeom, because as we had been in N.K. under Red puppet regime for five years we well know their deception....
>
> 4. Give us an opportunity of releasing so that we may be able to going to front lines to fight against Red and make revenge on Red and washed a triumphal knife with the water of the Doo-Han River.[107]

But before "shame" solidifies as the operative incentive behind these seeming exhortations of "till death" pronouncements, it is important to pause and consider this as an "act of writing." Who was the intended readership of this blood document?

These prisoners of war in 1953 were preempting any ambiguity in how they could be read by the US military and state. For the 478 different, individual Korean prisoners of war who signed their names with blood on large, separate sheets of paper, each act of signing must have been witnessed by the collective group. Moreover, the blood transformed the text into a performance of one's subjecthood, perfectly attuned to the demands on it.

Similar to the blood petition, Syngman Rhee himself was uncategorizable in the eyes of the US military and government. As US military head John Hodge complained in 1947 about Rhee, "Appears Syngman Rhee is completely off the reservation again and will use every effort to sabotage the work of the Joint Commission.... In his childish talk he repeatedly refers to alleged promises from General Hilldring that we would form a south Korean Govt and repeated accusations that the coming meeting of the Joint Commission is contrary to US policy and that if I go through with it I am violating orders given me by the US Govt."[108] But in 1953, when he ordered the mass release of the Korean anti-Communist POWs, Rhee was not necessarily primarily acting for the audience of the United States. It was a gesture to claim legitimate sovereignty over the Korean populace, in front of the Korean populace.

Although the blood document is quasi-quarantined away from the rest of the extensive paper archive on the Korean War in the National Archives, there remained a close relationship between the ACYL petition behind vault doors and the CIC and US military intelligence papers in the archival boxes. Indeed, the explicit performance of this blood document is instructive for us in how we survey the bureaucratic files of US military intelligence, which have served as a crucial basis for reconstructing the puzzle of the US occupation and war in Korea. The medium of blood for the writing and signatures demands our attention to the medium itself—the blood. In front of the seemingly more banal intelligence reports, summaries, and orders, what is the medium with which the authors wrote and constructed the narratives? The material for both acts of writing was the Korean person—whether as a preemptive bounding and claiming of the self as a subject in the blood document or as a constant insisting on and inventing of the Korean as fragmented, incoherent subject in the interrogation reports.

A Korean POW named Ju Yeong Bok had been in the Yŏngch'ŏn POW Camp on the mainland. But when the orders for the mass escape were issued, the lights were shut down, and everyone made a rush for the cut barbed-wire fence, Ju decided to stay.[109] Born in Manchukuo when it was under Japanese colonial rule, Ju had studied Russian literature in Harbin, and in 1945 he stepped foot for the first time on Korean soil to work as a translator for the Soviet occupying forces in the northern half of Korea. When the war broke out, Ju was an officer in the Korean People's Army. Captured early in the war, Ju had spent a great deal of time behind the United Nations' barbed-wire fences. He did not fully endorse or believe in the northern Communist state, but he also did not trust the anti-Communists in the south. He was tired of the violence, of the profound uncertainty of his own survival. So he did not leave the camp and decided to wait.

In July 1953, Ju was sent to the 38th parallel, where he entered the gates of yet another POW compound. But this time, the POW camp had been created by the Indian military. He would soon have to make a choice. To repatriate to the north, to not repatriate and go south, or to choose a "neutral country." A third choice.

6

On the 38th Parallel

THE THIRD CHOICE

ON JULY 27, 1953, at Panmunjom, UN Command representative US Lieutenant General William K. Harrison Jr. and Northern Command (NC) representative DPRK Lieutenant General Nam Il entered a hall built specifically for the purpose of the armistice signing ceremony. With the "mutter of artillery fire" coming through the "thin wooden walls," Harrison and Nam took their seats at separate tables and wordlessly signed nine copies of the armistice, which would take official effect within twelve hours later. In front of "Allied observers" and press from sixteen different United Nations countries as well as observers and thirty-five press members from different Communist countries, General Harrison finished signing at 10:10 A.M., with General Nam finishing one minute afterward. "The North Korean general glanced at his watch, rose and strode quickly from the hall, without a glance at the United Nations table," noted a *New York Times* article. Harrison exited more "leisurely," pausing to smile and pose for photographs, and "saluted the honor guard and greeted some United Nations representatives before he climbed into a helicopter to fly back to Munsan at 10:27 A.M."[1]

The cease-fire had been signed, but it seemed that everyone was quick to caution against considering the armistice as the "end" of the conflict. As President Eisenhower stated in an address broadcasted nationally:

> We have won an armistice on a single battleground, not peace in the world. We may not relax our guard nor cease our quest. Throughout the coming months, during the period of prisoner screening and exchange, and during the possibly longer period of the political conference which looks toward the unification of Korea, we and our United Nations allies must be vigilant against the possibility of untoward developments.[2]

The Korean War had not come to an official close—only a cease-fire pause. "Seventy-two hours after the signature of the armistice," the military troops of all sides withdrew "one and a quarter miles from the fighting line, and a neutral zone [was] established between the armies."[3] The Demilitarized Zone, representing the cease-fire, had become the setting for the next phase of the war—the exchange of prisoners of war.

In early October 1953, Indian General Kodandera Subayya Thimayya arrived at the 38th parallel in a US helicopter. "In the helicopter," he explained, "I had a superb view of the Korean landscape, and I was struck by the beauty of the country—until I got a glimpse of the DZ. The land here looked like a bleak, barren and blasted piece of hell."[4] On this very "piece of hell," what Thimayya called an "experiment in neutrality" took shape in the final prisoner of war complex of the Korean War, and the final iteration of the interrogation room, here called the "explanation room." India led the experiment with a resolution to the impasse at the armistice table over POW repatriation. Each POW would individually enter the "explanation room," and after listening to an "explanation" provided by a representative from the POW's prewar nation-state on why the POW should return home, the prisoner of war would choose to repatriate, to not repatriate, or to go to a yet undetermined "neutral country." The landscape of the 38th parallel had changed again as buildings and compounds were erected by both sides.

This carefully scripted encounter often broke down in actual practice. As Thimayya himself noted in his memoir, "Some amazing incidents occurred during the explanations." He recalled one young Korean man who had originally been from South Korea, but was now a prisoner of war in North Korea and refused to repatriate back to the south:

> In one instance, a prisoner entered the room to discover that the explainer was a late friend who had been in the same regiment. They greeted and hugged each other as old comrades would. The prisoner then asked if he could sit alongside the explainer, and the Chairman of the subordinate body had no objection. The two men started to reminisce and to tell stories about the old days, and the prisoner made enquiries about his mother.[5]

At this point, the explainer pulled out a photograph of the POW's mother, saying that he had just seen her before coming to the 38th parallel. "She wants you to come quickly," the explainer said. On seeing the photograph, the prisoner "burst into tears and said, 'Please give her my love. I will come back quickly. I will come back when Korea is free, and that is not very far off.' "[6]

In today's history books, the 38th parallel—or the Demilitarized Zone—appears more permanent than temporary, the line cutting across the Korean peninsula often being the most recognizable feature of Korea to the American mainstream public. But in 1953, even with the signing of the cease-fire agreement, no one—not Eisenhower, not Thimayya, not the Korean prisoner of war—considered the 38th parallel to be a permanent line of division. The immediate post-cease-fire phase of the war, namely, the exchange of prisoners of war at the 38th parallel, provides us an opportunity to refract the meaning of the Korean War not through the usual, overdetermined prism of Cold War politics where anti-Communism and Communism become the only stakes visible, but rather through the prism of neutrality, a different history that has been present on the Korean peninsula.

For India and Korea, the POW controversy was not the first time that India had played a role in the questions of applications of international law over political recognition in Korea through the United Nations. There were multiple interpretations of the significance of the northern KPA's crossing over the 38th parallel on June 25, 1950, and the Department of State followed the wide-ranging spectrum of reactions

and narratives of the conflict that was escalating on the Korean peninsula. India, in particular, concerned the US officials. "Three of four
Delhi English language papers ran prominent editorial comment on
Korean situation June 27," a telegram from New Delhi addressed to the
US secretary of state reported. The *Indian News Chronicle* stated, "The
North Koreans have a cause to fight for—national unity and a Communist regime. The Koreans in the south are called upon to fight in defense
of American capital—and human freedom. In these moves Moscow
has scored over Washington." The telegram report further noted that
the *Hindustan Times* voiced its opinion that the "dissolution of South
Korea [would be a] blow to UN prestige but [would have] 'saving
grace on bringing about Korean unity.'"[7] From the vantage point of an
independent India, the fate of the Korean peninsula held a great deal
of weight in terms of the futures of newly independent Asian nation-
states. India had been a member of the United Nations Temporary
Commission on Korea to oversee the 1948 elections that ended up establishing the southern Republic of Korea—and it was India that had
voiced reservations about ultimately failing to remove the 38th parallel
as a line of division. When the United Nations convened an emergency
session after northern KPA forces crossed the 38th parallel, Sir Benegal
Rau, the Indian permanent representative, raised "questions ... over
the use of the term 'act of aggression'" by the United States in their
draft resolution, arguing whether there was enough information available to place "all blame" on North Korea.[8] Nehru later refused to commit Indian military forces to the United Nations Command, since he
considered General Douglas MacArthur a "warmonger," and eventually
did send a field ambulance unit.[9]

The question of how the US-dominated Cold War vision would affect the postcolonial civil war on the Korean peninsula, not the 38th parallel per se, was the concern of the Indian government. Historian Manu
Bhagavan argues that Nehru saw "modern, sovereign nation-states" as
"stepping stones to the larger end": "a progressive global body" like the
United Nations, which would both counter "the totalitarian power of
the unlimited states," and "uphold and defend the fundamental rights
and common good of all humanity."[10] India's commitment to and in-

volvement in the POW controversy during the Korean War was part and parcel of this longer historical concern about the nature of the international nation-state system, and what would be the overarching vision guiding it.

On the Korean peninsula in September 1953, the United Nations Command was making preparations to move 7,900 anti-Communist Korean prisoners, who had not escaped during Rhee's dramatic release in June 1953, along with 15,000 Chinese prisoners to the final POW camp created by the Custodian Force of India on the 38th parallel. The US military handed out new clothing and blankets to the POWs for their journey and arrival at the 38th parallel for repatriation screening. Part of the bundle was a "160-Day-Calendar," given out of consideration for prisoners so they could remove one sheet each day and look forward to the day of release," recalled POW Ju Yeong Bok. And an "ordinary POW" would have been "happy to tear off one leaf of calendar each day, counting days before being released from the camp." However, "as the day of release drew nearer" for Ju, his "heart was torn." He was "pessimistic for [his] survival."[11]

Ju was one of seventy-six Korean prisoners of war who chose the third choice: a "neutral" country. This chapter also charts the more intimate cartographies of the prisoners of war as they navigated global geopolitics, and explores what "neutrality" might have meant for the prisoners. Born in Manchuria in the years before the Japanese military occupation and establishment of "Manchukuo," Ju later left his home when his parents encouraged him to go to Harbin to study Russian literature. His parents themselves, according to Ju, had left Korea because it had become difficult to survive after Japanese colonization. After his studies in Harbin, Ju then lived in Beijing for two years. He was twenty-two years old when the Japanese announced their unconditional surrender, and in his search for a means to survive economically, Ju stepped foot for the first time in his life on the Korean peninsula in 1945. Soon, he discovered, alongside many other young men, that the military provided the most immediate means for survival. Fluent in Korean, Japanese, Russian, and Mandarin, Ju served as a translator for the Soviet military occupation officials in the post-1945 years, and later became a major in the Korean People's Army. But disillusioned politically, he eventually surrendered and became a POW under UNC custody.

By the time the cease-fire was signed at Panmunjom, Ju Yeong Bok was tired. He had come under suspicion from both Communist and anti-Communist POWs repeatedly and relentlessly. Interrogation happened over and over again, whether in the POW compound or with the ROKA or US military intelligence. In September 1953, as a result of the Dodd kidnapping, the US military instituted a plan to segregate anti-Communist POWs from the Communist POWs, and Ju was one of approximately fifty thousand anti-Communist POW who were shipped off of Koje Island and sent to six different camps on the mainland. But at the first location, Ju recounted that the "fanatic" anti-Communist POW police arrested him, suspecting that he was a Communist. "The POW camp was really a nasty place," he said. Much to his relief, he was then sent to the Yŏngch'ŏn POW Camp, where he and his friends were recognized as anti-Communists. "I thought we would have a very quiet life in this camp, however, within a week I was summoned alone." Officials from the Central Intelligence Agency (CIA) wanted to interrogate Ju. The US authorities placed him in a detention camp near Pusan, and to Ju's chagrin, they had placed him in the same holding cell with "newly surrendered three officers—two were lieutenant colonels and the other a pilot major—who were completely 'red.' ... [Ju] was so irritated and vexed to have been put together with the Reds."[12]

The CIA kept Ju for two months of interrogation, and eventually brought in a "civilian in the Army who spoke Russian," with whom Ju spoke about the Soviet military instructors he had known. "The civilian was a very gentle and kind man," recalled Ju. And in fact, the Russian-speaking interrogator, who was traveling to Tokyo briefly, asked Ju if he would like something from Japan. Ju, revealing his terrific sense of political survival, asked for a "book of English lessons for self-study, written in Japanese." In an exchange for his information on the Soviets, Ju requested books that would enable him to learn English, a language that was now critical for him as an anti-Communist.[13]

At the 38th parallel, the interrogation and the beatings continued at the hands of other anti-Communist POWs. Having signaled that they were "neutral," Ju and his friends aroused the ire and suspicion from the other POWs. "We were neutral elements because we believed President Rhee and his government were worse criminals than the Communist Party. And as for Kim Il-sung and his government they were opportunists even more detestable than Capitalists and anti-revolutionists." This chapter follows the strategies of three groups of historical actors as they debated repatriation screening and the stakes involved in the choices at hand: the delegates at the United Nations, the anti-Communist Korean POWs, and the seventy-six Korean POWs as they journey to New Delhi and beyond. Ju soon concluded, "My political life was finished." We examine what was next for Ju, and how he imagined what was possible in the rapidly shifting global landscape of Cold War politics and the possibility of nonalignment.[14]

India's Recalibration of the Nation-State System for Decolonization

Right before he was scheduled to depart from India for Korea to take on his role as the chief delegate of the Neutral Nations Repatriation Commission (NNRC), General Thimayya met with his two "chief political advisors," B. N. Chakravarty and P. N. Haksar, "senior officers of the External Affairs Ministry," along with Krishna Menon, and Prime Minister Nehru. Starting with tea, the people at the meeting soon focused on the topic of Korea. Thimayya recalled that Prime Minister Nehru placed his hand on the bound copy of the Terms of Reference on the table. Nehru stated:

> This is your bible, ... the only guide you will have. No one can tell you what to do or how to do it.... Your job is to find some solution to the problem that is plaguing the world in Korea. A solution to that problem may mean that similar problems in other parts of Asia can be solved as well. Thus, your job can well mean peace in Asia and perhaps in the world.[15]

Nehru's instructions as remembered and reconstructed by Thimayya laid out two elements that were critical in how India had decided to approach the question of "neutrality." First, the notion of "international law" or an "international community" was to be affirmed—the Terms of Reference, here almost reverentially portrayed, were to be the parameters between which Thimayya had to invent "neutrality." Second, the "Korean problem" was brought to the fore as an important case study for the rest of Asia. Or as Thimayya himself stated in his memoir, "The basic pattern of the Korean war was being duplicated in the other Asian conflicts. A study of the Korean pattern, therefore, would have equal significance to the problems in Burma, Indo-China, Malaya and Indonesia."[16]

For India, the "Korean problem" at the United Nations—and specifically the POW repatriation controversy—presented an opportunity for an intervention in the operations of the international community. At the crossroads between an increasingly bipolar Cold War and indigenous struggles for self-determination, Korea had become a high-profile representative of dynamics that were in play all over the Asian continent. For Thimayya personally, the significance of the Korean War lay in how it seemingly heralded a new kind of war: "the significance of the conflicts in Asia is that the military is attempting to proselytize on a large scale."[17] The struggle was now over each side "proving the superiority of its ways of life." "What does history teach us about wars in which way of life was a basic aim?" Thimayya asked. "The Crusades come first to mind."[18]

What kind of "neutrality" did one have to fashion in front of such an emerging pattern of war—a war that was patently ideological? The ideological conflict was on full display at the seventh session of the General Assembly, where discussion on the Korean question instigated the creation of more concrete proposals on possible resolutions to the armistice negotiation impasse. A special report from the United Nations Command in Korea on the current status of the military and armistice activities began the discussion on October 18, 1952:

The differences between the United Nations Command and the communists which have prevented the conclusion of the armistice were narrowed, by the end of April 1952, to one question: whether all prisoners of war should be returned, by force if necessary. Final conclusion of an armistice under the terms of the present draft agreement now depends upon communist acceptance of a solution to the prisoner-of-war question consistent with humanitarian principles.[19]

Having raised the question of how to resolve this issue of the negotiation impasse, the United States representative presented a draft resolution, one that was sponsored by twenty-one states. This particular draft resolution was worded to have "the General Assembly to affirm the principle of non-forcible repatriation as representing the will of that body," to use the words of scholar Shiv Dayal. "*Notes with approval*," the draft resolution stated, "the principle followed by the United Nations Command with regard to the question of repatriation of prisoners of war, and the numerous proposals which the United Nations Command has made to solve the questions in accordance with this humanitarian principle." In essence, as Dayal has noted, the draft resolution aimed to frame the US policy of voluntary repatriation as a "humanitarian principle," as a way to counter the North Korean and Chinese accusations that such a principle went counter to the mandatory repatriation stipulated in the 1949 Geneva Conventions.[20]

However, during the course of the General Assembly session on Korea, three very specific draft resolutions dealing with the question of POW repatriation were placed on the table by representatives from Mexico, Peru, and India respectively. The Mexico resolution was primarily concerned with the particular categories applicable to the prisoners of war, to ensure that the prisoner of war was not rendered "stateless" as a result of the process. Although all prisoners of war who desired repatriation would be immediately repatriated, those who were "desirous of establishing temporary residence in other States, would not return to the country of their origin until the coming into force of the decisions that, in order to achieve a peaceful settlement of the Korean question." Regarding the states who had already agreed to accept POWs temporarily within their borders, the "authorities of that country shall grant them [the prisoners of war] a migratory status which will enable them to work in order to provide for their needs," prioritizing state "guarantees for the subsequent protection of their [prisoners of war] freedom and their lives."[21] In his follow-up letter to the secretary-general, Luis Padilla Nervo, the representative of Mexico, further explained that this granting of immigrant status would enable the POWs to "[raise their] social status by restoring to them the dignity that only free work can bestow. At the same time, a contribution to the progress of international law might be made by reaffirming the principle that prisoners of war are not to be treated as just a conglomeration of human beings whose fate as the authorities may decide at will, but on the contrary, that man's inalienable right to work out his own destiny freely should prevail."[22]

The Peru resolution focused on creating a commission that would decide the resolution over the POW repatriation issue.[23] The resolution proposed a commission composed of delegates from each of the "parties to the conflict," as well as two delegates selected by the General Assembly and one "neutral state," who was not a member of the United Nations. And notably, the non-UN member "neutral state" would serve as the chairman of this commission. Beginning the resolution with a statement affirming "the desire of mankind for an immediate just and honourable peace," the writers of the resolution ended with a different affirmation: "That in the performance of its functions, the Commission shall be guided by the principles of the United Nations Charter and by the Declaration of Human Rights." The Peru resolution was a recognition that the "international community" embodied by the United Nations did not, in fact, include all states or groups in the international community, but also extended the United Nations' claims to defining certain universals. It was a careful recalibration of the United Nations vis-à-vis the Korean peninsula and the globe.

India's draft resolution very explicitly positioned the 1949 Geneva Conventions as its point of departure: "*Affirms* that the release and repatriation of prisoners of war shall be effected in accordance with the Geneva Convention relative to the Treatment of Prisoners of War, dated 12 August 1949, the well-established principles and practice of international law and the relevant provisions of the draft Armistice Agreement."[24] The elaborately detailed proposal contained seventeen separate steps outlined in the process of resolving the POW repatriation issue. In the contested draft of the armistice, a "Committee for Repatriation of Prisoners of War" was already part of the provisions, and this committee's responsibilities were primarily logistical. However, the India resolution made a number of significant revisions and changes to the composition and duties of the committee. First, the India resolution stipulated that there would be four representatives on the committee: Czechoslovakia, Poland, Sweden, and Switzerland. And second, the committee was responsible for providing the following to all prisoners of war:

> 7. In accordance with arrangements prescribed for the purpose by the Repatriation Commission, each party to the conflict shall have freedom and facilities to explain to the prisoners of war depending upon them their rights and to inform the prisoners of war on any matter relating to their return to their homelands and particularly their full freedom to return.

The India proposal began from the premise that international law must be upheld—in the above quote, the proposal insists on the POWs' "full freedom to return," which echoes the 1949 Geneva Conventions of mandatory repatriation. In a sense, all of the meticulous details outlined in the proposal held the essential characteristics of later nonalignment—the objective of restraining excess by the different powers, which placed India in the role of determining when the United States or China, or any nation-state representative, had "crossed" over their proper bounds, and also an assertion of a moral authority to be able to determine "excess," "ideology," and "nationalism."

India's proposal challenged the US authorities' claim over the universalisms espoused through the United Nations, but the proposal did not pose a challenge to the legitimacy of the 38th parallel or to either states on both sides of the parallel. The General Assembly quickly passed the India resolution with an overwhelming majority vote. Later, Krishna Menon added new terms that facilitated the overcoming of the impasse that still existed at the negotiating table—the choice of a "neutral country" for the prisoner of war in the explanation room. As scholar Rosemary Foot notes, "the signature of the Korean armistice agreement in July 1953 has often been linked to the Eisenhower administration's threats, during the final stages of the negotiation, to launch nuclear war against the People's Republic of China (PRC), should there be continuing failure to agree to terms," an idea espoused and circulated by the Eisenhower administration itself in the years following the cease-fire.[25] However, Foot demonstrates that multiple other factors probably aided the quickening of the signing of the cease-fire. For example, China was to begin its Five-Year Plan in 1953, and for North Korea, the escalation in US bombing especially during the final year of the war had been devastating. US air bombs targeted wide swaths of land, civilian villages, and military targets such as dams and factories.

India's particular formulation of "neutrality" offered in the form of the Neutral Nations Repatriation Commission and the third choice of a "neutral country" also facilitated the signing of the cease-fire in that it provided a space where political recognition could be negotiated, deferred, and still remain intact. Menon and Nehru understood that the main issue on the negotiating table was the issue of recognition of the People's Republic of China and the Democratic People's Republic of Korea at the United Nations, with the United States being quite adamant about not allowing a possible seat to the PRC or DPRK. The choice of a "neutral country" enabled the political recognition issue embedded in the voluntary repatriation issue to appear less about the states' legitimacy and more about the individual POW's preference. It appeared to be more about the POW rendering him/herself an asylum seeker or a refugee, rather than being about the POW rejecting the state's claims on his/her subjecthood.

"Repatriation" Explained, Translated, and Performed

The entire proceedings of the Neutral Nations Repatriation Commission at the POW complex on the 38th parallel hinged on one concept: repatriation. The most crucial aspect of the "choice" rendered in these "explanation rooms" was the moment when the prisoner of war decided through which door he or she would exit—the door for repatriation, or the door for nonrepatriation:

> After each explanation session the prisoner was asked by the Indian chairman of the NNRC committee within each explanation tent if he

desired to be repatriated. This question was asked by the chairman through an interpreter. It had been specific in the Armistice Agreement that, to avoid misunderstanding, the act of delivery of a prisoner of one side to the other side would be called "repatriation" in English. The equivalent words in Chinese and Korean were also specified.[26]

But the various wars on the Korean peninsula with its disparate array of "prisoners of war," consisting of civilians and military personnel from both sides of the 38th parallel, had been complicating the notion of "repatriation" from the beginning of the debate. And in October 1953, when explanations began, the personnel involved in the explanations discovered a difficulty: "repatriation" could be interpreted differently depending on the POW's background. For a Communist soldier of the North Korean army who had been born in South Korea, the term "repatriation" more immediately meant returning to the soldier's hometown in South Korea rather than North Korea, which was where the soldier had been before the outbreak of the war. As Thimayya recalled, "This problem concerned the particular choice of words we had to use when we asked the prisoner if he wanted repatriation. These Chinese and Korean words that were used to signify the idea of repatriation had a literal meaning that suggested vaguely the idea of returning home.... Unquestionably, some confusion did exist in the minds of some of the prisoners."[27]

Debate over the interpretation of the different stipulations of the Terms of Reference had erupted along the 38th parallel. Building sites and the speed at which these compounds were built, the order in which the prisoners of war would be sent to the explanation rooms, whether or not prisoners of war would receive "explanations" in a collective group or individually—these were only a few of the overwhelming details that became a site of intense contestation. According to the Terms of Reference, the "bible" that Nehru had gestured to in front of Thimayya, the "explanation period" was mandated to ninety days. At the end of the ninety-day period, Thimayya reflected on the results: "Explanations were finished. Out of the 90-day period, ten days were used for explanations, and some 3,000 men out of 22,000 had been explained to. Of these 3,500 men, less than 150, or slightly more than 4% asked for repatriation. This was a much smaller number than the total who sought repatriation by escape from the compounds."[28] The issue that had been holding up the cease-fire agreement from being signed at Panmunjom for over eighteen months had now boiled down to only ten days of "explanations," where even the "choice" of repatriation or nonrepatriation seemed dubious.

Although the primary focus of debates, wrangling, and arguments at the 38th parallel was on whether or not "choice," "free will," "neutrality," or "objectivity" were properly supported and facilitated by the elaborate setups of the camp and explanation rooms, the actual fundamental concern of all state parties involved was not the exercise of "free will" in the explanation rooms but rather the proper performance of the relationship between the state and its subject and the mediation of the international community over that particular relationship. For the ninety-day period at the 38th parallel on the Korean peninsula, the states of the Republic of Korea, the Democratic People's Republic of Korea, the People's Republic of China, and the United States found themselves in an unprecedented situation in the conduct of warfare: the state had to "explain" to prisoners of war who had rejected repatriation why they should return. For the states involved, their own legitimacy—fragile and tenuous—was tested one by one in these individual explanations as the basic relationship between state and subject was laid bare and ambiguous. The prisoner of war, despite being heralded as the humanitarian focus of all states involved, was rather beside the point in the grand scheme of nation-states and the international community. The point was the allegorical performance of the explanation room itself, not the choice of repatriation or nonrepatriation.

The explanation room was a distilled scene of the nation-state system—each element represented by a body, some listening, others observing, one talking, but all judging. And the setting of the "stage" or the explanation room exemplified these dynamics, as evidenced in the following schematic images of the explanation room system created by the UNC for the anti-Communist Korean and Chinese nonrepatriates based on the Terms of Reference enforced by the Neutral Nations Repatriation Commission (see figures 6.1 and 6.2).

Neutrality, in the map, lay in the carefully calibrated and controlled movements of the POWs, punctuated with deliberate repetition of the

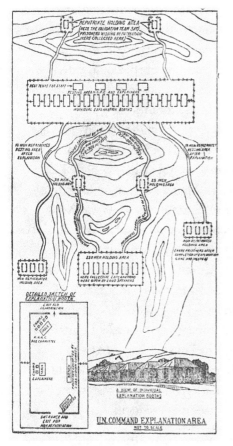

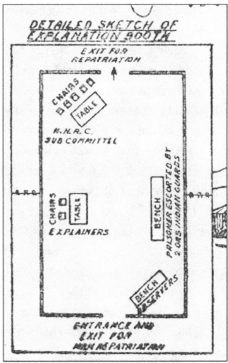

FIGURES 6.1 and 6.2 A map of the "U.N. Command Explanation Area" and "Detailed Sketch of Explanation Booth" from *History of the Custodian Force (India) in Korea, 1953–54* (1976)

"explanation" for clarity. According to the map, 250 POWs were first gathered in the holding area, located in the lower middle of the map, where "collective explanations were given by loudspeakers." Then, Indian soldiers took groups of twenty-five POWs at a time to the intermediate holding area, from where POWs were taken one by one to the individual "explanation booths" drawn in the top center of the map. Each explanation booth held a tableau of different actors—the prisoner of war sat on a bench accompanied by two or five Indian guards, facing the "explainers," who sat behind a table. In the far corner behind another table sat the five-member Neutral Nations Repatriation Commission inspection team—made up of delegates from Switzerland,

Sweden, Czechoslovakia, and Poland, with the head delegate from India. In the other corner, sitting on a bench were members of "observers" from the United Nations Command. Neutrality, in the explanation room, lay in the carefully calibrated encounters of speaking, listening, and observing—it was a scripted encounter, supposedly strong enough to mitigate any "excesses" enacted within the room.

Each side of the Cold War divide was reserving the ability to pass judgment on the maturity and the ability of the Korean explainer to interpolate their subject. Which Korea would it be—which Korea would be deemed appropriate to join a system of nation-state recognition? It was not just a room, as the POWs understood. It was a frontline competition of the politics of recognition in the Cold War. And it was a heated competition. On October 22, 1953, General A. K. Hamblen, the head of the United Nations Command Repatriation Group (UNCREG), received a memorandum from the headquarters of the NNRC. It reported that on October 17, 1953, one of the UNC representatives (according to the footnotes, it appears that it was a Lieutenant Colonel William R. Robinette) called "the Polish delegate to the NNRC 'a son of a bitch' after several arguments within the explanation tent." The performance aspect of the explanations is demonstrated fully in UNCREG's unpublished history's rendition of the incident:

> The incident occurred near explanation tent 15. The explanation to the prisoner in that tent had continued for over two hours. Because all other tents had completed explanations for the day, a crowd gathered near tent 15 to observe the outcome of the interview then in session. As the prisoner left the tent through the non-repatriation door, the crowd surged around the prisoner. The Communists present shouted for the prisoner to return to the tent and urged that he make his exit through the repatriation door. At this point a UNC Representative protested to Communists that they had no right to try to continue explanations outside the tent. It was during the ensuing melee that the offensive remark was alleged to have been made to the Polish representative by the UN representative.[29]

The willfulness on the part of those involved to perform their roles within the explanation room did not diminish the fact that the "choice"

FIGURE 6.3 Locations of explanation and holding areas
(National Archives and Records Administration)

the prisoner of war made had a very material and serious consequence. In fact, when examined more closely, the choice of nonrepatriation, repatriation, or a neutral country was a multivalent issue for the prisoners of war. It was not merely about "choosing" a particular state, but rather weighing and navigating an ever-shifting terrain of power. It was a question of discerning what was *still possible* or *now impossible* in the project of decolonizing Korea.

To set the proper stage for the explanations, the "bleak, barren, and blasted piece of hell" that Thimayya had seen from the window of his helicopter on arrival had to be transformed. The Demilitarized Zone was a "strip of land 4 kilometres in width running across the Korean peninsula." Divided into "two equal halves by the Military Demarcation

FIGURE 6.4 Captain Gilbert Ostrander (UNC representative) and Lieutenant
Colonel Ujjal Singh of the Indian Custodian Force at Panmunjom. January 1, 1954
(National Archives and Records Administration)

Line, the Demilitarized Zone was to be the site of the POW complex
for the explanation and repatriation proceedings—the northern half
was under the Northern Command, and the southern half was under
the United Nations Command."[30] In the middle along the DZ was the
explanation room system. On either side of the explanation room com-

plex were the POW camps of the nonrepatriates who were now under the custody of the Custodian Force of India (CFI). "Bounded on the South by the Imjim river and ... dominated by hills rising from 1,500 to 1,800 feet," this area of the DZ was "very heavily mined" since it had changed hands many times over the course of the war. In the southern part of the DZ, within "the vicinity of Tong-Jong-ni,"[31] the 22,600 Chinese and Korean prisoner of war nonrepatriates from the UNC were housed in what Thimayya noted was a "marvelous job of construction. All the huts were prefabricated and every plank for them had been shipped from the United States."[32] On the other side of the DZ, in the villages of Song-Gong-ni and Palsan-ni, were the lodgings of 359 prisoners—American, British, and Korean—who had decided not to repatriate. Although they lived with "less luxury than did the south camp POWs," these POWs "lived comfortably"—the Northern Command had whitewashed the small houses in the village—"Their quarters, with the neat vegetable patches beside the houses and with pumpkins ripening on the roofs, had a pleasant and peaceful atmosphere."[33]

When the "first batch" of prisoners arrived at 0800 on September 10, 1953, the 489 North Korean nonrepatriates from the Koje-do camp "marched in with flags waving and bands blaring ... shouting, screaming and gesticulating."[34] The flags were of South Korea and the United Nations.[35] General Thimayya judged that such a demonstration, if it did not interfere with the processing, was permissible. Present at the POW's arrival were representatives of the NNRC, press correspondents, and also observers from the Chinese People's Volunteer Army and KPA. A sudden melee broke out when some of the anti-Communist North Korean POWs spotted the uniformed members of the KPA-CPV observer teams. POWs hurled stones and spat at the observers as the Indian soldiers attempted to hold them back. Later, according to the official history of the Custodian Force of India, the anti-Communist POWs "explained [to the CFI] that their objection to the presence of the Communist observers was based on the fear that individual prisoners would be identified during the process of taking over and then their families would [be] harassed or punished by the Chinese and North Korean Govts."[36]

The anti-Communist Korean prisoners of war became the contingent that consistently challenged the work of the Neutral Nations Repatriation Commission and the authority of the Custodian Force of India, and thus, Thimayya accorded these POWs a great deal of attention in his memoir. He detailed their daily lifestyle and practices, which were instituted almost immediately on their arrival. They woke up every morning "between three and four A.M., and began the day briskly with a few marching songs vigorously accompanied by brass bands." Physical training exercises followed, and then the POWs sat down to their breakfast. The camps were "neat and spotless," and the afternoons were usually spent with sports or classes. What Thimayya called "political indoctrination" classes took place later in the day, and the "last event of the day would be a march-past, again with much music, flags, and slogan-shouting."[37] Such a disciplined lifestyle also was the creation of a solidified surveillance police structure that the POWs had developed during their time in the Koje-do Camp. Every compound had its own "guard tent," and the ruling organizations—namely, the Anti-Communist Youth League—held trials for offenses and reserved the right to exercise punishment by death.[38]

Mass demonstrations, insistence on negotiating the terms of entering the explanation rooms, and even kidnappings became part of the daily scene of the POW camp at the 38th parallel. Notably, Thimayya observed a difference between the Chinese and the Korean POWs' mass organizing: "The Chinese POWs were better disciplined, less noisy, and a bit more rational. They seemed to me like lost and abandoned children; the Koreans seemed like bewildered and angry children."[39] The mass rioting, according to Thimayya, was an attempt to garner attention, to "force recognition": "Sometimes they acted like neglected or rejected children, and the clamour they made was an almost pathetic attempt to force recognition of themselves as people rather than as pawns in a brutal game of politics," observed Thimayya in his memoir.[40] Thimayya attributed this level of desperation on the part of the POWs to the fact that "they all were fed up with being statistics.... [T]heir inclination was to try to increase the dissension in the hope of attracting more consideration of the individual problems."[41]

Thus, he framed the challenges the POWs issued to the India-led NNRC not as ultimate challenges to the legitimacy of the Indian "experiment in neutrality" but as a necessary element to overcome in order to achieve neutrality. He wrote,

> The Chinese and Korean soldiers, like our own, were mainly simple village folk, barely literate, and completely unsophisticated.... We did believe that an important function of our neutrality was to find out everything we could concerning the true desires of these non-repat POWs. By the time we had the whole lot in our custody, we were convinced that if anyone was going to begin thinking of these prisoners as human beings, it would have to be us.[42]

Thus, the "true desires of these non-repat POWs" was to be the province of the India-led NNRC and the CFI.

Kenneth Hansen, a colonel in the US Army Psychological Warfare Division, depicted a different portrait of the anti-Communist prisoners of war, dubbing them "Anti-Communist heroes" in his memoir, *Heroes behind Barbed Wire*, about his observations and experiences during the PsyWar operations and programs conducted in the POW camps of the Korean War. Hansen described the actions and choices of the nonrepatriate prisoners of war at the 38th parallel as the culminating climax of the "valiant and victorious struggle of the anti-communist heroes in Korea."[43] "For the prisoners of war," Hansen wrote, "it was a life and death struggle, replete with drama and pathos, and yet even to them not without flashes of their irrepressible humor. To participate in their ordeal was to become emotionally involved with them, without exception."[44] Hansen's narrative was also one of pedagogy, but it differed from Thimayya's in a fundamental, significant way—the story of the anti-Communist POWs Hansen provides was one of linear transformation catalyzed by the US Psychological Warfare educational programs. It was a story about liberal enlightenment, aspiration, and truth—in other words, the "anti-Communist hero" of Hansen's memoir was a subject who had learned and acquired the proper behavior and affect in front of the Cold War–inflected global order.

According to Hansen, the anti-Communist POWs had studied the armistice agreement meticulously and rigorously during their time in the Koje-do camp. Each anti-Communist prisoner of war received the full armistice agreement annex that contained the Terms of Reference regarding prisoners of war. "It was so important a document to the prisoners that those who could read it memorized it. Those who could not read it participated in so many discussion groups that they thoroughly knew the sense of it, and could point to the numbered paragraph under discussion at any time."[45] Hansen waxed almost poetic about the prisoners of war studying the Terms of Reference: "If ever a group deserved the U.S. Army slang designation of 'guardhouse lawyers,' it was the prisoners of war." He asserted that the prisoners, "in the end, were more familiar with the agreement as to their fate than many of the Indian officers who had the final say as to its administration."[46] Such an assertion was essentially an argument for the merits of the Psychological Warfare work within the POW camps—primarily an "educational" program conducted through the Civilian Information and Education (CIE) section. The anti-Communist Korean prisoners of war were publishing and distributing their own compound newspapers— for example, the newspaper titled *Flash* specifically dealt with information on the repatriation issue—and conducting their own discussion groups on the armistice agreement. To Hansen's delight, the POWs were now performing "democracy" as taught by the CIE program.

Hansen and his PsyWar team were not the only ones observing the prisoners of war for the duration of the war. Delegates from the International Committee of the Red Cross made regular visits to the camps to note the conditions, register any complaints, and ensure that the camp authorities were running the camp in accordance with the 1949 Geneva Conventions. One aspect of POW camp life the delegates especially took note of was the compound performances put on by the prisoners of war themselves for one another. The stage, built by the POWs themselves, often was the central focus of each POW compound. It was the site where the Korean People's Army and Chinese Volunteers Prisoners of War Representatives Association placed Brigadier

General Francis Dodd for their first official meeting. The stage was the site of People's Court trials in the Communist compounds, where individual POWs were called on to do public self-criticism in front of the other POWs—and disciplinary action could often follow. In the anti-Communist POW compounds, the more violent group disciplinary beatings took place in the CIE building, where the stage often was located. And the stage, for both anti-Communist and Communist compounds, was also the site of many entertainment performances staged by the POWs.

The stage was a site of pedagogy created, sustained, and circulated by the Korean prisoners of war. The performances that were for entertainment value—and perhaps the most visible element of POW daily life to outside visitors such as the ICRC delegates and PsyWar members—must be seen as part of the larger matrix of sovereign claims-making occurring on the grounds of the POW camp. Although not all Korean prisoners of war were members of the ACYL, the ACYL was effectively in charge of the compounds in which they had established themselves—and as Thimayya has noted in his memoir, the ACYL set down a similar structure of a state-like body in the camps on the 38th parallel. Surveillance, interrogation, disciplinary beatings, newspapers, educational programs, and even meal distribution fell under the jurisdiction of the ACYL. From the archival materials available, it is difficult to say that the ACYL also had control over the performance department of the compounds. However, a closer examination of the plays reveals a positionality that the POWs projected—and instructed others to inhabit—that Thimayya's and Hansen's formulations could not encompass.

In the compound of the prisoner of war Oh Se-hŭi, dramatic performances were the special forte. According to Hansen, the Compound 65 productions varied from one-man acting scenes to plays in "four acts and six scenes." The prisoners of war "built stage-settings out of cardboard and kraft paper boxes, hemp bags, poster paper, paper bags, tins cans and wooden ration boxes, dyed with tooth powder, clay, grass, lime and DDT!" exclaimed Hansen, pointing at the ingenuity of the anti-Communist Koreans. The list of play names—unfortunately only in English translation—that Hansen provided in his memoir run an interesting gamut of interests and entertainment. Plays such as *Blood-stained Sword*, *A Day in Seoul*, *Mr. Park Visits Seoul*, and *Dear Free Land* clearly referred to the Korean War experience. Romance plays also found their way onto the production bills: *Love at the Port*, *Son-in-Law Wanted*, *Princess Bell-Flower*, and *White Pearl*. However, as Hansen continued with his list of plays, it became evident that the plays were very much geared toward creating a narrative of the Korean nation: *Naivete*, *Justice*, *Sword of Wrath*, *My Homeland Where the Flowers Bloom*, *For the Cause of My Fatherland*, *Sons of the Republic of Korea*, *Going Home*, *Prop of the Republic of Korea*, and *Land of Passion*. Other plays referred explicitly—and perhaps in content described—aspects of camp and military life: *Quack's Hospital*, *Leaders*, *Cigarette Butts*. Comedies were also part of the roster; *Shanghai Typhoon* and *Foggy Shanghai*, according to Hansen, were "devoted to the struggles of political exiles during the Japanese occupation of Korea."[47]

When the prisoners of war were faced with the situation of the "explanations" that would take place at the 38th parallel, they had a few questions. "Would they receive explanations individually or in groups?" —this was the central question, according to Hansen. "Their solution was a series of plays, presented with variations in every Korean and Chinese compound," marveled Hansen in his memoir. "Compounds with particularly exhilarating versions—or exceptionally effective actors— toured other compounds, presenting their production to wild cheers and applause."[48] The setting was almost always invariably the same—"a table presided over by a turbaned actor who, so there could be no mistake, wore on his chest a sign proclaiming him the 'Indian Chairman.'" On his left were the Czech and Polish representatives—each "placarded and obviously in the role of minor villains." On his right were the Swedish and Swiss representatives—and also a UN representative, a UN observer, and a UN interpreter. The Korean POWs—and also the Chinese anti-Communist POWs—had staged according to the Terms of Reference their own tableau of the explanation room.

From offstage entered the Communist representative, observer, and interpreter—and finally, the Communist "explainer" entered and "took his seat." "Then, to an accolade which was invariably deafening, the HERO strode on stage."—the anti-Communist Korean prisoner of war entered the tableau. The "explainer" began his "explanation script," and the POWs, in writing the script, had "considered every possible angle which might be employed to persuade" a POW to repatriate to North Korea. But, "the hero had an answer for every approach." The answers often "confounded" the explainer—and in other instances, the "explainer," visibly moved by the POW's responses, would exit out of the tent through the nonrepatriation door, arm in arm with the POW. In "one version, even the Czech and Pole sought asylum."[49] And although such a play seemed to fall all too easily within certain categories of mapping Communists versus anti-Communists, these plays are remarkable in the sense that here it was the anti-Communist Korean POW who was the full agent of history on the world stage of political change, not the presiding committee assembled by the United Nations or China. And within the context of the previous performances and plays, the actions of the Korean prisoner of war were portrayed as part of a longer teleological history of anticolonialism and nationalism. It was the Korean prisoner of war who would enlighten others, and it was the Korean prisoner of war who would embody the South Korean state. Hansen's apparent delight with these dramatized "explanation room" performances misrecognized the dynamics of political articulation expressed in these plays. But the aims of the PsyWar section and the POWs' portrayal of the explanation room did converge in an important way—the "choice" of repatriation or nonrepatriation was not exercised, but rather performed in the explanation room.

When the Korean anti-Communist POWs arrived at the 38th parallel, the tactics of the POWs turned toward challenging the NNRC-structured explanations. Initially, the Korean nonrepatriate POWs refused to attend the explanations scheduled, and General Thimayya held discussions with them over a week-long period. Thimayya, it turned out, did have one very effective way of breaking the impasse in their discussion over the explanation structure and procedures. "Unquestionably, the best argument with the POWs was to play on the fear that their future never would be settled if they didn't cooperate with the NNRC and the CFI." Although the POW compound leaders were attempting to use their position as prisoners of war to make claims on the legitimacy of certain states, Thimayya's statement hit home on an unerring reality: the POWs' position as nonrepatriates had rendered them as essentially stateless. "They could not go on indefinitely being non-repats and until their future had been decided, they themselves would have no security and their very existence would be a threat to peace."[50] On October 31, 1953, when the Korean POWs finally agreed to attend the explanations individually, some had been able to bypass inspection with a "stone and occasionally a knife hidden in their clothes. They made serious attempts to attack the explainers."[51] As Thimayya noted, the North Korean POWs were "more violent than the Chinese in the explainers' huts."[52] Or among the Korean POWs who sat quietly in front of the explainer, many of them had "plugged their ears with cotton wool" to demonstrate their "refusal to listen to the explanations."[53] A few POWs did engage in exchange with the explainer: "For instance, the explainer might ask if he could give the prisoner a copy of the message which the Northern Command had for him. The prisoner would accept the leaflet and then blow his nose on it. Or the explainer might offer a cigarette; the prisoner, when reaching for it, would suddenly slap the explainer's face."[54] At the end of the first day of explanations with the Korean POWs, out of 459 POWs who had received explanations, twenty-one elected repatriation. The next day 483 POWs attended individual explanations, and only nineteen elected repatriation.

As Thimayya has observed, the North Korean nonrepatriate POWs used much more violent tactics than the Chinese POWs, and the particular tactics of the North Korean POWs point to the stakes involved for the Korean POWs in the explanation room and the question of repatriation. Although Hansen interpreted these gestures as transparent evidence of the POWs' desire for nonrepatriation—and thus, an affirmation of a US-framed anti-Communist state—these gestures of threats and insults also reveal the peculiar precarious position of the prisoner of war. The "choice" of whether or not to repatriate had been clearly made by the prisoners of war before entering the explanation room. The explanation room, thus, became a site where the North Korean prisoner of war had to perform his or her own legitimacy. It was indeed a performance of transparency, although one that was different from Hansen's vision. The majority of the North Korean nonrepatriate prisoners of war who were at the 38th parallel after the cease-fire were from UNC Camp #1, part of the population that remained on the island after the initial voluntary screening had been done to distinguish and separate the repatriates and nonrepatriates. The nonrepatriates had been sent to various camps on the mainland, while repatriates had remained on the island. The North Korean prisoners of war at the 38th parallel were a population of POWs who could possibly garner a great deal of suspicion under the Republic of Korea because they had "elected" nonrepatriation later during the war. Unlike Hansen's portrayal of the educational enlightenment of the POWs transforming them into idealized subjects, the POWs very well understood that they were marked as doubly suspicious for being from north of the 38th parallel and for deciding on nonrepatriation late in the war. It was ambiguity that would mean a certain social—and even possibly physical—death.

The claims of the DPRK state on these POW subjects were also clearly being challenged. After the first two days of expectations, the Northern Command switched their own tactics in explanations. Previously, the explainers had spent twenty to twenty-five minutes per POW in order to process through the approximately five hundred POWs that made up the population of one compound. The explainers had "merely read a written statement from the Supreme Northern Commander. If the prisoner then showed interest or asked a question a more detailed explanation was given." However, with the new version of explanations, "the prepared statement was read out continuously, over and over again," at times for a period extending to three to four hours. "According to their view, the prisoners had been under the influence of the UNC for two or three years, and the explainers therefore were entitled to a few hours in which to counteract the UNC's influence."[55] It was a move to invalidate the challenges issued by the POWs' resistance to the explanations by implicitly accusing the UNC of manipulating the "psyches" of the POWs.

Across the 38th parallel, the United Nations Command explanations commenced much later, on December 2, 1953. Compared to the activities south of the 38th parallel, the atmosphere of the UNC explanations seemed orderly and contained. The most prominent, distinguishing feature of the South Korean explanation rooms were the tape recorders—there was background music for the explanations. The recordings had three parts, evidence of Thimayya's comment in his memoir that "the explaining technique of the UN side leaned heavily on the sentimental."[56]

> 1st part: A conversation between a boy and a girl, showing their desire to have the prisoner in his mother country and amidst his family. They talked about their peaceful land "with streams, and paddy fields, where little calves jump about seeking their mothers" and requested the prisoner to "come back to your home land and cherished freedom."
>
> 2nd part: Korean music, generally beginning with the song "I want to go home."
>
> 3rd part: A female voice appearing on behalf of the prisoner's mother. She complained "that our strange fate does not permit me to reach my boy but I am sending a warm message to my son enclosed behind barbed wires without liberty." She went on to tell him the family anguish when they did not find him among the prisoners who returned earlier. "I looked in your room and found your sister crying in despair all day long." She assured him that no harm would befall him if he returned, and then sounded a note of warning: "If you keep believing in the North Korean Regime you will be only a half matured man." The appeal ended with the words "Walk to the fate of freedom, picturing your motherland in your mind."[57]

The strategy of the Republic of Korea was to present the relationship between the state and its subject through familial narratives. The allegory of the state appeared in the form of different family members—as voices of a young boy and girl and an older woman were meant to evoke memories and affective ties to siblings and mothers. The family, the motherland, and the state had been collapsed into one, and the ROK explainers were presenting the ROK as a naturalized nation-state, whose legitimacy had been already established through a genealogy of blood family ties.

Surrounded by the sound from the recordings, the South Korean explainers also had paid a great deal of attention to their uniforms and dress. "Dressed in American uniforms of rich material and fine cut," the explainers "made a show" of their expensive watches and "ostentatious" cigarette cases "with such nonchalance as to suggest that everyone in South Korea possessed it."[58] However, the South Korean nonrepatriate prisoners of war were eager to debate their explainers on this very issue. In fact, the prisoners in the Northern Camp, unlike their counterparts in the Southern Camp, "apparently were very anxious to receive explanations."[59] In Thimayya's opinion, the "prisoners were usually more politically educated than the explainers themselves," and rejected the sentimental music as a simple ploy.[60] They pointed to their POW uniforms and "brag[ged] that they were made in Korea," accusing the ROK explainers of being "American stooges." The prisoners wanted to engage in a debate with the explainers about the conditions in South Korea, and often "confused or embarrassed the explainers."

Soon, the ROK explainers adopted a tactic that was exactly the opposite of what their DPRK counterparts had done. When explanations commenced, the explainers allotted thirty to thirty-five minutes per POW. By December 8, 1953, none of the POWs had chosen repatriation, and the explainers began quickly dismissing the POW after only six or ten minutes. The POWs protested this practice and "complained that they were being treated lightly." One particular prisoner "wanted to know much more, for example, about South Korea's Five-Year Plan, about economic conditions there, about the reasons for the presence of the Americans and so on." Heated arguments often broke out, with the prisoner refusing to leave, and "in some cases remained for as long as two or three hours" until forcibly removed by the CFI.[61]

In the end, of the 359 Communist nonrepatriate POWs, only seven chose repatriation—five were South Koreans and two were Americans.

According to Thimayya, "These seven all claimed that they were real communists and that they left only because they did not like the way their camp was being run; they said the administration was not conducted along properly democratic lines, and some claimed to have been bullied by the camp leaders."[62] But there was one particular POW among the South Korean nonrepatriates whom Thimayya focused on in his memoir, where Thimayya described him as a "a young South Korean of unusual intelligence." "From the beginning, I felt that he would eventually opt for a neutral country," wrote Thimayya. As the days passed, Thimayya began to believe that this POW would indeed stay in North Korea. The POW did eventually decide to go to a neutral country, and Thimayya recorded the POW's response to his question about why he had made that decision:

> He answered that he did not approve of the North Korean communist regime any more than he did of the South Korean government. He felt that he could not be happy living under either regime. When he opted for a neutral country, his belief in communism was lessened, I think, but it had not disappeared altogether. He told me frequently that he was fed up with wars, and he wanted nothing more than to go where there was peace.... The Korean understood his own motives better, and whatever was the strength of his political beliefs, his desire for a peaceful existence was far greater.[63]

For Thimayya, the POW's choice of a "neutral country" was a choice for peace, an affirmation of India's own policy of neutrality.

The Seventy-Six POWs Who Chose a "Neutral Country"

Boarding the ship at Inchon harbor to head for India, the eighty-eight prisoners of war—seventy-six Korean and twelve Chinese—could still hear the message from the South Korean government being broadcasted from "loudspeakers in the surrounding hills" to the Korean prisoners of war, "an impassioned plea [for the Korean POWs] not to leave with the foreigners but to stay in their own country." "The prisoners seemed affected by the broadcast," General Thimayya noted, "but when we told them they could still choose to return they all refused to do so and continued the journey with our troops."[64] All eighty-eight prisoners of war had one thing in common—all of them had made a choice not to be repatriated to North Korea or South Korea, and not to China or Formosa, but rather to be sent to a "neutral country." At that moment, they were headed to India where they would wait for further information and news about which country or countries would be the possible "neutral country." In other words, the "neutral country" was still unknown and undecided—all eighty-eight POWs had chosen an idea, an abstraction, not a specific country.

The "explanations" were not the only thing that demanded an audience of the prisoners of war at the 38th parallel—loudspeakers in the POW compounds blared programming and announcements, dramas were staged by and for the POWs, educational programs that had been developed by the US PsyWar and Civilian Information and Education teams continued in the anti-Communist compounds, and consistent interrogation by POWs of fellow POWs also intensified at the 38th parallel. When the ship departed from Inchon harbor with the eighty-eight prisoners of war and the members of the Custodian Force of India, Ju Yeong Bok, a former major in the Korean People's Army, noted a moment of quiet pause, markedly different from the incredible volume of programming and announcements that had been directed at the POWs in the camps—"When we disembarked from Inchon, the Indian soldiers who had seemed to fill the entire deck of the ship went below to their cabins, and the remaining prisoners of war ... threw futile glances at their vanishing fatherland.... I looked out at the horizon until barely a speck was discernible," Ju wrote in his memoir. It took the strains of Indian music coming from the cabins of the soldiers below deck to shake Ju's focus on the horizon. "Now, I noticed that the music did not seem so unfamiliar to my accustomed ear. The sorrowful tone directly entered my soul, it seemed. Without quite realizing it, my body had been placed within Indian culture."[65] At the moment the Korean peninsula faded from view, Ju found that his ear had become "accustomed" to the Indian music, and that his body and soul fell into an empathetic consonance with the music.

Amid a sense of loss and isolation, there was no expression of fear—rather, Ju emphasized the sense of a measure of the possible, a kernel of the imaginable, for him to be able to live in the future land of the "neutral country." It became clear that the concept of a "neutral country" was not an empty category for Ju; thus, what did it mean for the seventy-six Korean prisoners of war to choose to go to a "neutral country" as they lived cordoned off in camps at the 38th parallel in 1953?

The prisoners of war who chose a "neutral country" would move from being one of the most oddly "hypervisible" subjects on the stage of struggles over political recognition to becoming one of the most oddly "invisible" subjects after the Korean War conflict receded into the past with the 1954 Geneva Conference on Korea and Indochina, where a different 38th parallel—the 17th parallel—was instituted. The eighty-eight prisoners of war, as they waited in India, soon discovered that they were essentially stateless persons, and it became incumbent on the prisoners of war themselves to gauge the geopolitical globe, propose possible countries for the category of "neutral country," and then petition the appropriate authorities. And survival once again hinged on a certain recognition by a state power—only instead of the violence experienced in the POW compounds as state-proxy organizations like the Anti-Communist Youth League sanctioned and enforced, the question of productive labor was on the table for these men in negotiating their future "neutral country."

Ju had been able to imagine a sense of his own future intertwined with India because India was indeed not "foreign" to Korea. The encounters between the Indian military personnel and the Korean prisoners of war within the POW camps belied an even longer history of being embedded in each other's colonial histories; at one point, two Korean prisoners of war called out to Brigadier Gurbaksh Singh Dhillon of the CFI. They had recognized him from a previous encounter in an earlier conflict—Dhillon "had been a prisoner of the Japanese in Singapore during World War II," and the two Korean POWs had been his guards, working under the Japanese colonial army.[66] It was this very history that enabled the CFI to communicate with the Korean prisoners of war without the aid of interpreters from either the UNC or Northern Command (NC). "Among our own personnel we had a number of men who could speak Japanese. Most of the prisoners, because of their experience with the Japanese during World War II, could understand a little of this language," wrote Thimayya in his memoir. The ability to communicate, however rudimentarily, with the POWs became critical when nine Korean prisoners of war, during a simple reprocessing assignment, suddenly broke out of the line and threw themselves at the CFI soldiers and asked for repatriation. "These men were terrified of the UN in general and of their recent comrades in particular," commented Thimayya. The Korean prisoners of war trusted neither the United Nations Command nor the ACYL nor the Republic of Korea to safeguard their lives.[67]

The choice of "neutrality" for the Korean nonrepatriate POWs occurred in a similar manner. Choosing neutrality usually did not occur in the space of the explanation room, although occasionally a POW did choose a "neutral country" at the end of his explanation. More often than not, the choice of a "neutral country" happened in these moments of rather desperate escape. For POW Ju Yeong Bok, his choice of a "neutral country" was exercised when he threw himself at the barbed-wire fence of his POW compound, in an effort to escape the constant interrogation and torture the POW compound leaders were exercising on him. According to his memoir, the POW compound leaders had been keeping close surveillance on who might choose repatriation or a neutral country. One night, someone woke up Ju by pulling his head up by the hair—they demanded to know who else he knew was intending to choose a neutral country. Refusing to speak, Ju was placed under surveillance with POW guards and then subject to routine interrogation.[68] Indeed, Ju must have seemed suspicious to the anti-Communist nonrepatriate POW compound leaders because he had been one of the first-round nonrepatriate POWs sent to the mainland camps, but he had not escaped from the camp during Syngman Rhee's mass organized release of POWs on June 18, 1953. In his memoir, Ju stated that he had purposefully not escaped because he had already decided to leave the

Korean peninsula for a "neutral country." "I did not like the idea of escaping," he wrote. "Or to put it more precisely, the thought of having my body attached to this land and living here made me anxious, and I disliked it. I wanted to go anywhere far, far away. I wanted to use my hands to cultivate land where there was neither red nor white [neither Communism nor right-wing anti-Communism]."[69] To the POW compound leaders, the choice of a "neutral country" reeked of an ambiguity that could not be tolerated.

On January 14, 1954, Ju was still under POW guard and surveillance. It was his birthday, and snow covered the ground. The guards were not as alert, he noticed, perhaps due to the cold and the snow. He made a mad run for the fence, startling the guards into pursuit. He saw a CFI soldier running toward him on the other side of the fence. "Don't shoot!" Ju called out in English. "Don't shoot!" When the Indian soldier was able to place his hands on Ju's body, pulling him out of the compound, Ju wrote of that moment: "I felt a comfort rise up from a mysterious place deep inside of me."[70] And, indeed, this moment marked the end of the very brief first chapter in his memoir, and opened what Ju clearly considered to be the important drama of the memoir—his time in India as an ex-prisoner of war.

Ju opened his memoir with a phrase that was suggestive of both statement and question: "Why did I choose a neutral country"—"It was a question I had asked myself thousands of times over the course of my lifetime," wrote Ju. But Ju's memoir was not a straightforward expository narrative providing a definitive answer to this question. The title of his memoir was *The 76 Prisoners of War*; Ju refracted the question of why he chose a neutral country through a sort of auto/biography of the cohort of the seventy-six Korean POWs who had all chosen a "neutral country." This particular narrative decision on Ju's part indicated two important facets of how Ju understood his experience as a "neutral country" POW.

First, in terms of understanding why he had chosen a neutral country, Ju's experience with the collective cohort functioned literally and figuratively as a pivotal part of how, when, and where the "neutral country" was defined. In their peculiar status of chosen statelessness, the prisoners of war formed strategies to make themselves visible to different states as viable candidates—they grouped themselves together accordingly. The vision of the "neutral country" was not an individual one, as POWs banded to ensure that no one individual would be left stranded. And it is through Ju's explication of other POWs' reasonings behind their decisions that the reader is able to glean a sense of Ju's possible motivations. Second, Ju and the other POWs were clearly aware of their particular status as the POWs who had chosen to go to a "neutral country." As "The 76 Prisoners of War," they held a symbolic importance for India; however, as time progressed, the POWs encountered a series of challenges in the increasing bipolarization of the geopolitical landscape. Ju's memoir was also a story about the incredibly disparate choices the POWs made in the years following the cease-fire. The search for the "neutral country" was perhaps even more difficult than the decision to choose a "neutral country."

After disembarking at Madras, the now ex-prisoners of war and members of the Indian CFI boarded a train that transported them to Delhi. Their arrival at Delhi was greeted by a mass of Indian citizens and government officials. In place of her father, Prime Minister Nehru, Indira Gandhi was there to offer an official welcome to the eighty-eight ex-POWs, making sure to shake each individual ex-POW's hand. Before boarding buses that would take them to their living quarters, the ex-POWs were split into two groups—those who had elected to stay in India as their "neutral country," and those who had elected to go to South or Central America for their possible "neutral country."[71] The ex-POWs had initially inquired about the possibility of Switzerland or Sweden as their receiving neutral countries, but both states had rejected the possibility. Ju had been a part of the group who had hoped to go to Central or South America.

Afterward, the ex-POWs arrived at their new living space in the New Delhi vicinity—a large, old hospital structure that had been erected by the British colonists. The Indian authorities in charge of the ex-POWs held a meeting with them, where the authorities made specific suggestions to the ex-POWs on how to organize their days. Classes on discipline, customs, public morals, domestic lifestyle, English language lessons, and dining manners, and also maintaining an organized daily life based on going to bed and rising early were all recommended.[72] It was clear that the Indian authorities viewed the ex-POWs as citizens-in-training and claimed responsibility for preparing these ex-POWs as proper subjects for whichever nation-state would become their future home. Education—in terms of language, trade, and behavior or composure—was considered to be important to transform the ex-POWs into proper subjects of the modern nation-state.[73]

However, finding a receiving "neutral country" had become much more complicated than anticipated. General Thimayya paid a visit to the ex-POWs' residence to convey the difficult news. The wait for a "neutral country" was most probably going to take a long time, much longer than anticipated, conveyed Thimayya. If any of the ex-POWs no longer wanted to wait to see if and which "neutral country" would be open to receiving them, then the Indian government would help them return to their original countries, whether China or North Korea. Otherwise, the only thing the ex-POWs could do in the meantime was to wait.[74]

Thimayya's words of caution about a long wait soon rang very true for the ex-POWs. It took at least another two years, until August 1956, for the majority of the ex-POWs to have a "neutral country" destination. Five months after Thimayya's initial talk with the ex-POWS, General Thorat, who had been the head of the CFI at the 38th parallel, came to discuss the situation with the ex-POWs. The situation had not changed ever since Thimayya's visit, and Thorat suggested that the most effective way to move the process forward was to have the ex-POWs petition states where they hoped to settle. After a meeting among the ex-POWs themselves, the resulting numbers were twenty-four for Mexico, twenty-two for Brazil, six for Argentina, and two for the Dominican Republic. Ju himself had selected Brazil, and he noted that the more anti-Communist-leaning ex-POWs had chosen Mexico and Argentina, while the more left-leaning ex-POWs had chosen Brazil and the Dominican Republic. For example, Ju portrayed one particular Korean ex-POW, Pak Gi-Chan, as a fervent anti-Communist—at this meeting with Thorat, Pak stood up and announced that all the ex-POWs must go to Mexico. Pak most probably considered Mexico to be safely anti-Communist because of its proximity and also "alliance" with the United States at that time. The ex-POWs were attempting to read the geopolitical landscape of Central and South America.

Over the next two years, the ex-POWs found themselves in an increasingly precarious situation. After the first round of petitions, Mexico was the only one who was willing to accept ex-prisoners of war; however, even Mexico was not willing to take all original twenty-four ex-POWs who had petitioned. There was constant reconfiguring and recalibrating among the ex-POWs, and eventually Brazil and Argentina also accepted a number of ex-POWS, although both states reserved the right to refuse the petitions of particular ex-POWs. By early 1956, the ex-POWs had received news about their possible destinations, but a collective letter sent by a number of Korean optees for Argentina to the United Nations conveyed a sense of their underlying anxiety:

> Most Honourable The U.N. Secretary-general, Dr. Dag Hammar-skijoeld
>
> From Korean ex-prisoners opted for Argentina
>
> It is really very happy that at last we are found our new home in beautiful country, Argentina after two year's waiting. Firmly we believe that it is only due to Your Excellency's favour and efforts through U.N. organization and direct and indirect contact with government concerned....
>
> Sir, in return for your Excellency's good office and the generous offer of Argentine government we will strive for the prosperity of Argentina along with her people.
>
> And it was said that our 57 Brazilian optees would leave here for Brazil on February 4.
>
> We hope that "very soon after that" we shall be able to leave for Argentina.[75]

The letter was signed as being "From all Argentine optees," but was specifically signed by Pak Sang Sin, Lim Ik Kam, Hong Il Seop, and Lee Chol Kyun. The letter was clearly an effort on the part of the ex-POWs to leverage some degree of pressure on the United Nations to ensure that their departure and acceptance by Argentina would happen. "We will strive for the prosperity of Argentina along with her people," they wrote, as they expressed their *desire* to become proper subjects of Argentina, their willingness to become productive citizens, if given the choice. The situation was a differently inflected situation of the explanation room for these former prisoners of war—rather than having their subjecthood explained by a member of the state, they found themselves in a position of having to explain their viable subjecthood for other states.

One major difficulty for a small subset of the ex-POWs was their background as officers in the Korean People's Army. Two particular ex-POWs, Hyeon Dong Hwa and Ji Ki Cheol, had applied for Argentina and Mexico respectively, but were repeatedly rejected. Ji had then tried to apply for Brazil, but because his application went in after the initial group of fifty-five had been sent, Brazil had refused his application also. In 1957, after the majority of ex-POWs had departed India, Hyeon Dong Hwa embarked on a letter-writing mission to the United Nations, sending letters dated April 25, May 7, October 22, and the final one on November 23. He wrote the letters to plead both his case and that of Ji Ki Cheol. In the first letter, Hyeon introduced him by immediately distancing himself from the possibility of being associated with Communism:

> I am a Korean ex-Prisoner of War who was brought here with Indian Custodian Troops in Feb. 1956. I came to India not because I am a pro-Communist or admirer of "Nehru's neutral policy" but because the injury which I got during the War and self-grieves were the main reason.[76]

And regarding Ji, Hyeon wrote, "It is beyond my conception that the Government of Argentina refuses the entry of one of most ardent anti-Communist fighter among our groups." He acknowledged that both he and Ji had been in the KPA, but he offered evidence of their "wills of fight with Communism." He had written a piece in the "reader's column in Hindustan Times in the Feb. 11th 1957 issue under the title of

'Korea Election,'" he stated in his letter, and the piece clearly communicated his anti-Communist beliefs.

Later, after Lennart Finnmark, the assistant to the secretary-general, suggested that they get in touch with the respective Argentine and Mexican embassies in New Delhi, Hyeon reported on his visit with the Argentine embassy, where "Mr. Falco, Chargé d'affaires of the Embassy, ... frankly told us that his government had refused to accept us because we were officers of North Korean army and were regarded as Communists."[77] Hyeon then stated, "Thereafter, we did everything in our power to obtain the materials that can prove us as anti-Communist and submitted them to him." The cases of Hyeon and Ji disappear from the United Nations archive after this final letter. But the series of letters written by Hyeon clearly demonstrates how the ex-POWs, although far away from the Korean peninsula, were still compelled to render themselves politically transparent in front of each state they wanted to petition. Being part of the "76 POWs" meant something different politically depending on from where in the geopolitical world one was looking.

The ex-POWs had also clearly made a strategy to render themselves visible to the state they were petitioning not only as individuals but also as a collective group. In a letter dated March 27, 1956, from Arthur S. Lall, permanent representative of India to the United Nations, to Mr. Dag Hammarskjöld, secretary-general of the United Nations, Lall forwarded lists of the men who had "expressed a desire to be resettled" in Mexico and Argentina and asked the secretary-general to forward the lists to the respective government representatives. Both lists provided the names of the petitioning ex-POW, sometimes also the ex-POW's age, and also the background and desired occupation of the ex-POW. An examination of the lists themselves reveals how the ex-POWs were preparing and trying to reinvent themselves for settlement in Mexico or Argentina. The Korean ex-POWs who had opted for Argentina all primarily wanted to work in the engineering sector, whether as a mechanical engineer, electrical engineer, or in chemistry.[78]

For the ex-POWs who opted for Mexico, the occupations of poultry farmer and camera mechanic were the choices of the majority. With such specific choices of occupations and training, the ex-POWs were hoping to travel with their specific group. Creating a life in a "neutral country" was not an isolated, individual vision at this point—the ex-POWs were presenting themselves as a collective specialized labor force and resource to each state.

The choice of a "neutral country" for these ex-prisoners of war had not happened spontaneously, but rather through debate, conversation, and discussion. In the "Indian Village," or "Hind Nagar,"at the 38th parallel, Ju Yeong Bok had a conversation with a friend, "Major KYM." Kym was thinking of choosing to go to a neutral country, and he "invited" Ju to join him. Kym made the argument that if they stayed in South Korea, they would not be able to secure "any decent jobs," and Ju quipped that they could become farmers of "potatoes or tomatoes at best." Kym noted that with his linguistic skills in Russian, Japanese, and Korean, and some English, Ju could possibly procure a position at a newspaper. Ju supposedly retorted, "Well ... two countries for one people, two sovereigns for one territory ... can a newspaper exist where there's no freedom of speech?" According to Ju's recollections, their conversation continued as follows:

> "Then, let's go to a free, wide world!" K said again.
> "But a month ago Sweden and Switzerland refused to receive POWs?" I reminded K.
> "There'll be other places ... Mexico, Argentina and Brazil in South America ... so let's go with hope!" K said.
> "We can build a large farm and work hard!" I said.

Kym enthusiastically agreed, "We'll all help one another and build a huge farm!"[79] In this recollection by Ju, "Major Kym" may not have so uncannily exactly predicted that Mexico, Argentina, and Brazil would indeed be the receiving countries, but it was clear that the POWs were discussing global politics in an attempt to discern which countries would possibly step in as "neutral" countries between the Cold War and nonalignment imperatives. Another important facet that this exchange highlighted was how the POWs clearly planned on creating small com-

TABLE 6.1. Status of Korean prisoners of war sent to India

Brazil	55	Arrived in Brazil according to letter from India Mission of March 27, 1956
Argentina	11	Opted for Argentina according to letter from India Mission of March 27, 1956; Argentine entry visa granted according to letter from the Argentine Mission of July 17, 1956
Mexico	9	Opted for Mexico according to letter from India Mission of March 27, 1956
India	7*	Opted for India
North Korea	4	Returned to North Korea
China	2	Returned to China
	88	

* One of these returned to North Korea according to Note Verbale from India Mission of August 17, 1956

munities together, building future plans on friendships forged in the POW camps.

In his memoir, Ju Yeong Bok depicted a conversation he had with another ex-POW, Yi Shinyeong, whom he had known ever since they met in the UNC camp at Yŏngch'ŏn in mid- or late 1952. They had become close, and Yi very willingly followed Ju. At some point, Ju had persuaded Yi to choose to go to a neutral country, but one night sometime after Thimayya's visit in 1954, Yi told Ju that he had decided to stay in India, rather than going to a country somewhere in Central or South America. Ju reconstructed Yi's words to him as follows:

> I decided on this after a great deal of thought. And this is not meant to be a reproach in any way to your proposal to go to a neutral country. Because I'm not an idiot, I have also thrown away everything "north" and "south." We left not because we were mistrustful of others but because we believed that we could leave behind the politics and ideologies and go to a foreign country where we could farm and have a successful life, no?

Yi believed that he would be able to "farm and have a successful life" in India rather than in Central or South America. He called the Indians very "pure and direct" and considered India to be "very democratic."

India had become the site of his vision of a "neutral country."[80] Although initially greatly surprised, Ju said that he wished him the best. Yi soon departed the ex-POW camp hospital, and two years later on February 4, 1956, ex-POW Ju Yeong Bok left India along with fifty-four other ex-POWs for Brazil.

The choice of a "neutral country" was neither assured asylum nor guaranteed immigration. The ex-POW was a stateless person, dependent on a discourse of humanitarianism to place strategic pressure on the United Nations and different states. The strategies they employed were multiple, and their choices revealed a longer history of imagining what a possible future might be. They exercised as much control as they possibly could over the seemingly haphazard structural shifts that determined their futures. They had to articulate themselves as proper subjects for an imagined nation-state. The demands of decolonization had not ended for them, just as the Korean War had not ended.

"A Neutral Country" and Decolonization

In his memoir, *The 76 Prisoners of War*, Ju Yeong Bok reflected on the possibilities neutrality could have opened up for politics on the Korean peninsula. He wrote, "8.15 Liberation. The joy of freedom and independence from the oppression of Japanese colonial rule had arrived. But the joy was shortlived." Almost immediately, the divided occupation of the Soviets and the Americans was imposed on the peninsula, and "another chain was tied around the neck of Koreans."[81] For Ju, Korea should have been a neutral nation, and at the time of writing his memoir, he also believed that Korea should become a permanent neutral nation. Neutrality, in this case, was a moment of Korea's history before the politics of the Cold War descended on the peninsula and co-opted the possible future in Korea. Scholar Theodore Hughes has noted how the massive, constant displacement of peoples through the colonial era and the divided occupation period resulted in a "sense of dislocation" for Koreans, which "made it easier to make the claim that one belonged neither" to South Korea nor North Korea. Hughes states that "this move toward nonbelonging represents a continuation of the calls for neutrality made in the 1945–1948 occupation period."[82] Ju completed his memoir in 1993, but perhaps when viewed through his thoughts on neutrality and Korean history, the choice that he made as a young man during the war to go to an undefined "neutral country" was a choice to go to a Korea that he believed should have been, one separate from the politics of the Cold War. But as Ju and the other seventy-five Korean prisoners of war very quickly discovered on their arrival in New Delhi, "neutrality" had already been tempered with the lens of the Cold War, and the vision of the "neutral country" evidently eluded more than just a few of them, as some elected to repatriate to North Korea eventually.

Ju Yeong Bok had not returned to North Korea. And although Ju no longer lived in Korea, the presence of the 38th parallel and the constant reminder of Korea's division still pained him. The dedication of his book reads: "This book is for my mother and all of the other mothers who had sent their sons to the front line and are still waiting for their return." Ju himself went on to write again and again, over and over his experiences of the war leading up to his choice to go to a neutral nation. His facility with languages—once used strategically to survive and navigate war—was then turned to survive a strange self-exile and diasporic life after the war. After his arrival in Brazil, Ju wrote what was possibly the first Korean-Portuguese dictionary. When his parents immigrated to Manchuria during the colonial era, Ju's father had found a job within a printing press shop. One wonders if this background, along with his parents' encouragement to study languages and literature, influenced how writing clearly became a critical instrument for Ju in his constant self-fashioning. He went on to write a two-volume memoir of his prewar and wartime experiences; he wrote a series of columns on the Korean War from his first-person accounts for the *Korea Times* in June 1980; and he recorded a torrent of memories—sometimes in Japanese, sometimes in English—for author John Toland, when Toland was gathering interviews and accounts for his book, *In Mortal Combat: Korea, 1950–1953*, which was published in 1991. Translation and narrative— these were continuous modes through which Ju grappled with his past.

Ju became a rigorous and patient scribe to all who had come before, telling his story this time not to an interrogator but to readers unknown, perhaps even in the hopes that one day his mother would read his dedication. Ju's life, his own archive, and the 38th parallel all acutely demonstrated the unending nature of the Korean War.

7

Above the 38th Parallel

THE US CITIZEN–POW

ACCORDING TO HIS CALCULATIONS, Arden Rowley, a twenty-three-year-old Mormon boy from the dairy farms and alfalfa fields of Arizona, had spent "32 months and 18 days" as a prisoner of war in Korea. On August 22, 1953, Rowley boarded the USNS *Marine Adder* for a two-week-long journey from the port of Inchon to San Francisco. At that point, it had only been four days since he had crossed over to US custody at the village of Panmunjom on the 38th parallel. When a US Army colonel had greeted him hours after his release and asked him what he would like to eat, Rowley requested "a big bowl of ice cream."[1] And in Inchon where the naval ships were docked, a "complete PX had been set up." Rowley was able to purchase "American goods for the first time in more than 3 years."[2] But the pleasure of 1950s America through the taste of ice cream and display of goods was brief. Once he boarded the *Marine Adder*, Rowley "was told ... to proceed to a certain room for ... interrogation and knock on the door."[3]

"About three days after we were freed," recalled Johnny Moore, another former POW, "we got on the ship. And thanks to the U.S. military, instead of flying us home as they should have, they took their own sweet time on the ocean, because they planned to interrogate us all the way across the ocean."[4] The US military had indeed prepared for these extensive interrogations by conducting some strategic "carpentry work" on these ships, to use the words of historian Raymond Lech. "Numerous booths, about four by four, were constructed," noted Lech, and each booth "contained a small field desk and two chairs." In essence, ships like Rowley's *Marine Adder* "became floating interrogation centers for the Counter Intelligence Corps (CIC) of the U.S. Army."[5] Michael Cornwell, one of the POW repatriates, said, "You could call what happened on the ship coming home debriefing or an interrogation, but it lasted all day long—some eight hours."[6] The soldier, who was supposedly a weapon of American warfare, had now become the target of American military intelligence.

During the Korean War, the prisoner of war emerged to eclipse the citizen-soldier as the dominant military figure in the American public's imagination of war-making. Arden Rowley was one of 4,428 US prisoners of war repatriated from the Chinese and North Korean camps during the war. Of these repatriates, 88 percent of them had been captured in the first year of the war, from July 1950 to June 1951, which meant that the majority of US POWs had been living in the Chinese and North Korean POW camps for almost three years, with some of them undergoing interrogation repeatedly. When these US POWs became repatriates and found themselves in a US military hospital in Tokyo or on a US naval ship headed for San Francisco, they quickly discovered that repatriation simply marked a turning point—rather than an end—to the demand on them to narrate their lives and experiences over and over again. For the next year or even up to four years, the US military demanded of these men details, chronologies, and names of men who had been either "collaborators" or "reactionaries." Agents of the CIC and the Federal Bureau of Investigation (FBI) followed these men far beyond the port of San Francisco. The entire apparatus of the US national security state was mobilized on both sides of the Pacific to diagnose, survey, and punish a domain of American warfare: the domestic militarized psyche. And "brainwashing" became the lit match that exploded the tinderbox of American anxiety over being unable to control the meanings of a war that was not a war.[7]

The Korean War was supposed to have been the "state of emergency" that held the real war—nuclear warfare with the Soviet Union—in abeyance. Jimmy Thompson was a member of the all-black 155th Howitzer Battalion; he was captured in late November 1950 by Chinese troops. He remembered the freezing temperatures all too acutely in his memoir. The US military had only given him light uniform clothing, despite the "20-degree below temperature." Thompson had been part of US General Douglas MacArthur's push northward past the 38th parallel, and everyone thought that they'd be "back home in time for Christmas turkey."[8] After all, "having fought a real world war against the Germans in France and Germany, Korea wasn't supposed to be any big deal."[9] American involvement supposedly operated as a deus ex machina on the Korean peninsula, its superior technology and knowledge enabling the US troops to move, disrupt, and reinvent the course of history. But the American POW, who seemed to be evidence of having been affected by the war, challenged this notion of war.

By the time Arden Rowley and other American POWs crossed into "Freedom Village" on the 38th parallel, the phrase "brainwashing" was in heavy rotation on the front pages of American newspapers, specifically in regard to the American POW. In April 1953, Neal Stanford, a correspondent for the *Christian Science Monitor*, published an article titled "Red 'Teaching' of Prisoners Stirs U.S.," where he concluded, "It is therefore not entirely fantastic to believe that when a voluntary exchange of PWs in Korea is actually arranged, there may be some Americans, as well as thousands of Communists, who will refuse to be exchanged.... And it would present the United States with a most serious problem—how to insist on the 'unwashing' of any Americans who may refuse to be repatriated so they can make a free and honest decision of their own."[10] During that very same month, Allen W. Dulles, the director of the Central Intelligence Agency, commented on the issue of "brainwashing" in a speech in front of Princeton University alumni: "The Communists are now applying the brain-washing techniques to American prisoners in Korea and it is not beyond the range of possibility that considerable numbers of our own boys there might be so indoctrinated as to be induced, temporarily at least, to renounce country and family."[11] With the signing of the cease-fire in July 1953, twenty-one US POWs announced that they had chosen to not repatriate to the United

States and would instead stay in China at the close of the fighting on the battlefields.

The American POW, under the specter of "Oriental" brainwashing, became a cipher for American unease about how the fast-moving backdrop of capitalism, the Cold War, and a decolonizing globe was challenging the seemingly assured coherence of the American individual self. "Choice" in the liberal individualistic sense was both the beacon of light and the litmus test for the full expression of selfhood. In order for this horizon of redemption to remain viable, the American soldier had to embody the teleological endpoint by being the manifestation of a secure individual selfhood with an imperial mastery over navigating the marketplace, warfare, and the everyday. The United States had offered "choice" to the Korean and Chinese prisoners of war, and thereby ensconcing the POW voluntary repatriation proposal within a halo of US-sanctioned redemption from which, depending on the choice made, the Korean or Chinese POW could emerge as aspiring liberal subjects. The American citizen-soldier was a priori coherent, whole, and present on the stage of history. But what if the American POW made a choice that rejected this premise?

When confronted with the twenty-one POWs who chose to stay in China—as well as reports that hundreds of American POWs had collaborated in some form with the Chinese and North Korean authorities in the camps—the US military, government, and public had to neutralize these American POWs and the potential visibility of their politics by rendering them again as "vulnerable" subjects. "Brainwashing" became the term that grabbed the media spotlight—and the American public's imagination for comprehending what had happened. In other words, these American POWs had essentially *not* made a choice and were instead victims of an Oriental Communist regime. Whether in the Hollywood film *The Manchurian Candidate* or Virginia Pasley's Pulitzer Prize–winning *21 Stayed*, the American POW of the Korean War was emblazoned publicly—with startling rapidity—as the symptom of a social malady, a national pathology, or an even deeper yet unidentified crisis of the United States.

Scholars have analyzed how and why the figure of the American POW incited and inspired such a fervor of sociocultural narratives, from psychiatry to journalism to film. The American cultural fascination and obsession with "brainwashing" exposed a nerve running through US imperial anxieties about the mutability of the domestic social order in relation to American projects of power abroad. Indeed, what happened if the subject transformed in the crucible of warfare was the American citizen-soldier, and not the intended "Oriental" everyman? The "brainwashing" anxiety around the US POW laid bare that a basic tenet of US imperial warfare vis-à-vis the global order had been challenged: the US was supposed to be the power that transformed the enemy in wartime encounters, not the other way around.

The figure of the "brainwashed" American POW was the product of a fundamental tension that lay in the fault lines between the American "war of intervention" that was to effect "freedom" in the postcolonial world and the Korean Communist revolution that was to fulfill the promise of liberation in postcolonial Asia. In this story about fashioning the decolonized subject for the post-1945 global order, we follow American prisoners of war through a series of prisoner of war camps north of the 38th parallel. Another cast of characters not usually present in the stories of the war come to the fore. Sons of working families in factories, on the railroads, or oil fields were in the North Korean and Chinese-run POW camps. The young men were from places like Puerto Rico, the Philippines, and the states of Louisiana, Ohio, and Texas. They were children of immigrant families—such as Japanese, Italian, or German—and they were children during the Great Depression. In the interrogation rooms, the North Korean interrogators were fluent and at ease in English, a number of them having attended college in the United States, and they were eager to talk with the POWs from working-class and racial minority backgrounds. Conversations about W.E.B. DuBois and Paul Robeson often took place within interrogation, as a North Korean vision of Third World internationalism began to take shape between the interrogator and the interrogated. How did one decolonize an American?

This study brings the inquiry into "brainwashing" back to the multiple encounters that had supposedly created and detected it and the multiple acts of narrative that each encounter demanded. The primary archival source consists of recently declassified US military interrogations of over one thousand US POW repatriates about their experiences of interrogation in the Chinese and North Korean POW camps north of the 38th parallel. To read the archive of the CIC vis-à-vis the US POW is to read about the US POW's negotiations with the "Oriental" interrogator, his own strategies in how to portray this encounter to the CIC agent, and how the CIC agent tried to evaluate the coherency not only of the story provided but also of the US POW sitting in front of him. And from these CIC reports, we can trace the patterns and contours of the Chinese and North Korean practices of interrogation, albeit with deep limitations.

The POW, the Psychiatrist, and the Interrogator

To show a therapist "how the men feel about things," a US POW repatriate brought a poem to a group therapy session held aboard the USS *General John Pope*. The therapist was twenty-seven-year-old Robert Lifton, one of the four psychiatrists assigned to 442 US POW repatriates who were making the journey across the Pacific from Inchon to San Francisco.[12] The poem, however, had been written before the USS *General John Pope* departed Inchon Harbor on August 26, 1953. Three prisoners, in anticipation of returning to the United States, had written it together in the camp.

In an academic article he published soon after his experience aboard the USS *General John Pope*, Lifton reproduced the poem verbatim in its entirety, but placed certain portions of the text in italics:

I know you are curious about my life in this strange land
As a prisoner of war in Korea, *but how could you understand?*

You ask about the treatment, was it good or was it bad?
I answer, it's all over now and I am very glad.

You ask if I was captured, if I was wounded too,
Yes, I was badly wounded, but *what does that mean to you?*

I realize your idle interest, curiosity and wonder too,
But even if I tried, I couldn't explain all this to you.

I hope this answers your questions, please forget you ever knew
That I was ever a prisoner, for I want to forget it too.[13]

This poem was not a description of their camp experience, nor was it a simple letter to those back home. The poem was supposed to have been an expression of "how the men feel about things," but the poem laid bare the men's feeling of the impossibility of communicating their experiences. Lifton himself was struck by the POWs' insistence that their experience was beyond the realm of storytelling. Their experiences defied being shaped into a story that both the teller and the listener could believe. The men *couldn't explain all this*, and *how could you understand?* To Lifton, they talked about "their unique forms of prison camp communication: "We spoke our own language up there—kind of a mixture of American 'bebop,' Korean, Chinese, and Japanese, and lots of four-letter words." They described how in the camps they "acted kind of crazy, like imitating a dog or a railroad train," and they explained: "You had to, to keep your spirits up. But back home, people might think we're peculiar."[14]

The US repatriate challenged a fundamental tenet of American interventionist and imperial warfare: military action was a discrete event, both temporally and geographically bounded. The American military was supposed to transform and affect the landscape, not vice versa. The "over there" of Asia seemed to be suddenly unsustainable, as these repatriates—molded by their experiences in the "Oriental" POW camps—were themselves not wholly "American" now. The crucible of wartime encounter with the enemy was supposed to have strengthened the masculine certainty of US liberal, democratic personhood. However, these repatriates were anticipating that other Americans would see them as "peculiar."

The third phrase in the above poem Lifton placed in italics revealed something else the POWs felt vis-à-vis their potential listener: "Yes, I was badly wounded, but *what does that mean to you?*" The authors of the poem expressed wariness about the intent behind the questions of the anticipated listener. Somehow, the standard storyline for the POW experience would not be sufficient for their experiences, and there would be repercussions for that insufficiency. The repatriates felt that, "they won't believe what we say back home anyhow. It's too fantastic." But more pressing than the issue of their own stories being outside the comprehensible purview of what constituted wartime experience was what other Americans would do if they could not understand: "People back home may think I'm a 'progressive,' or a Communist. If they accuse me of that, I'll sock them in the nose."[15]

The US POW repatriates were coming home to the United States, but felt that they were now unrecognizable, untranslatable, and incomprehensible. A career US military psychiatrist, William Mayer, observed the behavior of the repatriates who were convalescing in the hallways and rooms of a hospital in Tokyo before being shipped out to San Francisco. The men "did not wander around the hospital, or even their own wards"; instead, they were "passively waiting for whatever was to come next." When American Red Cross workers "offered the men the opportunity to call home to the U.S., at no cost, and talk to anyone they wanted," Mayer noted that "[to] everyone's astonishment, most of the returnees declined that offer."[16] For the three POWs who had written the poem, the reluctance to talk was more about an anticipated failure on the part of the listener to understand. In Mayer's opinion, the reluctance was a behavioral symptom of a deeper issue: "Oriental" brainwashing.

Mayer was a member of a board of "experts" organized by the US military to evaluate, analyze, and explain the US POW repatriate. The group was called the Joint Japan Processing Board (JJPB)—Mayer was joined by Robert K. Stull of the PsyWar division; Marion R. Panell from the Counterintelligence Corps (CIC); Steve Yamamoto, a representative from Military Intelligence (MI); Joseph S. Carusi, a legal representative; and Gordon R. Hatt from the US Air Force Office of Special Investigations. Given the task of understanding what had happened to the most basic weapon of war—the US soldier—the JJPB set up a precursor to the "floating interrogation centers" of the US naval ships. In the Tokyo hospital, the CIC conducted "approximately 850 interrogations," which involved 527 US repatriates, but the others included "personnel from Turkey, the Philippines Islands, Colombia, France, Greece, Belgium, and the Netherlands."[17] During the CIC routine interrogations of the repatriates who passed through the Tokyo hospital, the JJPB "decided to subject every third man to far more extensive questioning," which resulted in a "sample of more than a thousand" of the repatriates. "Unbeknownst to them or to anyone else in their group, these men were kept in the hospital several days longer than the others and interviewed in far greater detail."[18] During these interviews, "Every word of the questions and their answers was recorded, transcribed the same day, and delivered" to Mayer's research group the next morning.[19] A sense of patriotic mission pervaded the effort. As Mayer put it: "We had been charged with finding answers to questions that had shaken our whole military structure."[20]

The final report of the Joint Japan Processing Board confirmed the US POW repatriates' sense that they were already marked as somehow suspicious: "Every repatriated United States PW must be considered a potential threat to the security of the Armed Forces and the United States government until such time as his activities as a PW of the North Korean and Chinese Communists have been satisfactorily explained."[21] For the Counterintelligence Corps, similar to how the CIC had been tasked during the occupation and war to distinguish between the Communist and the anti-Communist Korean, the objective was to identify the collaborators among the returning former prisoners. And the substance through which they would make that judgment and assessment was narrative, whether in the form of questionnaires or summaries.

The challenge—and also the suspicion—lay in the fact that the body of the returning repatriate did not provide its own physical evidence or story of the experiences in the camp of the North Korean and Chinese militaries. As the US military psychiatrist William Mayer noted,

"Physically, the great majority was in surprisingly good condition. There was no physical evidence that they had been badly treated or fed poorly, although there were no fatties in the group.... What was first most striking was their silence and lack of any inter-action with one another as they stay, mainly on their beds on the wards, passively waiting for whatever was to come next."[22] If the body was an unreliable plane of evidence and the narrative given was not necessarily reliable, then how did one assess and come to the conclusion of "brainwashing"?

The US prisoner of war was the object of the JJPB's study, but it was a different figure in the Chinese and North Korean POW camps that caused a crisis in imagination for the board of experts. As narratives and questionnaires filled thousands on thousands of sheaves of paper, this archive of supposed evidence seemed to revolve less around the objective of understanding the US prisoner of war and much more around the aim to delineate a portrait of the "Oriental" interrogator. If the US POW was a symbol of a failed weapon of war, then the "Oriental" interrogator represented a new kind of warfare. Or at least the CIC and the JJPB constantly asserted this conclusion in their assessment of the countless interrogations they had conducted of the US POWs' own experiences of interrogation in the POW camps north of the 38th parallel.

> Our present concepts of acceptable behavior in captivity are based upon the assumption that while the enemy is a beast, he is more or less [an] honorable beast who treats his captives like men and leaves their feelings alone, even though he may employ physical brutality. It now appears that the new type [of] beast eschews physical torture and works on feelings and with better results.[23]

The "Oriental" interrogator who took shape in the reports clearly challenged the JJPB's idea of how an "Oriental" should have behaved. The more predictable Oriental "beast" would have embraced "physical torture." However, according to the POWs' narratives, the "physical measures" used during interrogation by the Chinese and North Korean militaries "consisted chiefly of isolation in a small space, maintenance of uncomfortable positions, a few sharp blows, relatively mild beatings, face slapping, denial of latrine privileges, reduced rations, etc. falling far short of the fingernail pulling, elaborate castration, and other Chinese tortures popularly associated with Oriental captivity."

The board's own assumptions of "Oriental captivity" certainly revealed the endurance and persistence of tropes in Western projected Oriental fantasies. But the board's insistence that the "Oriental" interrogator violated the "feelings" of American POWs, and therefore did not "treat" the American POWs "like men" pointed to a deeper anxiety the board members held. To employ "physical brutality" solely was supposedly an act of recognition on the part of the enemy that the American soldier was a man. A note of an odd nostalgia underlined this reasoning, as if the "Oriental" did not understand or fit into a traditional mode of warfare, where dignity, honor, and civilization were ideally always clear. Why would acting on "feelings" violate and rupture the coherent masculinity of the American soldier?

In the aftermath of World War II, such expressions of nostalgia for traditional warfare could have appeared strange and narrow-minded. But the US military's advice to American soldiers on how to resist enemy Japanese interrogation during World War II focused on maintaining a specific relational racial masculinity that could only be reaffirmed by the American POW actively rendering the Japanese military masculinity as incomplete, fraudulent, and—in the end—ridiculous. During World War II, the US military published a series of pamphlets that used cartoon images and humor to render essential survival skills, such as opening and operating a parachute, into an easy-to-remember script. In a World War II training pamphlet titled "Prisoner Sense," the authors counseled US soldiers when captured by the Germans or Japanese to disregard the "monkey-like expression on the Japanese faces" and the "beetling, stopped-up sewer look of the Germans," keeping in mind that the enemy had a "high degree of low cunning."

Especially with the Japanese officers, the US soldiers were advised to not worry about "threats of violence." "The Japs have been known to tell prisoners they were condemned to death, and then make all sorts of elaborate gestures to break down their morale," stated the pamphlet writers. To better illustrate this point, the writers noted that the

Japanese at times "merely made threatening gestures with their fists, flailing the air like men fighting mosquitoes." As this particular spectacle was occurring, the writers suggested that US troops occupy their minds on "random topics, preferably of a non-war variety." A few topics suggested were "sirloin steak, movies, football, women, and clubbing Japanese over their heads with baseball bats."[24] By re-experiencing American masculine bodily pleasures of consuming meat, viewing film and sports, and also a daydream fantasy of racial violence with an iconic American symbol, the American POW could supposedly ensconce himself safely within a discrete, superior American subjectivity. For the US military, the key element was to prevent the American POW from *feeling* distant from the United States, from *feeling* separated from or abandoned by US state power, one capable of protection, punishment, and rescue. It was the intimacy between the state and the citizen-soldier, the subtle collapse of state power on individual subjectivity, that the US military wanted to ensure was maintained.

The American POW repatriate from the Korean War presented a conundrum. All of his behaviors were suspect. There were so many behaviors that were supposedly abnormal for an American POW, according to Mayer: "why had so many men, known to have been captured, failed to come back; why had no one ever escaped and returned to our hands from almost unguarded village camps in a small, narrow peninsula country; why had so many collaborated with the enemy to make propaganda broadcasts to our units in the field; why hadn't a single one of our air-dropped escape and evasion 'rescue' specialists, sent to help people escape, even survived?"[25] The usual script of American warfare had been challenged by these US POWs' nonactions. Indeed, all of these behaviors were considered to be evidence of a deeper, underlying plot. The behaviors of these men had to be considered abnormal, unusual, and even exceptional. Warfare, in the American tradition, was supposed to be the forge for American manhood and manifest destiny. The sheer encounter with the "other"—whether an "Indian" in the conquest tradition of Jackson, or Secretary of State John Hay's "splendid little war" in the Philippines, or the war of eradication in the Asia-

Pacific theater of World War II—was the dynamic impetus for the forging of American manhood and nationhood.

In its effort to highlight what they considered to be model, "rational" behavior exhibited by American POWs in the camps, the members of the US military investigation board described "organizations [that] were formed for the purpose of resisting Communist indoctrination." The exemplary organization was:

> Ku Klux Klan (KKK): This organization was formed in most of the camps and the membership included a few well-meaning individuals who sent anonymous notes bearing the signature "KKK" to some of the better known "progressives" warning them to desist from collaborating with the enemy. Beatings were also administered to "progressives" and informers.[26]

In the eyes of the US military investigation board, the men who organized an informal KKK network in the camps had maintained an integrity of their subjectivity. There was practically no space for recognition for any kind of subject position between "collaborator" (assimilated into Orientalism) and the "KKK"—to the extent that only the KKK seemed to have maintained a recognizable subjectivity in the eyes of the board. In this report, the investigation board highlighted two characteristics of this KKK POW network: the members were "well-meaning" and they used tactics of intimidation, especially physical violence. These POWs of the KKK network had sustained an interior life, similar to that discussed in the pamphlet "Prisoner Sense," where a clear, racial disdain for the "Oriental" reinforced the POW's sense of white manhood. While the writers of "Prisoner Sense" had suggested to American POWs in World War II to imagine themselves clubbing their Japanese captors over the head with baseball bats, in the North Korean and Chinese POW camps of the Korean War, these American POWs had turned to their fellow POWs to demarcate racial orders with physical violence. According to this report, the measure of how successfully an American prisoner of war had endured wartime imprisonment was the degree to which he had continually maintained and replicated the everydayness of American life, even when they were thousands of miles away from the United States. There was much at stake in this kind of project for the American POW because the "everyday" of American life that the POW reproduced in the camps was also an encapsulation of the American society and values that he had been fighting for in the war. But the "everyday" of American life that was held up by the US military as the ideal was neither flexible nor varied.

In his review of the reports written by the CIC on their interrogations of the US POW repatriates, sociologist Albert Biderman provided a more nuanced demographic portrait of who the American POWs were in the Korean War. "The first world known by the large majority of these men was the Great Depression," wrote Biderman. "Relative to most Americans, few of them shared much" in the post–World War II "period of prosperity" marked by "neat suburbs." What they did know was "depression, war, and armed service," and a "considerable number of them had enlisted in the Regular Army to escape from the poverty and lack of opportunity of their back grounds." These POWs were from the "slums and 'nonwhite' ghettos of the city, tenant farm and barrio shacks and milltown" of America."[27] The backgrounds of the twenty-one American prisoners of war who chose to stay in China after the cease-fire matched Biderman's portrait. Of the twenty-one POWs, three of them had fathers who were railroad workers; others were from poor families who worked in oil fields or working-class families who worked in factories or lumber; and still others were from families who had migrated from rural areas to urban centers during the Great Depression in search of work.[28] Three of the twenty-one nonrepatriate POWs were African American. In front of media after the signing of the ceasefire, twenty-four-year-old Clarence Adams, who was from Memphis, Tennessee, made the following statement for media regarding his choice to not repatriate: "I am Clarence Cecil Adams of Memphis, Tennessee. My family and millions of other Negroes, plus myself, have suffered under the brutal attack of white supremacy and these cruel slave laws of the southern states."[29] The American "everyday" that these POWs brought with them to the camps along the Yalu River was one in which white-supremacist violence was present already and always. Historian

Tejasvi Nagaraja calls 1946 "a most violent year—with a wave of lynchings and riots against Black veterans in many incidents across the 48 states by police, military, guard and white-citizen agents, in a purposeful race-war against Black claims to first-class citizenship."[30] If these POWs, regardless of race, had mostly not experienced the postwar economic boom after World War II, then conversely they all had, inclusive of all races, experienced the postwar project of "reconversion" as a racial structuring via policing, vigilantism, and legal policies on the ground.

In the United States, under the pressure of having to cover up the deep stigma of racism in the Cold War competition over which society offered equality and democracy to its members, President Truman signed Executive Order 9981, which called for the desegregation of the US armed services. Christine Hong has noted how during the Korean War, US officials attempted to recast the war as one that heralded the democratizing effects of the military, especially in its putative racial desegregation, "in effect ideologically framing the US military as the vanguard of civil rights reform."[31] But in the POW camps of the war, such narratives fell flat. The "America" that was present was the one where the second rise of the Ku Klux Klan during the 1920s was far-reaching and the KKK was "never a secret organization." Historian Linda Gordon describes a KKK that "published recruiting ads in newspapers, its members boasted their affiliation, and it elected hundreds of its members to public office."[32] Although the KKK did make exaggerated claims to having four to six million members, Gordon points out that during the 1920s, the "Klan's program was embraced by millions who were not members, possibly even a majority of Americans." The Klan of the 1920s "seemed ordinary and respectable to its contemporaries."[33] The recreation of the KKK in the POW camps of the Korean War was not something entirely unimaginable. With the presence also of POWs from Puerto Rico and the Philippines, the everyday life within these POW camps mapped out much longer and broader histories of how race and warfare have been central cogs to the workings of US empire—at home and abroad. "Brainwashing"—although catapulted into American popular memory via *The Manchurian Candidate* as an artifact of the McCarthy era—had a longer genealogy of anxiety, fear, and power within

American imperial history. It came from a deep-seated anxiety on the part of Americans about what they would see if the lens of decolonization was turned back on them.

Battlefield to Camp

On the "cold, damp and weary night" of November 30, 1950, Jimmy Thompson, a self-described "black Arkansas farm boy," realized that he and other members of the all-black 155th Howitzer Battalion were in "serious trouble" when he saw the troops of the retreating Thirty-Eighth Infantry suddenly among them—"men, barely alive, with arms and legs blown off." The "units consisting mostly of blacks and Turkish soldiers were still being told to 'hold and cover the retreating forces,'" but when Thompson and others "observed retreating white officers removing their brass and insignia to protect their rank and identity if caught," those who were alive decided what they needed to do. Or as Thompson described the hour: "protect your own ass time."[34]

In an area somewhere 150 miles north of Pyongyang in northern Korea, Thompson spent the next twenty-four hours trying to evade the Chinese troops. With the "crackle of gunfire" echoing through the surrounding mountains, Thompson played a "game of cat and mouse" with the Chinese troops for what seemed to be a very long time. Until he could no longer. Thompson's leg was bleeding, and he had no weapon. "A soldier senses a very eerie feeling upon being captured," wrote Thompson in his memoir.[35]

Becoming a prisoner of war was not a moment of relief. The labor, intention, and identity of a US soldier like Thompson were invested entirely in the obliteration of the enemy soldier. To be granted another moment of life by this very same enemy soldier seemed almost perverse. "You lie on your belly day after day trying to blow the head off some poor bastard a mile away," explained Thompson. "You try to subject him to every conceivable horror of war imaginable. You burn his crops, destroy his supplies, set ablaze his homes and torture his friends." As a "black Arkansas farm boy" who lived under Jim Crow racial segregation at home, he understood how to read the cues about racially differentiated degrees of disposability of life on the battlefield—and when he could no longer trust the US military's official line.[36] In front of the Chinese troops, he himself was the terrain he needed to read preemptively to assess his vulnerability—how would the Chinese troops see and understand him? And what would make them decide to give him another moment of life?

Thompson's "very eerie feeling upon being captured" disclosed an understanding that this granting of another moment of life was an assertion of power. It was not a reprieve from the scenes of violence, death and warfare, but rather simply an extension of it. "They decided to take me and did.... I concluded that they wanted me alive."[37]

The postbattle landscape on the Korean peninsula was ghastly, and one that was still strange to the newly recruited or drafted US soldiers. "During the day a lot of Gooks had been killed," wrote Lloyd Pate. "The sun had shone on their bodies and caused gas to come up inside of them. The cool night air caused that gas to want to come out and it was making a rustling noise. All that night I kept hearing this noise. I'd holler, 'Halt! Who goes there?' And I was scared speechless, you might say."[38] Pate and Thompson were part of the two shifts in the battlefields during the first year of the war, which were the Inchon landing in September 1950 and the Chinese entrance into the war in November 1950 after US General Douglas MacArthur crossed northward over the 38th parallel. Just as the vast majority of Korean prisoners of war were taken in right after MacArthur's Inchon landing, the vast majority of American prisoners of war were taken in during and after the November 1950 involvement of the Chinese Communist Forces (CCF).

Capture and surrender in the midst of these relentless waves of violence across the peninsula became moments of unexpected exchange. When a "hand-grenade explosion" knocked Private First Class Francis Mosnicka "unconscious," two CCF soldiers moved him away from the hill, searched him, and then bandaged his wound. Mosnicka recalled that the two soldiers "appeared friendly and tried to talk to him ... 'hello' ... 'ok,' and laughed."[39] For George Barnett, the "Chinese tried to force him to yell to other UN troops to stop fighting and surrender because they would not be harmed."[40]

In late November, winter had begun. And it was brutal for the American prisoners of war. As the initial war for containment turned into a war for rollback, another kind of war commenced: carpet bombing. During the three years of battle, US airplanes dropped 635,000 tons of bombs on Korea—primarily on the north—a staggering amount that was even more than the 503,000 tons the United States dropped in the Pacific theater of World War II. It was indeed a different war. During the summer and fall of 1950, the North Koreans had virtually no air support or defenses of which to speak. The landscape of what had been the industrial heartland of Korea under Japanese colonial rule was reduced to dust and rubble within two years. An estimated 8,700 factories, 5,000 schools, 1,000 hospitals, and 600,000 homes were destroyed, according to DPRK statistics. The American prisoners of war noticed that the sound of airplanes would send North Korean soldiers and civilians scrambling for cover. In the early months of the war, the North Korean soldiers traveled via railroad with captured US prisoners of war, housing them in firehouses and schoolhouses in different cities and towns. But the US bombing critically changed how US POWs were taken to the north. Moving under the cover of darkness, the US POWs had to walk through the snow and freezing cold because roads and the railroad had either been destroyed or were likely targets for US bombing. Historian Charles Armstrong writes of this moment in the war: "Agriculture was devastated, and famine loomed. Peasants hid underground during the day and came out to farm at night."[41] As the US POWs traveled north, with their light fatigues, the freezing temperatures and the scant food supply soon resulted in an ongoing struggle to survive.

When they arrived at what the POWs would nickname "Bean Camp," because they were fed a diet primarily of various beans, the landscape of wars past was present. Alfred Banah, a US POW, recounted to the CIC interrogator that they stayed in "former Japanese Army barracks where World War II prisoners had been interned." In fact, one of the British POWs "had been a prisoner of the Japanese and was interned at this location until he was liberated by the Russians."[42] But the Chinese and North Korean militaries were intent on shuttling everyone farther and farther north, away from the 38th parallel.

Camp #5, the largest among the camps the Chinese and North Korean militaries established during the conflict, was on the uppermost North Korean shore of the Yalu River, with China on the other side of the water. Johnny Moore recalled arriving at the camp in January 1951. The camp consisted of homes of "people who had been evacuated from the lower part of the town.... Looking down we could see a peninsula. The river was frozen over, but you could see the ice, and it enveloped the land at the bottom and around each side.... We could see Manchuria on the other side of the river."[43] POWs estimated that there were about 3,400 prisoners in total living in the camp, and the prisoners were segregated by nationality, race, and grade. The first company was "American colored troops," the second company was Turkish troops, the third one was "American caucasian troops," the fourth one was "Spanish and Puerto Rican troops, and the fifth company was British troops.[44] Among these were other nationalities: Filipinos, Colombians, Japanese, Dutch, Greek, Australian, and Canadian. Although the POWs were divided into compounds of three or four homes, there was no fence dividing the camp from the rest of the town, only a few guards to patrol the area. Bartering with the Korean townspeople and nearby farmers happened occasionally, with cigarettes to buy items like UN leaflets the civilians had picked up or an item of food.

Beginning in January 1951, the Chinese military began educational programs for the prisoners of war, and the scheduling was intense. In the mornings, the instructors—who were Chinese usually—gave lectures, usually for the one hour before breakfast and then again for two and a half hours after breakfast. Over the course of the following months, POW George Sayre stated that "the entire US political system was discussed." In the afternoons and evenings, the camp instructors organized study groups, which were more casual and informal.[45] The lecture topics were wide-ranging:

American plans for world domination; how capitalism got started and why it should be stopped; how the U.S. controlled foreign countries through trade; how the Marshall Plan aid was designed to gain control of foreign governments by forcing them to be dependent on the U.S.; how the American big business men picked political candidates, put them in office, and then controlled them ... how China was progressing under the new government by improvements in education, methods of production and the position of women in China ... the burden that the U.S. taxpayer was shouldering in order to further war and aggression; that the better ways of American life, schools and public works, were being neglected in favor of rearmament; how all races, except the Caucasian, were suppressed in America and prevented from progressing ... that the peace treaty between the U.S. and Japan was a war treaty; that the people of all American occupied nations resented American occupation.[46]

The lectures, according to the POWs, were often handed down from the higher offices. But the portraits the US POWs provided to the CIC interrogators of the Chinese instructors pointed to social dynamics that could not entirely be controlled by the higher military offices and programs. One POW described a figure well known to the other POWs in Camp #5—a Chinese instructor nicknamed "Screaming Skull" by the POWs. George Sayre commented that Screaming Skull was a "good time Charley" and "appeared to like Americans. He smoked, drank, liked to play the trap drums," often joining POWs in "jam sessions." Screaming Skull, noted Sayre, spoke "good English" and frequently invited POWs to his quarters "after hours for drinking and talking." In fact, Sayre said that the POWs did not know what to make of Screaming Skull, and some were even suspicious that he might be an "American agent," but Sayre concluded that Screaming Skull was "reasonable; and, when some PW were in trouble, he often failed to report them and talked to them individually instead."[47]

Another instructor, nicknamed "Professor," "spoke excellent English and claimed to have attended Yale University." And indeed, the other instructors all laid out another facet of the unexpected group that had formed in Camp #5. POW Ray Dowe noted other instructors who had ties to the United States: there was Shu who was twenty-eight years old and "professed to have a sister residing in San Francisco who was disowned by the family for not returning to China." Shu's father was supposedly a former merchant in Shanghai who had ties to the government. Then there was Leon, possibly in his late twenties, who "spoke fluent English with a good knowledge of American slang," and he had supposedly attended the University of California, Los Angeles.[48] In Camp #1, POWs noted that from October 1951 until the spring of 1952, the POWs heard lectures on the topic of "Depression Years in U.S.," which were given by a "Comrade Young" who had been "reportedly in States at that time."[49]

In the postrepatriation interrogations with the US Counterintelligence Corps, especially in the interrogations conducted aboard the naval ships slowly sailing across the Pacific, certain US POW repatriates employed a specific strategy to establish their credibility in front of the CIC interrogator. They portrayed the "Orientals" at their camps and interrogation rooms much along the same lines as in the pamphlet "Prisoner Sense." Caricatures, rather than portraits, came to the fore in a number of the interrogations. The "Oriental" character was a foil to the asserted American male character of the POW repatriate. For example, there was "Sun," a Chinese instructor and platoon commander at Camp #5, who "spoke in high girlish voice, particularly when excited; walked with feminine air."[50] Or Wong, nicknamed "Shaky" by the POWs, could speak Russian and English, but "had to be treated as a small boy."[51]

It seems significant that the person who perhaps spent the most time on a regular basis with the POWs would be portrayed in a much more expected "Orientalist" manner. The composite portrait of "Screaming Skull" consisted of him being a "homosexual," who had "relations with PW" and "held hands with other Chinese."[52] He spoke "fluent English," but had a "high pitched screaming voice." Screaming Skull knew "a lot about U.S. history," but he was a "fanatical Communist."[53] The fanaticism was on display whenever he delivered speeches because he "would wave his hands wildly and stamp his feet."[54] By portraying Screaming Skull as an Oriental with an aberrant sexuality, the US POW affirmed the coherency of his own masculinity. If one could diagnose and condemn the pathological, then one was speaking from the safe confines of having maintained a normative masculinity in behavior and mentality.

The details, when conflicting, exposed either how much the US re-patriates desired to portray these "Orientals" as stereotypical carica-tures, or how much their own stereotypes had framed their memory and seeing. For the man nicknamed "Hatchet Man," the POWs gave conflicting family names—Wong, Li, and Chin.[55] The one common thing in descriptions of "Hatchet Man" was the pomaded black hair, but one POW noted his "slight build" along with a "stooped left shoulder" that "drooped,"[56] while another noted his "stocky build" with a "square" jaw,[57] and yet another recalled his "oval face."[58] However, Joseph Harri-son noted more fully in his observations that "Hatchet Man" was "re-puted to speak four to five languages; spoke English well; understood Korean," and he also "used American slang." Harrison had observed that "Hatchet Man" always took notes in Pitman shorthand, and "stud-ied on his own, studies not of a Communistic nature but for his own advancement," and even "lent his Pitman Shorthand Text to a POW to study in 52–53." Despite the unreliability of the descriptions of "Hatchet Man," Harrison's observation did reveal the everyday intimacy that de-veloped in the camps between the "Oriental" interrogators, guards, workers, and the US prisoner of war.

In the midst of the everyday life shaped by these lectures and study groups was the camp's library. The POW library in Camp #5 was one room, measuring about "thirty feet long and twelve feet wide." Richard Artesani Jr., a master sergeant in the US Army, served as the POW li-brarian, and he was responsible for operating and cleaning the library during regular hours, "usually from 1600 hrs to 2100 hrs." He described the layout and contents of the library: it had "one light, a pot bellied stove," and shelves that "extended along the room and contained space for about 150 books." Below the books were shelves for magazines and newspapers.[59]

In his CIC interrogation, Artesani took evident pride in the kind of space he had created for his fellow POWs. He told the Chinese camp officials that he needed flour "for making paste," and then he would "make dough out of it and make buns on his stove." Other POWs stole food from other places and brought it to Artesani to be cooked or heated. According to Artesani, "there was always a snack to be had in the library for anyone coming in to relax." But even more importantly,

Artesani used the library as a kind of hub. He worked as the POW librarian for approximately one year, during which time he had supposedly "called in about 150 men to see him." Artesani was able to monitor who was reading what, and if he felt that a particular POW was "reading too much on communism," he would invite the POW to come in "for a talk ... to discourage any further reading of this sort by pointing out [to] the man how trouble might ensue." Artesani, with the help of friends, also read through all of the books and removed pages that they deemed contained content that was "anti-religious." And POWs themselves "pulled out passages that disgusted them," or "inserted expressions" into the books for the next reader. He noted that "most of the books had pages missing," due to Artesani's pruning and the POWs' using book paper for cigarette paper. The POWs who indeed wanted to "read books of a political nature" were few in number; however, these POWs read the entire collection of the political books.[60]

Indeed, in their CIC interrogations, the POWs attested to the efficacy of the library over the lectures and study groups in terms of influencing the POWs' political views. US POW Manuel Castlewitz believed the "library to be the most effective means because PsW could become indoctrinated without being forced."[61] Everett Carpenter, a twenty-one-year-old from Verda, Kentucky, read "parts of books but felt it a bunch of 'bull': however, most men believed to be 'Pros' were men who had read a bunch of books."[62] A POW from Liberty, Kentucky, Edward Campbell, stated that "he read a good bit," and he called books such as *Tom Paine* and *Freedom Road* to be "good," while *Iron City* and *American Imperialism* were "bad."[63]

For the books themselves, Artesani stated that many of the books had been written during the Great Depression, and they "portrayed the life of the sharecropper in the United States ... in highly idealistic terms."[64] The books rotated between the different camps, and the composite portrait of the collection indicated a wide-ranging, even surprising selection of books:

Posthumous Tales of the Piquikillwick [Pickwick] *Club* (Dickens)
Grapes of Wrath
Citizen Tom Paine

Tom Sawyer
Anthology of American Negro Literature
Christmas Carols
Les Miserables
Freedom Road
Path of Thunder
The Negro in America
Masses in Mainstream (Herbert Aptheker)
Political Affairs
History of the Communist Party (Soviet and US)
Outline of Political History of Americas (Foster)[65]

There were also "articles by Paul Robeson; books by Dr. W. G. Dubois [W.E.B. Du Bois],"[66] "story books such as Robin Hood, Black Beauty, and the Three Musketeers,"[67] and even "non-political books by such authors as Edgar Allan Poe and O. Henry."[68] The Chinese and North Korean officials clearly held a deep knowledge of American culture and literature—this diverse collection addressed class and race in everyday life.

In Camp #5, the one-room library, with buns and snacks heating on a pot-bellied stove, was located right next to the Chinese interrogation room. Artesani stated that he "would eavesdrop on the conversations that the Chinese had" with the other prisoners. And if he ever heard the Chinese instruct the POW to go and write an article on a particular topic (or suffer some kind of punishment), Artesani would take it on himself to bring the men to the library and "help them to write the articles in a way that would not sound too un-American." Artesani seemed eager to convey to the CIC interrogator how he had worked effectively as a guiding arbiter to the other POWs as they navigated what was fast becoming a very blurred social everyday—one where the "Oriental" knew much more about the American already than vice versa, and one where casual exchanges were possible between the prisoners and the camp officials. As the POWs, who felt incredibly fraught and anxious about how people back "home" in the United States would perceive them, told Lifton in their group sessions later: "We spoke our own language up there—kind of a mixture of American 'bebop,' Korean, Chinese, and Japanese, and lots of four-letter words." The everyday life in the POW camp was indeed impacting the POWs' sense of self and collective, and Artensani viewed himself as someone who could essentially ensure that this "mixture" was not happening at the most fundamental level for the POWs. Artesani's policing and pedagogy was happening right at the heart of an ecosystem set up between interrogation, the book, and the pen.

"Hopes and Desires" in Interrogation

The Korean major who was responsible for individually questioning every POW who passed through the "Valley" was an "English-speaking Korean, twenty-five years of age," recalled Richard Artesani. On December 10, 1950, it was Artesani's turn to go through the preliminary interrogation process. The questions the major asked were checks on a "personal history statement" POWs had to fill out after surrender or capture: "name, rank and serial number, length of service, reason for enlisting (if enlisted), name of mother and father and their respective incomes." After one hour of interrogation, this Korean major posed a "last question" that was "identical with the last question of every other interrogation to which ARTESANI was exposed. This was: 'State your hopes and desires.'"

"He was very sincere and appeared to have no hatred for Americans," according to Artesani's description of him. And after posing the final question to Artesani, the major offered to explain his own "hopes and desires." The "major stated that his individual hopes and desires were for the Americans and Chinese to leave Korea and for the Koreans to live in peace." Artesani's interrogation concluded with the Korean major making a note "on the interrogation sheet his observation of the character of the interrogee. He wrote, 'This man is (or is not) sincere.'"[69]

On the part of the Chinese and North Korean armies, the aims of interrogation were threefold: tactical information, US intelligence systems, and the enlightenment of US POWs regarding Communism. Both the Chinese and North Korean interrogators required the American

POWs to fill out a basic personal history statement. And then quite a number of POWs, although not all, were asked repeatedly to write or tell their autobiographies during the course of their imprisonment.

However, a very interesting difference reveals itself between the working assumptions and frameworks of the Chinese interrogators and the North Korean interrogators. The Chinese interrogators worked from a place of omniscience, where they asserted that they knew everything already. For example, when US POW Alarich Zacherle underwent interrogation "within an hour after capture," the questions "were primarily tactical in nature." Zacherle refused to give any information beyond his name, rank, and serial number, and "he was neither threatened nor subjected to any violence at this time." The Chinese "boasted, however, that he already knew the answers; pointed at the patch on ZACHERLE's shoulder and identified it as the 2d Infantry Division insignia." Zacherle was told "that it was foolish not to answer, since, 'you cannot fool the CPV; they know everything.' Many times in the months to come, the prisoners were to hear this phrase."[70]

Because the Chinese military was the dominant force on the ground during the last two years of the war, it made sense that the Chinese interrogators were more invested and interested in extracting technical and tactical knowledge from the US prisoners of war. The Chinese also comprised the majority of the instructors in the political courses run at the POW camps, so this kind of division of interests between the tactical and the political may have been possibly strategic. The North Korean interrogators, on the other hand, worked from a place of intimacy, a potentially much more horizontal line of relating. They were the ones who provided a space for change, for reflection and pause. It is clear that the North Koreans had a slightly different set of stakes from the Chinese involved in the POW camps and interrogations.

In December 1951, US POW Shelton Foss underwent additional screening by North Korean officers at Camp #2. A lieutenant colonel named Kim "took FOSS to a Korean house outside the camp." There, Kim introduced Foss to another North Korean lieutenant colonel named Zun, who did not speak English. When Kim explained to Foss that they would like to talk with Foss, he replied that he "would not discuss military matters with them." In response, Kim and Zun explained that they "just wanted to have a talk with him on general matters pertaining to life in US and Korea."

Cigarettes and tea were offered to Foss, and the "opening conversation was about life in the U.S." Foss had grown up in Maine, so Kim wanted to learn about the "climate, industry, agriculture, customs, songs, sports, etc." In turn, Kim then talked about Korea, "the new order, improvements, etc." But songs ended up taking up much of that day's conversation. "KIM and ZUN knew the tunes of many American songs, and Kim knew the words of 'Home Sweet Home,' 'Home on the Range,' 'My Old Kentucky Home,' and 'You are my Sunshine.'" Kim asked Foss to write down the lyrics to the song "Come back, Little Sir Echo," and Foss noted in his CIC interrogation that he believed Kim had been "educated by American Missionaries" in order to be familiar with these songs.[71]

Kim and Zun soon regularly brought Foss to the Korean home outside the camp bounds. "Sometime in the afternoon, KIM took out a bottle of brandy, which was about half full and had Oriental writing on a yellow label, and offered him a drink." Foss apparently did not refuse—"It was good brandy, which he believed either American or British." He "accepted the drink, then the next, and so on, until the bottle was empty." Kim told Foss that he and Zun were sharing their liquor ration with him. Soon, the conversation "was taking a turn toward controversial political subjects; workers' plight in the UN, success of Communism in Korea; why not in the U.S., etc." Supposedly to goad Kim and Zun into revealing more information, Foss then "quoted excerpts from MARX and ENGELS," which was "a fact very pleasing to KIM and ZUN." Foss told the CIC interrogator that he excused himself to go to the latrine and vomit up the brandy "through fear of not knowing what he might say or do."[72]

When he returned to Kim and Zun, they said a few words to him before returning him to the camp at "2100 hours." They advised Foss not to tell the Chinese about "what they were discussing ... and told to say that he had undergone typical questioning." In Kim's words, the Chinese "did not understand the problem." Foss told the CIC interrogator that he believed that the CCF had granted permission to Kim and Zun to interrogate him "but that the true purpose of the interviews was not known by the CCF." And here in the competing claims over the US POW, a division opened up between the KPA and the CCF: Kim once told Foss that "the CCF were not as clever as they thought they were, and that the NK communists were closer to the desired level of development."

Soon, the three of them were meeting regularly. There was food, cigarettes, and Korean brandy, and they "played chess, sang American songs … and talked generally about the US and Korea." Eventually, Kim and Zun asked Foss "if he would like to be a 'leader' in his country (US) upon return." Foss came up with a different strategy at this point in dealing with their request: if he played along, Foss believed that they "might give him a chance to return to the UN lines," where he could then immediately give the information to the "nearest 'reliable' CIC officer." When they met again the following day, Foss told Kim and Zun "that he was willing to be a leader in the US." At that point, "he was asked to write his complete autobiography, which took him two days." The autobiography writing was followed by other acts of writing, and then an oath ceremony, where he pledged to "uphold the Friendship of the Korean and American Peoples." Before they last parted ways and Foss never saw Kim and Zun again, Kim had "advised FOSS to go to a university upon return to the U.S. and to study political science." The primary place discussed as a possibility was the University of New Mexico.

Although Foss did not know, or did not reveal, the personal background history of Lieutenant Colonel Kim, Kim's fluency in the English language, knowledge of US culture and institutions, all point to him working within a socialist internationalist frame. For the Korean Communist interrogator, the use of autobiography as a technology of the self was a recently transformed, postcolonial tool of the state, formed in the crucible of colonial police practices and revolutionary anticolonial collectivism. The Japanese colonial police, a highly well-organized structure that followed Korean anticolonial revolutionaries from the Korean peninsula to Manchukuo and beyond, demanded multiple, exhausting personal history statements to check the veracity

of a Korean colonial subject's claims of who he or she was. These statements were then kept on file, and Koreans under colonial rule were
trained to keep their narratives consistent, or strategically inconsistent,
depending on the situation and need.[73] In 1945, with liberation from
colonial rule, the practice of self-narration became a way to demonstrate evidence of full subjective rupture with the colonial past and to
narrate the individual into a collective future horizon with the postcolonial state. In her study of autobiographical writing practices during
the post-1945 liberation period in North Korea, historian Suzy Kim
notes, "Sharing common experiences of capitalist colonial modernity,
many of the autobiographies included similar stories of economic hard-
ship compounded by ethnic discrimination, which became one of the
main themes by which to plot one's life in the postcolonial period."[74]
The act of writing an autobiography provided "a necessary moment of
reflection and deliberation about the colonial past as a way forward."
Or as Theodore Hughes has examined in Korean postliberation literature written by proletarian authors, the narrative demanded that "what
must now occur is a movement—by way of introspection, self-critique,
confession—toward becoming a properly liberated subject prepared to
participate in the making of history."[75] When placed on the US POW,
this very practice of enacting a subjective, interior rupture with the
colonial past raises a question of how the imperial citizen would do so
vis-à-vis his own past, present, and future.

For the North Korean interrogators, offering a chance to the American POW to renarrate one's life story was an offer of a different kind
of template for thinking about historical agency. The North Korean
military focused on the notions of will and transformation. In his work
on post–Korean War criticism culture in North Korea, Andre Schmid
examines an article written by Ri Hongjon that was "published in the
same month as the armistice." Ri insisted on how "criticism ... served
as a vehicle for change," and in his words, criticism could "purge the
vestiges of colonial and feudal thought, as well as the remains of Japanese bourgeois thought."[76] The US POW like Foss was being brought
into the "long tradition of criticism" within socialism, but here, it was
the North Korean interrogators' familiarity with US society and culture

that was used to create a space of persuasion. The North Korean interrogators rendered their sense of historical socialist change as a possible template for the US POW to inhabit, so that the US POW could then project a future in which he acts politically within a global socialist and internationalist context. This kind of project was a possible precursor to the later North Korean project of internationalizing *juche*, the Korean notion of a revolutionary subjectivity forged through self-reliance, as a theory and practice for Third World subjects. Often seen by historians and political scientists as an ideology that reinforced the consolidation of the postcolonial North Korean state in the 1960s, the internationalist *juche* within the interrogation rooms of the early 1950s looks unexpectedly different and more open. It was still more practice than ideology, and the creation of a collective consciousness to thus imagine an expanded temporal and geographical framework for constant revolution was operating in the interrogation room.[77]

The American analysts of the CIC interrogation data often lumped the Chinese and the North Korean interrogators together under "Oriental," but more often than not the US analysts were preoccupied with the Chinese methods, as the US military and government believed that North Korea was the twice-over puppet state of both China and the Soviet Union. The JJPB obfuscated these kinds of relationships with North Korean interrogators by portraying the North Koreans as simple sadists: "The North Koreans generally lacked subtlety and finesse and were not politically minded. Their methods in contradistinction to the Chinese, who were subtle and predominantly political in their attitude, were primitive and direct."[78] Clearly, the JJPB understood that the US military and government were invested in creating an enemy, and here the enemy—nefarious, "Oriental," and unpredictable—was the Chinese. But the elision of the North Korean interrogation techniques such as those in Foss's experiences possibly signaled a deeper discomfort with—or perhaps simple dismissal of—the kind of intimacy that was claimed by the North Korean interrogators. Violence was threatened and practiced by both the North Koreans and Chinese interrogators, but the political lessons were conveyed in different registers and relational dynamics. Jimmy Thompson, the African American prisoner of war in Camp #5, recalled the demeanor of the Chinese interrogators during this one particular lecture they gave him. In Thompson's own words from his memoir:

[The Chinese told] me I had knowledge that could be put to use helping my people but that I wasn't doing a damn thing but wasting it. They suggested that my attitude was nothing but a total disgrace to my people, to the black race in particular, and to Third World Peoples in general. This "lecture" really got under my collar. I guess it wasn't so much what they said as how they said it. It was said in a very condescending manner.... Reminded me of too many well meaning patronizing whites back home in Arkansas.[79]

The experiences of American POWs in these kinds of North Korean interrogation rooms seemed for the most part to have taken place earlier during the war, during the first two years of captivity. It is most probable that after the proposal of voluntary repatriation was placed on the table at Panmunjom, the Chinese focused much of their energy on the political classes they conducted in the camps. After the signing of the cease-fire, the CCF appeared to have given similar "missions" as the North Koreans to US POWs. In their final report, the JJPB singled out three prisoners of war as "potential menaces" to the United States— one was an African American, the other a Filipino, and the third was a Nisei Japanese American.

Master Sergeant Preston E. Richie, an African American young man from Texas, was one of these "potential menaces." A thirty-two-year-old father of six, Richie had worked as a cook at the Kelly Field Officer's Club and then at the San Antonio Aviation Cadet Center. When he arrived in Korea in August 1950 with the 503rd Field Artillery Battalion, he was serving as the mess steward. Richie was captured by the Chinese Communist Forces on December 1, 1950, and remained a prisoner of war until September 1953. In early August 1953, Chu, a Chinese interrogator, talked with Richie individually "about the Negro race problem in the United States" for a period of five days. "RICHIE was asked if HE desired to fight segregation and discrimination, and RICHIE answered in the affirmative." Chu responded that "he could not make him a Communist," and that he could not tell him how to become a member of the Communist Party in the United States. But Chu did want to know if Richie would be willing to fight "race problems" in the United States "through the instrumentality of Communism."[80]

Chu laid out a plan for Richie to fight the "race problem." Richie was to leave the army by requesting a discharge, and once out of the army he "should study the American political situation, ally himself with 'progressives' and start agitating among Negroes for better housing, higher wages, equal education, and representation in the United States government." Chu dismissed both the Republican and Democratic Parties as "rich man's parties," and told Richie that the "Progressive Party was the only American political party that stood for the people and the masses." Richie was to "locate liberal-minded white Americans, and gain their confidence and friendship."

Chu then instructed Richie to move to the San Francisco Bay Area, where he would "file an application with the International Longshoremen's Union for a job with the Cooks and Stewards Division." After contacting "Harry Bridges and Al Trabadeux, the latter Colored," both union leaders, Richie would continue working with the workers, going to all meetings, and become acquainted with the workers. This was the plan that rendered Richie a "potential menace" in the words of the JJPB. But what exactly, in the eyes of the JJPB, was Richie's transgression?

"It was not Communism as we generally think of it," wrote the members of the JJPB regarding the aims of the North Koreans and Chinese in their interrogation rooms. "The material followed the Communist 'line,' it is true, but it is abundantly clear that the enemy was not operating an espionage or subversion school for Americans, nor was he as his primary mission attempting to make 'good Communists' out of them." If Richie's potential threat or "menace" to the United States did not consist of actually having become a Communist or an espionage agent, then what was the threat he and hundreds of other US repatriates presented? It was twofold according to the JJPB: the first element was a "distrust of American motives, actions, and institutions." But the second element was more destabilizing: internationalism. The JJPB noted:

> In addition there was a very persistent attempt to get across the idea that while the Communists have no specific intentions in America, they do have goals in oppressed and backward countries such as China, India, and Southeast Asia, where they wish only to improve the lot of the downtrodden, exploited masses. That they got this point across is attested to by the statement on dossier after dossier to the effect that while Communism would not work in the United States because we are too well off now, still it is a good thing for the backward, primitive countries like China, where it has done so much good.

The US military attempted to portray this internationalism the North Koreans and Chinese espoused—and its potential appeal to certain American POWs—as irrational desire. "Brainwashing" became the perfect trope with which to render these American POWs' "desires"— or politics, to be more exact—into a more familiar racialized narrative of the unwitting, innocent American being seduced by the mysterious "Oriental."

The "Oriental" Interrogator

Between the CIC interrogator or the US military psychiatrist and the US POW repatriate lay the unknown terrain of the POW's experience in North Korea. There were two levels of assessment and negotiation occurring between the US military interrogator/psychiatrist and the US POW repatriate. First, the question was, what kind of information did the POW give to these "Oriental" interrogators? Second—and more importantly—how did the POW interact with these interrogators? For the US interrogator, the objective of the interrogation session was to calculate and measure the degree of collaboration in the POW, as evidenced by his past behavior in the camp and his present behavior during questioning. And for the former prisoner of war, the objective was to narrate his experience in a way that expressed his own position, a way to preclude the interpretation of the interrogator. For example, US repatriate Shelton Foss explained in his questioning that he believed "that many U.S. prisoners attempted to escape primarily to be able to say upon return ... that they did their duty. This observation he bases on the fact that escapes by the US prisoners were made with little or no preparation, coordination, or planning."[81]

US prisoners of war felt compelled to demonstrate that they had maintained a racial superiority during their interrogation sessions with the Chinese and North Koreans. US POWs Dwight Coxe and Raymond Mendell explained their different tactics to maintain racial difference throughout the interrogation experience. For example, when a Chinese interrogator named "Chou" or "Chew (phonetic)" began a session with Coxe, it "seemed to be a period of mental fencing and COXE was not sure at the time whether he was being interrogated." The final part of his interrogation consisted of a request for narrative: "CHEW finally asked him to write an autobiography 'Like LINCONC' (LINCOLN)."

> COXE took him literally and wrote in very great detail, including the house where he was born, the trees, the sidewalks, the names of all his first play-mates, such as John, Mary, Helen, Joseph, etc and a little Chinese boy named Ching. He then told of his experiences in the first grade and repeated the list of play-mates (which he always ended with 'a little Chinese boy named Ching.') After about thirty pages of this, CHEW complained that he was writing in too much detail. COXE then quickly wrote a couple of pages covering his next thirty years. Later he had to expand this part of the autobiography.[82]

During his interrogations, Mendell was also "required to write two autobiographies in narrative form (on blank paper), following an outline given in a lecture at which he was required to take notes." He mentioned in his autobiography that he had enlisted at Fort Holabird, Maryland, so the interrogators 'accused' him "of being a CID agent." While the interrogator was accusing him of working for the Criminal Investigation Detachment (which operated also as an intelligence division), Mendell "stared at the interrogator, something which the interrogator intensely disliked, and the interrogator forced him to stand in the corner facing the wall. MENDELL feels that this is an aid to ease interrogations, and is probably due to an inferiority complex on the part of the orientals."[83]

But the US POW repatriates soon found a limit with this strategy on the whole. US POW repatriate Harrison commented that "there was no way to evade interrogation except to appear as ignorant as possible at all times." One could try to test the limits of the interrogator's English language ability by using "colloquial speech" to see if it would cause the interrogator "extreme difficulty," and "[disgust] the interrogator." But Harrison conceded that "most of the interrogators were of such a caliber that they could readily discern these attempts." It was clear to Harrison that the interrogators he encountered were "well trained," but he was unsure "whether they had attended a school to undergo instruction in this." However, "from hearsay, he gathered that a certain WONG (ph), known as the 'Hatchet Man,' (strong arm) had gained some experience working with the OSS in China during World War II."[84] The OSS, an acronym for the Office of Special Services, was the World War II precursor to the Cold War CIA. The "Hatchet Man" with his pomaded hair and his Pitman shorthand textbook not only already knew the US military and culture well but possibly also had learned intelligence gathering skills and practices from the US military less than a decade earlier.

Indeed, in the portraits of the "Oriental" interrogators, what eventually came to the fore was a stunning pattern. The Chinese and North Korean military interrogators spoke fluent English. Some of them had studied in universities and colleges in the United States. At first glance, it appeared that the JJPB and the CIC, along with the rest of the US military establishment, were panicked that they had incorrectly theorized the "Oriental" interrogator. But the deeper anxiety at the heart of this inquiry was that the "Oriental" interrogator had correctly theorized the American POW/soldier/citizen. Thus the fear underlying this massive undertaking was simple: What if the "Oriental" knew the American better than he did himself?

According to US military psychiatrist William Mayer in a speech he gave in 1956, the board had certain "intercepted" documents "which were written by Communists and which expressed the Communist

point of view about this raw material with which they had to work—
the average American, if there is such an average thing." The Communists had come up with the following portrait of this "raw material":
the average American was "materialistic and opportunistic" and was not
an innately loyal being. But the most damning judgment came down on
the American's own consciousness: "The average American not only
doesn't know anything about his own system, or about his enemy, he
doesn't know anything about how his system works, what his position
really is in it, what it guarantees him."[85]

The final report of the JJPB, completed in October 1953, used the
very same phrase—"raw material"—in describing what they considered to be the first step of "brainwashing," but the members of the JJPB
portrayed the American soldier to be transformed into "raw material"
when the Asian soldier acted in an unexpected manner:

> Here was the raw material of unutterable confusion when the Com-
> munist captor initially extended his hand and welcomed the "ex-
> ploited tool of the capitalist war-mongers," the poor GI, to the ranks
> of the "people."[86]

The Asian soldier was, according to this portrayal, disarming to the
American soldier because he was not immediately treating him as an
enemy. And—quite importantly—the Asian soldier in one gesture also
supposedly granted the American soldier an identity not as an American citizen but rather as an extension of a horizontal collective of a
"people."

If the Chinese and North Korean interrogation rooms were also
devoid of torture—as the Americans claimed that theirs were—a precarious proximity occurred between the liberal, bureaucratic space of
the American interrogation room and that of the North Koreans and
Chinese. In the final report, the JJPB concluded that the Chinese and
North Korean interrogation techniques, which played on "feelings,"
were "a lesson in the anatomy of seduction and subversion." The US
military argued that the Oriental interrogation techniques—although
not outright torture—were not rational and appealed only to base in-
stincts and desires. In fact, the Chinese and North Korean militaries

were approaching the POW in a parallel way that the United States had decided to approach the "Oriental" POWs under their aegis in the south. All parties were offering ways to dissolve the category of the "POW," making the POW a more ambiguous category of political potential.

What became clear through these CIC interrogations of US POW repatriates about their experiences of interrogation with the North Korean and Chinese militaries was that the US and the "Oriental" interrogation rooms were not complete foils to each other. As much as the United States military wanted to insist that the "Oriental" interrogators held intentions and practiced techniques that were utterly "foreign" to traditional and civilized notions of warfare, the United States was already conducting programs and studies parallel in intent in the United Nations Command POW Camps under its command in the south. Both the Chinese/North Korean and United States militaries attempted to glean and reproduce a universalized template of human agency. But the United States worked toward a logic that diverged fundamentally from the North Korean approach to renarrate and reembed the POW within an expanded context—and thus consciousness. The social scientists working with the United States military focused on distillation. How could one distill the human impulse, instinct, and reaction? In March and September 1951 in the far southern Korean island of Koje, a total of 5,101 prisoners, of whom 1,919 were Chinese and 3,182 were North Korean, underwent interviews for a Johns Hopkins–run study titled "A Study of North Korean and Chinese Soldier Attitudes toward Communism, Democracy, and the United Nations." On a five-choice spectrum from "Strongly Disagree" to "Strongly Agree," the Chinese and North Korean POWs had to respond to statements such as the following:

The UN is the hope and salvation of humankind.
The American type of democracy is the best form of government
   ever devised.
Since the American type of democracy respects the will of the
   majority it gives great happiness to its people.

American democracy is not an ideology of aggression.

The working class in a communist state leads a miserable slave life.

It was emphasized in all capital letters for the interviewers to convey to the POWs: "LET YOUR OWN PERSONAL EXPERIENCE OR FEELING DETERMINE YOUR ANSWER."[87]

Julius Segal, a senior research scientist at Johns Hopkins University at the time, was the head of this extensive research project at the Koje-do Camp. As Segal wrote in the report regarding the objectives of the research study:

> In planning psychological warfare operations, recognition has been taken of the importance of capitalizing on the tactical-military situation and other environmental factors in order to increase the effectiveness of our propaganda.... There is, however, an as yet unfulfilled need for establishing reliable and valid methods whereby purely psychological vulnerabilities of the enemy may be assessed readily in order, again, to direct and tailor our psywar in a maximally effective way.[88]

The "purely psychological vulnerabilities" so emphasized and desired in this study was a necessary object to locate in order to claim the efficacy and efficiency of the kind of warfare the United States was waging. The end goal was not simply to identify the "vulnerability" but to transform the POW: "The rationale underlying the assessment of enemy soldier attitudes has two aspects: the first for psychological warfare purposes, and the second for information and reorientation of the POW." Certainly, what the United States called "reorientation" was a kind of parallel to the "indoctrination" the JJPB described the Chinese and North Koreans as having implemented in the camps above the 38th parallel.

Julius Segal was commissioned by the US military to study the Oriental Communist prisoner of war, and after the signing of the cease-fire with the outrage around the "brainwashing" of American POWs, the US military again commissioned him for another study. But the studies this time focused on the American POW. The theorization of the "purely psychological vulnerabilities" in the Oriental Communist POW ended up being applied not necessarily solely to the American POW, but also—perhaps more significantly—to the Oriental Communist interrogator. The frustration expressed about the "Oriental" POW reflected (or echoed) the very same frustration around the "Oriental" interrogator. "The United States Army has never had to deal with this type of prisoner before," proclaimed the authors of a US military commissioned study titled, "The Oriental Communist Prisoner of War: A Study from the Intelligence Viewpoint."[89]

In a postwar study titled "Correlates of Collaboration and Resistance Behavior among U.S. Army POWs in Korea," Segal sampled 579 different "dossiers containing transcripts of interrogations of returning US POWs conducted by the Intelligence Branch of the Army."[90] "[Most] men behaved primarily out of emotion and self-interest," stated Segal. And although it "is true enough that upon repatriation, 45 per cent of the Americans who participated showed some 'sympathy' towards Communism as a way of life," he did not believe that such "sympathy" could have been the impetus for American POWs to participate willingly in POW camp life. And he noted that the "study concerns POWs *captured in a unique kind of war.* As members of a little understood UN 'police action' in which ultimate victory was not pursued, the motivation of troops in Korea may have been relatively lower than that of soldiers fighting a large-scale war."

The social science researchers on Oriental interrogation of American POWs all missed one critical element in their reading of the voluminous CIC interrogation reports: the "Oriental" interrogators themselves. If the US military's strategy to making psychological warfare efficacious was to remove and distill the Oriental POW from his social and historical context into "purely psychological vulnerabilities," then the Chinese and North Korean's strategy to disrupt the state's relation with the POW was to embed him into a temporally and geographically expanded social and historical context. The JJPB considered the handshake and an offer of a cigarette by a Chinese soldier to the American POW when he was captured to be the first step of a "brainwashing" process, but the more disarming experience for the American POW was most probably the realization that the "Oriental" interrogator had already been a part of his social and historical context.

Leonard Wilmeth had met an interpreter in Camp #3 in 1952 who had "studied in WACO Texas, deported in 1951, spoke fluent English; neat dresser." Shelton Foss mentioned "Zun" who had been in Camp #3—"low voice spoke slow; quiet and deliberate; attended the Univ of TOKYO; spoke Japanese and Russian ... joined the communist party as a student in Tokyo." And a political instructor at Camp #5, whom he characterized as having "a high-pitched voice" and "excitable," said to the American POWs that "he traveled and studied in the US but saw only slums."[91]

When US POW Zacherle arrived in mid-May 1951 to the North Korean Interrogation Center, which POWs had dubbed "Pak's Palace," he was interrogated every day by a North Korean officer called "The Professor." Zacherle was at "Pak's Palace" for a month, and he noted that there was "less of the indoctrination approach which had been evident at the Chinese counterpart interrogation centers; more of a 'friendly' and 'cooperative' attitude prevailed during the periods of questioning." Sometimes the interrogation lasted for about an hour, other times it would extend from the early morning hours until six o'clock in the evening. As Zacherle recalled, "The Professor usually began his interview with a smile and the homey comment, 'Now, we visit.' "[92]

"The Professor" was about forty years old with a slight build and wore glasses. Zacherle said that he "spoke fair English" and was supposedly a former university professor. In fact, "after 1945 he claimed to have worked for the Americans in SEOUL (advisory group) but due to their aggressive and immoral actions he went to PYOKTONG to join the NK." He had expressed to Zacherle his desire to write "a very comprehensive Korean-English dictionary." Characterized as a "mild person in general," the author of the report on Zacherle noted that "The Professor" was "liked by the POW."[93] Although described as "mild," the figure of "The Professor" may have unnerved the CIC and the members of the JJPB because of his claim to an easy familiarity with "Americanness." Neither intimidated nor naive, "The Professor" could speak with a certain authority on and experience of the US military and culture.

The Lives of Brainwashing

Clarence Adams, the young black soldier from Memphis, Tennessee, became the librarian at Camp #5 sometime after Artesani's tenure, at which point he estimated the library had grown to "more than a thousand books." In his memoir, Adams recalled, "Out of sheer boredom, I read nearly every book in the library, although I had never been much of a reader growing up." But he also noted that at Camp #5, there were American POWs who had arrived unable to read or write, and that study groups organized by the POWs helped these POWs develop literacy skills. In his study group were two other black prisoners— William C. White and Larance V. Sullivan—who would later choose not to repatriate to the United States and instead choose to make a life in China. And the Chinese instructors in these study groups, much to Adams's surprise, "were not army officers, but professors, editors [and] Some of them even had American college degrees."[94]

This change in attitude of Adams, White, and Sullivan did not go unnoticed by the white prisoners of war in Camp #5. "They still referred to us as 'niggers,'" wrote Adams, "but now they openly stated that we would never get back to the States alive, or if we did, they'd look us up and take care of us then." Adams recalled that previously, a white POW who had been labeled as a progressive by the others had been murdered in his sleep. "I always tried to keep awake at night and sleep during the day," Adams noted. Later, Adams resorted to sleeping in the library, with two other black POWs (who were both also from Memphis, but neither identified themselves as progressive) standing guard by the door while he slept.[95]

When Clarence Adams later declared at the 38th parallel that he had indeed chosen to go to China and not repatriate back to the United States, he stated that he could not return to the United States as long as Jim Crow and McCarthyism were in place. Branded as a traitor, Adams—along with White and Sullivan—was dismissed by the American public as having been "brainwashed" by the Chinese to spout such propaganda lines about American society. But Thompson's earlier experience on the battlefields of Korea demonstrated how he understood the disposability of black life over white life, and Adams's experience in Camp #5 demonstrated how Jim Crow had been re-created in the POW camps along the Yalu River. Memphis, Tennessee, and Camp #5 were both different and similar.

In all of the camps within the POW network, white prisoners of war created a myriad of different organizations to monitor whom they considered to be "progressive." The Ku Klux Klan was the most often cited one, but in their CIC interrogations, repatriated American POWs provided a variety of names of organizations: True Americans, Federated American Hearts, Screaming Eagles, Black Diamond, and Kill the Communists. POW Raymond Goodburlet, whom the Chinese had accused in Camp #1 of joining the Ku Klux Klan, explained the process and duties of the "reactionaries." For newcomers to the camp, "close observation and conversations ... were the only way to establish their reliability."[96] There was an entire vocabulary created to differentiate between the kinds of POWs within the camps: "rats" were for informers, "props" for prisoners "who seemed to believe the Communist propaganda, "pinkies" for those were just starting to believe the propaganda, "seeing the light" for "men who seemed doubtful about the U.S.," and "reactionaries" for POWs like Goodburlet "who resisted the Communist indoctrination." Notably, there was only one term used by POWs for those who adamantly refused indoctrination, but there was an entire spectrum of possible leanings and sympathies with Communism. Other terms used to describe progressives were "Chink-lovers" and "Lovebugs."[97] Beatings, according to Goodburlet, were meted out to progressives. As POW Walter Mayo commented, "isolation, surveillance, and interrogation" were the important practices of the POW reactionaries to control the POW population. The goals of these "clubs" were twofold: "to harass the progressives and Chinese and prevent the PsW from listening to the Chinese propaganda and believing it."[98] When the reactionaries identified a "questionable element," the prisoners of war "would form a group and talk with the man, warning him; they also wrote him notes."[99]

At Camp #5, the Chinese camp officials removed Artesani from his tenure as the camp librarian supposedly because they had accused him of using the library as a place for reactionaries. But the reactionary POW had other methods of communicating to those in other compounds within the camp. Goodburlet mentioned "grape vines and rumor chains" as effective means of communication as well as "placing notes in spots where they would be picked up."[100] The reactionaries created their own practices and infrastructure, but it was one that was wholly focused on controlling and punishing other prisoners of war. The surveillance set up by the reactionaries aimed to monitor the prisoners of war, but it was a difficult project to carry out since much of the interaction between the POWs and the Chinese and North Korean officials took place in study groups and interrogation. The camps themselves never had any clear fence surrounding them, and because of the everyday life enmeshed with the guards and monitors, all of the prisoners of war were in constant contact with these "Oriental" Communists.

As mentioned earlier, the Joint Japan Processing Board final report stated that organizations like the "Ku Klux Klan" had successfully resisted the "Oriental" Communists' attempts at brainwashing and had maintained a sense of American self-identity. But how did the CIC interrogators determine if an American POW was a "security risk"? In the report on Joseph Ramsey, a twenty-four-year-old white soldier from Las Vegas, the CIC interrogator noted that Ramsey was "well informed on Communist doctrine and theories," and deemed him a "definite security risk."[101] Another prisoner of war, William Freeman from Atlanta, Georgia, declared himself "a solid anti-communist, and … that HE would fight them again without hesitation." But the CIC interrogator described Freeman as having "great intimacy with the theories of communism, especially in HIS thorough understanding of its principles and its various aspects in life." But even more telling, according to the CIC interrogator, is that Freeman also declared himself a "union man, and always had been" and criticized the Taft-Hartley Act, a 1947 act that restricted the rights of labor unions regarding strikes and required union leaders to file declarations that they did not support the Communist Party. In the assessment of Freeman, the CIC interrogator labeled Freeman as having "ideological schizophrenia" and stated that it was difficult to know if Freeman was "actually insane or ... feigning insanity."[102]

The POW organizations like the KKK and the US military section of the Counterintelligence Corps were part of a continuous informal and formal structure of surveillance over the American prisoners of war. David Shay, a twenty-four-year-old POW from Erie, Pennsylvania, asked his CIC interrogator, "Are we all to be labeled as 'brain washed'?"[103] Shay was correct in his concern about whether or not US POWs would all be rendered suspicious in the eyes of the US state and military. Within the domestic United States, the FBI and even the House Un-American Activities Committee (HUAC) became involved in the questioning and surveillance of these POWs. When Clarence Adams arrived in San Francisco in 1966 with Liu Len Feng, his Chinese wife, and his two children, the FBI immediately took him in for questioning, and HUAC called him in for a closed-door session.

On August 13, 1955, President Dwight Eisenhower signed Executive Order number 10631, which was a "Code of Conduct" for US troops, emphasizing that "[every] member of the armed forces of the United States is expected to measure up to the standards embodied in this Code of Conduct while he is in combat or in captivity." In the aftermath of the POW "brainwashing" scandal, the US Congress had created a US Defense Advisory Committee on Prisoners of War, which in turn proposed this "Code of Conduct" in their August 1955 report. "As a serviceman thinketh so is he," concluded the members of the committee. Paraphrasing Carl von Clausewitz's theorization on war, the committee members wrote, "War has been defined as 'a contest of wills.' A trained hand holds the weapon. But the will, the character, the spirit of the individual—these control the hand. More than ever, in the war for the minds of men[,] moral character, will, spirit are important." The brief, five-part Code of Conduct was modeled on the catechism, a set of declarations, which the US soldier would learn, memorize, and internalize to fortify himself in battle and in captivity. The code began with: "I am an American fighting man. I serve in the forces which guard my country and our way of life. I am prepared to give my life in their defense." And it ended with a refrain of the first section in its final, fifth

FIGURE 7.1 "Sgt Preston Davis . . . shows the bass fiddle he made in POW camp to
marines Private First Class Raymond Mathis and Private First Class James Spagnolio,
Freedom Village, Korea." By Private First Class Joe Adams
(National Archives and Record Administration)

part: "I will never forget that I am an American fighting man, responsible for my actions, and dedicated to the principles which made
my country free. I will trust in my God and in the United States of
America."

The crisis over the POW during the Korean War had precipitated a
formal reconceptualization of the nature of warfare. "The battlefield of

FIGURE 7.2 Written in both Korean and English, the sign over the entrance to "Freedom Village" reads, "Welcome: Gate to Freedom." Frank Noel, an Associated Press photographer, arrives after being held as a prisoner of war in the Chinese and North Korean camps. (National Archives and Record Administration)

modern warfare is all inclusive," stated the advisory committee. "Today there are no distant front lines, remote no man's lands, far-off rear areas." Indeed, the American citizen, along with the American soldier, needed to understand this new, urgent logic of warfare. "Modern warfare has brought the challenge to the doorstep of every citizen, and so the Code we propose may well be a code for all Americans if the problem of survival should ever come to our own main streets." For the total warfare state of World War II, the ideal citizen was the citizen-soldier. He was eager for mobilization, and this eagerness was as seemingly infinite as free market capital. But for a state premised on wars of intervention, the citizen-POW became the important ideal.[104]

Conclusion

The Diaspora of War

THE WOODEN SLATS propped up against the wall in the photograph on the following page had been used as floorboards for many years in a small house in a fishing village located on the small island of Yongch'o. When the owner of the house pulled up the floorboards in order to install new ones, he noticed large Korean characters written boldly and in black on the underside of the boards. The authors of these writings had been Korean prisoners of war, and almost every house in the fishing village had these boards forming the walls or floors of their home. The small islands of Yongch'o and nearby Ch'ubong had been the site of top-secret POW camps during the Korean War. In place of official US military documents, the memories of the village residents and the physical, material remnants of the POW camps serve as the peculiar embodied archive of a war that has not ended.

When the prisoners of war were shipped to Panmunjom for repatriation or explanation after the signing of the cease-fire in July 1953, the local residents who lived near the POW camp carefully disassembled the camp materials, using what they could find. Wire, wooden planks, metal—all were precious commodities during a time of utter devastation. The residents had reassembled and reused these materials—the POW camp itself had an afterlife in the hands of the residents as it was transformed into small homes and other necessities. The traces of the POW camp can be found in the writing on the wooden planks, a large water reservoir created by the US Army, and stone partitions in various states of ruin dotting specific places on the island.

FIGURE C.1 Wooden slats from a POW camp that
had been used by local villagers as floorboards
in their homes (author's own photo)

But why the secrecy around these two prisoner of war camps? According to the histories recalled and told by the villagers, the camps
were created to house the most fervent Communist Korean POWs. In
the light of this study, it seems most probable that these camps were
installed after the Dodd kidnapping incident, when the US authorities,
especially camp commander Haydon Boatner, prioritized moving the
POWs into smaller, more manageable compounds. It was at this time
that all anti-Communist POWs were sent to the mainland, and the paratroopers were sent into the Communist Korean POW compounds to
discipline and punish the POWs for transgressing their position. It is
quite possible that the members involved in the Korean People's Army
and Chinese Volunteers Prisoners of War Representatives Association
had been placed there, along with other higher-ranking officers of the
KPA. But the villagers did not express any fear of or disgust with the
POWs themselves in their recollections—in fact, one of the POWs had

escaped the camp, and instead of going far away from the camp, he decided to stay in the surrounding village, where he ended up marrying a young woman in the village and became a farmer. The US Army, the villagers told me, could not recognize the difference between Koreans.

In other words, as the written-on wooden planks and the local villagers who had grown up around the POW camp could attest, the Korean War had never quite left the village. The writing on the wooden planks and the figure of the former POW who had become a local farmer point to particular ways to pay attention to the current lives and afterlives of war. Because although the Korean War had never left this village, different legacies from the war were also informing a world of constant warfare as the question of decolonization in Asia and the Pacific Islands continued. The written-on planks and the ex-POW farmer demonstrated the very real limits of the hegemonic reach of the US project on the Korean peninsula. Their desires and fears were not ultimately shaped by the US. The writing of the POWs was a demonstration of the POWs' *insistence* on articulating their own political subjectivities and imaginaries, to cover quite literally the space that was supposed to silence them through confinement in a visual, undeniable form—their presence and voice. The choice of the ex-POW to make a life under the shadow of the POW camp with the local villagers was a demonstration of a Korean subject *insisting* on his claims to shaping the everyday in spite of the constant "state of exception" touted by the United States and the newly formed Republic of Korea. It was an insistence to remember and return to the basic questions of self-determination, land, and what a liberated life was supposed to look like.

The Korean War continued—all over the globe. Geneva, Switzerland, was one site for the war. The final item of the July 1953 armistice agreement stipulated for a "political conference" where officials representing the different states involved in the war would "settle through negotiation the questions of the removal of all foreign forces from Korea, the peaceful settlement of the Korea question."[1] In April 1954, officials convened this promised conference in Geneva, where the objective was to address two political questions located at the nexus between decolonization and the Cold War: Korea and Indochina. Ho Chi

Minh had declared Vietnam's independence from French colonial rule in September 1945, and France reasserted its colonial claim with military force, with the eventual support of the United States. In the first week of May during the Geneva Conference, the French suffered a major military defeat at Dien Bien Phu, and in July 1954, the outcome was two lines drawn on the map. The 38th parallel remained on the Korean peninsula, and the "Korean question" was nowhere near solved. For Indochina, the 17th parallel became the demilitarized zone, dividing north and south zones. Clarence Adams, the former librarian of Camp #5 and one of the twenty-one prisoners of war who chose China, recalled that when he heard about President Lyndon B. Johnson sending American troops to Vietnam: "What was happening in Vietnam was all too familiar to me."[2] In August 1965, Radio Hanoi and loudspeakers were broadcasting Adams's message to US troops on the frontlines in Vietnam: "I am not broadcasting to the entire US Army, only to its black soldiers," said Adams in the recording. He described how his "all-black regiment had been sacrificed to save white units" during his time on the battlefields of Korea, and he pointed out the unerring contradiction between Jim Crow at home and the democracy espoused by US military intervention abroad.[3]

Memphis, Tennessee, was also ground for the unresolved Korean War. Adams, who had attended People's University of Beijing after the cease-fire, saw the political tides turn in the years leading up to the Cultural Revolution, and he eventually decided to leave China to return to the United States with Liu Lin Feng, his wife, and their two children. The US state created a dense series and network of interrogations around Adams and his family, from three months of interrogation by the State Department, to the CIA on the ship to the United States, and the FBI when the family arrived in Honolulu. Feeling that he at least "did know how to survive in Memphis," Adams took his family back to his hometown.[4] Plagued by the House Un-American Activities Committee (HUAC), constant FBI surveillance, threatening phone calls from the KKK, and branded as a "commie" by the community, Adams found it extremely difficult to find a decent, stable job and finally decided to open up the first chop suey restaurant in Memphis with his wife in 1972. And in the eight restaurants that would eventually comprise his family's chain of chop suey restaurants, black war veterans from Memphis would sometimes come in and say, "Hey, you were the guy who made those broadcasts." Korea, China, Vietnam, and Memphis were not as distant from one another for these black veterans of the Korean and Vietnam Wars.[5]

The US wars across the Pacific were also in Los Angeles, California. In the late 1970s, Ju Yeong Bok, who had been one of the seventy-six "neutral nation" Korean prisoners of war, moved to the United States from his life and home in São Paolo, Brazil. Ju and his family made their home in Los Angeles, where like many other Korean immigrants who found work in the garment and laundry industry at that time, Ju opened up a dry cleaners store.[6] Ju was in his mid-fifties, and he had made yet another migration—from Manchuria to Harbin to Beijing to Korea to India to Brazil, and now to Los Angeles. Sam Miyamoto, who was in his early forties at this time, was also living in the Los Angeles area, working in the import and export business between the United States and Japan. As a drafted interrogator for the US military during the Korean War, Sam Miyamoto had been at Koje Island during the war at the same time as Ju Yeong Bok, only on different sides of the barbed-wire fence at the United Nations Command Camp #1. According to Miyamoto, who had been an "enemy alien" behind barbed wire in the Poston internment camp and then a stateless adolescent trying to survive in Tokyo as a product of a "POW exchange" the United States had negotiated with Japan during World War II, the accumulation of wartime violence had also left its own physical imprint on his family. Miyamoto disclosed that the brother with whom he had traveled to Hiroshima later developed a brain tumor, most probably because they had unknowingly exposed their bodies to staggering levels of radiation as they walked through Hiroshima so soon after the United States had dropped the bomb, both teenagers stunned at what they saw in front of them.[7] The life survival choices Ju and Miyamoto had to make over and over again via warfare powerfully demonstrate how the figures of the Japanese American businessman and the Korean immigrant dry cleaners storeowner in America's racial imagination are forms of forgetting the Korean War, the Asia-Pacific Wars, and US expansionist ambitions in the Pacific—past, present, and projected. The Japanese American businessman and the Korean immigrant dry cleaners owner only become visible on the American social landscape by becoming evidence of the "American dream" story, where the individual Asian American or Asian immigrant strives to assimilate—to become "American." But Miyamoto and Ju had already experienced the violent limits of "becoming."

Telling the story of the Korean War through the interrogation room puts into stark relief the *productive* capabilities of war, not simply its destructive ones. What the POWs and interrogators understood intimately was that states used warfare not simply as political strategy but also as a form of governance. The violence enacted by militaries on the battlefields, through mass air bombings, and via torture in the interrogation rooms, must be viewed through a larger, implicating lens, where these acts are not simply rendered as "immoral," "evil," or "irrational." Torture and bureaucracy, killings and state-building, battlefields and international law—the profound intimacy between violence and the languages of liberalism lies at the heart of this study. Remaining at the level of an abstracted, universalizing sense of "horror" in front of war essentially denies a deeper violence enacted and facilitated by war—the fact that "war" is also supposed to produce "new subjects" through its crucible of mass violence. Clarence Adams, Ju Yeong Bok, and Sam Miyamoto had experienced precisely this violence of state and empire-building over and over at this node of warfare: the interrogation room.

The Korean War may have initially provided the neat, moral narrative needed to launch the NSC-68 fully to the extent Paul Nitze and Dean Acheson envisioned and desired, and thus "had a major impact on both domestic American politics and international affairs," states Mary Dudziak. "Korea was also the first major military conflict of the Atomic Age and exemplified the kind of warfare the United States would engage in for the rest of the twentieth century."[8] Determined to demonstrate its own relevance and authority within Truman's national security state in Washington, DC, the members of the Psychological

Strategy Board took it on themselves to define the contours and dynamics of this new kind of warfare. In a progress report dated October 30, 1952, the Psychological Strategy Board reviewed their strategies over the past few months on the project they had proposed in 1951: the POW voluntary repatriation proposal. At this point in the war, the Dodd kidnapping incident had exploded all over global media, along with reports of the unrest and killings behind the barbed-wire fences. The Korean Communist POWs were resisting repatriation interrogation. "Publicity on agitation in prisoner-of-war camps has provided the communists with additional effective propaganda material, despite U.S. attempts to present a contrary interpretation," encapsulated the PSB memo. As a countermeasure, the US military was implementing another program: "In Korea the conduct of a program to warn civilians residing in 78 North Korean cities of the impending bombing by the United Nations Command expresses the intent to save non-combatant lives, and at the same time is designed to increase the pressure on the communist negotiators at Panmunjom."[9] The PSB made an equivalence between the advance warnings to civilian populations and the voluntary repatriation proposal. The advance warnings, done via leaflet bombing, were a gesture of mercy and humanity on the part of the United States, just as the voluntary repatriation proposal was supposed to evidence the same to the world. And similar to the voluntary repatriation issue, the responsibility for whether one lived or died was transferred upon the individual as a supposed choice. If the Korean person decided not to leave the area before the bombing, then the burden of their death rested solely on their decision. With this logic, mass civilian death was the consequence of the Korean individual's choice on the ground, rather than the consequence of the US military's development of a mass bombing program targeting civilian populations in major urban areas in North Korea.

The hyperfocus on and the hypervalorization of the individual subject in these situations elided the massive scale of violence that was part and parcel of the same logic in conducting US liberal warfare. Targeting the civilian populations in seventy-eight cities fit with the earlier proposal of General Douglas MacArthur in 1950 to drop thirty or so atomic bombs "across the neck of Manchuria" in order to create a "belt of radioactive cobalt" to prevent a land invasion of Korea from the north. General Matthew Ridgeway, MacArthur's replacement who was considered to be less of a maverick, requested thirty-eight atomic bombs for his disposal.[10] Advance warning campaigns were leaflets, paper from the sky in advance of the bombs. The safe surrender leaflets, like the one Oh Se-hŭi had stowed away in the inside pocket of his jacket, was also supposed to save the soldier from certain death. Under the rubric of the CIC's "war of espionage," all Koreans were rendered suspicious. The mass bombing plan also placed the entire Korean civilian populace under suspicion. If Koreans chose to stay, then such a choice supposedly confirmed that they were the "enemy," and therefore were disposable.

The object of rescue could, at any minute, become the target of violence. Between bombs and paper, the interrogation room was the crucial cog in making this wartime dynamic operational. In a "war of intervention," the United States needed more than simply a foil or an enemy to mobilize both military bureaucracy and violence. The interrogation rooms of the Korean War worked on the premise that the "Oriental mind" was in a perpetual state of "in due course," to take the words from the Cairo Communiqué regarding Korean independence. The creation and maintenance of this very irresolution, this "almost, not-quite" state, were the objectives of interrogation in fashioning a subject who could also become a viable target for US wartime violence, if needed. The "Oriental" was suspicious and unreliable but at the same time aspirational and striving. Here, we can see how the usual Cold War binary formation of anti-Communism versus Communism is gravely insufficient, and that the questions of colonialism, sovereignty, and recognition over the twentieth century are more at the core of the Korean War on the ground. This is how the interiority of people became both the terrain and *jus ad bellum* for warfare in the Korean War.

The tallying of the numbers after the cease-fire regarding POW repatriation tells a deliberately narrow story, where the propaganda lines close the parameters of our field of vision. For the POWs who originated in North Korea before the start of the war, 75,823 chose to repatriate to North Korea, 7,826 chose not to repatriate, and 74 chose a "neutral nation." Among the Chinese POWs, 6,670 chose to repatriate, 14,692 chose not to repatriate, and 12 chose a "neutral nation." Under the custody of the Chinese and North Korean militaries, 3,746 US POWs chose to repatriate, and 21 chose not to repatriate. For the South Korean POWs, 8,321 POWs chose repatriation, 335 chose not to repatriate, and 2 chose a "neutral nation."[11] The North Korean POWs did not deliver a propaganda victory to the United States, but US officials pointed to the Chinese POWs instead. However, the history behind the Chinese POWs was not one of a simple accumulation of individual choices weighing Cold War politics among twenty thousand POWs. In his work on the Chinese POW experience of the war, David Cheng Chang lays out how the POWs' decisions "were directly related to their divergent pre-Korean War experiences in China under both the Nationalist and Communist."[12] The POWs themselves made undeniable the struggles over restructuring political power and material infrastructure in the East Asian region.

This book reached back to the early twentieth century when the question of Korea's sovereignty vis-à-vis the United States, China, and Japan became a strategic site for expansionist imperial ambitions. In the mid-twentieth century, Korea again became the critical flashpoint of claiming hegemonic power in the region, and thus, the larger Asia-Pacific area. The POW camps were a node for the larger network the US military had been creating across the Pacific region. The US Navy employed the offshore labor of the Japanese; Japanese factories served as the arsenal for the US military during the war; and the economic surge that resulted from Japan as the major site of US military command and troops prompted Japanese Prime Minister Yoshida Shigeru to call the Korean War "a gift of the gods."[13] But US CIC was operating across both Korea and Japan. When the CIC identified *zainichi* Korean leftists in Japan, US military officials seriously discussed sending these *zainichi* Korean leftists as prisoners to the POW camps on the Korean peninsula, as an attempt to repress not only dissent but also a political critique that effectively linked the US agenda to maintain the Japanese colonial order in the metropole to the business of the US war of intervention on the Korean peninsula.

These embedded networks, militarization policies, and established surveillance that operate on multiple scales will not surprise those familiar with the hallmarks of US empire-building in the twentieth century. Alfred McCoy has called the Philippines the "laboratory" for the US surveillance state; Greg Grandin has characterized Latin America as the "workshop" for US empire; Laleh Khalili has traced the long colonial history of asymmetrical warfare and counterinsurgency as practiced by the United States in sites all over the globe.[14] And certainly, the enduring and unending nature of the Korean War, most visibly demonstrated by the Demilitarized Zone on the peninsula, is exemplary of what Christine Hong has noted about how "warfare" is at the heart of US empire: "War figures redemptively ... as the enabling condition of democracy, which is typically deferred into an indeterminate future."[15] The US embrace of liberal warfare as a redemptive crucible is critical to how we must pay attention to these wars of intervention.

This book exposed how the first "hot war" of the Cold War—the "police action" called the Korean War—was a crucible for this kind of putatively rational warfare, otherwise known as wars of intervention. From inside the military interrogation rooms of the war, this book mapped out a landscape of liberal warfare different from the usual Cold War battlefields of struggles over borders and territory. The geography of war inside the interrogation room was the interior worlds of people. This struggle of political legitimacy waged over human psyches, souls, and desires using the rational tools of bureaucracy, social science, and political theorization revealed how the logic of liberal "wars of intervention" were borne out of a moment when the laws of war came into crisis in front of formal decolonization.

Through the prism of the interrogation room, this book was able to begin the story of the Korean War with the high stakes involved in the compressed intimate exchange between the interrogator and the prisoner. Interrogation, the most everyday event of war which also held the threat of extraordinary violence, opened up a way to tell the story of the Korean War that forced us to take seriously the experiences of ordinary people on the ground as political history. Often, the political histories of the Korean War stay within top-down narrative analysis of the war's events, personages, and consequences. The state officials, diplomats, and military personnel of those more familiar histories are within the pages of this book as well. In this book, however, the people who are navigating global geopolitics within the calculus between life and death are ordinary people. We had to take seriously the notions of liberation and decolonization that the peasant farmer turned POW held in the years after 1945, to take seriously the notions of war-making and nationalism held by Japanese American interrogators who had recently been also behind barbed-wire fences in the United States, and to take seriously the lived experiences of violence across the Pacific— by the Korean people in the years following official liberation from Japan and by the American people in the years of making a total warfare state. Paying attention to this kind of political history is critical in order to challenge the current paradigmatic form of warfare that is shaping global politics in the second millennium. If US empire fashions itself as the end telos, then US imperial warfare renders its forms of violence as inevitable. The narrative of unending war, constant threat, and pervasive suspicion pushes the war of intervention forward as the only possible logical act.

The Korean War has not yet come to an official end. The cease-fire armistice signed in July 1953, after eighteen months of continued fighting due to the POW repatriation controversy, is the one element that holds the war in a tense, fractured abeyance. The one still remaining "hot war" of the Cold War, the Korean War seems to confound the usual elements of historical narrative. The difficult contradictions one comes across when attempting to give shape to this war seem to multiply with every attempt. The Korean War is a war that is "forgotten" in the annals of United States history but that has been in plain sight of the world continuously through the latter half of the twentieth century into the second millennium in the form of the hypermilitarized

Demilitarized Zone (DMZ) on the Korean peninsula. The undergirding logic and impetus for the continued investment in the Korean War—national security—has become part of the everyday language and politics of Korea, East Asia, and the United States. The Korean War is a war that is simultaneously everywhere and nowhere. It is a war that is marked on territory and on consciousness.

ACKNOWLEDGMENTS

ANY ACCOUNT I CAN GIVE of my gratitude is, in the end, an insufficient one. But let me begin, at least, with my dissertation committee
members who have taught me a great deal about how to pay attention
to these stories we tell. Penny von Eschen has granted me perhaps one
of the most important lessons in scholarship—to write history un-
flinchingly, with a clarity that comes from a commitment to articulating the everyday human struggles over power and history. My own
growth as a scholar is indebted to Henry Em in his dedication to rethinking and relearning constantly in order to reimagine the relationship between ourselves and social change. Sarita See in her fearlessness
and brilliance was an inspiration for me as I grappled with the politics
and ethics of how to pay attention to the historical archive, and how to
write a history of war. Scott Kurashige always brought the key question
of integrity back to the table, as the most important task at hand—and
for that, I am thankful.

At the University of Michigan, I learned how asking these questions
about power, narrative, and experience could be a shared endeavor.
Meredith Woo, who was like a force of nature with her ability to inspire, brought me into the Center of Korean Studies soon after my arrival, and with David Chung, Nojin Kwak, Youngju Ryu, and Jiyoung
Lee, the center was an intellectual home for me throughout all of my
years at Michigan. The very first person to welcome me to the University of Michigan was Rebecca Scott, and indeed, it was a fortuitous
meeting. I thank Jean Hébrard for teaching me to appreciate all that is
in the marginal, gestural, and accidental in the archive, and introducing
me to the academic community at the École des hautes etudes en sciences sociales. At the Institute of the Humanities, with director Danny

Herwitz, I met a group of graduate students with whom I'd have an irrepressible, genuine bond: Eva Dubuisson, Amy Rodgers, Danna Agmon, Lembit Beecher. The Eisenberg Institute for Historical Studies, headed by Ron Suny, was another such space of inspired dialogue. Additional graduate funding for this project came from the Department of History and the Rackham School for Graduate Studies, the Korea Foundation, the Josephine de Karmàn Fellowship, the Fulbright IIE, and the Korea Society. But the coordination of these grants would not have been possible without the support of Lorna Altstetter, Sheila Coley, Kathleen King, and Diana Denney in the Department of History office. Any modicum of sanity of mine during my graduate studies is all thanks to them. And the true teachers were and continue to be the friends who shared countless conversations and meals with me: Isabela Quintana, LaKisha Simmons, Taymiya Zaman, Ji Li, Clay Howard, Jason Gavilan, Lily Geismer, Jinyeon Kang, Dean Saranillio, Sam Erman, Heijin Lee, Joel Mowdy, and Simona Vaitkosima.

Joan Scott and Christine Hong were early editors and interlocutors for some of the material in this book, and I thank them for helping me articulate both the contours and core of these pieces. Certain sections of Chapter 3 are expanded and elaborated parts from "Empire's Babel: U.S. Military Interrogation Rooms of the Korean War," *History of the Present: A Journal of Critical History*. 3:1 (Spring 2013), 1–28—and I thank University of Illinois for permission to draw upon this article for the book. Thanks is also due to Duke University Press for permission to publish revised sections of an article, "The Intelligence of Fools: Reading the US Military Archive of the Korean War," which was originally published in *positions*, Vol. 23:4, 695–728.

During the research for this project, I have depended on the generosity and willingness of archivists to share their knowledge and time with me. During the many months I spent at the National Archives in College Park, Maryland, I hugely benefited from the kindness and good humor of archivist Richard Boylan and the dedicated staff. I also thank Randy Sowell at the Truman Presidential Library, David Keogh at the Military History Institute, Fabrizio Bensi at the International Committee of the Red Cross archives in Geneva, Ken Klein at the Korean American archives at the University of Southern California, Christopher Abraham at the Eisenhower Presidential Library, and the archivists at the Hoover Institute at Stanford University for the conversations and support they provided me during my research trips. I thank Susan Uyemura for bringing me into the JA Living Legacy project and family during my time as a graduate student. Susan is an exemplary oral historian, who is firmly committed to ensuring that the voices often unheard will be recorded. I thank the Japanese American veterans who were willing to share their stories and experiences with me, often welcoming me into their homes more than once, or transforming a small corner of a conference hall into one of reflective personal history.

It was a privilege to spend my time in Korea as a fellow at the Asiatic Research Center at Korea University, under the mentorship of Choi Jang-jip. His commitment to fostering a critical intellectual dialogue on politics and democracy in Korea has been an inspiration for my work over the years. Chung Yong-wook at Seoul National University is a historian of the highest order; his deep understanding of the archives and also the political stakes in Korean historiography always pushed my own work further. I met Kim Dong-choon while he was a standing commissioner of the Truth and Reconciliation Commission of Korea, and over the years, his work on Korean War history and his political activism sparked important conversations that continue today. I also must thank Cha Cheol-uk of Pusan University and local historian and teacher Ju Yeong-Taek for embarking on research and interview trips with me along the southern coast of the peninsula. Lee Yong-choel of the Geoje City Hall administration provided me with a tour and access to the libraries. Ryu Suk-hyeon shared stories and a copy of her master's thesis on the Koje POW Camp with me early on in the research. Jen Gab-Saeng, with his journalistic and research knowledge, taught me a great deal about the regional history around Koje-do. As a researcher with Seoul National University's Institute for Peace and Unification Studies (IPUS), he also shared with me a multitude of photographs he had found while researching at the National Archives for the Korean War POW Camp Research Team. Many of those photos are included within the pages of this book. Park Sang-hoon provided insight, perspective, and knowledge at critical moments in the research, and I thank him for his exceptional, expansive, singular ability to cut to the heart of any matter. My time in Korea and beyond has been enriched by Pak Su-hyeon, Okhee Kwon, Hae Joo Kim, Ai Fukuda, Jamie Park, Song Myeon-gyu, Alex Lee, and Jae Won Chung.

Bruce Cumings and Kyeong-hee Choi welcomed me to the University of Chicago during my year as a Korea Foundation postdoctoral fellow, and Bruce has offered his steady encouragement and insightful advice throughout all of the life stages of this project. At the Penn Humanities Forum at University of Pennsylvania, I found myself working with a group of junior scholars who continue to energize me and my work with our shared enthusiasm: Laurent Dissard, Rossen Djagalov, Elidor Mëhilli, and Noah Tamarkin. Over the years, through formal invitations or informal conversations, others have expanded my own thinking on these pressing questions about the culture and infrastructure of war-making: Kavita Dayal, Eichiro Azuma, Deborah Solomon, Mitch Lerner, Dirk Hartog, Ted Hughes, Kim Brandt, Louise Young, Mark Selden, Nadine Attewell, Deborah Boehm, Junghyun Hwang, Charlie Hanley, JJ Suh, Jun Yoo, Namhee Lee, Olga Federenko, Nan Kim, Dagmar Herzog, Chris Dietrich, Rich Nisa, Wes Attewell, Ramsey Liem, Christophe Prochasson, Sophie de Schaepdrijver, Elena Bellina, Chunmei Du, Jennifer Jihye Chun, Judy Ju Hui Han, Takashi Fujitani, Lisa Yoneyama, Hyaewol Choi, Tessa Morris-Suzuki, Ruth Barraclough, David Cheng Chang, Jung Keun-sik, Jung Byung-joon, Lee Sunwoo, Kevin Gaines, and Ying Qian. I am indebted to the many excellent scholars, postgraduate and graduate fellows who were involved with Daniel Pick's "Hidden Persuaders" project at Birkbeck College, a multiyear conversation that involved an exciting project on the colonial histories and multidisciplinary approaches to "brainwashing." My time at the University at Albany, SUNY, expanded the sense of community. Richard Hamm and Nadia Kizensko were wonderful advocates as department chairs. My colleagues had a transformative impact as teachers and writers, and I continue my best to practice what I have learned from them—I thank Barry Trachtenberg, Jennifer Greiman, Ryan Irwin, Kori Graves, Carl Bon Tempo, Sheila Curran Bernard, among others.

This book has both been the starting point and the beneficiary of countless discussions I have had with my friends, colleagues, and students in the Department of History at NYU. With a feel for the central pulse of any project, my colleagues have also become very important interlocutors for these larger questions about race, empire, and the urgent question of political alternatives. I have benefited from their institutional advocacy, coteaching in the classroom, and the vibrant dynamic such collaboration fosters. I thank Barbara Weinstein, David Ludden, Nikhil Singh, Michele Mitchell, Linda Gordon, Martha Hodes, Fred Cooper, Stef Geroulanos, Robyn D'Avignon, Steven Hahn, Andrew Needham, Becky Goetz, along with many others. The care and effort of Karin Burrell, Danielle Hartounian, and Maura Puschek have also been pivotal to this project. I need to thank Barbara specifically for the work she did to grant me critical time to work on this very book, as well as organizing a workshop.

For invaluable feedback as invited workshop readers or discussants of the project, I thank Mark Bradley, Andre Schmid, Vince Rafael, and Laleh Khalili. Rebecca Karl deserves a special mention for her reading interventions on the manuscript at a critical juncture. My time as a member of the School of Social Science at the Institute for Advanced Study was crucial to allowing me the time and space to produce the full manuscript draft in the first place. The IAS brought together friends and comrades, new and old. I thank Joan Scott, David Eng, Didier Fassin, Brian Connolly, Miriam Ticktin, and Ilana Feldman for their engagement with the project. Carolyn Eichner, Beth Lew-Williams, Tod Hamilton, and Gena Camoosa provided much-needed support and perspective throughout the writing process. Eating food and writing together continues with Rhacel Parreñas, Enze Han, and Alice Goffman to this day. Sara Pursley and Colleen Woods both have sustained the writing of this book through the sheer force of their brilliance and their friendship—thank you for both. To Sylvain Perdigon, I thank him for the lucidity and depth of the registers he has inspired in the final drafting of this manuscript.

Brigitta van Rheinberg of Princeton University Press has believed in this book project from the very first conversation we had, and I thank her for her incredible support and championing. Amanda Perry has been a wonderful assistant editor, and she has edited and read the manuscript with a deft eye and touch. I am most grateful to Eric Crahan's astute and generous support as the book makes its way to readers. To the anonymous readers for PUP, I thank them for insights into the manuscript at different critical stages. I thank Shane Kelly for the terrific map needed of the Korean peninsula. Dawn Hall, the copyeditor for this project, worked on heroic levels with each draft, and I thank Mark Bellis for shepherding this book through production with extraordinary care and adroitness. Patricia Szobar translated Ernst Fraenkel's lecture on the Korean War and international law, and I thank her for putting her formidable skills to translating the text. And thank you to Dave Luljak for distilling and creating the index for this book.

Marilyn Young passed away before I could present her with a hardcover copy of yet another book on US empire whose author she had mentored and influenced greatly. In her address as president of the Society for Historians of American Foreign Relations, Marilyn offered these words: "I think our continuous task must be to make war visible, vivid, an inescapable part of the country's self-consciousness, as inescapable a subject of study as it is a reality." In front of Molly Nolan, Andrew Ross, Sonya Posmentier, Josh Fattal, Sarah Sklaw, Rachel Kuo, Angela Arias, others across campuses and the NYC community, Nodutdol, the scholars I have met through the Alliance of Scholars Concerned about Korea—I cannot adequately express what their solidarity and organizing work has helped me to challenge and develop in the pages of this book. Deokhyo Choi continues to be a true comrade through a shared dedication to a work that strives continuously against the ever-present momentum to simplify and mollify our stories about the past. Paula Chakravartty is a dragon slayer, and she is someone with whom I am always willing to take up the "continuous task."

Christine Hong has long been like family, but she is the wiser, more courageous older sister, and frankly words cannot express my gratitude for her ever-stunning and powerful insights and articulations about race and empire. Samita Sinha, Jesse Harold, and Isaac Chang have been the home for my soul and history for many, many years, and have nurtured me and this particular project with more meals, conversations, and celebrations than I can count. Betty Kim has witnessed many, many beginnings to this project from our childhood together, and I thank her for her capacious understanding of the urgency this project has held for me over the past decade.

And then, there are the people who understood the origins of this project even before I did, and supported me even when I could not see the project as clearly as I wanted. My respect and gratitude are immense toward my brother, Andy, as he constantly inspires me with his steadfast groundedness and clear commitment to civic service and the public good. This book has also seen my nephews, August and Austin, energizing my brother's work. My sister-in-law, Kammy Lai, has witnessed the project in its full trajectory, and I thank her for sharing each milestone.

In Korea, my aunt, my cousins, and my cousins' families opened their doors, hearts, and kitchens to me with laughter and love. When I arrived in Korea as an adult, so eager to learn and understand, they always showed such beautiful patience and enormous enthusiasm toward me and my project. They worked with me on my research, assisted me with Korean language homework, and made sure that I never lost sight of the bigger picture. I love them all so immensely, and I only wish that I could be more articulate in expressing my thanks.

I dedicate this work to my parents, for whom the legacies of the war were lived, embodied, and traversed, not simply studied, researched, and written. It has been an unexpectedly circuitous journey for me as I began to inquire about a history that seemed both everywhere and nowhere growing up, and my parents have even traveled with me to Washington, DC, Geneva, and Koje-do. They grounded me during the research and writing like no one else could—after all, the urge to tell stories, a curiosity about the workings of the world, and questions about justice began with them. I had to be able to tell this story to them and with them. And for that, I dedicate this book to my parents.

NOTES

Introduction: War and Humanity

1. Se-hŭi Oh, *Suyoungso 65* [Compound 65] (Taegu: Maninsa, 2000), 61–62.

2. On war as a "duel": Carl von Clausewitz, *On War*, ed. and trans. Michael Eliot Howard and Peter Paret (Princeton, NJ: Princeton University Press, 1989); "The President's News Conference," June 29, 1950. Part of the *Public Papers of the Presidents: Harry S. Truman, 1945–1953* of the Harry S. Truman Presidential Library, available at www.trumanlibrary.org/publicpapers, accessed May 21, 2011.

3. Frantz Fanon, *The Wretched of the Earth*, trans. Richard Philcox (New York: Grove Press, 2000), 2.

4. Dean Rusk, *As I Saw It* (New York: W.W. Norton, 1990), 123–124.

5. "Statement by the President on the Violation of the 38th Parallel," June 26, 1950. Part of the *Public Papers of the Presidents: Harry S. Truman, 1945–1953* of the Harry S. Truman Presidential Library, available at www.trumanlibrary.org/publicpapers, accessed May 21, 2011.

6. Report on Soviet official press release, June 27, 1950. From *Mi Kungmubu Hanguk kungnae sanghwang kwallyŏn munsŏ: The US Department of State Relating to the Internal Affairs of Korea* (Seoul: Kukpangbu Kunsa P'yŏnch'an Yŏn'guso, 2000–2002), vol. 1.

7. Meeting dated January 2, 1952. Minutes of Meetings of Subdelegates for Agenda Item 4 on Prisoners of War, 12/11/1951-02/06/1952; Korean Armistice Negotiation Records; Secretary, General Staff; Headquarters, United Nations Command (Advance); Record Group 333; National Archives at College Park, College Park, MD.

8. Kodendera Subayya Thimayya, *Experiment in Neutrality* (New Delhi: Vision Books, 1981), 39.

9. "Address on Foreign Policy at the Navy Day Celebration in New York City," October 27, 1945. Part of the *Public Papers of the Presidents: Harry S. Truman, 1945–1953* of the Harry S. Truman Presidential Library, available at www.trumanlibrary.org/publicpapers, accessed June 27, 2018.

10. "Special Message to the Congress on Greece and Turkey: The Truman Doctrine," March 12, 1947. Part of the *Public Papers of the Presidents: Harry S. Truman, 1945–1953* of the Harry S. Truman Presidential Library, available at www.trumanlibrary.org/publicpapers, accessed June 27, 2018.

11. Mimi Thi Nyugen, *The Gift of Freedom: War, Debt, and Other Refugee Passages* (Durham, NC: Duke University Press, 2014), 4.

12. "blueprint": Walter LaFeber, *America, Russia, and the Cold War, 1945–2006* (New York: McGraw-Hill, 2008), 106. "bible of American national security": Michael Hogan, *A Cross of Iron: Harry S. Truman and the Origins of the National Security State, 1945–1954* (Cambridge: Cambridge University Press, 1998), 12.

13. Hogan, *Cross of Iron*, 12.

14. "A Report to the National Security Council—NSC 68," April 12, 1950. President's Secretary's File, Truman Papers. Harry S. Truman Presidential Library, available at www.truman library.org/, accessed June 27, 2018.

15. Transcript of Princeton Seminar Discussion dated July 9, 1953. Princeton Seminars File, Dean Acheson Papers. Harry S. Truman Presidential Library, available at www.trumanlibrary .org/, accessed June 10, 2018.

16. Transcript of Princeton Seminar Discussion, dated October 11, 1953.

17. David Fautua, "The 'Long Pull' Army: NSC 68, the Korean War, and the Creation of the Cold War U.S. Army," *Journal of Military History* 61, no. 1 (1997): 94–95.

18. Aaron B. O'Connell, "An Accidental Empire?: President Harry S. Truman and the Origins of America's Global Military Presence," in *Origins of the National Security State and the Legacy of Harry S. Truman*, ed. Mary Ann Heiss and Michael J. Hogan (Kirksville: Truman State University Press, 2015), 197–98.

19. Maria Höhn and Seungsook Moon, "Introduction: The Politics of Gender, Sexuality, Race, and Class in the US Military Empire," in *Over There: Living with the US Military Empire from World War Two to the Present*, ed. Maria Höhn and Seungsook Moon (Durham, NC: Duke University Press, 2010), 8–11.

20. Bruce Cumings, *Dominion from Sea to Sea: Pacific Ascendancy and American Power* (New Haven, CT: Yale University Press, 2009), 485.

21. Ruth Oldenziel, "Islands: The United States as a Networked Empire," in *Entangled Geographies: Empire and Technopolitics in the Global Cold War*, ed. Gabrielle Hecht (Cambridge, MA: MIT Press, 2011), 19.

22. "National Security Council directive on Office of Special Projects" (NSC 10/2), in *Foreign Relations of the United States, 1945–1950, Emergence of the Intelligence Establishment*, ed. C. Thomas Thorne Jr. and David S. Patterson (Washington, DC: Government Printing Office, 1996), 715.

23. On the Chinese POW issue, see David Cheng Chang, *The Hijacked War: The Story of Chinese POWs in the Korean War* (Stanford, CA: Stanford University Press, 2019). For the US Military official history, see Walter G. Hermes, *Truce Tent and Fighting Front* (Washington, DC: Office of the Chief of Military History, United States Army, 1966). For an analysis of the education programs and politics of the UNC POW camps, see Grace Chae, "Captive Minds: Race, War, and the Education of Korean War POWs in US Custody, 1950–1953" (PhD diss., University of Chicago, 2010). On the subject of US POWs, see Charles Young, *Name, Rank, and Serial Number: Exploiting Korean War POWs at Home* (New York: Oxford University Press, 2014).

24. See James T. Sparrow, *Warfare State: World War II Americans and the Age of Big Government* (Oxford: Oxford University Press, 2011).

25. See Takashi Fujitani, *Race for Empire: Koreans as Japanese and Japanese as Americans during World War II* (Berkeley: University of California Press, 2011).

26. Carl Schmitt, *The Nomos of the Earth in the International Law of the Jus Publicum Europaeum*, trans. G. L. Ulmen (New York: Telos Press, 2003), 419.

27. Marilyn Young, "Bombing Civilians from the Twentieth to the Twenty-First Centuries," in *Bombing Civilians: A Twentieth-Century History*, ed. Yuki Tanaka and Marilyn Young (New York: New Press, 2009), 157.

28. Memoranda; Folder: Psywar Activities—Chief of Staff Papers; Box 7; General Correspondence; Psychological Warfare Section; Records of the General Headquarters, FEC, SCAP, and UNC–; Record Group 544; NARA, College Park, MD.

29. Oh, *Suyoungso 65* [Compound 65], 45.

30. Case #68, Box 4. POW Incident Investigation Case files, 1950–53; Office of the Provost Marshal; Office of the Assistant Chief of Staff, G-1; Headquarter, US Army Forces, Far East, 1952–57; Record Group 554; NARA, College Park, Maryland.

31. Case #64, Box 3. POW Incident Investigation Case files, 1950–53; Office of the Provost Marshal; Office of the Assistant Chief of Staff, G-1; Headquarter, US Army Forces, Far East, 1952–57; Record Group 554; NARA, College Park, Maryland.

32. Karma Nabulsi, *Traditions of War: Occupation, Resistance, and the Law* (Oxford: Oxford University Press, 1999), 12–13.

33. 181st CIC Detachment—1st Marine Division, SOP for Counterintelligence Operations; Folder: 228-01 181st CIC Detachment—Korea—SOP—1952; Box 12; Counter Intelligence Corps Collection; Assistant Chief of Staff, G-2 (Intelligence); RG 319; NARA, College Park, Maryland.

34. An eloquent and compelling work arguing for a consideration of the relationship between history-writing and the nature of the archive is Michel-Rolph Trouillot, *Silencing the Past: Power and the Production of History* (Boston: Beacon Press, 1995). See also Marisa Fuentes, *Dispossessed Lives: Enslaved Women, Violence, and the Archive* (Philadelphia: University of Pennsylvania Press, 2016); Natalie Zemon Davis, *Fiction in the Archives: Pardon Tales and Their Tellers in Sixteenth-Century France* (Stanford, CA: Stanford University Press, 1987); Thomas Richards, *The Imperial Archive: Knowledge and the Fantasy of Empire* (New York: Verso, 1993); Kathryn Burns, *Into the Archive: Writing and Power in Colonial Peru* (Durham, NC: Duke University Press, 2010).

35. On race and liberalism: see Nikhil Pal Singh, *Race and America's Long War* (Oakland: University of California Press, 2017); Denise Ferreira da Silva, *Toward a Global Idea of Race* (Minneapolis: University of Minnesota Press, 2007); Christine Hong, "Legal Fictions: Human Rights Cultural Production and the Pax Americana in the Pacific Rim" (PhD diss., University of California, Berkeley, 2007); Teemu Ruskola, David L. Eng, and Shuang Shen, eds. "China and the Human," special double issue of *Social Text*, no. 109–10 (Winter 2011/Spring 2012).

36. Albert Biderman, *March to Calumny: The Story of American POW's in the Korean War* (New York: Macmillan, 1963), 61.

Chapter One: Interrogation

1. I have given the details and spelling of Chang Sung Sum's location in accordance with the US military report. However, according to today's spelling and administrative unit breakdown, Chang's home is not located in the currently existing 38th parallel: Sangsunae-ri, Nam-myeon,

Inje-gun, Gangwon-do, Republic of Korea. The 1945 38th parallel had been farther south than the current one.

2. Mi kunjŏnggi chŏngbo charyojip: CIC (Pangch'ŏptae) pogosŏ, 1945.9–1949.1 (Kangwŏn-do Ch'unch'ŏn-si: Hallim Taehakkyo Asia Munhwa Yŏn'guso, 1995), vol. 1, report dated April 19, 1946, included in 971st CounterIntelligence Corps Detachment Annual Progress Report for 1947, 331. (Hereafter CIC 1945.9–1949.1.)

3. Bruce Cumings, The Origins of the Korean War, vol. 1, Studies of the East Asian Institute (Princeton, NJ: Princeton University Press, 1981–90), xxii.

4. Alexis Dudden, Japan's Colonization of Korea: Discourse and Power (Honolulu: University of Hawai'i Press, 2005).

5. Daniel Rodgers, Atlantic Crossings: Social Politics in a Progressive Age (Cambridge, MA: Belknap Press of Harvard University Press, 1998), 63.

6. Courrier de la Conférence de la Paix (dated Juin 30, 1907), from Swarthmore College Peace Collection.

7. Courrier de la Conférence de la Paix, Juillet 1, 1907.

8. Anthony Anghie, Imperialism, Sovereignty, and the Making of International Law (Cambridge: Cambridge University Press: 2005), 87.

9. Anghie, Imperialism, 87.

10. Thomas Joseph Lawrence, War and Neutrality in the Far East (Cambridge, MA: Harvard University Press, 1904), 23.

11. Patrick G. Hogan Jr. and Joseph O. Baylen, "Shaw, W. T. Stead, and the 'International Peace Crusade,' 1898–1899," Shaw Review 6, no. 2 (1963): 60–61; Kate Campbell, "W. E. Gladstone, W. T. Stead, Matthew Arnold, and a New Journalism: Cultural Politics in the 1880s," Victorian Periodicals Review 36, no. 1 (2003): 20–40.

12. Henry Em, The Great Enterprise: Sovereignty and Historiography in Modern Korea (Durham, NC: Duke University Press, 2013), 75.

13. Courrier de la Conférence de la Paix, Juillet 5, 1907.

14. Gordon Chang, "Whose 'Barbarism'? Whose 'Treachery'? Race and Civilization in the Unknown United States–Korea War of 1871," Journal of American History 89, no. 4 (2003): 1333. "American officers claimed that they had killed some 250 Korean soldiers; the number may have been twice as high."

15. Other articles gave Japan rights to search for new ports in five Korean provinces, survey Korean waters, conduct business and trade without interference, and protect its merchants in Korean ports under extraterritorial privileges. See Bruce Cumings, Korea's Place in the Sun: A Modern History (New York: W. W. Norton, 1997), 102.

16. Em, Great Enterprise, 40.

17. Em, Great Enterprise, 40–41.

18. The core of Em's argument in his analysis of what he calls the "semantics of sovereignty" involved in the Japanese attempts at closing and controlling the space of ambiguity concerning Korean sovereignty lies in elucidating how the Japanese positioned itself as the "preeminent translator of the new semantics of sovereignty in East Asia"; Em, Great Enterprise.

19. Dudden, Japan's Colonization of Korea, 7.

20. "Final Text of the Communiqué," *Foreign Relations of the United States: Diplomatic Papers, the Conferences at Cairo and Tehran*, eds. William M. Franklin and William Gerber (Washington, DC: United States Printing Office, 1961), Document 343.

21. "The Cairo Declaration did not end the territorial questions; it intensified them. For the subject of international trusteeship, the significance of the Cairo Declaration is clear and simple: Japan would be stripped of her Empire." From William Roger Louis, *Imperialism at Bay: The United States and the Decolonization of the British Empire, 1941–1945* (Oxford: Clarendon Press, 1977), 274.

22. From the Pacific War Council Minutes, January 12, 1944, Roosevelt Paper. (Quote taken from Louis, *Imperialism at Bay*, 355.)

23. "Bohlen Minutes," in *Foreign Relations of the United States, Diplomatic Papers, Conferences at Malta and Yalta, 1945*, ed. Bryton Barron (Washington, DC: United States Government Printing Office, 1955), Document 393.

24. Dean Rusk, *As I Saw It*, 1st ed. (New York: W. W. Norton, 1990).

25. Mi Kunjŏngch'ŏng kwanbo: *Official Gazette*, United States Army Military Government in Korea (Seoul: Wonju Munhwasa), Proclamation No. 1. (Hereafter *Official Gazette*.)

26. *Official Gazette*, Proclamation No. 2.

27. E. Grant Meade, *American Military Government in Korea* (New York: King's Crown Press, 1951), 67.

28. Ernst Fraenkel, "Entry 24 January 1946: Aufzeichnungen vom 15. bis 30. Januar 1946 über Fraenkels Ankunftszeit in Korea [1946]," in *Ernst Fraenkel: Gesammelte Schriften* (Baden Baden: Nomos Verlagsgesellschaft, 1999).

29. Gregory Henderson, *Korea: The Politics of the Vortex* (Cambridge, MA: Harvard University Press, 1968), 124.

30. Philip H. Taylor, "Military Government Experience in Korea: Part I; Administration and Operation of Military Government in Korea," in *American Experiences in Military Government in World War II*, ed. Carl Friedrich (New York: Rinehart, 1948), 357.

31. *History of the United States Armed Forces in Korea* (United States, Far East Command, published in 1948). Part III: Chapter 1, "Creating Military Government," 11. (Hereafter *HUSAFIK*.)

32. Ernst Fraenkel, "Aufzeichnungen vom 15. bis 30. Januar 1946 über Fraenkels Ankunftszeit in Korea [1946]," in *Ernst Fraenkel: Gesammelte Schriften* (Baden Baden: Nomos Verlagsgesellschaft, 1999).

33. Udi Greenberg, *The Weimar Century: German Émigrés and the Ideological Foundations of the Cold War* (Princeton, NJ: Princeton University Press. 2017), 98.

34. Greenberg, *Weimar Century*, 95.

35. Associated Press article, "Koreans March in Protest against Keeping Japanese; Officials in Washington Amazed at Army Action—State Department Disclaims Any Part in Move—MacArthur Bars Disorder," *New York Times*, September 11, 1945.

36. G-2 Periodic Report / United States Army Forces in Korea. Headquarters. G-2. 1945–1948 (Kangwŏn-do Ch'unch'ŏn-si: Hallim Taehakkyo Asia Munhwa Yŏn'guso); report dated September 12, 1945. (Hereafter G-2 Weekly.)

37. Report dated October 23, 1945, G-2 Weekly.

38. Report dated September 12, 1945, G-2 Weekly.

39. "Message to U.S.A. Citizens" included in report dated October 30, 1945, G-2 Weekly.

40. Meade, *American Military Government in Korea*, 59.

41. "Message to U.S.A. Citizens" signed by "The Central People's Committee of the People's Republic of Corea." (October 5, 1945, Seoul.) In G-2 Weekly, included in report dated October 30, 1945.

42. "Message to U.S.A. Citizens."

43. "Message to U.S.A. Citizens."

44. Ernst Fraenkel, "Aufzeichnungen vom 15. bis 30. Januar 1946 über Fraenkels Ankunftszeit in Korea [1946]," in *Ernst Fraenkel: Gesammelte Schriften* (Baden Baden: Nomos Verlagsgesellschaft, 1999).

45. Letter from Commander in Chief, US Army Forces, Pacific to Joint Chiefs of Staff, December 16, 1945. Folder: Papers of Harry S. Truman, SMOF: Selected Records on Korean War, Pertinent Papers on Korea Situation; Box 11; SMOF: National Security Files; Papers of Harry S. Truman; Harry S. Truman Library. Although the letter itself is from MacArthur to the JCS, he had enclosed a report made by Hodge on the current situation in Korea. The quote is from Hodge's report.

46. Dipesh Chakrabarty, *Provincializing Europe: Postcolonial Thought and Historical Difference* (Princeton, NJ: Princeton University Press, 2000), 8.

47. Report dated October 9, 1945, G-2 Weekly.

48. Report dated October 23, 1945, G-2 Weekly.

49. Meade, *American Military Government in Korea*, 72.

50. "Lyuh Woo Hyun" is the spelling used by the USAMGIK during the occupation. In McCune-Reischauer format, his name would be as follows: Yŏ Unhyŏng.

51. G-2 Weekly, report dated September 25, 1945. This particular report scrutinizes and narrates Lyuh's history and notes that Lyuh only accepted the Japanese colonial state's offer "under the following conditions: 1) The food for the coming three months should be guaranteed; 2) Political prisoners should be released; 3) Freedom of the press and speech should be guaranteed; 4) There should be no mobilization of the students for maintenance of peace; and 5) No interference from the Japanese."

52. *HUSAFIK*, vol. 3, chapter 4, part I, 50. Also quoted in Cumings, *Origins of the Korean War*, 1: 201–2.

53. *HUSAFIK*, chapter 3, part III, "American Arrival," 89.

54. Cumings, *Origins of the Korean War*, 1: 420. "From 1914 to 1938, the total number of farmers increased 11 percent but the number of tenants increased 66 percent. During the same period the proportion of tenants to the total number of farm households increased from 35 to 53 percent."

55. Quote is from Meade's *American Military Government in Korea*, 188.

56. Meade, *American Military Government in Korea*, 72.

57. Speech included in report dated October 30, 1945, G-2 Weekly.

58. *Official Gazette*, Ordinance 21.

59. Henderson, *Korea: The Politics of the Vortex*, 126.

60. Henderson, *Korea: The Politics of the Vortex*, 127.

61. *CIC 1945.9–1949.1*, vol. 1, CIC, vol. 1, US Army Intelligence Center, History of the Counter Intelligence Corps Volume XXX, "CIC during the Occupation of Korea (1959.3)," 15.

62. Donald Nichols, *How Many Times Can I Die?* (Brooksville, FL: Brooksville Printing, 1981), 116.

63. Nichols, *How Many Times Can I Die?*, 117.

64. "Interview with Kenneth E. MacDougall, Capt, MPC, on October 5, 1954, Bldg 22, Ft Holabird," Folder: 228-01 MacDougall, Kenneth E.—CIC during Occupation of Korea—(1947–1948) Box 6; Counter Intelligence Corps Collection; Assistant Chief of Staff, G-2 (Intelligence); RG 319; NARA, College Park, Maryland.

65. William Tigue, Folder: 228-01 EEI: CIC Operations in Korea (1952); Box 6; Counter Intelligence Corps Collection; Assistant Chief of Staff, G-2 (Intelligence); RG 319; NARA, College Park, Maryland.

66. Ernst Fraenkel, "Aufzeichnungen vom 15. bis 30. Januar 1946 über Fraenkels Ankunftszeit in Korea [1946]," in *Ernst Fraenkel: Gesammelte Schriften* (Baden Baden: Nomos Verlagsgesellschaft, 1999), 379–80.

67. *Official Gazette*, Ordinance 9.

68. *Official Gazette*, General Notice No. 1.

69. G-2 Weekly report, dated October 9, 1945.

70. G-2 Weekly report, dated October 30, 1945.

71. G-2 Weekly report, dated October 30, 1945.

72. G-2 Weekly report, dated October 30, 1945.

73. *Official Gazette*, Ordinance 19.

74. *Official Gazette*, Ordinance 19.

75. *Official Gazette*, Ordinance 19.

76. *Official Gazette*, Proclamation No. 2.

77. *Official Gazette*, Ordinance 72.

78. The twenty-eight stipulations are as follows: Numbers 13, 14, 15, 16, 17, 18, 19, 20, 21, 22,30, 31, 32, 33, 34, 47, 48, 49, 50, 51, 52, 53, 54, 57, 58,59, 60.

79. *Official Gazette*, Ordinance 72.

80. *Official Gazette*, Ordinance 72.

81. *CIC 1945.9–1949.1*, vol. 1, US Army Intelligence Center, History of the Counter Intelligence Corps Volume XXX, "CIC during the Occupation of Korea (1959.3)," 21.

82. *CIC 1945.9–1949.1*, vol. 1, US Army Intelligence Center, 22.

83. *CIC 1945.9–1949.1*, vol. 1, report dated April 19, 1946, included in 971st Counter Intelligence Corps Detachment Annual Progress Report for 1947.

84. *CIC 1945.9-1949.1*, vol. 1, report dated April 19, 1946.

85. 1948 Annual Progress Report of the 971st CIC Detachment in Korea; Box 14856; WWII Operations Report, 1941–48; Central Intelligence; RG 407; NARA; College Park, Maryland.

86. *CIC 1945.9–1949.1*, vol. 1, 971st Counter Intelligence Corps, 17.

87. MacDougall interview, NARA.

88. *CIC 1945.9–1949.1*, vol. 1, US Army Intelligence Center, History of the Counter Intelligence Corps Volume XXX, "CIC during the Occupation of Korea (1959.3), 1.

89. This quote is taken from the "USAFIK letter AG 322 (TFGBI) dated 30 April 1946." This document is one of four cited as explicating the "mission of the Counter Intelligence Corps" in the SOP: a) War Department letter AG 322, CIC (October 31, 1944) OB-S-B-M dated November 13, 1944, Subject: Counter Intelligence Corps. b) AFPAC regulations #100-10 dated August 1, 1945. C) AFPAC letter AG 322 (March 22, 1946), CI. Located in above citation.

90. *CIC 1945.9–1949.1*, vol. 1, CIC, vol. 1, US Army Intelligence Center, History of the Counter Intelligence Corps Volume XXX, "CIC during the Occupation of Korea (1959.3), 24.

91. 1948 Annual Progress Report of the 971st CIC Detachment in Korea; Box 14856; WWII Operations Report, 1941–48; Central Intelligence; RG 407; NARA; College Park, Maryland.

92. 1948 Annual Progress Report of the 971st CIC Detachment in Korea; Box 14856; WWII Operations Report, 1941–48; Central Intelligence; RG 407; NARA; College Park, Maryland.

93. 1948 Annual Progress Report of the 971st CIC Detachment in Korea, NARA.

94. 1948 Annual Progress Report of the 971st CIC Detachment in Korea, NARA.

95. MacDougall interview, NARA.

96. Second Lieutenant Joseph H. Farell of the 116th CIC Detachment; Folder: 228-01 EEI: CIC Operations in Korea (1952); Box 6; Counter Intelligence Corps Collection; Assistant Chief of Staff, G-2 (Intelligence); RG 319; NARA, College Park, Maryland.

97. Folder: 228-01 Griemann, Theodore E.—CIC during Occupation of Korea—(1947–49); Box 6; Counter Intelligence Corps Collection; Assistant Chief of Staff, G-2 (Intelligence); RG 319; NARA, College Park, Maryland.

98. Hee-Kyung Suh, "Atrocities before and during the Korean War," *Critical Asian Studies* 42, no. 4 (2010): 571.

99. John Dilworth, Box 6; Counter Intelligence Corps Collection; Assistant Chief of Staff, G-2 (Intelligence); RG 319; NARA, College Park, Maryland.

100. Interview with 1st Lt. Jack D. Sells, 111th Counter Intelligence Corps Detachment; Folder: 228-01 EEI: CIC Operations in Korea (1952); Box 6; Counter Intelligence Corps Collection; Assistant Chief of Staff, G-2 (Intelligence); RG 319; NARA, College Park, Maryland.

101. Interview with M/Sgt. Joseph P. Gorman; Folder: 228-01 EEI: CIC Operations in Korea (1952); Box 6; Counter Intelligence Corps Collection; Assistant Chief of Staff, G-2 (Intelligence); RG 319; NARA, College Park, Maryland.

102. Migun CIC chŏngbo pogosŏ : RG 319 Office of the Chief of Military history. (Sŏul : Chungang Ilbo Hyŏndaesa Yŏn'guso, 1996), Volume 2; "Korean War: CI Activities," Investigative Records Repository (IRR), Box #99/Case #ZF010482. Agent Report: Masan G2 Office, dated 14 March 1951. [hereafter *CIC RG319*]

103. *CIC RG319*, vol. 2, Agent Report: Masan G-2 Office, March 14, 1951.

104. Thomas Blom Hansen and Finn Steppputat, eds., *Sovereign Bodies: Citizens, Migrants, and States in the Postcolonial World* (Princeton, NJ: Princeton University Press, 2005), 11.

105. Historical Report for Period 1 November to 30 Number 1950; Folder: Historical Rpt 704 CIC Nov 1950; Box 4677; Army AG Commercial Reports; Record Group 407; NARA, College Park, Maryland.

106. Historical Report for Period 1 November to 30 Number 1950; Folder: Historical Rpt 704 CIC Nov 1950; Box 4677; Army AG Commercial Reports; Record Group 407; NARA, College Park, Maryland.

107. Joseph Vincent Lisiewski [Sgt, 7th Div., 32nd Inf Rgt.], enlisted in anticipation of the draft on 3-4-51: Korean War Veterans' Survey Questionnaire, Military History Institute Archives, Carlisle, Pennsylvania.

108. Robert H. Moyer [Staff Sgt, 3rd Inf. Div., 7th Inf. Regt., 3rd Battalion, Med company] enlisted on August 13, 1947: Korean War Veterans' Survey Questionnaire, Military History Institute Archives, Carlisle, Pennsylvania.

109. Charles Ehredt [1st Sgt., 1 Cav. Div, 16th Regiment] enlisted in 1949: Korean War Veterans' Survey Questionnaire, Military History Institute Archives, Carlisle, Pennsylvania.

110. Robert William Burr [2nd Inf div., 38th inf. Reg, 2nd battalion, Company E], Korean War Veterans' Survey Questionnaire, Military History Institute Archives, Carlisle, Pennsylvania.

111. Mu-ho Yi, Ŏnŭ cholbyŏng i kyŏkkŭn Han'guk chŏnjaeng [The Korean War Experienced by an Ordinary Soldier] (Sŏul-sl : Chisik Sanŏpsa, 2003).

112. "Normal procedure was to acquire the land for an indefinite period and without compensation to the owners. Clearance was generally a simple matter, requiring only the signature of the local governor. On occasions, however, local landowners protested the seizure of their land, verbal protests were sometimes backed with pitchforks, and demonstrations sometimes made necessary the procurement of the written approval of the ROK Minister of National Defense as well as that of the local governor. When native structures became an obstacle to the construction of POW facilities or constituted a security hazard, they were procured with the campsite property." From "The Handling of POW during the Korean War," Folder: Unclassified, S11-02, Korea; Box 16; Unclassified Records, 1969–75; POW/Civilian Internee Information Center; Records of the Provost Marshal General, 1941–; Record Group 389; NARA.

113. Ernst Fraenkel, *Korea: A Turning Point in International Law?*, trans. Patricia Szobar (Berlin: Gebrüder Weiss Publishers, 1951).

Chapter Two: The Prisoner of War

1. Reports by Bieri May 29 to June 9, 1951; Transmission des rapports de visites de camps aux Nations Unies, aux Etats-Unis et à la Corée-du-Nord, 16/01/1951–12/05/1952, B AG 210 056-021, Archive of the International Committee of the Red Cross.

2. Reports by Bieri May 29 to June 9, 1951; Transmission des rapports de visites de camps aux Nations Unies, aux Etats-Unis et à la Corée-du-Nord, 16/01/1951–12/05/1952, B AG 210 056-021, Archive of the International Committee of the Red Cross.

3. Reports by Bieri on June 8 and 9, 1951; Transmission des rapports de visites de camps aux Nations Unies, aux Etats-Unis et à la Corée-du-Nord, 16/01/1951–12/05/1952, B AG 210 056-021, Archive of the International Committee of the Red Cross.

4. Report on UN POW Camp No. 1 Koje-do and Pusan. Bieri: May 29 to June 9, 1951. Dr. Bessero May 29, 31, 1951.; Transmission des rapports de visites de camps aux Nations Unies, aux Etats-Unis et à la Corée-du-Nord, 16/01/1951–12/05/1952, B AG 210 056-021, Archive of the International Committee of the Red Cross.

5. Harry S. Truman to Secretaries of State and Defense, and Director of CIA, April 4, 1951; Psychological Strategy Board; Subject File; CF; Truman Papers, Student Research File: "Psychological Warfare." Harry S. Truman Presidential Library and Archives.

6. "Prepared Public Statement by the Director of PSB," Folder: 000.7, Box 1. SMOF: Psychological Strategy Board Files, Papers of Harry S. Truman, Harry S. Truman Presidential Library and Archives.

7. Memorandum for the Senior NSC Staff. "U.S. Courses of Action with Respect to Korea," in vol. 10 of *Documentary History of the Truman Presidency*, ed. Dennis Merrill (Bethesda, MD: University Publications of America, 1997), 29–32.

8. Closing Lecture, Psychological Warfare Seminar at University of North Carolina, August 15, 1952. Folder: 350.001 file #1—Dr. Raymond B. Allen Lecture [1 of 2], Box 29, SMOF: Psychological Strategy Board Files, Papers of Harry S. Truman, Harry S. Truman Presidential Library and Archives.

9. "The Oriental Communist Prisoner of War," POW/CI Center; Office of the Provost Marshal; Office of the Assistant Chief of Staff, G-1; Headquarter, US Army Forces, Far East, 1952–57; Record Group 554; NARA, College Park, Maryland.

10. Case file #64; Box 3; POW Incident Investigation Case Files, 1950–53; Office of the Provost Marshal; Office of the Assistant Chief of Staff, G-1; Headquarter, US Army Forces, Far East, 1952–57; Record Group 554; NARA, College Park, Maryland.

11. Case file #64.

12. Interview with Song Jeung Taik; Box 144; Series VI: "In Mortal Combat"; Toland Papers; Franklin D. Roosevelt Presidential Library and Archives.

13. Dean Acheson, *Present at the Creation: My Years in the State Department* (New York: W. W. Norton, 1969), 468–69.

14. Calculation of prisoners interned each month and captured rates (1952), Folder: Unclassified, 511-02, Korea; Box 19; Unclassified Records, 1969–75; POW/Civilian Internee Information Center; Records of the Provost Marshal General, 1941–; Record Group 389; NARA, College Park, Maryland.

15. Case file #40, Box 2; POW Incident Investigation Case Files, 1950–53; Office of the Provost Marshal; Office of the Assistant Chief of Staff, G-1; Headquarter, US Army Forces, Far East, 1952–57; Record Group 554; NARA, College Park, Maryland.

16. *Convention (III) relative to the Treatment of Prisoners of War. Geneva, 12 August 1949.* International Committee of the Red Cross, accessed January 21, 2018, https://ihl-databases.icrc .org/ihl.

17. The citation for the case files is as follows: POW Incident Investigation Case Files, 1950–53; Office of the Provost Marshal; Office of the Assistant Chief of Staff, G-1; Headquarter, US Army Forces, Far East, 1952–57; Record Group 554; NARA, College Park, Maryland.

18. Administrative Instructions Reference Handling Enemy Prisoners of War (Addressed to: Commanding General, Eighth Army), February 20, 1951, issued March 5, 1951; EPW/CI/D Gen Info Files—PW processing forms (1951); Unclassified/SS11-02/Korea; Box 14; Unclassified Records, 1969–75; POW/Civilian Internee Information Center; Records of the Provost Marshal General, 1941–; RG 389; NARA, College Park, Maryland.

19. Subject: Prisoners of War (this memo is a response to an inquiry received on April 15, 1952, from Merlin Nelson Major (MPC) Chief, Prisoner of War Branch, and is addressed to Lt. Colonel Vern E. Johnson of the Plans and Training Division); Folder: Unclassified/Prisoners

of War as re: Geneva Conventions; Unclassified/SS11-02/Korea; Box 15; Unclassified Records 1969–75; POW/Civilian Internee Information Center; Records of the Provost Marshal General, 1941; RG 389; NARA, College Park, Maryland.

20. Yi Chong-gyu, oral history interview by author, Seoul, Korea, January 11, 2008 (my translation).

21. Memorandum from 91st MP Bn to 2d Log Com, Vol V-Reference Files-Control of Prisoners of War-HQ KCOMZ; Box 1651; Enemy Prisoners of War Records, 1951–53, Final report: "The Handling of Prisoners of War during the Korean War," June 1960 to Control Prisoners of War, HQ KCOMZ; Eighth US Army, Military History Section; Records of US Army Operational, Tactical, and Support Organizations (World War II and thereafter); Record Group 338; NARA, College Park, Maryland.

22. I am culling this information from hundreds of ATIS reports and also POW and Civilian Internee Incident case files. Although it is well known that prisoners of war often did not divulge their identity during initial screenings, the information presented here appeared frequently enough to merit credence and attention.

23. Meeting dated December 22, 1951, Minutes of Meetings of Subdelegates for Agenda Item 4 on Prisoners of War, 12/11/1951–02/06/1952; Korean Armistice Negotiation Records; Secretary, General Staff; Headquarters, United Nations Command (Advance); Record Group 333; NARA, College Park, Maryland. Quote is from Admiral Libby speaking to General Lee.

24. Se-hŭi Oh, *Suyoungso 65* [Compound 65] (Taegu: Maninsa, 2000), 101.

25. Yeong-gyun Ko, *Jookumeo Gobilul Numuso* [Facing Death] (Seoul: Mokmin Publishing, 1997).

26. Yi Chong-gyu, oral history interview (my translation).

27. Fernando Coronil and Julie Skurski, *States of Violence* (Ann Arbor: University of Michigan Press, 2006), 84.

28. John Prados, *Safe for Democracy: The Secret Wars of the CIA* (Chicago: Ivan R. Dee, 2006), 80.

29. Prados, *Safe for Democracy*, 79.

30. Prados, *Safe for Democracy*, 81.

31. During World War II, the "CIAA [Coordinator for Inter-American Affairs], OWI [Office of War Information], and OSS [Office of Strategic Services], were the major organizations involved in American psychological warfare, but . . . the War Department also had a Psychological Warfare Branch and the Navy had a Special Warfare Section." From Scott Lucas, "Campaigns of Truth: The Psychological Strategy Board and American Ideology, 1951–1953," *International History Review* 18, no. 2 (1996): 253–504. After 1945, much of the psychological strategy revolved around the Marshall Plan and creating approval and consent among different populations in Western Europe, in particular Italy. For more of an overview of psychological warfare, see Rob Robin, *The Making of the Cold War Enemy: Culture and Politics in the Military-Intellectual Complex* (Princeton, NJ: Princeton University Press, 2001).

32. Folder 014.3 Social Science Research—Loomis Report [2 of 2]; Box 1; SMOF: Psychological Strategy Board files; Papers of Harry S. Truman; Harry S. Truman Presidential Library and Archives.

33. The PSB: Functional Relation to the President and the NSC (dated 1 July 16, 1951); Folder: 040 Centralizing Paramilitary Activity; Box 2; SMOF: Psychological Strategy Board files; Papers of Harry S. Truman; Harry S. Truman Presidential Library and Archives.

34. Manuscript of lecture: "Psychological-Political Strategy Re-examined" delivered at the National War College on February 15, 1952; Folder: 350.001 file #1—Dr. Raymond B. Allen Lecture [1 of 2]; Box 29; SMOF: Psychological Strategy Board files; Papers of Harry S. Truman; Harry S. Truman Presidential Library and Archives.

35. Preliminary estimate of the effectiveness of US Psychological Strategy [May 5, 1952]; Folder: File #1—Report by PSB on the Status of the Psychological Program [2 of 2]; Box 22; SMOF: Psychological Strategy Board files; Papers of Harry S. Truman; Harry S. Truman Presidential Library and Archives.

36. Status of POW Policy Review, 386.6 Report on Situation with Respect to Repatriation of Prisoners of War, Box 32, SMOF: Psychological Strategy Board Files, Papers of Harry S. Truman; Harry S. Truman Presidential Library and Archives.

37. Status of POW Policy Review, 386.6 Report on Situation with Respect to Repatriation of Prisoners of War, Box 32, SMOF: Psychological Strategy Board Files, Papers of Harry S. Truman; Harry S. Truman Presidential Library and Archives.

38. Memorandum for Mr. Barnes, December 18, 1951; Box 32, SMOF: Psychological Strategy Board Files; Papers of Harry S. Truman; Harry S. Truman Presidential Library and Archives.

39. This form of US-led "trusteeship" was enacted in 1947 with the "Trust Territory of the Pacific Islands," which had previously been the "South Pacific Islands," a League of Nations mandate that had been under Japanese administration before transferring to US control in 1944. In 1947, the territories came under UN-sanctioned "trusteeship." The Republic of the Marshall Islands, the Federated States of Micronesia, the Commonwealth of the Northern Mariana Islands, and the Republic of Palau—all established after US-administered trusteeship officially ended in the late 1970s (or early 1980s)—had all been under this particular trusteeship.

40. Document: Over-all Strategic Concept for our Psychological Operations (dated May 7, 1952); Folder: 091.412 File #2, "The Field and Role of Psychological Strategy in Cold War Planning" [2 of 2]; Box 15; SMOF: Psychological Strategy Board files; Papers of Harry S. Truman; Harry S. Truman Presidential Library and Archives.

41. Carl Schmitt, *The Nomos of the Earth in the International Law of the Jus Publicum Europaeum* (New York: Telos Press, 2003), 419. For a discussion on international humanitarian law that situates Schmitt's theories within a longer genealogy, see Martti Koskenniemi, *The Gentle Civilizer of Nations: The Rise and Fall of International Law, 1870–1960* (Cambridge: Cambridge University Press, 2002). The work of Nathaniel Berman also critically assesses the historical claims to universalism in international humanitarian law; see Nathaniel Berman, "Privileging Combat? Contemporary Conflict and the Legal Construction of War," *Columbia Journal of Transnational Law* 43, no. 1 (2004). On the changing nature of war as a legal institution, see David Kennedy, *Of War and Law* (Princeton, NJ: Princeton University Press, 2006).

42. Sibylle Schiepers, ed., *Prisoners in War* (Oxford: Oxford University Press, 2010), 2.

43. Schiepers, *Prisoners in War*, 7.

44. *Final Record of the Diplomatic Conference at Geneva of 1949, Vol II, Sec. A.* (Berne: Federal Political Department, 1963), 9.

45. Geoffrey Best, *War and Law since 1945* (Oxford: Oxford University Press, 1996).

46. *Final Record of the Diplomatic Conference at Geneva of 1949, Vol II, Sec. A.* (Berne: Federal Political Department, 1963), 9.

47. Jean S. Pictet, ed., *Commentary: The Geneva Conventions of 12 August 1949.* 4 vols. Geneva, ICRC, 1952, 1958, 1960. The quote is taken from volume 4, page 86.

48. Address in San Francisco at the Opening of the Conference on the Japanese Peace Treaty. September 4, 1951. Public Papers of Harry S. Truman, 1945–1953. Harry S. Truman Presidential Library and Archive. https://www.trumanlibrary.org/publicpapers, accessed May 21, 2018.

49. Operation Take Off; Box 35; Psychological Strategy Board Files; Papers of Harry S. Truman; Harry S. Truman Presidential Library and Archives.

50. For further historical analysis of the POW debate, see *A Substitute for Victory: The Politics of Peacemaking at the Korean Armistice Talks* (Ithaca, NY: Cornell University Press, 1990). In the collection *Child of Conflict: The Korean-American Relationship, 1943–1953* (1983); Barton J. Bernstein also provides analysis of the negotiations over the POW issue. A recent, very significant analysis is: Hakjae Kim, *P'anmunjŏm ch'eje ŭi kiwŏn: Han'guk Chŏnjaeng kwa chayujuŭi p'yŏnghwa kihoek* [The Origins of the Panmunjom Regime] (Seoul: Humanitas, 2015).

51. Harry S. Truman, "Address in San Francisco at the Opening of the Conference on the Japanese Peace Treaty." Part of the *Public Papers of the Presidents: Harry S. Truman, 1945–1953* of the Harry S. Truman Presidential Library, available at www.trumanlibrary.org/publicpapers, accessed June 20, 2018.

52. Acheson, *Present at the Creation*, 655.

53. See Giorgio Agamben, *Homo Sacer: Sovereign Power and Bare Life* (Stanford, CA: Stanford University Press, 1998) for Agamben's "bare life" concept, and Michel Foucault, *"Society Must Be Defended": Lectures at the Collège de France, 1975–76*, ed. Mauro Bertani and Alessandro Fontana; trans. David Macey (New York: Picador, 2003) for his "make live" concept.

54. Case File #60, Box 3; POW Incident Investigation Case Files, 1950–53; Office of the Provost Marshal; Office of the Assistant Chief of Staff, G-1; Headquarter, US Army Forces, Far East, 1952–57; Record Group 554; NARA, College Park, Maryland.

55. Case File #25, Box 1; POW Incident Investigation Case Files, 1950–53; Office of the Provost Marshal; Office of the Assistant Chief of Staff, G-1; Headquarter, US Army Forces, Far East, 1952–57; Record Group 554; NARA, College Park, Maryland.

56. Case file #87, Box 5, POW Incident Investigation Case Files, 1950–53; Office of the Provost Marshal; Office of the Assistant Chief of Staff, G-1; Headquarter, US Army Forces, Far East, 1952–57; Record Group 554; NARA, College Park, Maryland.

57. Case file #87.

58. Case file #87.

59. Case file #104, Box 5, POW Incident Investigation Case Files, 1950–53; Office of the Provost Marshal; Office of the Assistant Chief of Staff, G-1; Headquarter, US Army Forces, Far East, 1952–57; Record Group 554; NARA, College Park, Maryland.

60. Case file #17, Box 1, POW Incident Investigation Case Files, 1950–1953; Office of the Provost Marshall; Office of the Assistant Chief of Staff, G-1; Headquarter, US Army Forces, Far East, 1952–1957; Record Group 554; NARA, College Park, Maryland.

61. Case file #17.

62. Case file #17.

63. "Proceedings of Board of Officers appointed to investigate the death and injuries to civilian internees which occurred on 18 February 1952 at United Nations Prisoner of War Camp #1," POW Incident Investigation Case Files, 1950–1953; Office of the Provost Marshall; Office of the Assistant Chief of Staff, G-1; Headquarter, US Army Forces, Far East, 1952–1957; Record Group 554; NARA, College Park, Maryland.

64. "Proceedings of Board of Officers appointed to Investigate the death and injuries to civilian internees."

65. "Proceedings of Board of Officers appointed to Investigate the death and injuries to civilian internees."

66. "Proceedings of Board of Officers appointed to Investigate the death and injuries to civilian internees."

67. "Truman Endorses UN Truce Stand Rejected by Reds," New York Times, May 8, 1952.

Chapter Three: The Interrogator

1. Sam Shigeru Miyamoto, interview by author, March 1, 2007, Monterey Park, California. Earlier versions of certain portions of the following chapter appeared in Monica Kim, "Empire's Babel: US Military Interrogation Rooms of the Korean War," History of the Present (Spring 2013), 1–28.

2. With President Truman's executive order for the desegregation of the US Army in 1948, the categorization and identification of military personnel by "race" was no longer used, although according to some of my interviewees, the US Army circumvented the order by using photographs attached to personnel files. With such archival challenges, I have culled this number of "4,000" from the estimates given by members of the Japanese American War Veterans of the Korean War. The war veterans have invested a great deal of time tracking down Japanese Americans who had served in World War II and the Korean War, examining archival material of the US military and also relying on community memory. The number of "4,000" could be considered rather conservative by some standards—in his book on Japanese American linguists who had served with the Military Intelligence Service during World War II, James McNaughton notes that "by the spring of 1946 the school [Military Intelligence Service Language School] had graduated nearly 6,000 military linguists in the Japanese language." James McNaughton, Nisei Linguists: Japanese Americans in the Military Intelligence Service during World War II (Washington, DC: Department of the Army, 2007), preface. Not all of the 6,000 graduates would have been Japanese American; however, a sizable percentage was called back into service for the Korean War along with new draftees and volunteers.

3. Subcommittee on Korean War Atrocities, Korean War Atrocities, 83rd Congress, First Session, December 4, 1953, 152.

4. McNaughton's *Nisei Linguists* provides a detailed history of the Military Intelligence Service and Japanese American linguists from the perspective of an official Department of the Army narrative. Also see Eiichiro Azuma, "Brokering Race, Culture, and Citizenship: Japanese Americans in Occupied Japan and Postwar National Inclusion," *Journal of American-East Asian Relations* 16, no. 3 (2009): 183–211.

5. U.S. Department of State, *Papers Relating to the Foreign Relations of the United States: Japan, 1931–1941*, vol. 2 (Washington, DC: US Government Printing Office, 1943), 793–94.

6. Tohoru Isobe, interview by author, February 27, 2007, Los Angeles, California.

7. Miyamoto, interview.

8. From the Japanese American War Veterans online digital archive: https://java.wildapricot.org. Accessed April 2018.

9. Greg Robinson, *By Order of the President: FDR and the Internment of Japanese Americans* (Cambridge, MA: Harvard University Press, 2001), 4.

10. Arnold Yoshizawa, interview conducted by Susan Uyemura for the Japanese American Living Legacy Oral History Project, December 2, 2006, Carson, California. Robert Shiroishi, interview conducted by Susan Uyemura for the Japanese American Living Legacy Oral History Project, November 22, 2006, Cypress, California.

11. From a narrative and archival document compilation given to me by Atsushi "Archie" Miyamoto, the younger brother of Sam Miyamoto. Compiled and written in October 2006, Miyamoto titled the report, "The Gripsholm Exchanges: A Short Concise Report on the Exchange of Hostages during World War II between the United States and Japan as It Relates to Japanese Americans." Atsushi "Archie" Miyamoto, interview conducted by author, February 26, 2007, Harbor City, California.

12. Letter from Frank Knox to Mr. Joe J. Mickle, Secretary, Committee on East Asia. Folder: Japanese Govt Agreement; Box 81; Special War Problems Division; Department of State; Record Group 59; NARA, College Park, Maryland.

13. Quote from Bruce Elleman, *Japanese-American Civilian Prisoner Exchanges and Detention Camps* (New York: Routledge, 2006), 14.

14. The Spanish government became the mediating power on behalf of the Japanese, and the Swiss government became the mediating power on behalf of the United States.

15. Re: Expense of keeping Japanese officials in the United States prior to exchange, dated September 28, 1942; Folder: Japanese Int—United States Nov–Dec 1942; Box 86; Subject Files, 1939–1955 Gripsholm-Repatriation to Japanese Internees—United States; Special War Problems Division; Department of State; Record Group 59; NARA, College Park, Maryland.

16. Letter from Special Division; Box 86; Subject Files, 1939–1955 Gripsholm-Repatriation to Japanese Internees—United States; Special War Problems Division; Department of State; Record Group 59; NARA, College Park, Maryland.

17. Bruce Cumings, "Archaeology, Descent, Emergence: Japan in British/American Hegemony, 1900–1950," in *Japan in the World*, ed. Masao Miyoshi and Harry Harootunian (Durham, NC: Duke University Press, 1993).

18. Louise Young, *Japan's Total Empire: Manchuria and the Culture of Wartime Imperialism* (Berkeley: University of California Press, 1998). As historian Louise Young has charted in her

work: "By the end of World War I, the [Japanese] empire included Taiwan, Korea, the Pacific island chains the Japanese called Nan'yo, the southern half of Sakhalin, as well as participation in the unequal treaty system with China" (Young, *Japan's Total Empire*, 2). After the 1931 Manchurian Incident, Japan would move aggressively to expand its territory to China and Southeast Asia, engaging in challenges to the British Empire, the United States, and Russia.

19. Elleman, *Japanese-American Civilian Prisoner Exchanges and Detention Camps*, 12–13.

20. May 18 Telegram to Bern; Box 86; Subject Files, 1939–55 Gripsholm-Repatriation to Japanese Internees—United States; Special War Problems Division; Department of State; Record Group 59; NARA, College Park, Maryland.

21. Note dated March 27, 1943; Box 86; Subject Files, 1939–55 Gripsholm-Repatriation to Japanese Internees—United States; Special War Problems Division; Department of State; Record Group 59; NARA, College Park, Maryland.

22. Takashi Fujitani, *Race for Empire: Koreans as Japanese and Japanese as Americans during World War II* (Berkeley: University of California Press, 2011), 128.

23. Taken as quoted in Fujitani, *Race for Empire*, 127.

24. Fujitani, *Race for Empire*, 127.

25. Fujitani, *Race for Empire*, 134.

26. Elleman, *Japanese-American Civilian Prisoner Exchanges and Detention Camps*, 6.

27. Historian Mae Ngai argues that the project of the internment was, in fact, at the crossroads of differently inflected political projects, rather than the object of a monolithic power: Mae Ngai, *Impossible Subjects: Illegal Aliens and the Making of Modern America* (Princeton, NJ: Princeton University Press, 2004), and also Mae Ngai, "An Ironic Testimony to the Value of American Democracy: Assimilationism and the World War II Internment of Japanese Americans," in *Contested Democracy: Freedom, Race, and Power in American History*, ed. Manisha Sinha and Penny von Eschen (New York: Columbia University Press, 2007).

28. Above quotes from Sam Miyamoto are from an unpublished typescript narrative Miyamoto had written about his experience, and a copy is in the author's possession. All following excerpts from and summaries of letters are located at the following: Box 86; Subject Files, 1939–1955 Gripsholm-Repatriation to Japanese Internees—United States; Special War Problems Division; Department of State; Record Group 59; NARA, College Park, Maryland.

29. All letter recipients in this paragraph were interned at Fort Sill, Oklahoma.

30. Eiichiro Azuma, *Between Two Empires: Race, History, and Transnationalism in Japanese America* (Oxford: Oxford University Press, 2005).

31. Yuji Ichioka, *The Issei: The World of the First Generation Japanese Immigrants, 1885–1924* (New York: Free Press, 1988).

32. Thomas Takane and Thomas Tanaka, interview conducted by Susan Uyemura for the Japanese American Living Legal Oral History Project, November 9, 2006, Honolulu, Hawai'i.

33. Howard Okada, interview conducted by Susan Uyemura for the Japanese American Living Legacy Oral History Project, November 9, 2006, Honolulu, Hawai'i.

34. Roy Shiraga, interview conducted by author at the Japanese American Veterans Association 2007 All Wars Conference, February 24, 2007. Roy Shiraga, interview conducted by author, March 2, 2007, Hacienda Heights, California. Also based on an interview conducted by Susan Uyemura of the Japanese American Living Legacy Oral History Project on August 10,

2006, also in Hacienda Heights, California. The information about Jim Yanagihara's father is from an interview with the Reverend Jim Yanagihara "Gopher" conducted by Susan Uyemura for the Japanese American Living Legacy Oral History Project, January 14, 2006, at San Diego Buddhist Church. Yanagihara later became a medic during the Korean War.

35. Azuma, *Between Two Empires*, 2.

36. Azuma, *Between Two Empires*, 64.

37. Okada oral history interview; Roy Matsuzaki, interview conducted by Susan Uyemura for the Japanese American Living Legacy Oral History Project, March 3, 2006, Japanese American Museum and Library in San Jose, California; Katsuya "Kats" Nakatani, interview conducted by Susan Uyemura for the Japanese American Living Legacy Oral History Project, November 29, 2005, Pico Rivera, California. Oral history interview with Nakatani also conducted by author, February 24, 2007, at the All Wars Conference for the Japanese American Veterans Association in Los Angeles, California.

38. Azuma, *Between Two Empires*, 63. As Eiichiro Azuma noted, "Japanese dependency was the most common pattern of racial subordination, especially in rural districts of the West, where a majority of Issei engaged in agricultural pursuits. Prior to 1941, the nature of relations between Issei and whites was often predicated on a shifting mode of farming and land tenure."

39. Azuma, *Between Two Empires*, 79. The Issei—as they repositioned themselves within the Japanese empire and the American one—created a "racialized reinvention of a collective self—concomitantly as American frontiersmen and as Japanese colonists/colonialists—acceptable to both their adopted country and homeland," 90.

40. "With better luck, some Japanese founded similar colonial enterprises in Brazil, a popular destination of emigrants from Japan after the Gentleman's Agreement. Nagata Shigeshi, a one-time Issei who had taken over Shimanuki Hyodayu's emigration society called Rikkokai, was most responsible for the re-migration of these Issei to South America.... Following the passage of the 1924 Immigration Act, Nagata had a tight network of Issei Rikkokai alumni spread propaganda to encourage Japanese to leave racist America for friendly Brazil, where experienced Issei farmers could take the lead in creating a colonial utopia with their compatriots from Japan." Azuma, *Between Two Empires*, 81.

41. George Taniguchi, interview conducted by author, March 6, 2007, phone interview.

42. Nakatani, interview conducted by author.

43. George Tsuda, interview by author, February 28, 2007, Fullerton, California. "We had been encouraged to collect tin foils from the cigarette packages, make them into a ball and take it to the hall on designated days. These were sent to Japan where they were used for airplane construction, we were told. Around 1937, some of the guys who discard the packing would spit into it before discarding to prevent us from collecting." George Tsuda, who had served in ATIS in US-occupied Japan and also the Korean War, has also written an unpublished autobiography. Extensive in length and detail, he also included a chronology of his life in the typescript copy of the autobiography. Although I have not quoted directly from the autobiography itself, I do draw much information from Tsuda's autobiography.

44. From Atsushi "Archie" Miyamoto's report on the SS *Gripsholm* exchange.

45. By reporting the births of their children to the administrations of their home village or town, many Issei parents were able to create a dual citizenship for their Nisei children. However,

Sam Miyamoto's parents had not reported his birth to their hometown local administrative authorities—and thus, Miyamoto and his siblings did not have Japanese "citizenship."

46. Miyamoto, interview conducted by author.

47. Rinjiro Sodei, *Were We the Enemy? American Survivors of Hiroshima* (Boulder, CO: Westview Press, 1998). Smaller numbers of Chinese, Southeast Asian, and Europeans numbered among those killed.

48. Sodei, *Were We the Enemy?*, 50.

49. Sodei, *Were We the Enemy?*, 53.

50. According to Sodei, "since this figure was only for southern California, where there was the largest concentration of Japanese Americans on the mainland, we might estimate the total figure for the mainland United States at roughly five thousand." *Were We the Enemy?*, 57.

51. "Arlington Honor Paid to Two Heroic Nisei," *Los Angeles Times*, June 5, 1948, and "Tribute Paid to Nisei Heroes," *Washington Post*, June 5 1948.

52. Caroline Chung Simpson, *An Absent Presence: Japanese Americans in Postwar American Culture, 1945–1960* (Durham, NC: Duke University Press, 2001). For further work on the anxiety on the part of the US government concerning the contradictions between domestic race relations and its putative benevolence abroad in foreign policy, see Mary L. Dudziak, *Cold War Civil Rights: Race and the Image of American Democracy* (Princeton, NJ: Princeton University Press, 2000); Thomas Borstelmann, *The Cold War and the Color Line: American Race Relations in the Global Arena* (Cambridge, MA: Harvard University Press, 2001).

53. Yoshizawa, interview.

54. Yanagihara, interview.

55. Shiraga, interview.

56. The magazine-reading Nisei was from Fresno, as Shiraga could recall. It was most likely that although Shiraga, who was from Washington State, did not have to go to the internment camps during World War II, the other Nisei in the room had gone to the camps and later returned when California was again open to Japanese Americans.

57. Yoshizawa, interview.

58. Shiraga, interview.

59. McNaughton's *Nisei Linguists* provides a detailed history of the Military Intelligence Service and Japanese American linguists from the perspective of an official Department of the Army narrative. His access to both archival material and select interviews is wide-ranging. Eiichiro Azuma, "Brokering Race, Culture, and Citizenship: Japanese Americans in Occupied Japan and Postwar National Inclusion," *Journal of American–East Asian Relations* 16, no. 3 (2009): 183–211.

60. Okada, interview.

61. Yanagihara, interview.

62. Nakatani was later sent to Korea as part of a team who did highly dangerous activities during war: defusing bombs.

63. "Some Aspects of Interrogation of Oriental POWs," lecture notes and transcript delivered by Bartlett, Folder: Trainee Interrogation—General 0131; Box 18; Office of Naval Intelligence—POW Desk, Operational Section, 1949–54; Records of the Chief of Naval Operations; RG 38; NARA, College Park, Maryland.

64. Derived from copies of the lecture and also the subsequent pamphlet created.

65. "Techniques for Interrogating Orientals"; Folder: Trainee Interrogation—General 0131; Box 18; Office of Naval Intelligence—POW Desk, Operational Section, 1949–54; Records of the Chief of Naval Operations; RG 38; NARA, College Park, Maryland.

66. "Techniques for Interrogating Orientals."

67. AP Dispatch 148 by John Fujii; Folder: ITGP—500; Journals —500th Military Intelligence Group; Box 6177; Army AG Commercial Reports; RG 407; NARA, College Park, Maryland.

68. Folder: ITGP—500; Journals—500th Military Intelligence Group; Box 6177; Army AG Commercial Reports; RG 407; NARA, College Park, Maryland.

69. Miyamoto, interview.

70. Mamoru "Steve" Yokoyama, interview conducted by Colleen Wakai for the Japanese American Living Legacy Oral History Project, October 14, 2006, California. Yokoyama was present at the Japanese surrender in the Philippines, and as a Hawaiian-born Japanese interrogator, he witnessed the end of Japanese empire.

71. Yokoyama, interview.

72. Taniguchi, interview.

73. For more on the history of Japanese repatriates, see Lori Watt, *When Empire Comes Home: Repatriation and Reintegration in Postwar Japan* (Cambridge, MA: Harvard University Asia Center, distributed by Harvard University Press, 2009).

74. Tsuda, interview and unpublished autobiography.

75. Tsuda relates this with a laugh, in recognition of how random this process was. The Japanese term "hakujin" used can mean "foreigner" or "non-Japanese." In this case, the term references a white American military official.

76. Taniguchi, interview.

77. Giorgio Agamben, *Homo Sacer: Sovereign Power and Bare Life*, ed. Werner Hamacher and David E. Wellbery (1995), 21.

Chapter Four: Koje Island

1. Murray Schumach, "Gen. Dodd Is Freed by Koje Captives Unhurt and Happy," *New York Times*, May 11, 1952.

2. Details from Case File #33; Box 8; Post Capture Summaries; Historical Reports of the War Crimes Division, 1952–54, War Crimes Division, Records of the Office of the Judge Advocate General; Record Group 153; NARA, College Park, Maryland (hereafter "Case File #33").

3. Alexander Liosnoff Collection, Box 1, Folder: Korean War Press Releases and Wire Service Teletypes (Brigadier General Francis T. Dodd), Hoover Institution Archives. (A version of Zalburg's narrative appears in the *Chicago Daily Tribune* on May 12, 1952, in the article titled, "20 Tanks Scare Reds into Freeing Dodd: Army Rushes Force to POW Island by Ships." At that time, Zalburg was working as an International News Service correspondent.)

4. "A Time to Pause and Reflect," *Madison Press*, Madison County, OH, May 23, 2009.

5. "A Time to Pause and Reflect."

6. "Use Force to Release Hostage if Necessary, Gen. Ridgway Rules," *Los Angeles Times*, May 9, 1952; "UN Rejects Red Terms to Free General," *Atlanta Daily World*, May 10, 1952; "Koje Fantastic," *New York Times*, May 11, 1952.

7. Lindesay Parrott, "U.S. General Seized by Red Prisoners at Koje as Hostage," *New York Times*, May 9, 1952.

8. "UN Rejects Red Terms to Free General," *Atlanta Daily World*, May 10, 1952.

9. Murray Schumach, "General Believed Unhurt," *New York Times*, May 10, 1952.

10. Alexander Liosnoff Collection, Box 1, Folder: Korean War Press Releases and Wire Service Teletypes (Brigadier General Francis T. Dodd), Hoover Institution Archives.

11. Special to the *New York Times*, "TRUMAN ENDORSES U.N. TRUCE STAND REJECTED BY REDS; He Denounces as 'Repugnant' to World Foe's Insistence on Repatriation of Captives BACKS RIDGWAY 'PACKAGE' Acheson and Foster Also See Allies Offering Fair Terms for Cease-Fire Accord TRUMAN ENDORSES KOREA TRUCE STAND," *New York Times*, May 8, 1952.

12. Although there is still a lack of scholarship on the application of international humanitarian law during the Korean War specifically, there is a great deal of scholarship examining and analyzing the development of international humanitarian law especially after 1945. For a more general overview, please see Geoffrey Best, *War and Law since 1945* (Oxford: Clarendon Press, 1997) and his other monograph, *Humanity in Warfare* (New York: Columbia University Press, 1980). Another good overview narrative on the development of law and conflict is Yoram Dinstein, *The Conduct of Hostilities under the Law of International Armed Conflict* (Cambridge: Cambridge University Press, 2004).

13. Case File #33; Box 8; Post Capture Summaries; Historical Reports of the War Crimes Division, 1952–54, War Crimes Division, Records of the Office of the Judge Advocate General; Record Group 153; NARA, College Park, Maryland.

14. Case File #33, Interrogation of Dodd at Pusan, at the US Army Hospital, June 21, 1952.

15. "Subject: Letter of Instructions, TO: Brigadier General Haydon L. Boatner, G-15641," Tab 250. Volume III—Reference Files—Control of Prisoners of War—HQ KCOMZ; Box 1651; Enemy Prisoner of War Records, 1951–53; Eighth U.S. Army, Military History Section; Record Group 338; NARA, College Park, Maryland.

16. Case File #153; Box 8; POW Incident Investigation Case Files, 1950–53; Office of the Provost Marshal; Office of the Assistant Chief of Staff, G-1; Headquarter, US Army Forces, Far East, 1952–57; Record Group 554; NARA, College Park, Maryland.

17. Lee Hak Ku's letter was enclosed in a memorandum addressed to Dr. Otto Lehner of the ICRC from a Lt. Col. Henry S. Daughtery. Mauvais traitements lors de la capture. Témoignages, notes juridiques, 21/02/1951–14/03/1952. B AG 210 056-011. Archive of the International Committee of the Red Cross.

18. Box 7; Post Capture Summaries; Historical Reports of the War Crimes Division, 1952–54, War Crimes Division, Records of the Office of the Judge Advocate General; Record Group 153; NARA, College Park, Maryland.

19. Case File #33.

20. Case File #33.

21. Case File #33.

22. ATIS interrogation report no. 1468.

23. Charles Armstrong, *The North Korean Revolution* (Ithaca, NY: Cornell University Press, 2003), 9. Historian Charles Armstrong states, "It is important to understand the history of the guerilla struggle in Manchuria in order to make sense of the DPRK in 1950, or even in 2000. A new state and society for Korea had been imagined at the interstices of colonial control and unregulated frontier, at the meeting point of rootless intellectuals, political exiles, foreign influence, and a poor but mobile and relatively independent peasantry." Before the creation of "Manchukuo" in 1932 by the Japanese colonizers, Manchuria had been home to many Korean peasant farmers, most of whom had migrated due to the pressures of the famines and peasant uprisings of the latter half of the nineteenth century in Korea. With the advent of Japanese colonial rule, Korea and Manchuria became interconnected by the steel railroad and the constant need for labor—and by 1945, close to two million Koreans were residing in Manchuria.

24. Case File #33.

25. All quotes directly from interrogation transcripts in Case File #33.

26. Case File #33.

27. Transcribed copies of these statements are contained as evidence within Case File #33.

28. Case File #33.

29. Case File #33.

30. Case File #33.

31. William Hitchcock, "Human Rights and the Laws of War: The Geneva Conventions of 1949," in *The Human Rights Revolution: An International History*, ed. Akira Iriye, Petra Goedde, and William Hitchcock (Oxford: Oxford University Press, 2012), 99–100.

32. Hermes, *Truce Tent and Fighting Front*, 112.

33. C. Turner Joy, *How Communists Negotiate* (New York: Macmillan, 1955), 8.

34. John Dunham Kelly and Martha Kaplan, *Represented Communities: Fiji and World Decolonization* (Chicago: University of Chicago Press, 2001), 9.

35. Dean Acheson, *Present at the Creation: My Years in the State Department*, 1st ed. (New York: Norton, 1969), 533. Secretary of State Dean Acheson writes in his memoir, "The case for military talks through commanders in the field was strong for the following reasons: First, because neither the Chinese nor the North Korean authorities were official entities recognized by the United States."

36. The other agenda items were: (1) the setting of the agenda for the talks themselves, (2) the demarcation line and demilitarized zone, (3) cease-fire arrangements and inspection provisions, (4) prisoner of war repatriation, (5) referral of political questions (an agreement to hold a political conference after the armistice signing in order to settle "the questions of the withdrawal of all foreign forces from Korea, the peaceful settlement of the Korean question, etc." From, *Historical Dictionary of the Korean War* (New York: Greenwood Press, 1991), 7–12.

37. Hermes, *Truce Tent and Fighting Front*, 140.

38. Horace G. Underwood was the official interpreter for the United Nations Command. Underwood would later become a key figure in US-Korea relations, especially regarding education.

39. Meeting dated December 11, 1951, Minutes of Meetings of Subdelegates for Agenda Item 4 on Prisoners of War, 12/11/1951–02/06/1952; Korean Armistice Negotiation Records;

Secretary, General Staff; Headquarters, United Nations Command (Advance); Record Group 333; National Archives at College Park, Maryland (hereafter *MMS*).

40. In March 1951, approximately 50,000 prisoners of war were claiming that they had been residents of Korea south of the 38th parallel before the outbreak of the war and had been forcibly drafted into the KPA. As later stated during the meetings at Panmunjom, the US Army had captured people of a wide-ranging circumstances—guerrillas and Communist sympathizers. Some had been "taken into custody as a security measure," and still others had become prisoners of war "through the confusion of war." Soon, the category of "civilian internees" (CI) was made available to the camp population, and the US military and the ROKA initiated a screening process to sift through the claimants (*MMS*).

41. December 29, 1952, *MMS*.

42. December 29, 1952, *MMS*.

43. Dean Rusk, *As I Saw It* (New York: W.W. Norton, 1990), 123–24.

44. For scholarship on the activities of Koreans along the trans-border of Korea and Manchuria, please see Hyun Ok Park, *Two Dreams in One Bed: Empire, Social Life, and the Origins of the North Korean Revolution in Manchuria* (Durham, NC: Duke University Press, 2005); Charles Armstrong, *The North Korean Revolution, 1945–1950* (Ithaca, NY: Cornell University Press); Dae-Sook Suh and Edward J Shultz, eds., *Koreans in China* (Honolulu: Center for Korean Studies, University of Hawaiʻi, 1990). For a monograph on Korean labor in Hawaiʻi during the twentieth century, please see *From the Land of Hibiscus: Koreans in Hawaiʻi, 1903–1950* (Honolulu: University of Hawaiʻi Press, 2007).

45. Armstrong, *North Korean Revolution*, 216, The Republic of Korea was created in the south through UN-sponsored elections on August 15, 1948, three years exactly from the date of liberation from Japanese colonial rule in 1945. However, on September 9, with the creation of the Democratic People's Republic in Pyongyang, "North Korean authorities attacked the South Korean elections as illegitimate and claimed that underground elections had been held in the south."

46. December 27, 1951, *MMS*.

47. January 26, 1952, *MMS*.

48. January 8, 1952. *MMS*.

49. January 11, 1952. *MMS*.

50. January 14, 1952. *MMS*.

51. Summary for Case File #33.

52. Summary for Case File #33.

53. All quotes from interrogation reports located in Case File #33.

54. ATIS interrogation report no. 1293 dated September 24, 1950, contains Field Report (164-MIS-0930) dated September 21, 1950. From an unpublished data research collection compiled for a special documentary series produced by MBC (Cultural Broadcasting Company) in the Republic of Korea in 2004. The documentary special was called *Han'guk Chŏngaenggwa Poro* [The Korean War and the Prisoner of War], and it was a series special on a program called *Igaenŭn Marhalsu Itta* [Now We Can Speak] (hereafter *Now We Can Speak* compilation).

55. ATIS Interrogation report no. 1468 dated September 29, 1950, contains Field Report (ADVATIS-0900) dated September 25, 1950. From the *Now We Can Speak* compilation.

56. Elaine Scarry, *The Body in Pain: The Making and Unmaking of the World* (New York: Oxford University Press, 1985), 12.

57. The Handling of POW during the Korean War, Folder: Unclassified, S11-02, Korea; Box 16; Unclassified Records, 1969–75; POW/Civilian Internee Information Center; Records of the Provost Marshal General, 1941–; Record Group 389; NARA, College Park, Maryland.

58. Typed unpublished manuscript; Box 7; Haydon Boatner Collection. Hoover Institution Archives.

59. Typed unpublished manuscript; Box 7; Haydon Boatner Collection. Hoover Institution Archives.

60. "Statement to all Prisoners of War," Tab 2-19. Volume VI—Reference Files—Control of Prisoners of War—HQ PW; Box 1652; Enemy Prisoner of War Records, 1951–53; Eighth U.S. Army, Military History Section; Record Group 338; NARA, College Park, Maryland.

61. "Statement to all Prisoners of War."

62. Carl Schmitt, *The Concept of the Political,* trans. George Schwab (Chicago: University of Chicago Press, 1996), 33.

63. Correspondence of POW Division Relating to Enemy POWs; Box 1-4; Headquarters, U.S. Army Forces, Far East; Record Group 554; NARA, College Park, Maryland.

64. Murray Schumach, "3 Days of Captivity Described by Dodd," *New York Times,* May 13, 1952.

65. "Rapport Confidentiel Au C.I.C.R. Concernant La Crise Actuelle des Relations entre Puissance Detentrice et Prisonnier de Guerre en Corée du Sud [Confidential Report to the ICRC Concerning the Real Crisis between the Detaining Power and the Prisoner of War in South Korea]." B AG 119 056 016 (my translation).

66. "Rapport Confidentiel."

67. "Dodd Sakŏnoe ŭimi [The Meaning of the Dodd Incident]," *Dong-a Ilbo,* May 16, 1952.

Chapter Five: Below the 38th Parallel

1. Hyo-Soon Song, *The Fight for Freedom* (Republic of Korea: Korean Library Association, 1980), 206–7. Earlier versions of portions in the following chapter appeared in Monica Kim, "The Intelligence of Fools: Reading the US Military Archive of the Korean War" in *positions: asia critique* (23:4), 695–728.

2. Hyo-Soon Song, *Fight for Freedom,* 212.

3. "Press Release of the Office of Public Information, Republic of Korea." *Foreign Relations of the United States, 1952–1954, Korea, Volume XV, Part 2,* Document 607.

4. "Memorandum of Discussion at the 150th Meeting of the National Security Council, Thursday, June 18, 1953." *Foreign Relations of the United States, 1952–1954, Korea, Volume XV, Part 2,* Document 609.

5. Memorandum of Discussion at the 150th Meeting.

6. Case file #255 (UNC Camp Masan #7, dated June 18, 1953), Box 13, POW Incident Investigation Case files, 1950–53; Office of the Provost Marshal; Office of the Assistant Chief of Staff, G-1; Headquarter, US Army Forces, Far East, 1952–57; Record Group 554; NARA, College Park, Maryland.

7. Gregory Henderson, *Korea: The Politics of the Vortex* (Cambridge, MA: Harvard University Press, 1968), 140.

8. Jonson Nathaniel Porteux, "Police, Paramilitaries, Nationalists, and Gangsters: The Processes of State Building in Korea" (PhD diss., University of Michigan, 2013), 73. For more on anti-Communist nationalism and youth groups, see Chong-myong Im, "The Korean National Defense Student Defense Corps and the Manufacturing of Warrior-type Students in Its Incipient Days," *International Journal of Korean History* (Vol. 17, No.1, Feb 2012).

9. Henderson, *Korea: The Politics of the Vortex*, 141.

10. See Bruce Cumings, *The Origins of the Korean War*, vol. 2 (Princeton, NJ: Princeton University Press), 1981; Chong-myong Im, "The Making of the Republic of Korea as a Modern Nation-State, August 1948–May 1950" (PhD diss., University of Chicago, 2004).

11. Henderson, *Korea: The Politics of the Vortex*, 140.

12. Folder: 228-01 181st CIC Detachment—Korea—SOP—1952 (Part 2 of 2); Box 12; Records of the Army Staff; Assistant Chief of Staff, G-2 (Intelligence); Counter Intelligence Collection; Record Group 319; NARA, College Park, Maryland.

13. 1948 Annual Progress Report of the 971st CIC Detachment in Korea; Box 14856; WWII Operations Report, 1941–48; Central Intelligence; RG 407; NARA; College Park, Maryland.

14. Gregory Henderson, "Korea, 1950," in *The Korean War in History*, ed. James Cotton and Ian Neary (Atlantic Highlands, NJ: Humanities Press International, 1989), 175.

15. Interview with Gregory Henderson, June 13, 1987; Box 141; Series VI: "In Mortal Combat"; Toland Papers; Franklin D. Roosevelt Presidential Library and Archives.

16. Interview with Park Ki Byung; Box 143; Series VI: "In Mortal Combat"; Toland Papers; Franklin D. Roosevelt Presidential Library and Archives.

17. Allan R. Millett, "Captain James H. Hausman and the Formation of the Korean Army, 1945–1950," *Armed Forces and Society* 23, no. 4 (1997): 506. See also Jong-Myeong Yim, "Korean National Youth Corps (1946.10–1949.1) and Its Connection with 'Future Korean Leader' Policy by United States Army Military Government in Korea," *The Journal of Korean History* (95), 1996.12, 179–211.

18. Simeon Man, *Soldiering through Empire: Race and the Making of the Decolonizing Pacific* (Oakland: University of California Press, 2018), 23.

19. Millett, "Captain James H. Hausman and the Formation of the Korean Army, 1945–1950," 515.

20. Interview with James Hausman; Box 141; Series VI: "In Mortal Combat"; Toland Papers; Franklin D. Roosevelt Presidential Library and Archives.

21. Dong-choon Kim, "The Social Grounds of Anticommunism in South Korea: Crisis of the Ruling Class and Anticommunist Reaction," *Asian Journal of German and European Studies* 2, no. 7 (2017): 7. Also see Sung-hyun Kang, "Conversion, Surveillance, Mobilization and Massacre—Study on the National Guidance Alliance," *Yeoksa Yeongu [The Journal of History]*, (14) 2004.12, 55–106.

22. Kim, "Social Grounds of Anticommunism in South Korea," 9.

23. "Subject: Report of Educational and Informational Survey Mission to Korea, June 20, 1947, From Headquarters—United State Army Forces in Korea, To: Department of State," Reel

XIV, "Internal Affairs of Korea, 1945–1949" Microfilm. Department of State Decimal File 895. Records of the U.S. Department of State relating to the Internal Affairs of Korea, 1945–1949.

24. Henderson, "Korea, 1950," 175.

25. *CIC 1945.9–1949.1*, Volume 2, CIC Monthly Information Report, dated 1947.1.18.

26. "The Korean governor of North Kyŏngsang could write with equanimity that there were in his province some 3,000 native leftist leaders, 'strong men, ingenious, courageous, and ready to die.' Americans could not stomach suppressing such people unless they could perceive a tie to the Soviets." Cumings, *Origins of the Korean War*, 1: 375.

27. Cumings, *Origins of the Korean War*, 1: 367.

28. *CIC 1945.9–1949.1*, Volume 1, US Army Intelligence Center, History of the Counter Intelligence Corps Volume XXX, "CIC During the Occupation of Korea (1959.3)," 17.

29. *CIC 1945.9–1949.1*, Volume 1, report dated April 19, 1946, included in 971st Counter Intelligence Corps Detachment Annual Progress Report for 1947, 386.

30. *CIC 1945.9–1949.1*, Volume 1, US Army Intelligence Center, History of the Counter Intelligence Corps Volume XXX, "CIC During the Occupation of Korea (1959.3)," 21.

31. *CIC 1945.9–49.1*, Volume 1, US Army Intelligence Center, History of the Counter Intelligence Corps Volume XXX, "CIC During the Occupation of Korea (1959.3)," 22.

32. *CIC 1945.9–1949.1*, Volume 1, US Army Intelligence Center, History of the Counter Intelligence Corps Volume XXX, "CIC During the Occupation of Korea (1959.3)," 17.

33. *CIC 1945.9–1949.1*, Volume 1, US Army Intelligence Center, History of the Counter Intelligence Corps Volume XXX, "CIC During the Occupation of Korea (1959.3)," 15.

34. Among the refugees, only those people willing to talk were considered to be of any use to the Positive Intelligence Mission. *CIC 1945.9–1949.1*, Volume 1, 971st Counter Intelligence Corps Detachment Annual Progress Report for 1947, 259.

35. *CIC 1945.9–1949.1*, Volume 2, Weekly Information Bulletin dated 1947.6.19, 259.

36. Donald Nichols, *How Many Times Can I Die?* (Brooksville, FL: Brooksville Printing, 1981), 119.

37. *CIC 1945.9–1949.1*, Volume 2, Weekly Information Bulletin dated 1947.11.6, 505.

38. *CIC 1945.9–1949.1*, Volume 1, US Army Intelligence Center, History of the Counter Intelligence Corps Volume XXX, "CIC During the Occupation of Korea (1959.3)," 24.

39. *CIC 1945.9–1949.1*, Volume 1, US Army Intelligence Center, History of the Counter Intelligence Corps Volume XXX, "CIC During the Occupation of Korea (1959.3)," 24.

40. William J. Tigue; Box 6; Records of the Army Staff; Assistant Chief of Staff, G-2 (Intelligence); Counter Intelligence Collection; Record Group 319; NARA, College Park, Maryland.

41. 1947 Annual Progress Report of the 971st CIC Detachment in Korea; Box 14856; WWII Operations Report, 1941–48; Central Intelligence; RG 407; NARA; College Park, Maryland.

42. *CIC 1945.9–1949.1*, Volume 2, Weekly Information Bulletin dated 1947.4.23, 174.

43. *CIC 1945.9–1949.1*, Volume 2, Weekly Information Bulletin dated 1947.5.22, 221.

44. *CIC 1945.9–1949.1*, Volume 2, Weekly Information Bulletin dated 1947.8.28, 364.

45. *CIC 1945.9–1949.1*, Volume 2, Weekly Information Bulletin dated 1947.5.22, 221.

46. *CIC 1945.9–1949.1*, Volume 2, Weekly Information Bulletin dated 1947.4.23, 174.

47. *CIC 1945.9–1949.1*, Volume 2, Weekly Information Bulletin dated 1947.5.22, 221.

48. *CIC 1945.9–1949.1*, Volume 2, Weekly Information Bulletin dated 1947.8.28, 367.

49. *CIC 1945.9–1949.1*, Volume 2, Weekly Information Bulletin dated 1947.8.21, 353.

50. *CIC 1945.9–1949.1*, Volume 2, Weekly Information Bulletin dated 1947.5.1, 184.

51. *CIC 1945.9–1949.1*, Volume 2, Weekly Information Bulletin dated 1947.9.11, 397.

52. Nichols, *How Many Times Can I Die?*, 119–120.

53. Nichols, *How Many Times Can I Die?*, 120.

54. Nichols, *How Many Times Can I Die?*, 120.

55. Interview with Hausman.

56. Millett, "Captain James H. Hausman and the Formation of the Korean Army, 1945–1950," 522.

57. Su-kyoung Hwang, *Korea's Grievous War* (Philadelphia: University of Pennsylvania Press, 2016), 29.

58. Hwang, *Korea's Grievous War*, 38.

59. Chalmers Johnson, Blowback: The Costs and Consequences of American Empire (New York: Henry Holt, 2004), 99.

60. Hwang, *Korea's Grievous War*, 29.

61. Porteux, "Police, Paramilitaries, Nationalists and Gangsters: The Processes of State Building in Korea," 76.

62. Report written by Major George T. Gregory—see Nichols, *How Many Times Can I Die?*, 149.

63. Folder: 206-02.2 CIC Operations in Korea—CIC School (November 15, 1951); Box 6; Counter Intelligence Corps Collection; Assistant Chief of Staff, G-2 (Intelligence); Records of the Army Staff; RG 319; NARA, College Park, Maryland.

64. Interview with Hausman.

65. Interview with Hausman.

66. Interview with Hausman.

67. Nichols, *How Many Times Can I Die?*, 135.

68. Nak-Chung Paik, *The Division System in Crisis: Essays on Contemporary Korea*, trans. Myung-hwan Kim, June-Kyu Sol, Seung-chul Song, and Young-joo Ryu (Berkeley: University of California Press, 2011), 5.

69. Folder: 228-01 181st CIC Detachment—Korea—SOP—1952 (Part 2 of 2); Box 12; Records of the Army Staff; Assistant Chief of Staff, G-2 (Intelligence); Counter Intelligence Collection; RG 319; NARA, College Park, Maryland.

70. Folder: 228-01 181st CIC Detachment. On refugees: Janice C.H. Kim, "Living in Flight: Civilian Displacement, Suffering, and Relief during the Korean War, 1945–1953," *Sahak Yonku: The Review of Korean History* (100), 285–329.

71. Folder: 206-02.2 CIC Operations in Korea—CIC School (15 November 1951); Box 6; Records of the Army Staff; Assistant Chief of Staff, G-2 (Intelligence); Counter Intelligence Collection; RG 319; NARA, College Park, Maryland.

72. "Statement from Captain Samuel E. Walton Jr," EEI: Lt. Colonial Verne O. Jackson; Box 6; Records of the Army Staff; Assistant Chief of Staff, G-2 (Intelligence); Counter Intelligence Collection; RG 319; NARA, College Park, Maryland.

73. EEI: 1st Lt. Arnold J. Lapiner, 2nd CIC Detachment, 2nd Infantry Division; Box 6; Records of the Army Staff; Assistant Chief of Staff, G-2 (Intelligence); Counter Intelligence Collection; RG 319; NARA College Park, Maryland.

74. *Interviews with 24 Korean POW Leaders.* Prepared by Research, Analysis, and Evaluation Division, Psychological Warfare Section, United States Army Forces, Far East, Headquarters. Dated May 13, 1954. Unpublished manuscript.

75. Mass Behavior in Battle and Captivity: The Communist Soldier in the Korean War. Research studies directed by William C. Bradbury. Eds. Samuel Meyers and Albert D. Biderman (Chicago: University of Chicago Press: 1968), 280–81.

76. Mass Behavior, 280–81.

77. "Memorandum to Secretary of State, Washington; from Office of U.S. Political Adviser, Seoul, Korea, Hqs., XXI Corps), date May 12, 1948; Reel XIII, "Internal Affairs of Korea, 195-1949" Microfilm. Department of State Decimal File 895. Records of the U.S. Department of State relating to the Internal Affairs of Korea, 1945–49.

78. "Memorandum to Secretary of State, Subject: The Establishment of the 'Great Korean Youth Corps' in Connection with the Korean Cabinet," date December 30, 1948; Reel XIII, "Internal Affairs of Korea, 195-1949" Microfilm. Department of State Decimal File 895. Records of the U.S. Department of State relating to the Internal Affairs of Korea, 1945–49.

79. "Memorandum for the Ambassador, date December 27, 1948, by Bertel Kuniholm" Reel XIII, "Internal Affairs of Korea, 195-1949" Microfilm. Department of State Decimal File 895. Records of the U.S. Department of State relating to the Internal Affairs of Korea, 1945–49.

80. Above National Assembly discussion is pulled from Memorandum from Meetings. (Reference made specifically to two documents: No. 603, dated December 31, 1951, and No. 40 dated January 23, 1952, where discussion of a petition sent from Lee Kwang Soon's POW youth group takes place.) Records of the National Assembly, National Archives of Korea; Mass Behavior, 304–5.

81. Mass Behavior, 305.

82. *Interviews with 24 Korean POW Leaders.* Prepared by Research, Analysis, and Evaluation Division, Psychological Warfare Section, United States Army Forces, Far East, Headquarters. Dated May 13, 1954.

83. *Interviews with 24 Korean POW Leaders.*

84. *Interviews with 24 Korean POW Leaders.*

85. *Interviews with 24 Korean POW Leaders.*

86. See Grace Chae, "Captive Minds: Race, War, and the Education of Korean War POWs in U.S. custody, 1950–1953" (PhD diss., University of Chicago, 2010).

87. Evaluation Branch, January 17, 1952; Box 4591; UN Command, Civil Information and Education; Record Group 554; NARA, College Park, Maryland.

88. "A New Life" Essay, Box 4591; UN Command, Civil Information and Education; Record Group 554; NARA, College Park, Maryland.

89. Ou-Byung Chae, "Homology Unleashed: Colonial, Anticolonial, and Postcolonial State Culture in South Korea, 1930–1950," *Positions: East Asia Cultures Critique* 23, no. 2 (2015): 335.

90. Maggie Clinton, *Revolutionary Nativism, Fascism, and Culture in China, 1925–1937* (Durham, NC: Duke University Press, 2017), 24. See also Chong-myong Im, "The New Life Movement in Post-Liberation Days of South Korea," *Critical Studies on Modern Korean History* (27), 2012.4, 219–265.

91. *Interviews with 24 POW Leaders.*

92. [Case Number 264] Communist Indoctrination of ROKA PW Returnees. Dated June 13, 1952; Box 104; Office of the Assistant Chief of Staff for Intelligence, G-2; RG 319; NARA; College Park, Maryland.

93. [Case Number 266] Communist Indoctrination of ROKA PW Returnees. Dated June 15, 1952.

94. [Case Number 268] Communist Indoctrination of ROKA PW Returnees. Dated June 16, 1952.

95. [Case Number 268] Communist Indoctrination of ROKA PW Returnees. Dated June 16, 1952.

96. Lieutenant Colonel Verne O. Jackson of the 210th CIC Detachment; Folder: 228-01 EEI: CIC Operations in Korea (1952); Box 6; Counter Intelligence Corps Collections, Assistant Chief of Staff, G-2 (Intelligence); RG 319; NARA, College Park, Maryland.

97. Second Lieutenant Joseph H. Farell of the 116th CIC Detachment; Folder: 228-01 EEI: CIC Operations in Korea (1952); Box 6; Counter Intelligence Corps Collection; Assistant Chief of Staff, G-2 (Intelligence); RG 319; NARA, College Park, Maryland.

98. "Military Application of Polygraph Technique," Folder: Correspondence Korea Classified 1951, Box 1; Records Relating to Korea; Provost Marshal's Section; RG 544; NARA, College Park, Maryland.

99. Mass Behavior, xvii.

100. Mass Behavior, 285.

101. Mass Behavior, 286.

102. Case #125. Box 7; POW Incident Investigation Case Files, 1950–53; Office of the Provost Marshal; Office of the Assistant Chief of Staff, G-1; Headquarter, US Army Forces, Far East, 1952–57; Record Group 554; National Archives at College Park, Maryland.

103. Case #134. Box 7; POW Incident Investigation Case Files, 1950–53; Office of the Provost Marshal; Office of the Assistant Chief of Staff, G-1; Headquarter, US Army Forces, Far East, 1952–57; Record Group 554; National Archives at College Park, Maryland.

104. Due to its fragile and "unclassifiable" medium of blood and paper, this blood document is filed in a vault at the National Archives in College Park, Maryland. I have kept all of the original spelling and idiosyncrasies.

105. Blood document.

106. Blood document.

107. Blood document.

108. "To: Secretary of State, Rec'd May 17, 1947 2:38 PM [from Hodge]," Reel IX, "Internal Affairs of Korea, 195-1949" Microfilm. Department of State Decimal File 895. Records of the U.S. Department of State relating to the Internal Affairs of Korea, 1945–49.

109. Yeong Bok Ju, *76 P'orodŭl* [The 76 Prisoners of War] (Seoul: Daegwan Publishing, 1993).

Chapter Six: On the 38th Parallel

1. Lindesay Parrot, "Ceremony is Brief—Halt in 3-Year Conflict for a Political Parley Due at 9 A.M. Today," *New York Times*, July 27, 1953, 1.

2. "Texts of Eisenhower and Dulles Broadcasts on Truce," *New York Times*, July 27, 1953, 4; Drafts of "Statement of the President upon Korean Armistice" in Folders Korean 1953 (1) & (2), Box 35, International Series; Whitman File; Papers as President 1953–61; Dwight D. Eisenhower Library and Archives.

3. Parrot, "Ceremony Is Brief."

4. Kodendera Subayya Thimayya, *Experiment in Neutrality* (New Delhi: Vision Books, 1981), 47.

5. Thimayya, *Experiment in Neutrality*, 192.

6. Thimayya, *Experiment in Neutrality*, 192.

7. Telegram from New Delhi to secretary of state. Date 1950, June 28. Sent by Henderson. From *Mi Kungmubu Hanguk kungnae sanghwang kwallyŏn munsŏ: The US Department of State Relating to the Internal Affairs of Korea* (Seoul: Kukpangbu Kunsa P'yŏnch'an Yŏn'guso, 2000–2002), vol. 1.

8. Robert Barnes, "Between the Blocs: India, the United Nations, and Ending the Korean War," *Journal of Korean Studies* 18, no. 2 (2013): 266.

9. Barnes, "Between the Blocs," 267.

10. Manu Bhagavan, "A New Hope: India, the United Nations, and the Making of the Universal Declaration of Human Rights," *Modern Asian Studies* 44, no. 2 (2010): 328.

11. Young-bok Ju, Series VI: In Mortal Combat, B Interviews: Bussey-Ju. Box 146. Toland Papers. Franklin Delano Roosevelt Presidential Archives, Hyde Park, New York.

12. Young-bok Ju, Series VI: In Mortal Combat.

13. Young-bok Ju, Series VI: In Mortal Combat.

14. Young-bok Ju, Series VI: In Mortal Combat.

15. Thimayya, *Experiment in Neutrality*, 39.

16. Thimayya, *Experiment in Neutrality*, 24.

17. Thimayya, *Experiment in Neutrality*, 23.

18. Thimayya, *Experiment in Neutrality*, 22.

19. UN, Document A/2228 (note dated October 18, 1952, from the permanent representative of the United States of America addressed to the Secretary General, transmitting a special report by the United Nations Command in Korea).

20. Shiv Dayal, *India's Role in the Korean Question: A Study in the Settlement of International Disputes under the United Nations* (Delhi: S. Chand, 1959), 110.

21. UN, Document A/C.1/730 (Mexico: draft resolution) dated November 1, 1952.

22. UN, Document A/C.1/731 (letter dated November 1, 1952, from the permanent representative of Mexico addressed to the Secretary General).

23. UN, Document A/C.1/732 (Peru: draft resolution) dated November 3, 1952.

24. UN, Document A/C.1/734 (India: draft resolution) dated November 17, 1952.

25. Rosemary Foot, "Nuclear Coercion and the Ending of the Korean Conflict," *International Security* 13, no. 1 (1988–89): 92.

26. Draft of a history of the UNCREG operations at the 38th parallel; Box 1; The Jack Tydal Papers; United States Army Military History Institute, Carlisle, Pennsylvania.

27. Thimayya, *Experiment in Neutrality*, 82.

28. Thimayya, *Experiment in Neutrality*, 190.

29. Draft history of UNCREG, USAMHI.

30. *Custodian Force*, 21.

31. *Custodian Force*, 22.

32. Thimayya, *Experiment in Neutrality*, 83.

33. Thimayya, *Experiment in Neutrality*, 114.

34. Thimayya, 74. However, the *Custodian Force (India) of Korea* history states that the number of arriving prisoners of war was 499.

35. *Custodian Force*, 30.

36. *Custodian Force*, 31.

37. Thimayya, *Experiment in Neutrality*, 113.

38. Thimayya, 114. As the *Custodian Force (India) in Korea* history narrated, "The prisoners maintained a soldierly routine even in the POW camps, in order to keep up their health and spirits. The cooking party in the anti-Communist compounds started preparing breakfast for its 500 inmates as early as 0330 hours each morning. Everybody got up by 0430 hours in the pre-dawn bitter cold of the Korean winter. By 0600 hours PT was finished and breakfast was served an hour later. The main meals of the day were taken between 1100 and 1200 hours, and again between 1700 and 1800 hours (36–37).

39. Thimayya, *Experiment in Neutrality*, 109.

40. Thimayya, 90.

41. Thimayya, 104.

42. Thimayya, 92.

43. Kenneth K. Hansen, *Heroes behind Barbed Wire* (Princeton, NJ: Van Nostrand, 1957), vi.

44. Hansen, *Heroes behind Barbed Wire*, 175.

45. Hansen, 121.

46. Hansen, 121.

47. Hansen, 75–76.

48. Hansen, 145.

49. Hansen, 146.

50. Thimayya, *Experiment in Neutrality*, 181.

51. Thimayya, 182.

52. Thimayya, 182.

53. *Custodian Force*, 56.

54. Thimayya, *Experiment in Neutrality*, 182.

55. Thimayya, 187.

56. Thimayya, 190–91.

57. *Custodian Force*, 60.

58. Thimayya, *Experiment in Neutrality*, 191.

59. Thimayya, 61.

60. Thimayya, 191.

61. Thimayya, 192.

62. Thimayya, 115.

63. Thimayya, 115.

64. Thimayya, 206

65. Yeong Bok Ju, *76 P'orodŭl* [The 76 Prisoners of War] (Seoul: Daegwan Publishing, 1993), 47.

66. Thimayya, *Experiment in Neutrality*, 110.

67. Thimayya, 79.

68. Ju, *76 P'orodŭl*, 39.

69. Ju, 37–38.

70. Ju, 44.

71. Ju, 111.

72. Ju, 116.

73. "Nevertheless, we are trying to teach them languages and trades that will enable them to fit into our society. They have adjusted easily to our food. Our climate still is difficult for them and we have to send them to the mountains during the hottest part of the summers. Marriage for them will be a problem, but if they adjust in other ways perhaps that also can be arranged" (Thimayya, *Experiment in Neutrality*, 208).

74. Ju, *76 P'orodŭl*, 170.

75. [Miscellany—Correspondence and reports concerning the Neutral Nations Repatriation Commission 1954], United Nations Archive, New York.

76. Army Head Quarter Camp, National Stadium, New Delhi, Apr. 25th 1957, to: Director of U.S.I.A.; from [Miscellany—Correspondence and reports concerning the Neutral Nations Repatriation Commission 1954], United Nations Archive, New York. For developing, important work on the 76 Korean POWs, Jung Keun-sik and Jung Byung-joon have been conducting oral history research and interviews with the former POWs. Notably, Lee Sunwoo has followed Ji Ki-Chul's life history. Jung Byung-Joon has also done critical work on Choi In-hun, the author of one of the most widely read novels (often assigned in school curricula) titled *The Square* (1960), which focuses on the Neutral Nations POWs of the Korean War.

77. [Miscellany—Correspondence and reports concerning the Neutral Nations Repatriation Commission 1954], United Nations Archive, New York.

78. Attached to a letter sent by Arthur S. Lall, Permanent Representative of India to the United Nations, to Mr. Dag Hammarskjold, Secretary General of the United Nations. Dated March 27, 1956. (For the following lists that had been included with Lall's letter, I have placed my own emphasis in bold on the "remarks" section of each list.) from [Miscellany—Correspondence and reports concerning the Neutral Nations Repatriation Commission 1954], United Nations Archive, New York.

79. Young-bok Ju. Series VI: In Mortal Combat, B Interviews: Bussey-Ju. Box 146. Toland Papers. Franklin Delano Roosevelt Presidential Archives, Hyde Park, New York.

80. Ju, *76 P'orodŭl*, 176.

81. Ju, *76 P'orodŭl*, 29.

82. Theodore Hughes, *Literature and Film in Cold War South Korea: Freedom's Frontier* (New York: Columbia University Press, 2012), 92.

Chapter Seven: Above the 38th Parallel

1. Arden Allen Rowley, *Korea-POW: A Thousand Days with Life on Hold, 1950–1953* (Mesa, AZ: Tanner Publishing, 1997), 1.

2. Rowley, *Korea-POW*, 111.

3. Rowley, *Korea-POW*, 113.

4. Johnny Moore and Judith Fenner Gentry, *I Cannot Forget: Imprisoned in Korea, Accused at Home* (College Station: Texas A&M University Press, 2013), 171.

5. Raymond Lech, *Broken Soldiers* (Urbana: University of Illinois Press, 2000), 205.

6. Lewis H. Carlson, *Remembered Prisoners of a Forgotten War: An Oral History of Korean War POWs* (New York: St. Martin's Press, 2002), 220.

7. See Albert Biderman, *March to Calumny: The Story of American POW's in the Korean War* (New York: The Macmillan Company), 30 & 113. Biderman takes these numbers from US Department of Defense records as well as from a study done by Julius Segal. See also Charles Young, *Name, Rank, and Serial Number: Exploiting Korean War POWs at Home and Abroad* (Oxford University Press, 2014). The numbers of captured, casualties, and missing were highly politicized and uncertain. "Early estimates of the death toll were exaggerated—there were about 12,000 MIAs, and this figure was sometimes conflated with the number taken prisoner ... The real total captured was 7,000, but in October 1953 the US Information Agency widely reported an incongruous 6,113 'murdered, tortured, and starved,' which would not leave enough for nearly 4,000 to come back" (118). But as Young notes, "mortality was high by any count," and both Young and Biderman provide accounts for the deaths due to freezing, malnutrition, bombing, and what the POWs recount as the deadly march northwards towards the Yalu River when many POWs died.

8. James Thompson, *True Colors: 1004 Days as a Prisoner of War* (Madison, WI: Ashley Books, 1989), 11.

9. Thompson, *True Colors*, 12.

10. Neal Stanford, "Red 'Teaching' of Prisoners Stirs U.S.," *Christian Science Monitor*, April 7, 1953.

11. Arthur Krock, "In the Nation: Allen W. Dulles Describes 'Warfare for the Brain.'" *New York Times*, April 16, 1953.

12. From these experiences working with US POWs from the Korean War, Lipton would go on to become one of the foremost analysts and theorists of thought reform and warfare in the twentieth century.

13. R. J. Lifton, "Home by Ship: Reaction Patterns of American Prisoners of War Repatriated from North Korea." *American Journal of Psychiatry*, 110, no. 10 (1954): 737.

14. Lifton, "Home by Ship," 737.

15. Lifton, "Home by Ship," 737.

16. William E. Mayer, *Beyond the Call: Memoirs of a Medical Visionary*, vol. 1 (Albuquerque: Mayer Publishing Group International, 2009), 350.

17. Mayer, *Beyond the Call*, 350.

18. Mayer, 350.

19. Mayer, 350.

20. Mayer, 352.

21. Japan Joint Intelligence Processing Board Final Report, October 1953, vols. 1–2 ZA017695; Records of the Investigative Records Repository, Intelligence and Investigative Dossiers— Impersonal File, 1939–80, Box 47, RG 0319 Army Staff, NARA, College Park, Maryland.

22. Mayer, *Beyond the Call*, 349–50.

23. Japan Joint Intelligence Processing Board Final Report, October 1953. Following quotes on page are from this source.

24. Pamphlet: Prisoner Sense (Training Division, Bureau of Aeronautics, United States Navy), May 1943.

25. Mayer, *Beyond the Call*, 352.

26. Japan Joint Intelligence Processing Board Final Report, October 1953.

27. Albert Biderman, *March to Calumny: The Story of American POW's in the Korean War* (New York: Macmillan, 1963), 154.

28. Virginia Pasley, *21 Stayed: The Story of the American GI's Who Chose Communist China* (New York: Farrar, Straus, and Cudahy, 1955).

29. Quote from archival footage shown in following documentary film: Shui-Bo Wang, *They Chose China* (2005; Brooklyn: First Run/Icarus Films).

30. Tejasvi Nagaraja, "Soldiers of the American Dream: Midcentury War Work, Jim Crow, and Popular Movements Amidst Global Militarization" (PhD diss., New York University, 2017), 303–4.

31. Christine Hong, "The Unending Korean War," in a special issue, "The Unending Korean War," *positions: asia critique* 23, no. 4 (2015): 606.

32. Linda Gordon, *The Second Coming of the KKK: The Ku Klux Klan of the 1920s and the American Political Tradition* (New York: Liveright Publishing, 2017), 2.

33. Linda Gordon, *Second Coming of the KKK*, 2.

34. Thompson, *True Colors*, 14–15.

35. Thompson, *True Colors*, 18.

36. Thompson, 19.

37. Thompson, 18.

38. Lloyd Pate, *Reactionary!* (New York: Harper, 1956), 15.

39. Francis Mosnicka; 950774-RECAP-K; Intelligence Document File, Assistant Chief of Staff, G-2 (Intelligence); Box 1034, RG 0319 Army Staff, NARA, College Park, Maryland.

40. George Barnett; 950774-RECAP-K; Intelligence Document File, Assistant Chief of Staff, G-2 (Intelligence); Box 1025, RG 0319 Army Staff, NARA, College Park, Maryland.

41. Charles Armstrong, "The Destruction and Reconstruction of North Korea, 1950–1960," *Asia-Pacific Journal* 8, no. 51 (2010).

42. Alfred P. Banash; 950774-RECAP-K; Intelligence Document File, Assistant Chief of Staff, G-2 (Intelligence); Box 1025, RG 0319 Army Staff, NARA, College Park, Maryland.

43. Moore and Gentry, *I Cannot Forget*, 96.

44. Howard Beadleson; 950774-RECAP-K; Intelligence Document File, Assistant Chief of Staff, G-2 (Intelligence); Box 1025, RG 0319 Army Staff, NARA, College Park, Maryland.

45. George Sayre; 950774-RECAP-K; Intelligence Document File, Assistant Chief of Staff, G-2 (Intelligence); Box 1037, RG 0319 Army Staff, NARA, College Park, Maryland.

46. Millard Kaessner; 950774-RECAP-K; Intelligence Document File, Assistant Chief of Staff, G-2 (Intelligence); Box 1032, RG 0319 Army Staff, NARA, College Park, Maryland.

47. Sayre, 950774-RECAP-K.

48. Ray Dowe; 950774-RECAP-K; Intelligence Document File, Assistant Chief of Staff, G-2 (Intelligence); Box 1027[??], RG 0319 Army Staff, NARA, College Park, Maryland.

49. Manuel Castlewitz; 950774-RECAP-K; Intelligence Document File, Assistant Chief of Staff, G-2 (Intelligence); Box 1027, RG 0319 Army Staff, NARA, College Park, Maryland.

50. Michael Lorenzo Folder: 950774 ASCIR 0049 27 Apr 54; Box 1025, Intelligence Document File, Assistant Chief of Staff, G-2 (Intelligence); Records of the Army Staff; Record Group 319; –NARA, College Park, Maryland.

51. Frank Page Folder: 950774 ASCIR 0055; Box 1025, Intelligence Document File, Assistant Chief of Staff, G-2 (Intelligence); Records of the Army Staff; Record Group 319; –NARA, College Park, Maryland.

52. Leonard Wilmeth. Folder: 950774: ASCIR 0051 27 Apr 54; Box 1025, Intelligence Document File, Assistant Chief of Staff, G-2 (Intelligence); Records of the Army Staff; Record Group 319; NARA, College Park, Maryland.

53. Richard Artesani. Folder: 950774: ASCIR 0056 9 June 54; Box 1025, Intelligence Document File, Assistant Chief of Staff, G-2 (Intelligence); Records of the Army Staff; Record Group 319; NARA, College Park, Maryland.

54. Raymond Mendell; Folder: 950774: ASCIR 0052 20 May 54; Box 1025, Intelligence Document File, Assistant Chief of Staff, G-2 (Intelligence); Records of the Army Staff; Record Group 319; NARA, College Park, Maryland.

55. Joe Harrison claimed that the real name was "Wong," Michael Lorenzo said it was "Li," and Alarich Zacherle said that it was "Chin."

56. Alarich Zacherle. Folder: 950774: ASCIR 0062 11 June 54; Box 1025, Intelligence Document File, Assistant Chief of Staff, G-2 (Intelligence); Records of the Army Staff; Record Group 319; NARA, College Park, Maryland.

57. Joseph Harrison. Folder: 950774: ASCIR 0065 17 June 54; Box 1025, Intelligence Document File, Assistant Chief of Staff, G-2 (Intelligence); Records of the Army Staff; Record Group 319; NARA, College Park, Maryland.

58. Lorenzo, Folder: 950774, NARA.

59. Artesani, Folder: 950774, NARA.

60. Artesani, Folder: 950774, NARA.

61. Castlewitz, 950774-RECAP-K.

62. Everett Carpenter; 950774-RECAP-K; Intelligence Document File; Assistant Chief of Staff, G-2 (Intelligence); Box 1027, RG 0319 Army Staff, NARA, College Park, Maryland.

63. Edward Campbell; 950774-RECAP-K; Intelligence Document File; Assistant Chief of Staff, G-2 (Intelligence); Box 1027, RG 0319 Army Staff, NARA, College Park, Maryland.

64. Artesani, Folder: 950774, NARA.

65. Willie Polee; 950774-RECAP-K; Intelligence Document File; Assistant Chief of Staff, G-2 (Intelligence); Box 1035, RG 0319 Army Staff, NARA, College Park, Maryland.

66. Daniel Johnson; 950774-RECAP-K; Intelligence Document File; Assistant Chief of Staff, G-2 (Intelligence); Box 1031, RG 0319 Army Staff, NARA, College Park, Maryland.

67. Marvin Moore; 950774-RECAP-K; Intelligence Document File; Assistant Chief of Staff, G-2 (Intelligence); Box 1034, RG 0319 Army Staff, NARA, College Park, Maryland.

68. Kaessner, 950774-RECAP-K.

69. Artesani, Folder: 950774, NARA.

70. Zacherle, Folder: 950774, NARA.

71. Shelton Foss, Folder: 950774: ASCIR 0060 26 May 54; Box 1025, Intelligence Document File; Assistant Chief of Staff, G-2 (Intelligence); Records of the Army Staff; Record Group 319; NARA College Park, Maryland.

72. Foss, Folder: 950774, NARA.

73. See Kim San and Nym Wales, *Song of Ariran: The Life Story of Korean Rebel* (New York: John Day, 1941).

74. Suzy Kim, *Everyday Life in the North Korean Revolution, 1945–1950* (Ithaca, NY: Cornell University Press, 2013), 142.

75. Theodore Hughes, *Literature and Film in Cold War South Korea: Freedom's Frontier* (New York: Columbia University Press, 2012), 68.

76. Andre Schmid, "'My Turn to Speak': Criticism Culture and the Multiple Uses of Class in Postwar North Korea," *International Journal of Korean History* 21, no. 2 (2016): 129.

77. For more on *juche*, see Heonik Kwon and Byung-Ho Chung, *North Korea: Beyond Charismatic Politics* (Lanham, MD: Rowman and Littlefield 2012); Jae-Jung Suh, ed., *Origins of North Korea's Juche: Colonialism, War, and Development* (Lanham, MD: Lexington Books, 2013); Benjamin Young, "Juche in the United States: The Black Panther Party's Relations with North Korea, 1969–1971," *Asia-Pacific Journal* 13, issue 12, no. 2 (March 30): 2015; Cheehyung Kim, "Total, Thus Broken: Chuch'e Sasang and North Korea's Terrain of Subjectivity," *The Journal of Korean Studies* (17:1) Spring 2012, 69–96.

78. Japan Joint Intelligence Processing Board Final Report, October 1953. "Al Trabadeux, the latter Colored" referenced in Richie's report most probably refers to Al Thibodeaux.

79. Thompson, *True Colors*, 85.

80. Japan Joint Intelligence Processing Board Final Report, October 1953.

81. Foss, Folder: 950774, NARA.

82. Dwight Coxe. Folder: 950774: ASCIR 0059 10 June 54; Box 1025, Intelligence Document File; Assistant Chief of Staff, G-2 (Intelligence); Records of the Army Staff; Record Group 319; NARA, College Park, Maryland.

83. Raymond Mendell. Folder: 950774: ASCIR 0052 20 May 54; Box 1025; Intelligence Document File; Assistant Chief of Staff, G-2 (Intelligence); Records of the Army Staff; Record Group 319; NARA, College Park, Maryland.

84. Harrison, Folder: 950774, NARA.

85. William Mayer, "Brainwashing: The Ultimate Weapon," October 4, 1956. Speech given to the "officers and supervisors of the San Francisco Shipyard in the Naval Radiological Defense Laboratory."

86. Japan Joint Intelligence Processing Board Final Report, October 1953.

87. "A Study of North Korean and Chinese Soldier Attitudes toward Communism, Democracy, and the United Nations," by Julius Segal—Technical Memorandum ORO-T-42(FEC)—Received: 16 February 1954; Box 19; Unclassified Records, 1969–75; POW/Civilian Internee Information Center; RG 389, NARA, College Park, Maryland.

88. "Study of North Korean and Chinese Soldier Attitudes."

89. "The Oriental Communist Prisoner of War: A Study from the Intelligence Viewpoint," Folder: Unclassified 511-02; Box 19; Unclassified Records, 1969–75; POW/Civilian Internee Information Center; RG 389, NARA, College Park, Maryland.

90. Julius Segal, "Correlates of Collaboration and Resistance Behavior among US Army POWs in Korea," *Journal of Social Issues* (13:3).

91. Artesani, Wilmeth, Foss, Folder: 950774, NARA.

92. Zacherle, Folder: 950774, NARA.

93. Zacherle, Folder: 950774, NARA.

94. Clarence Adams, *An American Dream: The Life of an African American Solider and POW Who Spent Twelve Years in Communist China* (Amherst: University of Massachusetts Press, 2007), 56.

95. Adams, *An American Dream*, 59–60.

96. Raymond Goodburlet; 950774-RECAP-K; Intelligence Document File; Assistant Chief of Staff, G-2 (Intelligence); Box 1030, RG 0319 Army Staff, NARA, College Park, Maryland.

97. Gerard Brown; 950774-RECAP-K; Intelligence Document File; Assistant Chief of Staff, G-2 (Intelligence); Box 1027, RG 0319 Army Staff, NARA, College Park, Maryland.

98. Jimmy Chavez; 950774-RECAP-K; Intelligence Document File; Assistant Chief of Staff, G-2 (Intelligence); Box 1027, RG 0319 Army Staff, NARA, College Park, Maryland.

99. Gerard Brown, 950774-RECAP-K.

100. Goodburlet, 950774-RECAP-K.

101. Joseph Ramsey; 950774-RECAP-K; Intelligence Document File; Assistant Chief of Staff, G-2 (Intelligence); Box 1036, RG 0319 Army Staff, NARA, College Park, Maryland.

102. William Freeman; 950774-RECAP-K; Intelligence Document File; Assistant Chief of Staff, G-2 (Intelligence); Box 1029, RG 0319 Army Staff, NARA, College Park, Maryland.

103. David Shay; 950774-RECAP-K; Intelligence Document File; Assistant Chief of Staff, G-2 (Intelligence); Box 1037, RG 0319 Army Staff, NARA, College Park, Maryland.

104. Dwight D. Eisenhower: "Executive Order 10631—Code of Conduct for Members of the Armed Forces of the United States," August 17, 1955; "POW: The Fight Continues after the Battle," The Report of the Secretary of Defense's Advisory Committee on Prisoners of War, August 1955.

Conclusion: The Diaspora of War

1. See Appendix C for text of Armistice Agreement, in Walter Hermes, *Truce Tent and Fighting Front* (Washington, DC: Office of the Chief of Military History, United States Army, 1966).

2. Clarence Adams, *An American Dream: The life of an African American Soldier and POW Who Spent Twelve Years in Communist China* (Amherst: University of Massachusetts Press, 2007), 103.

3. Adams, *American Dream*, 104. Also see Susan Carruthers, *Cold War Captives: Imprisonment, Escape, and Brainwashing* (Berkeley: University of California Press, 2009).

4. Adams, *American Dream*, 111.

5. Adams, *American Dream*, 104.

6. Joo Young-Bok, oral history interview, Korean American Archives at University of Southern California, available at https://digitallibrary.usc.edu, accessed July 1, 2018.

7. Sam Shigeru Miyamoto, interview by author, March 1, 2007, Monterey Park, California.

8. Mary Dudziak, *War Time: An Idea, Its History, Its Consequences* (Oxford: Oxford University Press, 2012), 85.

9. Progress Report on the National Psychological Effort for the Period July 1, 1952 through September 30, 1952. Dated October 30, 1952. Folder: File #1 Report by PSB on the Status of the Psychological Program [2 of 2]; Box 22; SMOF: Psychological Strategy Board Files; Papers of Harry S. Truman. Harry S. Truman Presidential Library and Archives.

10. Young, "Bombing Civilians," 159.

11. See Appendix B in Hermes, *Truce Tent*.

12. David Cheng Chang, "To Return Home or 'Return to Taiwan': Conflicts and Survival in the 'Voluntary Repatriation' of Chinese POWs in the Korean War" (PhD diss., University of California, San Diego, 2011), 7.

13. Deokhyo Choi, "Fighting the Korean War in Pacifist Japan," *Critical Asian Studies* 49, no. 4 (2017): 1. These *zainichi* Korean leftists were a part of the population of Koreans who had been brought forcibly—or under the stress of penury—during the colonial era to the metropole to work in factories and mines, their labor essential to the operations of the Japanese economy.

14. Alfred W. McCoy, *Policing America's Empire: The United States, the Philippines, and the Rise of the Surveillance State* (Madison: University of Wisconsin Press, 2009); Greg Grandin, *Empire's Workshop: Latin America, the United States, and the Rise of the New Imperialism* (New York: Metropolitan Books, 2006); Laleh Khalili, *Time in the Shadows: Confinement in Counterinsurgencies* (Stanford, CA: Stanford University Press, 2013).

15. I thank Christine Hong for sharing with me her unpublished manuscript.

BIBLIOGRAPHY

Primary Sources

Archival Collections

United States National Archives and Record Administration, College Park, Maryland (NARA)
International Committee of the Red Cross Archives, Geneva, Switzerland
United States Army Military History Institute, Carlisle, Pennsylvania
Harry S. Truman Presidential Library and Archives, Independence, Missouri
Dwight D. Eisenhower Presidential Library and Archives, Abilene, Kansas
Franklin D. Roosevelt Presidential Library and Archives, Hyde Park, New York
Hoover Institution, Stanford University
National Archives of Korea
Korean American Archive, University of Southern California
United Nations Archives, New York, New York
Swarthmore College Peace Archives

Oral Histories

CONDUCTED BY AUTHOR

Isobe, Tohoru. Interview by author, February 27, 2007, Los Angeles, California.
Ju Yeong-taek. Oral history interview, Pusan, Republic of Korea, July 6, 2008.
Miyamoto, Atsushi "Archie." Interview conducted by author, February 26, 2007, Harbor City, California.
Miyamoto, Sam Shigeru. Interview by author, March 1, 2007, Monterey Park, California.
Nakatani, Katsuya "Kats." Interview conducted by author, February 24, 2007, at the All Wars Conference for the Japanese American Veterans Association in Los Angeles, California.
Shiraga, Roy. Interview conducted by author at the Japanese American Veterans Association 2007 All Wars Conference, February 24, 2007.
———. Interview conducted by author, March 2, 2007, Hacienda Heights, California.
Son Ku-wŏn. Oral history interviews, Seoul, Republic of Korea, May 28, 2008, and June 21, 2008.
Taniguchi, George. Interview conducted by author, March 6, 2007, phone interview.
Tsuda, George. Interview by author, February 28, 2007, Fullerton, California.
Yi Chong-gyu. Oral history interview, Seoul, Republic of Korea, January 11, 2008.

CONDUCTED BY JA LIVING LEGACY

Matsuzaki, Roy. Interview conducted by Susan Uyemura for the Japanese American Living Legacy Oral History Project, March 3, 2006, Japanese American Museum and Library, San Jose, California.

Nakatani, Katsuya "Kats." Interview conducted by Susan Uyemura for the Japanese American Living Legacy Oral History Project, November 29, 2005, Pico Rivera, California.

Okada, Howard. Interview conducted by Susan Uyemura for the Japanese American Living Legacy Oral History Project, November 9, 2006, Honolulu, Hawai'i.

Shiraga, Roy. Interview conducted by Susan Uyemura of the Japanese American Living Legacy Oral History Project on August 10, 2006, Hacienda Heights, California.

Shiroishi, Robert. Interview conducted by Susan Uyemura for the Japanese American Living Legacy Oral History Project, November 22, 2006, Cypress, California.

Takane, Thomas, and Thomas Tanaka. Interview conducted by Susan Uyemura for the Japanese American Living Legal Oral History Project, November 9, 2006, Honolulu, Hawai'i.

Yanagihara, Reverend Jim "Gopher." Interview conducted by Susan Uyemura for the Japanese American Living Legacy Oral History Project, January 14, 2006, at San Diego Buddhist Church.

Yoshizawa, Arnold. Interview conducted by Susan Uyemura for the Japanese American Living Legacy Oral History Project, December 2, 2006, Carson, California.

Unpublished Primary Sources

"The Gripsholm Exchanges: A Short Concise Report on the Exchange of Hostages during World War II between the United States and Japan as It Relates to Japanese Americans." Written by Atsushi "Archie" Miyamoto. Copy given to author.

"Interviews with 24 Korean POW Leaders." Prepared by Research, Analysis, and Evaluation Division, Psychological Warfare Section, United States Army Forces, Far East, Headquarters. Dated May 13, 1954. Unpublished manuscript.

Tsuda, George. Unpublished autobiography. Copy given to author.

Unpublished data research collection compiled for a special documentary series produced by MBC (Cultural Broadcasting Company) in the Republic of Korea in 2004. The documentary special was called Han'guk Chŏngaenggwa Poro [The Korean War and the Prisoner of War], and it was a series special on a program called Igaenŭn Marhalsu Itta [Now We Can Speak].

Published Multivolume Primary Source Material Collections

Documents of the Division of Historical Policy Research of the US State Department. Korea project file: Miguk Kungmubu Chŏngch'aek Yŏn'gukwa munsŏ. Seoul: Kukpangbu Kunsa P'yŏnch'an Yŏn'guso, 1998.

G-2 Periodic Report/United States Army Forces in Korea. Headquarters. G-2. 1945–48. Kangwŏn-do Ch'unch'ŏn-si: Hallim Taehakkyo Asia Munhwa Yŏn'guso.

Merrill, Dennis, ed. *Documentary History of the Truman Presidency*. University Publications of America, 1997.

[Proclamations and ordinances] Official gazette, United States Army Military Government in Korea: Mi Kunjŏngch'ŏng kwanbo. Sŏul: Wonju Munhwasa.

[Records of the Counterintelligence Corps] Mi kunjŏnggi chŏngbo charyojip: CIC (Pangch'ŏptae) pogosŏ, 1945.9–1949.1. Kangwŏn-do Ch'unch'ŏn-si: Hallim Taehakkyo Asia Munhwa Yŏn'guso, 1995.

[Records of the Counterintelligence Corps] Migun CIC chŏngbo pogosŏ: RG 319 Office of the Chief of Military History. Sŏul: Chungang Ilbo Hyŏndaesa Yŏn'guso, 1996.

Records of the policy planning staff of the Department of State: Mi Kungmubu Chŏngch'aek Kihoeksil munsŏ. Seoul: Kukpangbu Kunsa P'yŏnch'an Yŏn'guso, 1997.

Selected legal opinions of the Department of Justice, United States Army Military Government in Korea: Opinions rendered in the role of legal adviser to the military government of Korea and covering a period from March 1946 to August 1948: Migunjŏnggi Chŏngbo Charyojip: Pŏmmuguk Sabŏppŭi Pŏphaesŏk Pogosŏ. Seoul, Korea: Department of Justice, Headquarters, United States Army Military Government in Korea, 1948; reprint, Kangwŏn-do Ch'unch'ŏn-si: Hallim Taehakkyo Asia Munhwa Yonguso, 1997.

US Department of State, Papers Relating to the Foreign Relations of the United States. Washington, DC: US Government Printing Office.

US Department of State relating to the internal affairs of Korea: Mi Kungmubu Han'guk kungnae sanghwang kwallyŏn munsŏ. Seoul: Kukpangbu Kunsa P'yŏnch'an Yŏn'guso, 2000–2002.

Published Primary Sources—Korean Language

Ju, Yeong Bok. *76 P'orodŭl* [The 76 Prisoners of War]. Seoul: Daegwan Publishing, 1993.

Ju, Yeong Bok. Nae ka kyŏkkŭn Chosŏn chŏnjaeng. [The Korean War I Lived] Volumes 1 and 2. Sŏul: Koryŏwŏn, 1990–1991.

Ko, Yeong-gun. *Jookumeo Gobilul Numuso* [Facing Death]. Seoul: Mokmin Publishing, 1997.

Oh, Se-hŭi. *Suyoungso 65* [Compound 65]. Taegu: Maninsa, 2000.

Yi, Mu-ho. Ŏnŭ cholbyŏng i kyŏkkŭn Han'guk chŏnjaeng [The Korean War Experienced by an Ordinary Soldier]. Seoul: Chisik Sanŏpsa, 2003.

Published Primary Sources—English, French, German Language

Biderman, Albert. *March to Calumny: The Story of American POW's in the Korean War*. New York: Macmillan, 1963.

Fraenkel, Ernst. *Gesammelte Schriften*. Baden Baden: Nomos Verlagsgesellschaft, 1999.

———. "Korea: A Turning Point in International Law?" Translated by Patricia Szobar. Berlin: Gebrüder Weiss Publishers, 1951.

History of the United States Armed Forces in Korea. United States, Far East Command, Published in 1948.

Interviews with 24 Korean POW Leaders. Prepared by Research, Analysis, and Evaluation Division, Psychological Warfare Section, United States Army Forces, Far East, Headquarters. May 13, 1954.

Lifton, R. J. "Home by Ship: Reaction Patterns of American Prisoners of War Repatriated from North Korea." *American Journal of Psychiatry* 110, no. 10 (1954).

Mass Behavior in Battle and Captivity: The Communist Soldier in the Korean War. Research studies directed by William C. Bradbury. Edited by Samuel Meyers and Albert D. Biderman. Chicago: University of Chicago Press: 1968.

[Pamphlet] Prisoner Sense (Training Division, Bureau of Aeronautics, United States Navy), May 1943.

Pasley, Virginia. *21 Stayed: The Story of the American GI's Who Chose Communist China*. New York: Farrar, Straus, and Cudahy, 1955.

Memoirs and Collections

Adams, Clarence. *An American Dream: The Life of an African American Solider and POW Who Spent Twelve Years in Communist China*. Amherst: University of Massachusetts Press, 2007.

Acheson, Dean. *Present at the Creation: My Years in the State Department*. 1st ed. New York: Norton, 1969.

Carlson, Lewis H., ed. *Remembered Prisoners of a Forgotten War: An Oral History of Korean War POWs*. New York: St. Martin's Press, 2002.

Clark, Mark W. *From the Danube to the Yalu*. New York: Harper, 1954.

Daugherty, William E. *A Psychological Warfare Casebook*. Baltimore: Published for Operations Research Office, Johns Hopkins University, by Johns Hopkins Press, 1958.

Hansen, Kenneth K. *Heroes behind Barbed Wire*. Princeton, NJ: Van Nostrand, 1957.

Joy, C. Turner. *How Communists Negotiate*. New York: Macmillan, 1955.

Mayer, William E. *Beyond the Call: Memoirs of a Medical Visionary*, vols. 1 and 2. Albuquerque: Mayer Publishing Group International, 2009.

Moore, Johnny, and Judith Fenner Gentry. *I Cannot Forget: Imprisoned in Korea, Accused at Home*. College Station: Texas A&M University Press, 2013.

Nehru, Jawaharlal. *India's Foreign Policy: Selected Speeches*. [Delhi]: Publications Division, Ministry of Information and Broadcasting, Government of India, 1961.

Pate, Lloyd. *Reactionary!* New York: Harper, 1956.

Prasad, Sri Nandan, and Birendra Chandra Chakravorty. *History of the Custodian Force (India) in Korea, 1953–54*. Armed Forces of the Indian Union. [New Delhi]: Historical Section, Ministry of Defence, Government of India, 1976.

Rowley, Arden Allen. *Korea-POW: A Thousand Days with Life on Hold, 1950–1953*. Mesa, AZ: Tanner Publishing, 1997.

Rusk, Dean. *As I Saw It*. 1st ed. New York: W. W. Norton, 1990.

Song, Hyo-sun. *The Fight for Freedom: The Untold Story of the Korean War Prisoners*. Seoul: Korean Library Association, 1980.

Thimayya, Kodendera Subayya. *Experiment in Neutrality*. New Delhi: Vision Books, 1981.

Thompson, James. *True Colors: 1004 Days as a Prisoner of War*. Madison, WI: Ashley Books, 1989.

Truman, Harry S. *Memoirs*. Garden City, NY: Doubleday, 1955.

United States Government. *Japanese Evacuation from the West Coast, 1942: Final Report*. The Asian Experience in North America: Chinese and Japanese. New York: Arno Press, 1978.

———. *Personal Justice Denied Report of the Commission on Wartime Relocation and Internment of Civilians: Report for the Committee on Interior and Insular Affairs*. Washington, DC: US GPO, 1992.

Vatcher, William H. *Panmunjom: The Story of the Korean Military Armistice Negotiations*. New York: Praeger, 1958.

Yoneda, Karl G. *Ganbatte: Sixty-Year Struggle of a Kibei Worker*. Los Angeles: Resource Development and Publications, Asian American Studies Center, University of California, Los Angeles, 1983.

Zellers Larry. *In Enemy Hands: A Prisoner in North Korea*. Lexington: University Press of Kentucky, 1991.

Geneva Conventions Records

Final Record of the Diplomatic Conference at Geneva of 1949. Berne: Federal Political Department, 1963.

Pictet, Jean S., ed. *Commentary: The Geneva Conventions of 12 August 1949*. 4 vols. Geneva, ICRC, 1952, 1958, 1960.

Newspapers

Atlanta Daily World
Chicago Daily Tribune
Dong-A Ilbo (Korea)
Los Angeles Times
Madison Press (Madison County, Ohio)
New York Times
Washington Post

Secondary Sources

Agamben, Giorgio. *Homo Sacer: Sovereign Power and Bare Life*. Meridian: Crossing Aesthetics. Stanford, CA: Stanford University Press, 1998.

———. *State of Exception*. Chicago: University of Chicago Press, 2005.

Anghie, Antony. *Imperialism, Sovereignty, and the Making of International Law*. Cambridge: Cambridge University Press, 2004.

Appleman, Roy Edgar. *South to the Naktong, North to the Yalu: June–November 1950*. United States Army in the Korean War, 2nd vol. Washington, DC: Office of the Chief of Military History, Department of the Army, 1961.

Arendt, Hannah. *On Revolution*. New York: Viking Press, 1963.

———. *The Origins of Totalitarianism*. New ed. New York: Harcourt, Brace and World, 1966.

Armstrong, Charles. "The Cultural Cold War in Korea, 1945–1950." *Journal of Asian Studies* 62, no. 1 (2003): 71–99.

———. *The North Korean Revolution, 1945–1950*. Studies of the East Asian Institute. Ithaca, NY: Cornell University Press, 2003.

———. *Tyranny of the Weak: North Korea and the World*. Ithaca, NY: Cornell University Press, 2013.

Azuma, Eiichiro. *Between Two Empires: Race, History, and Transnationalism in Japanese America*. Oxford: Oxford University Press, 2005.

———. "Brokering Race, Culture, and Citizenship: Japanese Americans in Occupied Japan and Postwar National Inclusion." *Journal of American–East Asian Relations* 16, no. 3 (2009): 183–211.

Bacevich, Andrew J. *The New American Militarism: How Americans Are Seduced by War*. New York: Oxford University Press, 2013.

Balakrishnan, Gopal. *The Enemy: An Intellectual Portrait of Carl Schmitt*. London: Verso, 2000.

Barnes, Robert. "Between the Blocs: India, the United Nations, and Ending the Korean War." *Journal of Korean Studies* 18, no. 2 (2013).

———. *The US, the UN, and the Korean War: Communism in the Far East and the American Struggle for Hegemony in the Cold War*. New York: I. B. Tauris, 2014.

Berman, Nathaniel. "Intervention in a 'Divided World': Axes of Legitimacy." *European Journal of International Law* 17, no. 4 (2006): 743.

———. "Privileging Combat? Contemporary Conflict and the Legal Construction of War." *Columbia Journal of Transnational Law* 43, no. 1 (2004): 1–71.

Best, Geoffrey. *War and Law since 1945*. Oxford: Clarendon Press, 1996.

Bhagavan, Manu. *India and the Quest for One World: The Peacemakers*. Basingstoke: Palgrave Macmillan, 2013.

Borgwardt, Elizabeth. *A New Deal for the World: America's Vision for Human Rights*. Cambridge, MA: Belknap Press of Harvard University Press, 2005.

Borstelmann, Thomas. *The Cold War and the Color Line: American Race Relations in the Global Arena*. Cambridge, MA: Harvard University Press, 2001.

Bose, Sugata, and Ayesha Jalal. *Nationalism, Democracy, and Development: State and Politics in India*. New York: Oxford University Press, 1997.

Botsman, Daniel. *Punishment and Power in the Making of Modern Japan*. Princeton, NJ: Princeton University Press, 2005.

Bourke, Joanna. *An Intimate History of Killing: Face-to-Face Killing in Twentieth Century Warfare*. New York: Basic Books, 1999.

Bradley, Mark. *Imagining Vietnam and America: The Making of Postcolonial Vietnam, 1919–1950*. New Cold War History. Chapel Hill: University of North Carolina Press, 2000.

Caprio, Mark. *Japanese Assimilation Policies in Colonial Korea, 1910–1945*. Seattle: University of Washington Press, 2009.

Carlson, David, Drucilla Cornell, and Michel Rosenfeld, eds. *Deconstruction and the Possibility of Justice*. New York: Routledge, 1992.

Carruthers, Susan. *Cold War Captives: Imprisonment, Escape, and Brainwashing*. Berkeley: University of California Press, 2009.

Casey, Steven. *Selling the Korean War: Propaganda, Politics, and Public Opinion in the United States, 1950–1953*. New York: Oxford University Press, 2008.

Chae, Grace. "Captive Minds: Race, War, and the Education of Korean War POWs in U.S. Custody, 1950–1953." PhD diss., University of Chicago, 2010.

Chakrabarty, Dipesh. *Provincializing Europe: Postcolonial Thought and Historical Difference*. Princeton Studies in Culture/Power/History. Princeton, NJ: Princeton University Press, 2000.

Chang, David Cheng. *The Hijacked War: The Story of Chinese POWs in the Korean War*. Stanford, CA: Stanford University Press, 2019.

Chang, Gordon H. "Whose 'Barbarism'? Whose 'Treachery'? Race and Civilization in the Unknown United States–Korea War of 1871." *Journal of American History* 89, no. 4 (2003): 1331–65.

Chatterjee, Partha. *Nationalist Thought and the Colonial World: A Derivative Discourse*. Minneapolis: University of Minnesota Press, 1993.

Cho, Grace M. *Haunting the Korean Diaspora: Shame, Secrecy, and the Forgotten War*. Minneapolis: University of Minnesota Press, 2008.

Cho, Sŏng-hun. *Han'guk Chŏnjaeng kwa p'oro* [The Korean War and the Prisoner of War]. Sŏul-si: Sŏnin, 2010.

Choi, Deokhyo. "Crucible for the Post-Empire: Decolonization, Race, and Cold War Politics in US-Japan-Korea Relations, 1945–1952." PhD diss., Cornell University, 2013.

Chŏng, Pyŏng-jun. *Han'guk chŏnjaeng: 38-sŏn ch'ungdol kwa chŏnjaeng ŭi hyŏngsŏng* [The Korean War: Confrontations at the 38th Parallel and the Formation of the War]. Kyŏnggi-do P'aju-si: Tol Pegae, 2006.

Chŏng Yong-uk. *Haebang chŏnhu Miguk ŭi Taehan chŏngchaek: Kwado chŏngbu kusang kwa chungganpa chŏngchaek ŭl chungsim ŭro* [The Policies of the United States on Korea before and after Liberation: Through a Focus on Transitional Government Initiatives and Mid-term Policies]. Seoul: Sŏul Taehakkyo Ch'ulp'anbu, 2003.

Clinton, Maggie. *Revolutionary Nativism, Fascism, and Culture in China, 1925–1937*. Durham, NC: Duke University Press, 2017.

Connelly, Matthew James. *A Diplomatic Revolution: Algeria's Fight for Independence and the Origins of the Post-Cold War Era*. New York: Oxford University Press, 2002.

Coronil, Fernando, and Julie Skurski. *States of Violence*. Comparative Studies in Society and History Book Series. Ann Arbor: University of Michigan Press, 2006.

Cover, Robert M. *Narrative, Violence, and the Law: The Essays of Robert Cover*. 1st ed. Law, Meaning, and Violence. Ann Arbor: University of Michigan Press, 1995.

Cumings, Bruce. *Child of Conflict: The Korean-American Relationship, 1943–1953*. Seattle: University of Washington Press, 1983.

———. *Dominion from Sea to Sea: Pacific Ascendancy and American Power*. New Haven, CT: Yale University Press, 2010.

———. *North Korea: Another Country*. New York: New Press, 2004.

———. *The Origins of the Korean War.* Vols. 1 and 2. Studies of the East Asian Institute. Princeton, NJ: Princeton University Press, 1981–90.

———. *Parallax Visions: Making Sense of American–East Asian Relations at the End of the Century.* Asia-Pacific, Culture, Politics, and Society. Durham, NC: Duke University Press, 1999.

———. *War and Television.* Haymarket Series. London: Verso, 1992.

Daniels, Roger. *Concentration Camps USA: Japanese Americans and World War II.* New York: Holt, Rinehart and Winston, 1971.

Dayal, Shiv. *India's Role in the Korean Question: A Study in the Settlement of International Disputes under the United Nations.* Delhi: S. Chand, 1959.

Denning, Michael. *Culture in the Age of Three Worlds.* London: Verso, 2004.

Dower, John W. *Cultures of War: Pearl Harbor, Hiroshima, 9-11, Iraq.* New York: W. W. Norton; New Press, 2010.

———. *Embracing Defeat.* New York: W. W. Norton, 2000.

———. *War without Mercy: Race and Power in the Pacific War.* New York: Pantheon Books, 1986.

Drinnon, Richard. *Keeper of Concentration Camps: Dillon S. Myer and American Racism.* Berkeley: University of California Press, 1987.

Duara, Prasenjit. *Decolonization: Perspectives from Now and Then.* Rewriting Histories. London: Routledge, 2004.

———. *Sovereignty and Authenticity: Manchukuo and the East Asian Modern.* State and Society in East Asia Series. Lanham, MD: Rowman and Littlefield , 2003.

Dudziak, Mary L. *Cold War Civil Rights: Race and the Image of American Democracy.* Princeton, NJ: Princeton University Press, 2000.

———. *War Time: An Idea, Its History, Its Consequences.* Oxford: Oxford University Press, 2012.

Elleman, Bruce A. *Japanese-American Civilian Prisoner Exchanges and Detention Camps, 1941–45.* Routledge Studies in the Modern History of Asia 37. London: Routledge, 2006.

Em, Henry. *The Great Enterprise: Sovereignty and Historiography in Modern Korea.* Durham, NC: Duke University Press, 2013.

Evans, Humphrey. *Thimayya of India: A Soldier's Life.* New York: Harcourt, Brace, 1960.

Fanon, Frantz. *The Wretched of the Earth.* Translated from the French by Richard Philcox. Introductions by Jean-Paul Sartre and Homi K. Bhabha. New York: Grove Press, 2004.

Feldman, Ilana. *Governing Gaza: Bureaucracy, Authority, and the Work of Rule, 1917–1967.* Durham, NC: Duke University Press, 2008.

Foot, Rosemary. "Nuclear Coercion and the Ending of the Korean Conflict." *International Security* 13, no. 3 (1988): 92–112.

———. *A Substitute for Victory: The Politics of Peacemaking at the Korean Armistice Talks.* Cornell Studies in Security Affairs. Ithaca, NY: Cornell University Press, 1990.

Foucault, Michel. *The Archaeology of Knowledge.* New York: Harper and Row, 1976.

———. *Discipline and Punish: The Birth of the Prison.* New York: Vintage Books, 1995.

———. *Security, Territory, Population: Lectures at the Collège de France, 1977–78.* Translated by Michel Senellart, François Ewald, and Alessandro Fontana. Basingstoke: Palgrave Macmillan; République Française, 2007.

———. *"Society Must Be Defended": Lectures at the Collège de France, 1975–76.* Translated by Mauro Bertani, Alessandro Fontana, and David Macey. New York: Picador, 2003.

Ffytche, Matt, and Daniel Pick, eds. *Psychoanalysis in the Age of Totalitarianism*. London: Routledge, Taylor Francis Group, 2016.

Fujitani, Takashi. *Race for Empire: Koreans as Japanese and Japanese as Americans during World War II*. Berkeley: University of California Press, 2011.

Gaddis, John Lewis. *The Long Peace: Inquiries into the History of the Cold War*. New York: Oxford University Press, 1987.

———. *We Now Know: Rethinking Cold War History*. Oxford: Clarendon Press, 1997.

Gauthier, Brandon. "The Other Korea: Ideological Constructions of North Korea in the American Imagination, 1948–2000." PhD diss., Fordham University, 2016.

Goodrich, Leland M. *Korea: A Study of U.S. Policy in the United Nations*. New York: Council on Foreign Relations, 1956.

———. *The United Nations*. New York: Crowell, 1959.

Gordon, Linda. *The Second Coming of the KKK: The Ku Klux Klan of the 1920s and the American Political Tradition*. 1st ed. New York: Liveright Publishing, 2017.

Grandin, Greg. *Empire's Workshop: Latin America, the United States, and the Rise of the New Imperialism*. New York: Metropolitan Books, 2006.

Graves, Kori. "Domesticating Foreign Affairs: The African-American Family, Korean War Orphans, and Cold War Civil Rights." PhD diss., University of Wisconsin–Madison, 2011.

Ha, Yong-ch'ul, Hong Yung Lee, and Clark W. Sorensen, eds. *Colonial Rule and Social Change in Korea, 1910–1945*. Seattle: University of Washington Press, 2012.

Halberstam, David. *The Coldest Winter: America and the Korean War*. New York: Hyperion, 2007.

Hanley, Charles J., Sang-Hun Choe, and Martha Mendoza. *The Bridge at No Gun Ri: A Hidden Nightmare from the Korean War*. New York: Henry Holt, 2001.

Hansen, Thomas Blom, and Finn Stepputat. *Sovereign Bodies: Citizens, Migrants, and States in the Postcolonial World*. Princeton, NJ: Princeton University Press, 2005.

Hara, Kimie, ed. *The San Francisco System and Its Legacies: Continuation, Transformation, and Historical Reconciliation in the Asia-Pacific*. Asia's Transformations. Hoboken, NJ: Taylor and Francis, 2014.

Haruki, Wada. *The Korean War: An International History*. Translated by Frank Baldwin. New York: Rowman and Littlefield, 2014.

Hasegawa, Tsuyoshi. *Racing the Enemy: Stalin, Truman, and the Surrender of Japan*. Cambridge, MA: Harvard University Press, 2005.

Hayashi, Brian Masaru. *Democratizing the Enemy: The Japanese American Internment*. Princeton, NJ: Princeton University Press, 2004.

Hermes, Walter G. *Truce Tent and Fighting Front*. United States Army in the Korean War 2. Washington, DC: Center of Military History, United States Army, 2005.

Hobbes, Thomas. *Leviathan*. Rev. student ed. Cambridge Texts in the History of Political Thought. Cambridge: Cambridge University Press, 1996.

Hogan, Michael J. *A Cross of Iron: Harry S. Truman and the Origins of the National Security State, 1945–1954*. Cambridge: Cambridge University Press, 1998.

Hogan, Michael J., ed. *The Ambiguous Legacy: U.S. Foreign Relations in the "American Century."* Cambridge: Cambridge University Press, 1999.

Höhn, Maria, and Seungsook Moon. *Over There: Living with the U.S. Military Empire from World War Two to the Present*. Durham, NC: Duke University Press, 2010.

Hong, Christine. Introduction, "The Unending Korean War. Special issue of *Positions: Asia Critique* 23, no. 4 (2015): 597–617.

———. Introduction to "Reframing North Korean Human Rights." Coedited with Hazel Smith. Thematic issue of *Critical Asian Studies* 45, no. 4 (2013): 511–32.

———. "Legal Fictions: Human Rights Cultural Production and the Pax Americana in the Pacific Rim." PhD diss., University of California, Berkeley, 2007.

Horne, Gerald. *Black and Red: W.E.B. Du Bois and the Afro-American Response to the Cold War, 1944–1963*. SUNY Series in Afro-American Society. Albany: State University of New York Press, 1986.

Howland, Douglas, and Luise White, eds. *The State of Sovereignty: Territories, Laws, Populations*. Bloomington: Indiana University Press, 2009.

Hua, Ch'ing-chao. *From Yalta to Panmunjom: Truman's Diplomacy and the Four Powers, 1945–1953*. Ithaca, NY: East Asia Program, Cornell University, 1993.

Hughes, Theodore. *Literature and Film in Cold War South Korea: Freedom's Frontier*. New York: Columbia University Press, 2012.

Hussain, Nasser. *The Jurisprudence of Emergency*. Ann Arbor: University of Michigan Press, 2003.

Hwang, Junghyun. "Specters of the Cold War in America's Century: The Korean War and Transnational Politics of National Imaginaries in the 1950s." PhD diss., University of California, San Diego, 2008.

Hwang, Su-kyoung. *Korea's Grievous War*. Philadelphia: University of Pennsylvania Press, 2016.

Ichioka, Yuji. *Before Internment: Essays in Prewar Japanese American History*. Edited by Gordon H. Chang and Eiichiro Azuma. Asian America. Stanford, CA: Stanford University Press, 2006.

———. *The Issei: The World of the First Generation Japanese Immigrants, 1885–1924*. New York: Free Press, 1988.

Iriye, Akira. *After Imperialism: The Search for a New Order in the Far East, 1921–1931*. Cambridge, MA: Harvard University Press, 1965.

———. *Global Community: The Role of International Organizations in the Making of the Contemporary World*. Berkeley: University of California Press, 2002.

Irwin, Ryan. *Gordian Knot: Apartheid and the Unmaking of the Liberal World Order*. Oxford: Oxford University Press, 2012.

Jager, Sheila Miyoshi. *Brothers at War: The Unending Conflict in Korea*. New York: W. W. Norton, 2013.

Jian, Chen. *China's Road to the Korean War: The Making of the Sino-American Confrontation*. U.S. and Pacific Asia. New York: Columbia University Press, 1994.

Khalili, Laleh. *Time in the Shadows: Confinement in Counterinsurgencies*. Stanford, CA: Stanford University Press, 2013.

Kaplan, Amy, and Donald Pease, eds. *Cultures of United States Imperialism*. New Americanists. Durham, NC: Duke University Press, 1993.

Kawashima, Ken C. *The Proletarian Gamble: Korean Workers in Interwar Japan*. Durham, NC: Duke University Press, 2009.

Kelly, John Dunham, and Martha Kaplan. *Represented Communities: Fiji and World Decolonization*. Chicago: University of Chicago Press, 2001.

Kennedy, David. *Of War and Law*. Princeton, NJ: Princeton University Press, 2006.

Kennedy, Paul M. *The Parliament of Man: The Past, Present, and Future of the United Nations*. New York: Random House, 2006.

Kim, Dong-choon. *The Unending Korean War: A Social History*. Honolulu: University of Hawai'i Press, 2009.

Kim, Jeong-Min. "Intimate Exchanges: Korean Women, American GIs, and the Making of the Wartime Political Economy of South Korea during the Korean War." PhD diss., New York University, 2017.

Kim, Jodi. *Ends of Empire: Asian American Critique and the Cold War*. Minneapolis: University of Minnesota Press, 2010.

Kim, Richard S. *The Quest for Statehood: Korean Immigrant Nationalism and US Sovereignty, 1905–1945*. Oxford: Oxford University Press, 2011.

Kim, Suzy. *Everyday Life in the North Korean Revolution, 1945–1950*. Ithaca, NY: Cornell University Press, 2013.

Kim, T'ae-u. *P'okkyŏk: Mi konggun ŭi kongjung p'okkyŏk kirok ŭro ingnŭn Han'guk chŏnjaeng* [Bombing: Reading the Korean War through the Aerial Bombing Records of the United States Air Force]. Kyŏnggi-do P'aju-si Ch'angbi, 2013.

Kim, Tŭk-chung. *"Ppalgaengi" ŭi tansaeng: Yŏsun sakŏn kwa pangong kukka ŭi hyŏngsŏng* [The Birth of the "Red Commie": Yosu and the Formation of the Anti-Communist State]. Seoul: Sŏnin, 2009.

Koskenniemi, Martti. *The Gentle Civilizer of Nations: The Rise and Fall of International Law, 1870–1960*. Cambridge: Cambridge University Press, 2002.

Kramer, Paul A. *The Blood of Government: Race, Empire, the United States, and the Philippines*. Chapel Hill: University of North Carolina Press, 2006.

Kurashige, Scott. *The Shifting Grounds of Race: Black and Japanese Americans in the Making of Multiethnic Los Angeles*. Politics and Society in Twentieth-Century America. Princeton, NJ: Princeton University Press, 2008.

Kuzmarov, Jeremy. *Modernizing Repression: Police Training and Nation-Building in the American Century*. Amherst: University of Massachusetts Press, 2012.

Kwon, Heonik. *The Other Cold War*. New York: Columbia University Press, 2010.

Kwon, Heonik, and Byung-ho Chung. *North Korea: Beyond Charismatic Politics*. London: Rowman and Littlefield, 2012.

Lankov, A. N. *From Stalin to Kim Il Sung: The Formation of North Korea, 1945–1960*. New Brunswick, NJ: Rutgers University Press, 2002.

Lee, Chong-Sik. *Syngman Rhee: The Prison Years of a Young Radical*. Institute for Modern Korean Studies Monograph Series 4. [Seoul]: Yonsei University Press, 2001.

Lee, Christopher J. *Making a World after Empire: The Bandung Moment and Its Political Afterlives*. Athens: Ohio University Press, 2010.

Lee, Steven Hugh. *Outposts of Empire: Korea, Vietnam, and the Origins of the Cold War in Asia, 1949–1954*. Montreal: McGill-Queen's University Press, 1995.

Leffler, Melvyn P. *For the Soul of Mankind: The United States, the Soviet Union, and the Cold War*. New York: Hill and Wang, 2007.

———. *A Preponderance of Power: National Security, the Truman Administration, and the Cold War*. Stanford Nuclear Age Series. Stanford, CA: Stanford University Press, 1992.

Lipman, Jana K. *Guantánamo: A Working-Class History between Empire and Revolution*. Berkeley: University of California Press, 2009.

Louis, William Roger. *Imperialism at Bay: The United States and the Decolonization of the British Empire, 1941–1945*. Oxford: Clarendon Press, 1977.

Lowe, Lisa, and David Lloyd, eds. *The Politics of Culture in the Shadow of Capital*. Post-contemporary Interventions. Durham, NC: Duke University Press, 1997.

Lucas, Scott. "Campaigns of Truth: The Psychological Strategy Board and American Ideology, 1951–1953." *International History Review* 18, no. 2 (1996): 253–504.

Man, Simeon. *Soldiering through Empire: Race and the Making of the Decolonizing Pacific*. Oakland: University of California Press, 2018.

Manela, Erez. *The Wilsonian Moment: Self-Determination and the International Origins of Anticolonial Nationalism*. Oxford: Oxford University Press, 2007.

Matray, James A. *The Reluctant Crusade: American Foreign Policy in Korea, 1941–1950*. Honolulu: University of Hawai'i Press, 1985.

Mazower, Mark. *No Enchanted Palace: The End of Empire and the Ideological Origins of the United Nations*. Princeton, NJ: Princeton University Press, 2009.

McCoy, Alfred W. *Policing America's Empire: The United States, the Philippines, and the Rise of the Surveillance State*. Madison: University of Wisconsin Press, 2009.

———. *A Question of Torture: CIA Interrogation from the Cold War to the War on Terror*. New York: Metropolitan Books, 2006.

McMahon, Robert J. *The Cold War on the Periphery: The United States, India, and Pakistan*. New York: Columbia University Press, 1994.

McNaughton, James. *Nisei Linguists: Japanese Americans in the Military Intelligence Service during World War II*. Washington, DC: Department of the Army, 2007.

Merrill, John. *Korea: The Peninsular Origins of the War*. Newark: University of Delaware Press, 1989.

Millett, Allan R. "Introduction to the Korean War." *Journal of Military History* 65, no. 4 (2001): 921–35.

———. *The War for Korea, 1945–1950: A House Burning*. Modern War Studies. Lawrence: University Press of Kansas, 2005.

———. *The War for Korea, 1950–1951: They Came from the North*. Modern War Studies. Lawrence: University Press of Kansas, 2010.

Morris-Suzuki, Tessa, ed. *The Korean War in Asia: A Hidden History*. New York: Rowman and Littlefield, 2018.

Muller, Eric L. *American Inquisition: The Hunt for Japanese American Disloyalty in World War II*. Chapel Hill: University of North Carolina Press, 2007.

Muthanna, I. M. *General Thimmayya (Former: Chief of Army Staff, India; Chairman, N.N.R.C., Korea; Commander, U.N. Forces, Cyprus)*. Bangalore: Orient Power Press, 1972.

Nabulsi, Karma. *Traditions of War: Occupation, Resistance, and the Law*. New York: Oxford University Press, 1999.

Nagaraja, Tejasvi. "Soldiers of the American Dream: Midcentury War Work, Jim Crow, and Popular Movements Amidst Global Militarization." PhD diss., New York University, 2017.

Ngai, Mae M. *Impossible Subjects: Illegal Aliens and the Making of Modern America*. Princeton, NJ: Princeton University Press, 2004.

Nguyen, Mimi Thi. *The Gift of Freedom War, Debt, and Other Refugee Passages*. Durham, NC: Duke University Press, 2012.

Oh, Bonnie B. C., ed. *Korea under the American Military Government, 1945–1948*. Westport, CT: Praeger, 2002.

Oliver, Robert Tarbell. *Syngman Rhee and American Involvement in Korea, 1942–1960: A Personal Narrative*. Seoul: Panmun Book, 1978.

———. *Syngman Rhee: The Man behind the Myth*. New York: Dodd, Mead, 1954.

Paik, A. Naomi. *Rightlessness: Testimony and Redress in U.S. Prison Camps since World War II*. Chapel Hill: University of North Carolina Press, 2016.

Paik Nak-Chung. *The Division System in Crisis: Essays on Contemporary Korea*, trans. by Myung-hwan Kim, June-Kyu Sol, Seung-chul Song, and Young-joo Ryu. Seoul-California Series in Korean Studies. Berkeley: University of California Press, 2011.

Pak, Ch'an-p'yo. *Han'guk ui kukka hyongsong kwa minjujuui : Mi kunjonggi chayu minjujuui ui ch'ogi chedohwa* [Korean State Formation and Democracy:] Soul-si : Koryo Taehakkyo Ch'ulp'anbu, 1997.

Pak, Myŏng-nim. *Han'guk chŏnjaeng ŭi palbal kwa kiwŏn* [The Sources and Origins of the Korean War]. Sŏul: Nanam Ch'ulp'an, 1996.

Pang, Kie-Chung, and Michael Shin, eds. *Landlords, Peasants, and Intellectuals in Modern Korea*. Ithaca, NY: East Asia Program, Cornell University, 2005.

Park, Hyun Ok. *Two Dreams in One Bed: Empire, Social Life, and the Origins of the North Korean Revolution in Manchuria*. Durham, NC: Duke University Press, 2005.

Pierpaoli, Paul G. *Truman and Korea: The Political Culture of the Early Cold War*. Columbia: University of Missouri Press, 1999.

Prados, John. *Safe for Democracy: The Secret Wars of the CIA*. Chicago: Ivan R. Dee, 2006.

Prashad, Vijay. *The Darker Nations: A People's History of the Third World*. A New Press People's History. New York: New Press, distributed by W. W. Norton, 2007.

Rafael, Vicente L. *Motherless Tongues: The Insurgency of Language amid Wars of Translation*. Durham, NC: Duke University Press, 2016.

———. *White Love and Other Events in Filipino History*. Durham, NC: Duke University Press, 2000.

Rejali, Darius M. *Torture and Democracy*. Princeton, NJ: Princeton University Press, 2007.

Robin, Ron Theodore. *The Barbed-Wire College: Reeducating German POWs in the United States during World War II*. Princeton, NJ: Princeton University Pres, 1995.

———. *The Making of the Cold War Enemy: Culture and Politics in the Military-Intellectual Complex*. Princeton, NJ: Princeton University Press, 2001.

Robinson, Greg. *By Order of the President*. Cambridge, MA: Harvard University Press, 2001.

———. *A Tragedy of Democracy: Japanese Confinement in North America*. New York: Columbia University Press, 2009.

Ryu, Suk-hyeon. "Kŏje-do P'orosuyongsoŭi Shilsanggwa P'oroŭi Songhwan Shimsa" [The Reality in the Koje-do Prisoner of War Camp and the Repatriation Screening of Prisoners of War]. Master's thesis, Yonsei University, 2008.

Scarry, Elaine. *The Body in Pain: The Making and Unmaking of the World*. New York: Oxford University Press, 1985.

Schaller, Michael. *The American Occupation of Japan: The Origins of the Cold War in Asia*. New York: Oxford University Press, 1985.

Scheper-Hughes, Nancy, and Philippe Bourgois, eds. *Violence in War and Peace*. Blackwell Readers in Anthropology 5. Malden, MA: Blackwell, 2004.

Scheipers, Sibylle, ed. *Prisoners in War*. Oxford: Oxford University Press, 2010.

Schmid, Andre "'My Turn to Speak': Criticism Culture and the Multiple Uses of Class in Postwar North Korea." *International Journal of Korean History* 21, no. 2 (2016).

———. *Korea between Empires, 1895–1919*. New York: Columbia University Press, 2002.

Schmitt, Carl. *The Concept of the Political*. Chicago: University of Chicago Press, 2007.

———. *The Crisis of Parliamentary Democracy*. Studies in Contemporary German Social Thought. Cambridge, MA: MIT Press, 1985.

———. *The Nomos of the Earth in the International Law of the Jus Publicum Europaeum*. New York: Telos Press, 2003.

———. *Political Theology: Four Chapters on the Concept of Sovereignty*. Studies in Contemporary German Social Thought. Cambridge, MA: MIT Press, 1985.

Schrecker, Ellen. *Many Are the Crimes: McCarthyism in America*. 1st ed. Boston: Little, Brown, 1998.

Schrecker, Ellen, ed. *Cold War Triumphalism: The Misuse of History after the Fall of Communism*. New York: New Press, distributed by W. W. Norton, 2004.

See, Sarita Echavez. *The Decolonized Eye: Filipino American Art and Performance*. Minneapolis: University of Minnesota Press, 2009.

Selden, Mark, and Alvin Y. So. *War and State Terrorism: The United States, Japan, and the Asia-Pacific in the Long Twentieth Century*. Lanham, MD: Rowman and Littlefield, 2004.

Shaw, Angel Velasco, and Luis Francia, eds. *Vestiges of War: The Philippine-American War and the Aftermath of an Imperial Dream, 1899–1999*. New York: New York University Press, 2002.

Shepard, Todd. *The Invention of Decolonization: The Algerian War and the Remaking of France*. Ithaca, NY: Cornell University Press, 2006.

Shibusawa, Naoko. *America's Geisha Ally: Reimagining the Japanese Enemy*. Cambridge, MA: Harvard University Press, 2006.

Shigematsu, Setsu, and Keith L. Camacho, eds. *Militarized Currents: Toward a Decolonized Future in Asia and the Pacific*. Minneapolis: University of Minnesota Press, 2010.

Shin, Gi-Wook. *Ethnic Nationalism in Korea: Genealogy, Politics, and Legacy*. Stanford, CA: Stanford University Press, 2006.

Shin, Gi-Wook, and Michael Robinson, eds. *Colonial Modernity in Korea*. Cambridge, MA: Harvard University Asia Center, distributed by Harvard University Press, 1999.

Simpson, Bradley. *Economists with Guns: Authoritarian Development and US-Indonesian Relations, 1960–1968*. Stanford, CA: Stanford University Press, 2008.

Simpson, Caroline Chung. *An Absent Presence: Japanese Americans in Postwar American Culture, 1945–1960*. New Americanists. Durham, NC: Duke University Press, 2001.

Singh, Nikhil Pal. *Race and America's Long War*. Oakland: University of California Press, 2017.

Sinha, Manisha, and Penny von Eschen, eds. *Contested Democracy: Freedom, Race, and Power in American History*. New York: Columbia University Press, 2007.

Smith, Aminda M. *Thought Reform and China's Dangerous Classes: Reeducation, Resistance, and the People*. Asia/Pacific/Perspectives. Lanham, MD: Rowman and Littlefield, 2013.

Sŏ, Chung-sŏk. *Cho Pong-am kwa 1950-yŏndae* [Cho Pong-Am and the 1950s]. Vols. 1 and 2. Seoul: Yŏksa Pip'yŏngsa, 1999.

———. *Yi Sŭng-man ŭi chŏngch'i ideollogi* [The Policies and Ideology of Syngman Rhee]. Sŏul-si: Yŏksa Pip'yŏngsa, 2005.

Sodei, Rinjirō. *Were We the Enemy?: American Survivors of Hiroshima*. Transitions—Asia and Asian America. Boulder, CO: Westview Press, 1998.

Sparrow, James. *Warfare State: World War II Americans and the Age of Big Government*. Oxford: Oxford University Press, 2011.

Spillers, Hortense J. *Black, White, and in Color: Essays on American Literature and Culture*. Chicago: University of Chicago Press, 2003.

Stoler, Ann Laura, ed. *Haunted by Empire: Geographies of Intimacy in North American History*. American Encounters/Global Interactions. Durham, NC: Duke University Press, 2006.

Stone, I. F. *The Hidden History of the Korean War, 1950–1951*. A Nonconformist History of Our Times. Boston: Little, Brown, 1988.

Straus, Ulrich. *The Anguish of Surrender: Japanese POW's of World War II*. Seattle: University of Washington Press, 2003.

Stueck, William. *The Korean War: An International History*. Princeton Studies in International History and Politics. Princeton, NJ: Princeton University Press, 1995.

———. *Rethinking the Korean War: A New Diplomatic and Strategic History*. Princeton, NJ: Princeton University Press, 2002.

Suh, Jae-Jung, ed. *Origins of North Korea's Juche: Colonialism, War, and Development*. Reprint edition. Lanham, MD: Lexington Books, 2014.

Tanaka, Yuki, and Marilyn Blatt Young, eds. *Bombing Civilians: A Twentieth-Century History*. New York: New Press, 2009.

Toland, John. *In Mortal Combat: Korea, 1950–1953*. New York: Quill/William Morrow, 1993.

Trouillot, Michel-Rolph. *Silencing the Past: Power and the Production of History*. Boston: Beacon Press, 2015.

Uchida, Jun. *Brokers of Empire: Japanese Settler Colonialism in Korea, 1876–1945*. Cambridge, MA: Harvard University Asia Center, 2014.

Von Eschen, Penny M. *Race against Empire: Black Americans and Anticolonialism, 1937–1957*. Ithaca, NY: Cornell University Press, 1997.

Watt, Lori. *When Empire Comes Home: Repatriation and Reintegration in Postwar Japan*. Harvard East Asian Monographs. Cambridge, MA: Harvard University Asia Center, distributed by Harvard University Press, 2009.

Weglyn, Michi. *Years of Infamy: The Untold Story of America's Concentration Camps*. New York: Morrow, 1976.

Westad, Odd Arne. *The Global Cold War: Third World Interventions and the Making of Our Times*. Cambridge: Cambridge University Press, 2005.

Williams, William Appleman. *The Tragedy of American Diplomacy*. New York: W. W. Norton, 1988.

Woods, Colleen. "Bombs, Bureaucrats, and Rosary Beads: The United States, the Philippines, and the Making of Global Anti-Communism, 1945–1960." PhD diss., University of Michigan, 2012.

Yoneyama, Lisa. *Cold War Ruins: Transpacific Critique of American Justice and Japanese War Crimes*. Durham, NC: Duke University Press, 2016.

Yoo, Theodore Jun. *It's Madness: The Politics of Mental Health in Colonial Korea*. Oakland: University of California Press, 2016.

Young, Charles. *Name, Rank, and Serial Number: Exploiting Korean War POWs at Home and Abroad*. New York: Oxford University Press, 2014.

Young, Louise. *Japan's Total Empire: Manchuria and the Culture of Wartime Imperialism*. Berkeley: University of California Press, 1998.

Young, Marilyn Blatt. *American Expansionism: The Critical Issues*. Critical Issues in American History Series. Boston: Little, Brown, 1973.

Yuh, Ji-Yeon. *Beyond the Shadow of Camptown: Korean Military Brides in America*. New York: New York University Press, 2002.

Zhihua, Shen. *Mao, Stalin and the Korean War: Trilateral Communist Relations in the 1950s*. Cold War History Series. Hoboken, NJ: Taylor and Francis, 2012.

INDEX

Note: Page numbers in italic type indicate illustrations.

A NOTE ON THE TYPE

This book has been composed in Arno, an Old-style serif typeface in the classic Venetian tradition, designed by Robert Slimbach at Adobe.